D1479498

The African American Encyclopedia

Second Edition

The African American Encyclopedia

Second Edition

Volume 5
Hil-Lee

Editor, First Edition
Michael W. Williams

Consulting Editor, Supplement to First Edition
Kibibi Voloria Mack

Managing Editor, Second Edition
R. Kent Rasmussen

Marshall Cavendish
New York • London • Toronto • Sydney

Project Editor: McCrea Adams
Production Editor: Cindy Beres
Assistant Editor: Andrea Miller
Research Supervisor: Jeffry Jensen
Photograph Editor: Philip Bader
Page Layout: William Zimmerman

Marshall Cavendish Corporation
99 White Plains Road
Tarrytown, New York 10591-9001

Printed in the United States of America
09 08 07 06 05 04 03 02 01 5 4 3 2 1

Library of Congress Cataloging-in-Publication Data

The African American encyclopedia.—2nd ed. / managing editor, R. Kent Rasmussen.
p. cm.
Includes bibliographical references and index.
1. Afro-Americans—Encyclopedias. I. Rasmussen, R. Kent.
E185 .A253 2001
973'.0496073'003—dc21
ISBN 0-7614-7208-8 (set) 00-031526
ISBN 0-7614-7213-4 (volume 5) CIP

∞ This paper meets the requirements of ANSI/NISO Z39.48-1992 (R1997)
Permanence of Paper for Publications and Documents in Libraries and Archives

Contents

The African American Encyclopedia

Second Edition

Hill, Herbert (b. January 24, 1924, New York, New York): Educator and CIVIL RIGHTS activist. Hill's career took two principal directions, that of a labor leader with the NATIONAL ASSOCIATION FOR THE ADVANCEMENT OF COLORED PEOPLE (NAACP) and that of a scholar. He received a B.A. from New York University in 1945, did graduate work at the New School for Social Research in 1946 and 1947, and, having worked as a researcher and organizer for the United Steelworkers of America during 1947 and 1948, began his long association with the NAACP in 1948. First he was special assistant to the executive director (1948-1952), then national labor secretary (1952-1960), and later national labor director.

Across three decades, he was involved in virtually every NAACP suit filed against workplace (and intraunion) discrimination, against racially biased pay differentials, and against employer antilabor activity that especially affected black workers. That fact, together with an unbroken commitment to civil rights, voter registration, and school and housing desegregation, made him a highly respected black community leader.

Hill's academic side was no less energetic. His university affiliations include the New School for Social Research, the University of California at Irvine and at Santa Cruz, Princeton University, and the University of Wisconsin. As a labor historian, he compiled a roster of key publications in his name, including *Citizen's Guide to Desegregation: A Study of Social and Legal Change in American Life* (1955, with Jack Greenberg), *No Harvest for the Reaper: The Story of the Migratory Agricultural Worker in the United States* (1960), *Employment, Race, and Poverty* (1967, with Arthur Ross), and *Race, Work, and the Law* (1985), volume one of *Black Labor and the American Legal System*. The last book notes that although slaves were not recognized as persons legally, they were forced to perform the creative human tasks of work. Hill's literary interests, equally long-standing, are reflected in edited anthologies such as *Soon One Morning: New Writing by American Negroes, 1940-1962* (1963) and *Anger and Beyond: The Negro Writer in the United States* (1966).

See also: Civil rights and congressional legislation; Racial discrimination; Segregation and integration.

Hill, Lauryn (b. May 26, 1975, East Orange, New Jersey): Singer, RAP artist, and actor. Hill is one of the HIP-HOP artists given credit for helping assimilate hip-hop into mainstream music. Encouraged to sing by her parents at an early age, Hill was soon also acting in minor roles on television and in films. She began her professional singing career with the Fugees (whose members also included Wyclef Jean and Prakazrel Michel) at the age of thirteen. The Fugees (short for "refugees") achieved major success in 1996 when their second al-

In 1999 Lauryn Hill won five Grammy Awards, including best new artist of the year. *(AP/Wide World Photos)*

bum, *The Score*, sold well over a million copies. The title was a reference to a film score, and each song was meant to represent a separate scene.

In 1998 Hill released a debut solo album, *The Miseducation of Lauryn Hill* (1998), that propelled her to the top as a solo artist. Producing the album and writing or cowriting all the songs, she successfully integrated rap, SOUL MUSIC, REGGAE, and RHYTHM AND BLUES into her sound. The single "Doo Wop (That Thing)" was heavily played on the radio and featured on music video programs. Hill rapidly became a national media icon, appearing on the cover of such magazines as *Time*, *Esquire*, and *Teen People*.

At the 1999 Grammy Awards, Hill won five Grammies, for album of the year, best new artist, best female R&B vocal performance, best R&B song, and best R&B album. She was also the top winner at the 1999 MTV Awards later in the year. Hill's other work in 1998 and 1999 included harmony vocals and arrangements on Aretha FRANKLIN's *Rose Is Still a Rose* (1998) and Mary J. Blige's *Mary* (1999).

—*Alvin K. Benson*

Hilliard, Asa Grant, III (b. August 22, 1933, Galveston, Texas): Educator. Hilliard performed studies focused on the learning process of black CHILDREN. His degrees, from the University of Denver, include a B.A. in psychology (1955), an M.A. in counseling (1961), and an Ed.D. in educational psychology (1963).

From 1955 to 1960, Hilliard taught in the public schools in Denver, COLORADO. He became a teaching fellow at the University of Denver in 1960 and kept that position until 1963, when he finished his doctorate there. San Francisco State University hired Hilliard as a professor of EDUCATION in 1963. He had risen to the position of dean of education by the time he left the school in 1983. He was named distinguished professor of education at Georgia State University in 1980. From 1973 to 1975, Hilliard was on the board of directors of the National Black Child Development Institute.

Hilliard's studies found that white children are more likely than black children to tell stories in a linear fashion. White children's stories often progress chronologically, while those of black children tend to take a spiral pattern, circling the main topic before addressing it directly. When telling stories, black children often will introduce several apparently irrelevant topics before returning to the theme of their story and describing how the previously introduced topics relate to it.

Hilliard, David (b. May 15, 1942, Mobile, Alabama): Member of the BLACK PANTHER PARTY (BPP). Brought into the BPP by Huey NEWTON

David Hilliard during an interview with the media on the occasion of Eldridge Cleaver's death in May, 1998. *(AP/Wide World Photos)*

in 1967 and considered to be one of its cofounders, Hilliard became BPP chief of staff within a year. With Eldridge CLEAVER exiled and Newton in jail by 1969, Hilliard became BPP chairman. Hilliard achieved notoriety when he denounced President Richard Nixon at a San Francisco, California, antiwar rally in 1969, calling for Nixon's death. Hilliard was arrested by federal agents, but the case dissolved six months later, after the government refused to disclose details concerning wiretapping activities. When Newton was released from jail, Hilliard again became BPP chief of staff. *This Side of Glory: The Autobiography of David Hilliard and the Story of the Black Panthers* was published in 1992.

Hilliard, Earl Frederick (b. April 9, 1942, Birmingham, Alabama): Politician, attorney, and U.S. congressman. After receiving his bachelor's degree from Morehouse College in 1964, Hilliard went on to earn his J.D. from HOWARD UNIVERSITY School of Law in 1967. He served as assistant to the president of Alabama State University from 1968 to 1970, and earned his master's in business administration from ATLANTA UNIVERSITY School of Business in 1970.

Hilliard began working as a regional fellow with the BIRMINGHAM Legal Aid Society from 1970 to 1972 while serving as a representative in the ALABAMA state legislature. In 1972 he entered private practice as a partner in the firm of Pearson & Hilliard. He began serving as president of the American Trust Life Insurance Company in 1977 and accepted the post of president of the American Trust Land Company in 1980. Hilliard returned to the political scene in 1980, when he was elected to serve as a state senator in Alabama. While in the state legislature, Hilliard served as chairman of the Alabama Black Legislative Caucus and was active in the local chapter of the NATIONAL ASSOCIATION FOR THE ADVANCEMENT OF COLORED PEOPLE (NAACP).

In 1992 Hilliard ran for Congress from Alabama's Seventh Congressional District and was elected to fill the vacancy left by retiring representative Claude Harris. With his victory, Hilliard became the state's first black congressional representative since Jeremiah Haralson left Congress in 1877. Upon taking office, Hilliard was appointed to the House committees on Agriculture and Small Business. Hilliard won reelection in 1994 with a decisive victory over Republican opponent Alfred J. Middleton, Sr. He was again reelected in 1996 and 1998.

See also: Congress members; Politics and government.

Himes, Chester Bomar (July 29, 1909, Jefferson City, Missouri—November 12, 1984, Moraira, Spain): Novelist, short-fiction writer, essayist, and social analyst. His family moved frequently until he was fifteen, finally settling in Cleveland, OHIO. Himes graduated from Glenville High School in January of 1926 and made extensive plans to enter Ohio State University in the next fall term as a pre-med student. In the interim, he secured a position as a busboy in a local hotel. Shortly thereafter, he fell down an elevator shaft, permanently injuring himself.

As a result of the fall, Himes was in physical pain, but when he entered Ohio State he felt another pain—racism—that he describes eloquently in the first part of *The Quality of Hurt: The Autobiography of Chester Himes, Volume I* (1972). His academic performance was poor, and he dropped out after two quarters. He began associating with petty criminals, eventually being convicted of forgery, breaking and entering, and armed robbery. He was sentenced to serve twenty years at hard labor when he was nineteen years old.

In the Ohio State penitentiary, Himes began his writing career. His major break came with the publication of "Crazy in the Stir" in

Author Chester Himes during the 1940's. *(Library of Congress)*

Esquire (1934). He was paroled in 1936 and published his first and most successful novel, *If He Hollers Let Him Go* (1945). It is a complex novel about prejudice in the Los ANGELES, CALIFORNIA, shipyards during the height of WORLD WAR II. *Lonely Crusade* (1947) is another novel about the paranoia of an African American man living in white America.

Himes also was successful in writing detective novels, after he became an expatriate in 1953. He created the famous black detective duo of Grave Digger Jones and Coffin Ed Johnson, who operate in HARLEM, New York. Nine of these novels were published, the most successful being *Cotton Comes to Harlem* (1965), made into a successful film in 1970. In 1957 Himes was awarded the Grand Prix de Littérature Policière. He was far more appreciated in Europe than in the United States. His novel *Pinktoes* (1961) was one of his most controversial works. It is a satirical study of racial relations, centering on sex and food.
See also: Literature.

Hine, Darlene Clark (b. February 7, 1947, Moorley, Missouri): Historian, educator, and college administrator. Hine earned her undergraduate degree from Roosevelt University in CHICAGO and was awarded the master's and doctorate in history at Kent State University in OHIO. In 1972 Hine began her career as an assistant professor at historically black South Carolina State College in Orangeburg, SOUTH CAROLINA. She taught history and coordinated the black studies program. In 1974 she moved to Purdue University in Lafayette, Indiana, where she rose through the ranks from assistant to full professor in the department of history. In addition, Hine served as interim director of Purdue's Africana Research Center and worked as vice provost from 1981 to 1986. She went to Michigan State University in 1987 as John A. Hannah Professor of American History. During the 1989-1990 academic year, she taught in the women's studies department of the University of Delaware as a visiting distinguished professor.

During the 1980's, Hine became one of the best-known and most respected African Americans in the history profession. Although in her first book, *Black Victory: The Rise and Fall of the White Primary in Texas* (1979), she examined a southern political issue, she is best known for her scholarship in African American women's history. She developed a special interest in black women in the health care professions. Her *Black Women in White: Racial Conflict and Cooperation in the Nursing Profession, 1890-1950* (1989) was named Outstanding Book by the Gustavus Myer Center for the Study of Human Rights. From the 1970's to the 1990's, Hine published well over fifty articles on various aspects of black history.

Hine's 1990's publications include two edited works; she was primary editor of *Black Women in America: An Historical Encyclopedia* (1993) and coedited, with Wilma King and Linda Reed, *"We Specialize in the Wholly Impossible": A Reader in Black Women's History* (1995).

She also authored one of the three essays in *Black Studies in the United States: Three Essays* (1990); the other two were by Robert L. Harris, Jr., and Nellie McKay.

In 1991 she received the distinguished alumni award from Kent State. Her study on blacks in nursing also earned the Lavinia L. Dock Book Award from the American Association for the History of Nursing (1990) and the Letitia Woods Brown Book Award from the Association of Black Women Historians (1990).

See also: Health care professionals; Women.

Hines, Earl "Fatha" (December 28, 1905, Duquesne, Pennsylvania—April 22, 1983, Oakland, California): Pianist, bandleader, and composer. Earl Kenneth "Fatha" Hines was the most technically advanced and possibly the most musically sophisticated of the early JAZZ pianists. Because of the technique he developed with his right hand, his playing is usually described as "trumpet" style.

From his first recordings in the early 1920's, Hines was an important figure, but once he became the pianist in trumpeter Louis ARMSTRONG's Hot Five and Hot Seven later that decade, his reputation solidified. Although the groups made many memorable recordings, including "West End Blues" (1928), Hines and Armstrong performed most spectacularly together on their duet performance of "Weather Bird" (1928). The demands of that song are great, and few other musicians of the time could have performed at so high a musical and technical level.

Also in 1928, Hines formed a big band that played for years at the Grand Terrace club in CHICAGO, ILLINOIS. Because of the band's live radio broadcasts beginning in 1934, it became one of the most famous of all jazz bands, even though it performed in Chicago and not NEW YORK CITY. The band featured Hines's playing, but other excellent musicians contributed to its success, including saxophonist Budd JOHNSON and arranger Gerald Valentine.

Because of a wartime recording ban instituted by the American Federation of Musicians in the early 1940's, what was probably one of the greatest bands in the history of jazz remains undocumented musically. Hines led this band, which included some of the most important young musicians of the time, instrumentalists such as saxophonist Charlie PARKER and trumpeter Dizzy GILLESPIE, who would soon revolutionize improvised music with what became known as BEBOP.

Hines remained active throughout the remainder of his life, primarily, in later years, as a solo pianist. The most famous of his numerous compositions is "Rosetta" (1928). He made several European performance trips in the late 1950's and 1960's, and between trips he played at his own club in OAKLAND, CALIFORNIA.

See also: Music.

Earl "Fatha" Hines (left) entertaining troops at a training base during World War II. *(National Archives)*

Hines, Gregory (b. February 14, 1946, New York, New York): Tap dancer and actor. Steered toward DANCE by his mother, Gregory Hines, at the age of six, performed at the APOLLO THEATER with his brother, Maurice, in an act called the Hines Kids. He soon came under the tutelage of tappers Howard "Sandman" Sims and Teddy Hale.

In 1954 the Hines boys were cast in the Broadway musical *The Girl in Pink Tights*. Under the guidance of Broadway tap coach Henry LeTang, they rapidly became an international attraction. Upon reaching their teens, they called themselves the Hines Brothers, and during a brief period with singer and pantomimist Johnny Brown, they performed as Hines, Hines, and Brown. In 1963 they became Hines, Hines, and Dad, with Gregory playing comedian, Maurice playing straight man, and their father serving as percussionist. The trio became well known; they guested on the *Ed Sullivan Show* and the *Tonight Show* and toured the United States and Europe.

Hines landed a tap-dancing part in 1978 in a Broadway-bound revue, *The Last Minstrel Show*. Later that year, the brothers both appeared in *Eubie!* (1978), the Broadway musical paying homage to composer Eubie BLAKE, tap-choreographed by Henry LeTang. Hines won several awards for his performance, including the Outer Critics Circle award and a Tony nomination for outstanding featured actor in a musical. In 1979 Hines earned his second straight Tony nomination playing Scrooge in a Broadway musical version of *A Christmas Carol* entitled *Comin' Uptown*.

Maurice Hines (left), Terry and Deborah Burrell, and Gregory Hines in New York, where they were all performing in *Eubie!* in 1979. *(AP/Wide World Photos)*

In early 1980, he choreographed an Off-Broadway production, *Blues in the Night*. Later that year, a pair of his tap shoes was placed on the Wall of Fame at the famous Manhattan dance hall, the Roseland, alongside those of Fred Astaire, Ruby Keeler, and other greats. In 1981 Hines earned a third Tony nomination for the Broadway production *Sophisticated Ladies*.

On screen, Hines took roles that fostered recognition of black dance. His dance film credits include *The Cotton Club* (1984), *White Nights* (1985), in which he challenge-dances a renowned Soviet émigré ballet dancer played by Mikhail Baryshnikov, and *Tap* (1989). In 1986 he was teamed with Billy Crystal in the comedy-action film *Running Scared*. In addition, he made numerous public appearances to celebrate tap, including the public television documentary *Tappin': The Making of Tap* (1989).

Musically, Hines tap-danced to the bass playing of Stanley Clarke on the recording *If This Bass Could Only Talk* (1988). Reaching further afield, Hines sang on his own solo album, entitled *That Girl Wants to Dance with Me* (1988).

In 1992 Hines won a Tony Award for his Broadway portrayal of early jazz musician Jelly Roll MORTON in the well-received musical *Jelly's Last Jam*. Hines's films in the early 1990's included *Eve of Destruction* (1991) and *A Rage in Harlem* (1991). Later in the decade he took small roles in major films including *Waiting to Exhale* (1995) and *The Preacher's Wife* (1996), and in 1999 he starred in a low-budget, independent film, *The Tic Code*. In the 1997-1998 television season he starred in *The Gregory Hines Show*.

Hinton, William Augustus (December 15, 1883, Chicago, Illinois—August 8, 1959, Canton, Massachusetts): Physician and educator. He achieved worldwide recognition for his discovery of a method of testing for syphilis. In 1949 he became the first African American professor at Harvard Medical School. His book *Syphilis and Its Treatment* (1936) is one of the standard reference works on the subject. *See also:* Medicine.

Hip-hop: The terms "RAP" and "hip-hop" are sometimes used interchangeably to describe a musical genre, but hip-hop also encompasses a subculture with its own styles of dress, dance, and art. Rap and hip-hop originated in the 1970's in NEW YORK CITY's South Bronx, a desolate section of the city plagued by urban decay. The young people of South Bronx, mostly African Americans but some Hispanics as well, found their musical and cultural outlets in the streets.

The dance style that became known as BREAK DANCING evolved as youths danced to the music of street DJs. Playing music through their portable outdoor sound systems, these DJs created live dance mixes influenced by music styles brought by JAMAICAN immigrants. Soon DJs such as Cool Herc, said to have pioneered the technique of "breaking," or stopping a record while rapping over it, and Grandmaster Flash, said to have initiated "scratching," brought rap and hip-hop to New York's attention. Graffiti art evolved as a visual reflection of hip-hop culture. Works were painted on walls, subway cars, and abandoned buildings, and eventually on stage sets for DJs and rap performances.

In 1979, the success of the Sugar Hill Gang's "Rapper's Delight" helped popularize rap on the West Coast and elsewhere, and by the early 1980's, rap—and with it hip-hop culture—was spreading throughout the country. Artists such as RUN-D.M.C. (with their crossover hit "Walk This Way"), Whodini, and Salt-N-Pepper brought rap into the mainstream. From the beginning, rap lyrics were often gritty and looked at the seamier side of African American urban life, including drug use, crime, teenage promiscuity, prostitution, and prison. Many Americans first encountered hip-hop culture in a series of low-budget films, including *Breakin'* (1984), *Breakin' II* (1984), and *Krush Groove* (1985).

Suddenly rap became big business, and the street ethos of the music and of hip-hop culture in general ran straight into American consumer culture. Consumer items such as jewelry, expensive Nike shoes, and Tommy Hilfiger clothing became a part of the hip-hop look. Expensive and stylish rap videos showcased hip-hop dance and clothing styles on the Music Television (MTV) and BLACK ENTERTAINMENT TELEVISION (BET) cable networks. By the 1990's, hip-hop culture and American YOUTH CULTURE almost seemed synonymous. Hip-hop also developed its own vocabulary of new slang terms, which evolved throughout the 1980's and 1990's. In the 1990's, the majority of people who bought rap music were white youths, and suburban white teens began to adopt hip-hop language and wear hip-hop clothing. The trend was satirized by the white rock band Offspring in their 1999 hit "Pretty Fly (for a White Guy)."

Despite their huge popularity, rap music and elements of hip-hop culture remained controversial among many middle-class whites and blacks alike. Rap, notably gangsta rap, was assailed as antisocial vitriol performed by artists who were little more than rhyming thugs who ceaselessly used profanity, emphasized disrespect for women, and advocated drug use and defiance of authority. Rap aficionados argued that hip-hop culture was being unjustly criticized—particularly considering that the illegal or antisocial activities of white musicians received considerably less scrutiny. Rap lyrics, the artists themselves argued, honestly reflected the language and realities of inner-city life. Regardless of such debates, hip-hop styles dominated the look of America's youth in the 1990's.

—*Michael Polley*

See also: Graffiti and tagging.

Suggested Readings:

Fernando, S. H. *The New Beats: Exploring the Music, Culture, and Attitudes of Hip-hop*. New York: Anchor Books/Doubleday, 1994.

George, Nelson. *Buppies, B-boys, Baps and Bohos: Notes on Post-Soul Black Culture*. New York: HarperPerennial, 1994.

_______. *Hip Hop America*. New York: Viking Press, 1998.

_______, et al. *Fresh: Hip Hop Don't Stop*. New York: Random House, 1985.

Hager, Steven. *Hip Hop: The Illustrated History of Break Dancing, Rap Music, and Graffiti*. New York: St. Martin's Press, 1984.

Potter, Russell A. *Spectacular Vernaculars: Hip-Hop and the Politics of Postmodernism*. Albany: State University of New York Press, 1995.

Historically black colleges: From the pre-Civil War years through the 1990's, black colleges have been indispensable to the progress of African Americans. Some critics lose sight of the fact that historically black colleges and universities continue to fulfill a bona fide need for an underserved population. These schools have an outstanding record, but keeping them open and competitive is increasingly difficult.

Challenge of Funding

The most pressing problem is the perpetual concern about adequate funds to continue operating these historically black institutions. Lack of financial and political support, and sometimes outright opposition in the guise of desegregation and budget cutting, have made existence tenuous for these schools. Some black schools have been on the verge of closing. Others have closed or lost their identity through forced merger with nonblack institutions.

Over the years, the United Negro College Fund (UNCF) has given much-needed financial assistance to historically black colleges and universities. The fund was created in 1944 solely for the purpose of running a fund-raising campaign to support all 117 of these schools in nineteen states, mostly in the South. The UNCF has been one of the most successful nonprofit organizations because it keeps administration and fund-raising costs low and is able to generate contributions through extremely successful programs and campaigns such as the "Lou Rawls Parade of Stars," watched worldwide.

Private Funding

Because of its reputation for integrity, the UNCF has been able to receive large donations from all over the world. For example, the UNCF negotiated a donation of $50 million from publisher and philanthropist Walter H. Annenberg—the largest donation the fund ever received.

(continued on page 1206)

Historically Black Colleges and Universities

The following colleges and universities either were founded as institutes of higher learning for African Americans or have predominantly African American student bodies. The date in parentheses indicates the year that the institution was founded.

ALABAMA
Alabama A&M University (1875)
Alabama State University (1874)
Bishop State Community College (1927)
Concordia College (1922)
Lawson State Community College (1973)
Miles College (1905)
Oakwood College (1896)
Selma University (1878)
Stillman College (1876)
Talladega College (1867)
Tuskegee Institute (1881)

ARKANSAS
Arkansas Baptist College (1884)
Philander-Smith College (1877)
Shorter College (1886)
University of Arkansas, Pine Bluff (1873)

CALIFORNIA
Charles R. Drew University of Medicine and Science (1978)
Compton Community College (1927)

DELAWARE
Delaware State College (1891)

DISTRICT OF COLUMBIA
Howard University (1867)
University of the District of Columbia (1976)

FLORIDA
Bethune-Cookman College (1904)
Edward Waters College (1866)
Florida A&M University (1887)
Florida Memorial College (1879)

GEORGIA
Albany State College (1903)
Atlanta Metropolitan College (1974)
Clark Atlanta University (1869)
Fort Valley State College (1895)
Interdenominational Theological Center (1958)
Morehouse College (1867)
Morehouse School of Medicine (1975)
Morris Brown College (1881)
Paine College (1882)
Savannah State College (1890)
Spelman College (1881)

ILLINOIS
Chicago State University (1867)

KENTUCKY
Kentucky State University (1886)
Simmons Bible College (1879)

LOUISIANA
Dillard University (1869)
Grambling State University (1901)
Southern University and A&M College (1880)
Southern University—New Orleans (1959)
Southern University—Shreveport (1964)
Xavier University of Louisiana (1915)

MARYLAND
Bowie State University (1865)
Coppin State College (1900)
Morgan State University (1867)
Sojourner-Douglass College (1972)
University of Maryland, Eastern Shore (1886)

MASSACHUSETTS
Roxbury Community College (1973)

MICHIGAN
Highland Park Community College (1918)
Lewis College of Business (1929)
Wayne County Community College (1968)

MISSISSIPPI
Alcorn State University (1871)
Coahoma Community College (1949)
Hinds Community College—Utica Campus (1903)
Jackson State University (1877)
Mary Holmes Junior College (1892)
Mississippi Valley State University (1946)
Natchez Junior College (1885)
Prentiss Normal & Industrial Institute (1907)
Rust College (1866)
Tougaloo College (1869)

MISSOURI
Harris-Stowe State College (1857)
Lincoln University of Missouri (1866)

NEW YORK
Medgar Evers College of the City University of New York (1969)

NORTH CAROLINA
Barber-Scotia College (1867)
Bennett College (1873)
Elizabeth City State University (1891)

Fayetteville State University (1867)
Johnson C. Smith University (1867)
Livingstone College, Hood Theological Seminary (1879)
North Carolina A&T State University (1891)
North Carolina Central University (1910)
St. Augustine's College (1867)
Shaw University (1865)
Winston-Salem State University (1892)

OHIO
Central State University (1887)
Cuyahoga Community College (1963)
Wilberforce University (1856)

OKLAHOMA
Langston University (1897)

PENNSYLVANIA
Cheyney State University (1837)
Lincoln University of Pennsylvania (1854)

SOUTH CAROLINA
Allen University (1870)
Benedict College (1870)
Claflin College (1869)
Clinton Junior College (1894)
Denmark Technical College (1948)
Morris College (1908)
South Carolina State College (1896)
Voorhees College (1897)

TENNESSEE
Fisk University (1866)
Knoxville College (1875)
Lane College (1882)
LeMoyne-Owen College (1870)
Meharry Medical College (1876)
Morristown College (1881)
Tennessee State University (1912)

TEXAS
Bishop College (1881)
Huston-Tillotson College (1875)
Jarvis Christian College (1912)
Paul Quinn College (1872)
Prairie View A&M University (1876)
Southwestern Christian College (1949)
Texas College (1894)
Texas Southern University (1947)
Wiley College (1873)

VIRGIN ISLANDS
College of the Virgin Islands (1963)

VIRGINIA
Hampton University (1868)
Norfolk State University (1935)
St. Paul's College (1888)
Virginia State University (1882)
Virginia Union University (1865)

WEST VIRGINIA
West Virginia State College (1891)

In addition to receiving support from government and the UNCF, each individual black college or university conducts its own fund-raising campaigns. For example, in the early 1990's, the AT&T Foundation donated more than $5 million in money and equipment to Howard University alone. Bill Cosby donated $20 million to Spelman College in Atlanta. He also donated $1.3 million to Fisk University and millions more to at least six other schools.

The UNCF has continued to receive celebrity help. Scholarship funds have been established by Yoko Ono and Spike Lee. Sports legend Earvin "Magic" Johnson annually sponsors a benefit basketball game for the UNCF. Money has been raised through proceeds from concerts and record sales by artists such as Prince, Whitney Houston, and Michael Jackson. In 1993 alone, the UNCF raised a record $58 million in its annual campaign.

Government Support
President Franklin D. Roosevelt began the tradition of White House support by endorsing the UNCF. John D. Rockefeller, Jr., chaired one of its committees, lending his name to a charity for the first time in his life. During the 1990's, the brother of former president George Bush served as chairman of the UNCF's national board. President Bill Clinton repeatedly reiterated his commitment to black colleges and universities regarding funding, appointing Catherine LeBlanc to head the White House Initiative on Historically Black Colleges and Universities.

All this government support, however, has never been translated into an equitable government funding distribution. Earlier allocations to black institutions of higher learning fell victim to partisan posturing. The federal financial and policy support of such schools was severely criticized. Allocated funds received by these schools in the form of grants, contracts, and awards have been small in comparison to what "majority institutions" receive.

Attracting African American Students

Howard University, one of the strongest of the historically black colleges, is struggling to stay competitive. This university's struggle is representative of the challenges facing all black colleges and universities: trying to remain academically competitive while remaining open to as many students as possible. The most pressing problem has been the intense competition to attract promising black students from better-funded nonblack universities.

Before the 1960's, the most promising black medical students in the United States applied to the College of Medicine at Howard. Now, many of the best black medical students are going to nonblack universities. The statistics at Howard University Medical School are a compelling illustration of the overall condition of black universities. In the pre-1960's era, Howard trained half of the nation's black doctors. By the early 1990's, only 17 percent of the nation's black medical students were graduates of the nation's four predominantly black medical schools. Surprisingly, as more African Americans enroll in nonblack universities, students who are not African Americans are finding Howard increasingly attractive and affordable.

College Closures

In July of 1992, the U.S. Supreme Court issued *United States v. Fordice*, a landmark decision declaring that Mississippi had not succeeded in integrating its state-run system of higher education. This decision was good news for the nineteen states that operate black colleges and universities. One way of interpreting the *Fordice* decision is that black colleges enhance choice rather than limit it; thus they are in line with the ruling. From the standpoint of African American students, strong black educational institutions increase choice. Similarly, historically black colleges and universities offer white students a chance to experience a different environment, widening the range of choice for them as well.

On the other hand, the Court's emphasis on desegregation could easily justify the closure of black colleges. In 1992 the state of Mississippi proposed to comply with *Fordice* and the Court's 1954 decision in Brown v. Board of Education by closing one black college and merging a second with a traditionally white university. The state justified these actions on the grounds that private black colleges segregate blacks on their own campuses in the era in which diversity and multicultural values are at the center of educational debate.

Unique Status

Black colleges and universities are working with the UNCF in recruiting alumni to "give something back" to their alma maters. African American alumni are invited not only to help financially but also to help publicize the accomplishments of these schools. It is hoped that a clearer image of these accomplishments will woo superior black students as well as top-quality teachers and scholars.

These black institutions want the public and the politicians to know that they have always been leaders in international development. The Peace Corps program, for example, was modeled after the Crossroads Africa program, a once-flourishing exchange program offered at black colleges and universities.

Another little appreciated fact about these schools is their cost-effectiveness. In 1993 the

The Heritage Bowl

Most historically black colleges are located in southern states, where rigid segregation long prevented African American athletes from playing for white institutions. By the 1980's, however, desegregation had so changed this situation that the football and basketball teams of most formerly all-white institutions were becoming dominated by black players. One negative consequence of this otherwise positive change was a severe dilution of athletic talent enrolling in traditionally black institutions. To help promote historically black colleges, the National Collegiate Athletic Association approved creation of a new postseason football game especially for teams in the historically black Mid-Eastern Athletic and Southwestern Athletic Conferences. First held in December, 1991, the game soon came to be known as the Heritage Bowl. Since the 1994 season, it has been played in Atlanta's Georgia Dome.

SCORES

1991	Alabama State 36, North Carolina A&T 13
1992	Grambling 45, Florida A&M 15
1993	Southern 11, South Carolina State 0
1994	South Carolina State 31, Grambling 27
1995	Southern 30, Florida A&M 25
1996	Howard University 27, Southern 24
1997	Southern 34, South Carolina State 28
1998	Southern 28, Bethune-Cookman 2
1999	Hampton 24, Southern University 3

average cost of tuition and other fees at black colleges was $4,848, which was considerably lower than the national average for other private colleges. During the 1990's, Spelman College was recognized as one of the most affordable schools in the country by both *U.S. News and World Report* and *Money* magazines.

One strong argument in favor of continuing existence and progress of such institutions is that they enroll 17 percent of black college students who receive bachelor's degrees, and 43 percent of black students who earned doctorates did their undergraduate work at black institutions. In Mississippi, ALABAMA, and LOUISIANA—the three states that were in litigation in 1992 over whether they had desegregated their higher-education systems—nearly 60 percent of the blacks who graduated each year from public colleges received their degrees from historically black institutions. Those institutions therefore are best understood as indispensable in providing college opportunities for many blacks who would not otherwise have them.

Historically black colleges and universities have made the American landscape richer for more than a century. These schools have molded great minds that influenced the growth of America and the entire world. The single most convincing argument in favor of supporting these institutions is the singularly distinguished list of their alumni— a virtual who's who of great African Americans, including Martin Luther KING, Jr., Leontyne PRICE, Andrew YOUNG, Maynard JACKSON, Hazel O'LEARY, Joycelyn ELDERS, Nikki GIOVANNI, Spike Lee, Toni MORRISON, Justice Thurgood MARSHALL, L. Douglas WILDER, David DINKINS, Debbie ALLEN, and others.

William H. Gray III, president of the UNCF, expressed the value of these schools best when he said: "The Harvards and Yales can take a diamond and make it shine brighter. But we can take a piece of coal and turn it into a diamond."

—Chogallah Maroufi

See also: Clinton administration; Education; Roosevelt administration, Franklin D.

Suggested Readings:

Bowman, J. Wilson. *America's Black and Tribal Colleges*. 3d ed. Skyland, N.C.: R. J. Enterprises, 1999.

Christy, Ralph D., and Lionel Williamson, eds. *A Century of Service: Land-Grant Colleges and Universities, 1890-1990*. New Brunswick, N.J.: Transaction, 1992.

Elbert, Marian M. *The Politics of Educational Decision Making: Historically Black Colleges and*

Universities and Federal Assistance Programs. Westport, Conn.: Praeger, 1996.

Hill, Levirn, ed. *Black American Colleges and Universities: Profiles of Two-year, Four-year, and Professional Schools.* Detroit: Gale Research, 1994.

Hoffman, Charlene, Thomas D. Snyder, and Bill Sonnenberg. *Historically Black Colleges and Universities, 1976-1994.* Washington, D.C.: U.S. Government Printing Office, 1996.

Kennard, Toni H. *The Handbook of Historically Black Colleges and Universities: Comprehensive Profiles and Photos of Black Colleges and Universities.* 2d ed. Wilmington, Del.: Jireh & Associates, 1995.

Roebuck, Julian B. *Historically Black Colleges and Universities: Their Place in American Higher Education.* Westport, Conn.: Praeger, 1993.

Sagini, Meshack M. *The African and the African American University: A Historical and Sociological Analysis.* Lanham, Md.: University Press of America, 1996.

Sims, Serbrenia J. *Diversifying Historically Black Colleges and Universities: A New Higher Education Paradigm.* Westport, Conn.: Greenwood Press, 1994.

Historic landmark and neighborhood preservation: Since their arrival in America, blacks have developed their own unique culture. Blending the traditions of their African homelands with the evolving American experience, they created their own LITERATURE, MUSIC, art, and FASHION. In the second half of the twentieth century, historians and preservationists recognized that many sites and landmarks associated with African American culture were falling into disrepair or being demolished. The National Park Service and the National Register of Historic Places instituted programs to encourage greater interest in and greater efforts toward preserving this culture.

One such program has provided state historic preservation offices with funds to survey landmarks and sites associated with the black community. The ultimate goal of such surveys is to document the history of properties deemed worthy of inclusion in the National Register of Historic Places. State historic preservation offices, in turn, are able to offer grant money to local groups and professional historians to research, review, and survey the culture and heritage of African Americans in small communities, rural areas, and in inner-city neighborhoods throughout the United States.

The Historic Sites Act, passed by Congress in 1935, originally gave recognition primarily to those properties which had been most closely associated with the achievements of various European immigrants who came to America. In 1966 the National Historic Preservation Act broadened this perspective and made an effort to include sites associated with all ethnic and racial groups living in the United States. Passage of this act coincided with a new interest among historians and other scholars in examining American history "from the bottom up" by including the achievements of people whose names were largely unknown but whose contributions to American society merited attention. As a result of this new interest in social history, preservationists sought to include the experiences and achievements of ordinary people from all walks of life—bus drivers, housewives, factory workers, teachers, mechanics, and sharecroppers.

This interest in what some people have called "pots and pans" history gave energy and hope to small museums and private groups who were dedicated to preserving historical records of African American life. These organizations began to focus attention on local history and family history. They gathered information from old church records, from the minutes of various clubs and community organizations, and from family Bibles, letters, and other documents. Cities with large African American populations, including New York and Atlanta, began working to preserve neighborhood buildings that were of local significance.

Legislation Helps Protect Black History

The efforts to preserve African American culture were significantly enhanced by the passage of the National Historic Preservation Act Amendments of 1992. This amendment to Public Law 102-575 is commonly known as the Fowler Bill because its principal sponsor was Senator Wyche Fowler, Jr., of Georgia. The bill was signed into law on October 30, 1992, by President George Bush. The 1992 act strengthened the power of preservationists and increased the protections afforded to all endangered historic structures. One significant phase of the amendments established financial penalties to be assessed against anyone found engaging in the intentional destruction of historic properties to avoid federal historic preservation reviews.

Although designed to protect all historic preservation projects regardless of their origins, the new amendment provided special help in preserving structures associated with the nation's African American cultural heritage. The 1992 act made clear that historic preservation grants could be used to assist in the preservation of religious properties listed in the National Register as long as such aid was secular in nature and did not promote religion. From the early colonial period through the Civil War and beyond, African Americans developed close ties with their churches, whether the congregation met in a building, a private home, or a brush arbor. In these churches, millions of African Americans had free access to training in oratory, education, and leadership. The church was often their only public stage for self-expression.

Churches often served as social and cultural centers as well as religious centers in the black community. In an article published in *African American Historic Places* in 1994, A. Lynn Bolles referred to the social significance of black churches as vehicles for upward mobility and achievement within the black community. Throughout American history, black families with strong religious ties produced many artists, composers, singers, entrepreneurs, politicians, civil rights leaders, and other prominent individuals. The church not only gave African Americans moral and spiritual security but also served as a means of communication between members and between congregations of different religious denominations. Ambitious and talented African Americans used the church as a base of support in their endeavors to succeed in the secular world.

Fraternal Organizations

In addition to black churches, there were other important institutions within the African American community, particularly in urban neighborhoods. Fraternal societies such as the Freemasons served as centers of black social life. Black Freemasonry began in New England under the guidance of Prince Hall, a minister and activist living in Boston. In 1787 he organized the first group of black Masons as the African Lodge No. 459. One of the primary goals of the black Freemasons was to encourage African Americans to establish and operate their own businesses. Fraternal organizations were most effective in the years between the Civil War and the beginning of World War II—a period when segregation was at its height and separate black institutions flourished. Before the advent of the New Deal and the government relief programs associated with it, the black community relied heavily on private aid provided by fraternal organizations and benevolent associations. With help and encouragement from Freemasons and other social organizations, African Americans founded businesses such as cafés, barber shops, banks, garages, beauty parlors, pool halls, and funeral homes.

Public and Private Support

By the time the 1992 amendment was signed, interest in the preservation of African American culture was widespread. One of the leading supporters of this movement was the National Trust, a private, nonprofit organization established by Congress to encourage public participation in the preservation of historically significant sites. The National Trust began to take a special interest in preservation of inner-city neighborhoods as examples of cultural and ethnic diversity. It sponsored meetings and workshops throughout the country to promote interest in and awareness of such preservation efforts. In 1992 the National Trust conference was organized around the theme "Cultural Diversity in Historic Preservation." In addition to offering scholarships to advance public knowledge of African American culture, the National Trust published pamphlets and books about the preservation of black landmarks.

As private organizations and individuals became involved in the preservation movement, the public became more aware of the physical landmarks associated with black culture. According to records for 1995, more than three-fourths of all properties listed in the National Register of Historic Places were owned by private citizens. Even though such privately owned properties are often not open to the public, the preservation and recognition that comes with being placed in the National Register of Historic Places is all-important.

Because it is responsible for administering the historic preservation efforts on the federal level, the National Park Service became involved in promoting the preservation of black culture even before the passage of the 1992 amendment. Among its many activities, the Park Service supported the HISTORICALLY BLACK COLLEGES and Universities Program, which offered student internships, architectural drawing courses, curriculum development in historical preservation and planning, and many other educational programs on historic preservation within the black community. The National Conference of State Historic Preservation Officers also joined the efforts to preserve black culture. This group established its own task force on minority participation in state programs. The work of this task force has been a major factor in the dramatic growth of black cultural properties being studied, surveyed, and ultimately listed in the National Register of Historic Places.

Public awareness of America's black cultural heritage increased in other ways. Tourist literature has begun to feature historic landmarks and properties associated with African American history, and many museums

Since 1962 the National Park Service has preserved the Frederick Douglass House in Washington, D.C., as a historic site. *(Library of Congress)*

dedicated to the presentation and preservation of black history have been established or rejuvenated. Other museums have established permanent displays and traveling exhibits featuring black achievements and lifestyles. Thanks to these advances, Americans from diverse cultural backgrounds began to learn more about African American history and the role that the black community played in the development of the United States. Many people learned that black men were among the first cowboys in the American West and that many useful inventions and important scientific discoveries were made by African Americans. School textbooks began to incorporate information about the role of black soldiers during the Civil War and World War II and about the contributions of black laborers in building the nation's canals, railroads, and bridges.

Grassroots Preservation Efforts
With the advent of a new emphasis on the historic contributions of ordinary people, the number of black-related properties listed in the National Register of Historic Places expanded rapidly. The increase was encouraged through the efforts of many state historic preservation offices. The state of Missouri serves as a typical example of this expansion. Between 1990 and 1994, the National Register inserted at least ten new listings from Missouri related to African American history. The new listings included a community center, several churches, two schools, Kansas City's famous 18th and Vine Historic District (where black commerce and jazz have a glorious history), a Young Men's Christian Association (YMCA) building, and a private home. These listings joined such famous Missouri black landmarks as the George Washington Carver National Monument, the John W. "Blind" Boone House, the Scott Joplin House, and the Jefferson Nation Expansion Memorial National Historic Site (home of the St. Louis Arch and site of the old federal courthouse where the second Dred Scott trial was held).

In the early 1990's, the Missouri Historic Preservation Program included several grants for black-related studies and surveys. In 1993 these grants included one awarded to Lincoln University for an archaeological inventory of historic black communities throughout the state and another to Colored Paths, an organization conducting a survey of slave burials in Warren County, Missouri. The state program also printed several feature articles on black history in its bimonthly publication *Preservation Issues*. One article told about the widely publicized 1939 sharecroppers' demonstrations held in the southern region of the state known as the Bootheel. These black Missouri sharecroppers protested their eviction from their homes by landlords who were abandoning the share and rental system of farm production in favor of day labor. Other articles highlighted the experiences of more than eighty-four hundred blacks who served in the Union army during the Civil War, and the history of the Pennytown Project, a predominantly black community in Missouri's Saline County.

An Ongoing Process
New historic sites are constantly under consideration by preservationists. For example, in October, 1992, a federal law established the Brown v. Board of Education National Historic Site to commemorate the landmark 1954 U.S. Supreme Court decision aimed at ending segregation in public schools. Located in Topeka, Kansas, the site is the Monroe Elementary School, the segregated school that was attended by the lead plaintiff's daughter, Linda Brown, when the lawsuit was initially filed in 1951.

Interest in black history and culture has brought to light the important roles that African Americans have played in the development of the United States. This heightened his-

(continued on page 1215)

Historic Sites

Alex Haley House (Henning, Tenn.). Author Alex HALEY's house, which recaptures the 1920's era, opened as a museum in 1986. Haley spent his summers here, visiting with family and absorbing the stories that became the basis for his best-selling book *Roots: The Saga of an American Family* (1976).

Allensworth State Park (Allensworth, Calif.). In an attempt to help African Americans escape from racial animosity in the East during the early twentieth century, Colonel Allen ALLENSWORTH established a BLACK TOWN in Northern California. The town died out when large-scale agriculture moved into the area. Allensworth's home and a school have been restored, and a museum in the park describes local history.

Auburn Avenue/Martin Luther King, Jr., Birthplace Historic district in ATLANTA, GEORGIA. In 1980 the National Park Service, by invitation of the King family, began to administer the new Martin Luther KING, Jr., Historic District, a parcel of 23 acres that includes King's birthplace, grave, and the EBENEZER BAPTIST CHURCH. In the mid 1990's, the relationship between the two parties became strained when the Park Service revealed plans for a new visitors' center.

The agency signed an agreement with the church in which the church deeded control to the agency in exchange for a new church to be built to the congregation's specifications. Separately, the city of Atlanta deeded a piece of property to the Park Service for the purpose of constructing a new visitors' center in time for the 1996 Summer Olympics. The King family accused the agency of being land-hungry, but the heart of the controversy involved the deeper question of who should control the public interpretation of history. While some African American leaders supported the King family, the black community in Atlanta sided almost unanimously with the National Park Service. Many in the Auburn Avenue Historic District complained that the King family was aloof and uncaring about the concerns of local residents.

Beale Street Historic District (Memphis, Tenn.). The primary site of the BLUES culture during the 1920's, this district began to undergo renovation in the 1970's. It features places of entertainment as well as historical markers on every corner outlining the area's history and indicating landmark buildings.

Boston African American National Historic Site. Located in BOSTON's Beacon Hill neighborhood, the site features fifteen pre-Civil War structures relating to the history of Boston's nineteenth century African American community. One structure is the African Meeting House, constructed in 1806 and the oldest standing black church in the United States. As the CIVIL WAR neared, it became a center of political activity, and most abolitionist leaders spoke from the church's pulpit. All of the structures are linked by the 1.6-mile Black Heritage Trail, which also features Augustus Saint-Gaudens's bronze memorial to the FIFTY-FOURTH MASSACHUSETTS COLORED INFANTRY.

Charlotte Hawkins Brown Memorial (Sedalia, N.C.). Memorial located on the former campus of Palmer Institute. In 1902 Brown founded Palmer Institute as a vocational school, but it expanded into academics and later was accredited as a secondary school. It survived until 1971, ten years after its founder's death. In 1987 the campus and Charlotte Hawkins BROWN's residence were made into a memorial.

Civil Rights Memorial (Montgomery, Ala.). Commissioned by the SOUTHERN POVERTY LAW CENTER, designed by sculptor Maya Lin—who also designed the Vietnam War Memorial in Washington, D.C.—and dedicated in 1989, the memorial consists of two pieces of black granite, a circular stone on which the names of forty civil rights martyrs are inscribed, and a wall of rushing water.

Fort Pillow (near Henning, Tenn.). National historical landmark commemorating one of the worst massacres of the Civil War. On April 12, 1864, Confederate soldiers under the command of General Nathan Bedford Forrest captured and subsequently killed the approximately two hundred African American troops who were among those defending the fort. The action strengthened the resolve of other African American soldiers fighting for the Union. Forrest later helped organize the KU KLUX KLAN.

Fort Scott National Historic Site (Kansas). Frontier military post built in 1843. During the Civil War, the

(continued)

state of Kansas took the early lead in forming black military units to fight for the Union. By the fall of 1861, individual black men—mostly freedmen or runaway slaves—were being enrolled. The First Kansas Colored Volunteer Infantry Regiment was formally mustered into the U.S. Army at Fort Scott on January 13, 1863. It was the fifth black regiment to be formed in the entire Union Army, and it was soon followed by the Second Kansas Colored Volunteer Infantry Regiment. Throughout the war, both regiments were commended for their bravery, discipline, and gallantry under fire.

Fort Wagner (Morris Island, S.C.). Site of a Civil War battle, July, 1863. Troops from the Fifty-fourth Massachusetts Colored Infantry, under the command of white abolitionist Robert Gould Shaw, unsuccessfully attacked this Confederate fort. Although more than one-quarter of the regiment suffered casualties and Shaw was killed, the battle proved that African American troops fought with distinction. The battle was dramatized in the 1989 film *Glory*.

Freetown Village of the Indiana State Museum. Established in 1982 as a living history museum, Freetown Village attempts to re-create life in a typical African American community in INDIANA around 1870, after the end of the Civil War. Visitors interact with guides who perform in the roles of African Americans of this period going about their daily lives.

Joe Louis Memorial Sculpture DETROIT has two sculptures honoring heavyweight boxing champion Joe LOUIS. Robert Graham's controversial twenty-four-foot bronze arm and clenched fist was unveiled in September of 1986, at the intersection of Woodward and Jefferson Avenues. It was a gift to the city from *Sports Illustrated* magazine. In 1987 Edward Hamilton's twelve-foot bronze likeness of Louis in a crouched boxing stance (commissioned by the city in 1984) was installed in the atrium of Cobo Center, on Washington Boulevard.

Louis Armstrong Park and the Old U.S. Mint Museum. Two historic sites dedicated to African American culture and located near the French Quarter in NEW ORLEANS, LOUISIANA. Louis Armstrong Park is dedicated to the memory of jazz musician ARMSTRONG, who began his trumpet playing and singing in the bars and brothels of Basin Street in the Storyville district. Formerly known as Congo Square, the site was once a popular Sunday afternoon gathering place for local African American residents. After the Civil War, it was renamed Beauregard Square to honor Confederate General P. G. T. Beauregard, who supported desegregation during Reconstruction.

In 1980 the park was rededicated as Louis Armstrong Park and underwent extensive landscaping. It features lagoons, bridges, fountains, and a twelve-foot statue of Armstrong created by noted sculptor Elizabeth CATLETT. The 1826 Preservation Hall building has also been preserved.

The building that houses the Old U.S. Mint Museum served as a federal mint from 1838 until 1861, when it was taken over by the Confederacy. After the war, the building again housed a federal mint until 1909. Taken over by the state in 1966, it is now home to the New Orleans Jazz and Carnival Museum, the world's largest Mardi Gras exhibit, and the Historical Center.

Memorial to the Massachusetts Fifty-fourth Regiment (Boston, Mass.). This bronze relief sculpture located on the edge of the Boston Common was designed by Augustus Saint-Gaudens and completed in 1897. It commemorates the Civil War's first enlisted black regiment, which was devastated in an assault on Fort Wagner, South Carolina, in 1863. The regiment was the inspiration for Robert Lowell's poem "For the Union Dead" (1960). The sculpture, which features Colonel Robert Gould Shaw more prominently than his anonymous black soldiers, has sparked controversy, though many critics and viewers have admired the courage etched into the faces of the troops.

W. C. Handy Birthplace, Museum, and Library (Florence, Ala.). Historic site located a few blocks from the St. Paul AFRICAN METHODIST EPISCOPAL ZION CHURCH, where Handy's grandfather and father served as pastors. The restored two-room log cabin and museum house exhibits including annotated musical scores, recordings, musical instruments, and other mementos associated with the man known as the "Father of the Blues."

torical awareness has grown to include other minority groups and led to a greater appreciation of all ethnic peoples as well as a greater recognition of the contributions that have been made by women of all colors.

Historic preservation offices hope that gains made by African Americans and other minorities in the late twentieth century will continue to give them the financial means and the desire to continue efforts to preserve America's cultural heritage. Preservationists find comfort in the knowledge that the growth of multiethnic and multicultural awareness has built a firmer base for the national support of such preservation efforts.

—*Kay Hively*

Suggested Readings:

Bolles, A. Lynn. "From the 'Mystic Years' to the Harlem Renaissance: Art and Community in African America." In *African American Historic Places*, edited by Beth L. Savage. Washington, D.C.: Preservation Press, 1994.

Curtis, Nancy C. *Black Heritage Sites: An African American Odyssey and Finder's Guide*. Chicago: American Library Association, 1996.

Frazier, E. Franklin. *The Negro Church in America*. New York: Schocken Books, 1964.

Grossman, James R. "From Place to Place: African American Migration and Historic Sites." In *African American Historic Places*, edited by Beth L. Savage. Washington, D.C.: Preservation Press, 1994.

Haskins, James. *Hippocrene U.S.A. Guide to Historic Black South: Historical Sites, Cultural Centers, and Musical Happenings of the African-American South*. New York: Hippocrene Books, 1993.

Loth, Calder. *Virginia Landmarks of Black History: Sites on the Virginia Landmarks Register and the National Register of Historic Places*. Charlottesville: University Press of Virginia, 1995.

Lyon, Elizabeth A., and Frederick C. Williamson. "The Preservation Movement Rediscovers America." In *African American Historic Places*, edited by Beth L. Savage. Washington, D.C.: Preservation Press, 1994.

McCullough, David. "A Sense of Time and Place." In *Past Meets Future: Saving America's Historic Environments*, edited by Antoinette J. Lee. Washington, D.C.: Preservation Press, 1992.

Thum, Marcella. *Hippocrene U.S.A. Guide to Black America: A Directory of Historic and Cultural Sites Relating to Black America*. New York: Hippocrene Books, 1991.

Wright, John A., Jean E. Meeh Gosebrink, and Candace O'Connor. *Discovering African-American St. Louis: A Guide to Historic Sites*. St. Louis: Missouri Historical Society Press, 1994.

Historiography: African American historiography is primarily the study of the crafting of history by and about people of African descent in the United States. Many African American historians have been motivated to respond to the distortion or negation of black history and culture in white historical studies. As early as the 1820's, David WALKER, an abolitionist in Boston, insisted in his *Appeal to the Coloured Citizens of the World* (1829) that Africans must challenge white writers' racial depictions:

> The refutations written down by white friends are not enough—they are whites—we are blacks. We, and the world, wish to see the charges of [inferiority] refuted by blacks themselves.

One of the major areas addressed by early historiographers was negative white depictions of Africa. A number of black scholars recognized the great importance of Africa and used African history to rebut allegations of black inferiority.

Some of the first records of African American history were created by Africans who wrote and published manifestos, testimonials, and petitions to colonial legislatures asking for freedom, protesting their treatment in the colonies, and rebutting negative depictions of Africa and Africans. Using the language of the Declaration of Independence, black people in MASSACHUSETTS sent a petition to the colonial legislature in 1774 asking for a law giving them what they considered their natural right—freedom—and liberty for their children. The manifesto argues that Africans were unjustly stolen from Africa, "a populous, pleasant and plentiful country" and forced into enslavement "within the bowels of a free and christian Country."

Paul CUFFE, a wealthy Massachusetts mariner and emigrationist, helped compose petitions in the late 1700's protesting black taxation without black representation. He called attention to the contributions of Africans to American society, especially during the AMERICAN REVOLUTION, to attempt to influence white public opinion and public policy.

Slave Narratives and Personal Histories

Autobiography or personal narrative characterized the ensuing trend in African American historiography. Enslaved Africans who escaped to freedom often wrote or dictated narratives about their experiences. Their chronicles served as an indictment of a system that not only oppressed Africans but also avoided facing that oppression honestly.

It is estimated that approximately six thousand SLAVE NARRATIVES were written. One of the best known is *The Interesting Narrative of the Life of Olaudah Equiano: Or, Gustavus Vassa, an African* (1790), in which EQUIANO told of being kidnaped from Benin in what later became Nigeria in West Africa, and described the horrible experiences he suffered before he was able to purchase his freedom in PHILADELPHIA, PENNSYLVANIA. The famous abolitionist Frederick DOUGLASS penned a narrative, an autobiography, and numerous articles and essays. Harriet Jacobs wrote in *Incidents in the Life of a Slave Girl* (1860) of the sexual, physical, and emotional abuse she suffered as an enslaved woman. William Wells BROWN, an antislavery worker, authored several volumes, including a personal narrative in 1842; a novel, *Clotel: Or, The President's Daughter* (1853), about MISCEGENATION; and a history, *The Black Man: His Antecedents, His Genius, and His Achievements* (1863). Their narratives, created primarily for white audiences, were usually crafted using a formula prescribed by the abolitionist organizations which reproduced and used them in their antislavery work. Again, it was public policy that was being addressed.

A later writer to use the personal narrative method was Ida B. WELLS (Wells-Barnett), who led the fight against LYNCHING at the turn of the twentieth century. She wrote her autobiography, *Crusade for Justice*, in 1928 "for the young people who have so little of our race's history recorded . . . because there is such a lack of authentic race history of RECONSTRUCTION times written by the Negro himself." As a part of her antilynching campaign, she recorded and investigated lynching incidents and used the record she compiled to gain international support for her crusade. The leading black intellectual of the early twentieth century, W. E. B. DU BOIS, also used his own story as a barometer of the African American experience when he wrote *Dusk of Dawn* (1940) and his *Autobiography*, published posthumously in 1968.

The Historical Narrative

The next phase of African American historiography involved historical narratives. These records were designed to combat negative white depictions and to confirm the humanity of Africans by reporting on the contributions blacks made to America's history and culture. William C. NELL, author of the 1855 book *Colored Patriots of the American Revolution*, was one of the first to publish materials of this sort. Participants in the CIVIL WAR wrote chronicles of the contributions black people made during the conflict. Among them were Joseph T. Wilson,

Black Phalanx (1890), Susie King Taylor, *Reminiscences of My Life in Camp with the 33d United States Colored Troops* (1902), and George Washington WILLIAMS, *A History of the Negro Troops in the War of Rebellion, 1861-1865* (1888). In his landmark 1883 study, *History of the Negro Race in America 1619-1880*, Williams served as the benchmark for this period. He wrote that "not as a blind panegyrist of my race, nor as a partisan apologist, but for a love for the 'truth of history' I have striven to record the truth, the whole truth and nothing but the truth."

William J. Simmons followed shortly after with his *Men of Mark* (1887), which gave the biographies of 177 nineteenth-century African Americans who were rarely included in other sources. Hallie Q. BROWN, in 1926, published *Homespun Heroines and Other Women of Distinction* (1926), which provided 60 biographical sketches of African American women.

W. E. B. Du Bois

Writing for a primarily white audience, sociologist W. E. B. Du Bois, a well-established and productive intellectual, used both history and personal narrative to explore what it meant to be an alien in the land of one's birth. He coined the terms "double consciousness" or "the veil" to refer to this phenomenon, a "sense of always looking at one's self through the eyes of others." After his exposure to noted white anthropologist Franz Boas, he was one of the first twentieth-century black academicians to declare that enslavement had not erased all African American retention of traditional African culture.

Du Bois produced a prodigious amount of material on Africa and the AFRICAN DIASPORA that showed African people in the best possible light by concentrating on the contributions they made to the world. In addition to his best-known work, *Souls of Black Folk* (1903), he wrote *The Gift of Black Folk: Negroes in the Making of America* (1924), *Africa: Its Place in Modern History* (1930), *Black Reconstruction: An Essay Toward a History of the Part Which Black Folk Played in the Attempt to Reconstruct Democracy in America, 1860-1880* (1935), *The World and Africa: An Inquiry into the Part Which Africa Has Played in World History* (1947), and other works. He was working on the massive "Encyclopedia Africana," a project aimed at compiling African and diasporan history into one work, when he died in Ghana in 1963. Du Bois's dream for an encyclopedia was finally realized in 1999, with the publication of *Africana: The Encyclopedia of the African and African American Experience* prepared under the direction of Harvard scholars Kwame Anthony Appiah and Henry Louis GATES, Jr.

Du Bois's importance to African American historiography is apparent in the impact he

First published in 1947, John Hope Franklin's *From Slavery to Freedom* has become the standard general history of African Americans. *(Arkent Archive)*

had on black intelligentsia, including John Hope FRANKLIN, who published the definitive one-volume history of African Americans, *From Slavery to Freedom* (1947; and many later editions). While a history instructor at St. Augustine College in NORTH CAROLINA, Franklin sought Du Bois's help in 1940 for a paper he was composing as he worked on his Ph.D. at Harvard University. Another intellectual Du Bois influenced was William Leo Hansberry, who instituted the first college-level courses in African American studies at HOWARD UNIVERSITY in 1922. Hansberry was an early proponent of the contention that civilization began in Africa. Leading intellectuals from the continent of Africa, including Nnamdi Azikiwe of Nigeria, Kwame Nkrumah of Ghana, Jomo Kenyatta and Tom Mboya of Kenya, and Julius Nyerere of Tanganyika (later Tanzania) also sought Du Bois's advice.

Du Bois's primary vehicle for chronicling African American history was the NATIONAL ASSOCIATION FOR THE ADVANCEMENT OF COLORED PEOPLE (NAACP)'s organ, THE CRISIS, but he also wrote for major mainstream publications such as the *American Journal of Sociology*. He also was the editor of such erudite journals as *Phylon* and *Moon* and, from 1898 to 1913, directed the ATLANTA UNIVERSITY Publications on the Study of Negro Problems, a monograph series designed to study black people scientifically.

In 1984 the U.S. Postal Service celebrated Carter G. Woodson's contributions to historiography with this stamp. *(Arkent Archive)*

Carter G. Woodson

One of Du Bois's associates, Carter G. WOODSON, is considered the father of African American history. He ushered in the next phase of historiography, in which highly credentialed individuals produced scholarly historical material. Woodson, who received a Ph.D. in history from Harvard University in 1912 and studied at the Sorbonne in Paris, was a prolific writer. He authored, among many titles, *The Education of the Negro Prior to 1861* (1915), *A Century of Negro Migration* (1918), *The Negro in Our History* (1922), *Negro Orators and Their Orations* (1925), *Free Negro Heads of Families in the United States in 1830* (1925), *The African Background Outlined* (1936), and *African Heroes and Heroines* (1939).

Woodson saw the need to redress what he referred to as the "mis-education" of African American people. In *Mis-education of the Negro* (1933), he contended that blacks should develop an educational system of their own that would serve their needs, arguing that

> The same educational process which inspires and stimulates the oppressor with the thought that he is everything and has accomplished everything worthwhile, de-

> presses and crushes at the same time the spark of genius in the Negro by making him feel that his race does not amount to much and will never measure up to the standards of other peoples.

A strong grounding in African history was Woodson's solution. He stated that children should be taught about the ancient African and Egyptian contributions to science, mathematics, and the arts; African languages; the fact that Greek art and science were influenced by Egypt; and the political significance of African American history.

Woodson founded the Association for the Study of Negro Life and History (ASNLH) in Washington, D.C., in 1915. He founded the JOURNAL OF NEGRO HISTORY in 1916 and the NEGRO HISTORY BULLETIN in 1930. Both were devised to promote black history through the publication of heavily documented and meticulously researched academic work on the African American experience. The *Journal of Negro History* was aimed at scholars, while the *Negro History Bulletin* targeted the general public and schoolchildren. Woodson also organized Associated Publishers, which published the works of major intellectuals. He is perhaps best known, however, for pioneering Negro History Week in 1926. Fifty years later, in keeping with the activism of the 1960's and 1970's, it became BLACK HISTORY MONTH.

Wesley, Greene, Brawley, Frazier

Charles WESLEY was one of the highly accredited academicians generating historical information during the 1930's. He received a Ph.D. in history from Harvard University in 1925 and studied primary documents on slavery in the British Empire in London on a Guggenheim Fellowship. His training allowed him to become a scrupulous researcher and scholar. Wesley wrote numerous books and articles on black history, taught history at Howard University, and was the executive director of Carter Woodson's ASNLH.

Another was Lorenzo Johnston Greene, whose most well-known work is *The Negro in Colonial New England* (1942). Greene trained directly under Woodson, working as his assistant. Woodson, in turn, reviewed Greene's work in the *Journal of Negro History*, giving Greene needed academic exposure. Benjamin BRAWLEY, who produced *A Short History of the American Negro* (1913), *A Social History of the American Negro* (1921), *Early Negro American Writers* (1935), and *Negro Builders and Heroes* (1937), was another well-credentialed scholar. E. Franklin FRAZIER, trained as a sociologist, wrote works including *The Free Negro Family: A Study of Family Origins Before the Civil War* (1932).

John Hope Franklin

John Hope Franklin, with his 1947 seminal work, *From Slavery to Freedom*, legitimized Af-

Historian John Hope Franklin in 1956. *(AP/Wide World Photos)*

rican American historiography. This book, a meticulously researched assessment of African American history published by a major press, has gone through many revisions and editions and continues to be a preeminent text in the field.

White reviewers applauded Franklin's work, one labeling it "Negro history without a chip on its shoulder." The wide acceptance of the book by whites, though, caused many African Americans to be suspicious of it—there were complaints that it was too free of anger. Franklin's work spurred other historians to produce similar surveys, comprehensive studies, or narratives of the African American experience. Saunders Redding wrote *They Came in Chains* (1950), and Rayford Logan wrote *The Negro in American Life and Thought: the Nadir, 1877-1901* (1954); Logan also served as an editor of the *Journal of Negro History*. In the 1990's Franklin's longevity and scholarship were honored by President Bill Clinton, who appointed him chairman of the advisory board of the President's Initiative on Race and Reconciliation.

Black Studies Comes into Its Own

From Slavery to Freedom's publication coincided with growing black activism, as the modern Civil Rights movement was beginning to blossom. In the following decades, African Americans became much more militant. Two notable historiographical trends emerged: a more widespread defiance of Eurocentric depictions of African people and the production of new works of history intended for the masses. *Introduction to Afro-American Studies: A People's College Primer* (1973) is an example. As a matter of principle, no authors or editors were listed on the title page of this text—which was designed for community education and black studies courses—because "the united front around a committed scholarship" was considered more important than highlighting individual scholars.

Coupled with the development of black studies programs in colleges and universities were community education programs. For instance, the Black Panther Party made knowledge of African American history a central part of its platform. Malcolm X and the Nation of Islam promoted black history as essential for the re-education and self-reliance of the African American community. Scholars produced works such as Lerone Bennett, Jr.'s *Before the Mayflower: A History of the Negro in America* (1962; later editions retitled *Before the Mayflower: A History of Black America*), founded, as Bennett stated, "on the work of scholars and specialists [but] designed for the average reader."

The labor of this generation of historians also encompassed the production of historical analyses or reinterpretations of specific aspects of African history. Well-known historians during this era included Benjamin Quarles, the author of *The Negro in the American Revolution* (1961) and *Black Abolitionists* (1969); Dorothy Porter Wesley, curator of Howard University's Moorland Foundation Library of Negro Life and History and the compiler of numerous bibliographies on African Americans in the late 1960's and early 1970's; and C. Eric Lincoln, who wrote *The Black Muslims in America* (1961) and *The Negro Pilgrimage in America* (1967).

The driving force behind this phase was the need to redefine black history from the perspective of those who experienced it. John W. Blassingame, for example, departed from the traditional white interpretations of enslaved Africans when he used primary source material to interpret the experience of enslavement from the perspective of the enslaved in *The Slave Community* (1972). *Black Odyssey: The Afro-American Ordeal in Slavery* (1977) by Nathan Huggins took a similar approach. Lerone Bennett, Jr., wrote in the 1987 edition of *Before the Mayflower* that he had revised earlier editions of his text by detaching "epochal black events—the Founding of Black America, for example—from the white shell" and reinserting them "into a black time-line extending from the African past to the transformation of Black America in the twentieth century."

Self-Published and Lay Historians

This period also saw the rise of lay and self-published historians who, by virtue of the wide acclaim they received among the masses, affected African American historiography and scholarship. Most of these writers eschewed traditional academic systems and, much as Woodson had proposed, engaged in the intensive study of African people without the benefit, or liability, of an educational system that did not particularly value African and African American history and culture. Yosef BEN-JOCHANNAN explained this position in *Africa: Mother of Western Civilization* (1971) by contending,

> The only credentials necessary in the presentation of African history . . . are the documented facts and the sources from whence they are taken. . . . Titles and/or degrees, although having their merits, do not make history correct.

Among Ben-Jochannan's books is *Black Man of the Nile* (1970).

John G. Jackson, Joel A. ROGERS, and George G. M. James are among those in this school of historians. Jackson wrote *Christianity Before Christ* (1938), *Ethiopia and the Origin of Civilization* (1939), and *Pagan Origins of the Christ Myth* (1941) before writing the text for which he is best known, *Introduction to African Civilizations* (1970). Rogers was the author of *From Superman to Man* (1917), *One Hundred Amazing Facts About the Negro with Complete Proof* (1934), *Sex and Race* (1940), *World's Great Men of Color* (1946), and *Africa's Gift to America* (1961). James wrote *Stolen Legacy* (1954). John Henrik CLARKE, the first teacher to be licensed in the state of New York to teach African and African American studies, was responsible for bringing most of these scholars (who were writing long before this phase began) into the public arena through his own work in black studies at Hunter College in New York. Clarke was a critic and writer who also served as editor of *Freedomways* magazine.

A number of later historians nevertheless used academic settings to bring diversity to African American historiography. Sterling STUCKEY wrote about the foundations of black nationalist thought in *Slave Culture* (1987). The Marxist approach informs Manning MARABLE's work, such as *How Capitalism Underdeveloped Black America* (1983). Vincent HARDING brought his own experience as a social activist to bear in *The Other American Revolution* (1980) and *There Is a River: The Black Struggle for Freedom in America* (1981). Harold Cruse challenged the black intelligentsia in 1967 with *Crisis of the Negro Intellectual* and again in 1987 with *Plural but Equal*.

Afrocentric Perspectives

A trend in African American historiography that has been particularly notable since the 1980's is AFROCENTRICITY, the African-centered perspective, which insists that any discussion of the African diaspora be conducted from the viewpoint of African people. C. T. Keto, one of the articulators of this position, says in his *African-Centered Perspective of History* (1989) that such an approach is necessary because it recognizes that black people are naturally endowed with inalienable rights, including the right to freedom, and that there should be no equivocating about the historical conventions of the time to excuse oppression.

These scholars have returned to the earlier practice of linking the primacy and vibrancy of ancient Africa to modern civilization, especially to African American culture. They do not shy away from unpleasant, uncomfortable, or controversial aspects of the African experience. Molefi K. ASANTE, Jacob Carruthers, Asa HILLIARD, Marimba Ani, Tony MARTIN, Maulana KARENGA, Chancellor WILLIAMS, and Linda James-Myers are among the African-centered scholars. Another, Ivan Van Sertima, builds on the earlier work done by Jackson, James, Ben-Jochannan, and Rogers in *They Came Before Columbus: The African Presence in Ancient America* (1976).

Like the nationalists of the 1960's, African-centered scholars did not confine their work to the academic arena. This work appealed to the general public, resulting in a boom in African American publishing companies seeking to capitalize on a market often neglected by mainstream publishers. Africa World Press, Third World Press, and Black Classics Press were three of these publishers.

Black Women's Studies

A parallel trend has been the development of African women's studies, which combines the African-centered perspective with a focus on women. Historians in this field concentrate on covering an often overlooked aspect of the black experience, black women's history. Such work can be, as Paula Giddings says in *When and Where I Enter: The Impact of Black Women on Race and Sex in America* (1984), "at once a personal and objective undertaking." Giddings explains that black women historians have a mission to fulfill because "we have been perceived as token women in Black texts and as token Blacks in feminist ones." Gloria Hull, Darlene Clark HINE, and Nell PAINTER are among the female historians who produce works that can be considered black women's studies.

African American historiography, then, mirrors the historical trends that characterize the concerns of the black community, especially those involving public policy. Black history has covered a wide range of experiences, from the continent of Africa to modern American concerns, but African American historians have always been absorbed by a single issue—telling their own story about what it means to be black in the United States.

—Ella Forbes

See also: African cultural transformations; Higher education; Intellectuals and scholars.

Suggested Readings:

Ben-Jochannan, Yosef. *Africa: Mother of Western Civilization.* New York: Alkebu-lan Books, 1971.

Bennett, Lerone, Jr. *Before the Mayflower: A History of Black America.* 6th ed. Chicago: Johnson, 1987.

Franklin, John Hope, and Alfred A. Moss, Jr. *From Slavery to Freedom: A History of African Americans.* 7th ed. New York: McGraw-Hill, 1994.

Hine, Darlene Clark, ed. *The State of Afro-American History: Past, Present, and Future.* Baton Rouge: Louisiana State University Press, 1986.

Karenga, Maulana. *Introduction to Black Studies.* Los Angeles: Kawaida Publications, 1984.

Keto, C. T. *Africa-Centered Perspective of History.* Blackwood, N.J.: K.A. Publications, 1989.

Meier, August, and Elliott Rudwick. *Black History and the Historical Profession, 1915-1980.* Urbana: University of Illinois Press, 1986.

Ogunleye, Tolagbe. "African American Folklore: Its Role in Reconstructing African American History." *Journal of Black Studies* 27 (March, 1997): 435-455.

Parish, Peter J. *Slavery: History and Historians.* New York: Harper & Row, 1989.

Salzman, Jack, David L. Smith, and Cornel West, eds. *Encyclopedia of African-American Culture and History.* New York: Simon & Schuster Macmillan, 1996.

Smith, John D. *Slavery, Race, and American History: Historical Conflict, Trends, and Method, 1866-1953.* Armonk, N.Y.: M. E. Sharpe, 1999.

Woodson, Carter G. *Mis-Education of the Negro*. Washington, D.C.: Association for the Study of Negro Life and History, 1933.

Hodge, Derek M. (b. October 5, 1941, Frederiksted, Virgin Islands): Territorial senator. Hodge grew up in the Virgin Islands and attended college in the United States. He received his bachelor of arts degree from Michigan State University in 1963 and graduated from Georgetown University Law Center with a J.D. degree in 1971. Hodge began private practice as an attorney in 1972.

Hodge's first political campaign occurred in 1984, when he was elected to serve in the Virgin Islands territorial senate for a two-year term, during which Hodges served as senate president. In 1986 he was elected lieutenant governor of the islands.

See also: Politics and government.

Saxophonist Johnny Hodges when he was performing with the Duke Ellington Orchestra. *(Frank Driggs/Archive Photos)*

Hodges, Johnny (July 25, 1907, Cambridge, Massachusetts—May 11, 1970, New York, New York): Alto and soprano saxophonist. Nicknamed "Rabbit" and "Jeep," John Cornelius "Johnny" Hodges, known for his long tenure with the Duke Ellington Orchestra, is considered one of the finest alto saxophonists of all time because of his impeccable tone and abilities as a soloist. Introduced to both drums and piano in his youth, he began playing the soprano saxophone at the age of thirteen, having been given the instrument by Sidney Bechet, his first music teacher.

During the 1920's, Hodges worked in Harlem with Willie "the Lion" Smith, Bobby Sawyer, Lloyd Scott, Chick Webb, Luckey Roberts, and Sidney Bechet. Hodges joined Duke Ellington in 1928 and performed at the Cotton Club. Hodges's early recordings with Ellington include "Yellow Dog Blues/Tishomingo Blues" (1928) and "It Don't Mean a Thing" (1932), as well as the later solo feature, "Warm Valley" (1940). Hodges also was featured on "In a Sentimental Mood" and "Passion Flower." During the 1930's, Hodges recorded as well with Benny Goodman and Lionel Hampton, but his primary affiliation was with Ellington's band. Hodges's recordings as a leader during this period include "Jeep's Blues" (1938) and "Things Ain't What They Used to Be" (1941).

Hodges was the recipient of numerous awards, including the *Esquire* Gold Award (1945), the *Down Beat* poll (1940-1949), the *Metronome* poll (1945-1947), and the *Down Beat* critics' poll (1959). Hodges also is credited with writing compositions in collaboration with Duke Ellington, such as "Cotton Club Stomp" (1943) and "It Shouldn't Happen to a Dream" (1946). Hodges published a collection of his own compositions, *Sax Originals* (1945).

In 1951 Hodges left Ellington and started his own group with Lawrence Brown and Sonny Greer, both Ellingtonians. For a time, Hodges's small group included John COLTRANE. Hodges's small group of the 1950's recorded "Castle Rock" (1951), which became a RHYTHM-AND-BLUES hit. Hodges also recorded with Earl Hines and Wild Bill Davis. During Hodges's absence from the Ellington Orchestra, he appeared on Ted Steele's *Cavalcade of Bands* television show. In 1955 Hodges rejoined Ellington, remaining with Ellington's band until the end of his own career.
See also: Jazz; Music.

Holiday, Billie (Eleanora Fagan Holiday; April 7, 1915, Philadelphia, Pennsylvania—July 17, 1959, New York, New York): JAZZ singer. Her first recording, "Your Mother's Son-in-Law," with Benny Goodman in 1933, made it apparent that she had a unique musical talent. Unlike Ella FITZGERALD, Holiday did no SCAT SINGING (singing meaningless syllables instead of words, usually at a brisk tempo); unlike Sarah VAUGHAN, she did not possess a wide vocal range. She was not given to insincere emoting. Rather, Holiday's singing was limited, intimate, and understated, concerned more with nuance than with dramatics. When she first recorded with tenor saxophonist Lester YOUNG in 1937, at a recording session led by pianist Teddy WILSON, she began an intermittent association that would endure until 1957. Vocalist and saxophonist shared a similar legato conception and cared more about whispers than about shouts. Young called her Lady Day; she called him Prez, for president. They were known thereafter by these names.

Holiday enhanced her recordings by using superior supporting musicians. In addition to Wilson and Young, she employed such indisputably great instrumentalists as trumpeters Buck Clayton and Roy ELDRIDGE and saxophonists Chu Berry, Benny CARTER, Coleman HAWKINS, and Ben WEBSTER. No vocalist has had more consistently superior accompaniment. Some of her best known songs include "Strange Fruit," a hit record in 1939, and "God Bless the Child."

Holiday's troubled life—her humble beginnings, her narcotics problems—provided better material than many scriptwriters can concoct. Singer Diana Ross starred as Holiday in *Lady Sings the Blues*, a 1972 film based loosely on Holiday's 1956 autobiography of the same title. Holiday's own magnificent live performances also have been captured on film, in *The Sound of Jazz*, a television program broadcast on CBS in 1957. That film features

In 1972 Diana Ross portrayed Billie Holiday in *Lady Sings the Blues*. *(Museum of Modern Art, Film Stills Archive)*

Billie Holiday in 1949. *(Library of Congress)*

Holiday singing her own composition "Fine and Mellow." This was her last great performance, enhanced by many of her old instrumental colleagues.
See also: Music.

Holland, Endesha Ida Mae (b. August 29, 1944, Greenwood, Mississippi): Dramatist, educator, and activist. Born to a mother who worked as a midwife and ran a Mississippi boardinghouse that was actually a house of prostitution, Holland never knew the identity of her father. As a youngster, she worked as a babysitter to help her mother make ends meet. Raped by a white employer when she was only eleven years old, Holland dropped out of school at thirteen and worked as a prostitute to help pay her family's rent.

In 1962 Holland came in contact with the local office of the Student Nonviolent Coordinating Committee (SNCC) and began working as a volunteer. Her activities with SNCC involved traveling throughout the country as a civil rights activist, and she was arrested a number of times along with other SNCC members. Holland's high profile within the organization incurred the wrath of Greenwood's white residents; a firebomb killed her mother and destroyed her mother's home in 1965.

After this incident, Holland left Mississippi and attended college part-time at the University of Minnesota. There, she helped organize a black studies program and founded a prison aid program called Women Helping Offenders (WHO). After completing her undergraduate degree in 1979, Holland went on to earn her Ph.D. in 1986. She accepted an appointment to teach at the State University of New York at Buffalo in the school's American studies department.

Holland's play *From the Mississippi Delta*, opened Off Broadway at the Circle in the Square theater in November of 1991. Based on Holland's life experience and that of her mother, the play was adapted from an earlier script entitled *The Second Doctor Lady*, which had been performed by the Negro Ensemble Company in 1979 before being produced at several regional theaters and at the Old Vic Theater in London. The play testifies to the ability of African Americans— particularly women—to overcome poverty and abuse.

In recognition of her accomplishments as an activist and an educator, Holland's hometown of Greenwood declared October 16 as Dr. Endesha Ida Mae Holland Day in 1991.

Holland, Jerome H. (b. January 9, 1916, Auburn, New York): Educator and political appointee. Holland received his B.S. and M.S. degrees from Cornell University in 1939 and 1941, respectively. He taught at Lincoln University from 1939 to 1942 and received his Ph.D. from the University of Pennsylvania in 1950. Holland was an administrator at Tennessee A&I State University from 1946 to 1951 before becoming president of Delaware State College in 1953. He left Delaware State to become president of Hampton Institute in 1960. He was known for his skill in mediating disputes between student radicals and college authorities at Hampton during the late 1960's.

President Richard Nixon appointed Holland to serve as U.S. ambassador to Sweden in 1970. Holland resigned from this post in 1972 to become the first African American member of the Board of Directors of the New York Stock Exchange. He later served on the boards of many prominent corporations, including AT&T, Chrysler Corporation, General Foods, Union Carbide, and Manufacturers Hanover Trust.

See also: Diplomats.

Holman, M. Carl (June 27, 1919, Minter City, Mississippi—August 9, 1988, Washington, D.C.): Poet, civil rights leader, and president of the National Urban Coalition. Often described as the "godfather" of the Civil Rights movement, Holman grew up in St. Louis, Missouri, and graduated magna cum laude from Lincoln University in 1942. He earned a master's degree from the University of Chicago (1944) and a master of fine arts degree from Yale University (1954). He taught at Hampton Institute and at Lincoln University before beginning a fourteen-year term as an English professor at Clark College in Atlanta, Georgia, in 1949.

During the 1950's, Holman was active in the early developments of the Civil Rights movement in the South, serving as adviser to civil rights leaders and strategist for student demonstrators participating in sit-ins and freedom rides. He was a published poet and wrote extensively on African American and urban issues for magazines and newspapers. He was also editor of the *Atlanta Inquirer*, an award-winning newspaper reporting on civil rights activities. In 1962 Holman moved to Washington, D.C., to become an information officer at the U.S. Commission on Civil Rights, an organization considered to be the unofficial African American cabinet of the Kennedy and Johnson administrations. He became special assistant to the staff director in 1965 and deputy director in 1966.

In 1971 Holman succeeded John Gardner as president of the National Urban Coalition, a national advocacy organization for a variety of urban interests. From then until his death from cancer, Holman was a major figure in urban politics, serving as spokesman for the poor and underprivileged and calling attention to city problems ranging from inadequate housing and a declining tax base to unemployment.

Holman was a compassionate leader, trusted by radicals and conservatives alike. He was known for an uncanny ability to form coalitions and find ways for diverse groups to work together for a common purpose. Particularly concerned about improving educational opportunities for young African Americans, Holman promoted a "dual literacy" program in his later years. This learning program emphasized not only reading, writing, and speaking, but also skills in science, math, and technology.

Homicide: Homicide is a severe problem in urban areas, especially in the inner-city neighborhoods where many African Americans live in poverty. The American media promulgate news stories of gang killings, especially those in which bystanders are heedlessly killed, and other violent crimes committed by blacks. Regardless of the focus of such coverage, white Americans commit more crimes overall than blacks do. On the other hand, blacks do commit violent crimes, including homicide, in numbers that significantly exceed their percentage of the U.S. population, and in 1997 more than half of the people arrested for murder were black.

Although blacks comprised between 12 and 13 percent of the population in 1997, about 56 percent of the murder suspects arrested that year were African Americans. By far, most victims of African American murderers are also African American. In 1997 blacks represented 49 percent of the country's murder victims.

Between 1976 and 1997, 94 percent of black victims were killed by blacks; 85 percent of white victims were killed by whites. Blacks were seven times more likely than whites to be murdered. The difference for young men was even greater: A young black man was eleven times more likely to be murdered than a young white man. In the 1990's homicide was the leading cause of death among young black men.

Homicides sometimes occur in the course of another crime, such as robbery, that is poorly executed. Black men between the ages of sixteen and twenty-four represented roughly 1 percent of the population age twelve or older in the 1990's, but they experienced about 5 percent of all violent victimizations. African American youths were more likely than white youths to be victims of crimes involving guns. Black male teenagers, sixteen to nineteen, were four times more likely than teenage whites to be victimized by someone with a handgun.

Homicide Deaths per 100,000 People, 1970, 1980-1995

	Homicide Rate			
	White		*Black*	
Year	*Male*	*Female*	*Male*	*Female*
1970	6.8	2.1	67.6	13.3
1980	10.9	3.2	66.6	13.5
1981	10.4	3.1	64.8	12.7
1982	9.6	3.1	59.1	12.0
1983	8.6	2.8	51.4	11.3
1984	8.3	2.9	48.7	11.2
1985	8.2	2.9	48.4	11.0
1986	8.6	3.0	55.0	12.1
1987	7.9	3.0	53.3	12.6
1988	7.9	2.9	58.0	13.2
1989	8.2	2.8	61.1	12.9
1990	9.0	2.8	69.2	13.5
1991	9.3	3.0	72.0	14.2
1992	9.1	2.8	67.5	13.1
1993	8.6	3.0	69.7	13.6
1994	8.5	2.6	65.1	12.4
1995	7.8	2.7	56.3	11.1

Source: U.S. National Center for Health Statistics.

Risk Factors and Contributing Causes

Between 1977 and 1997, the homicide victimization rate for black men between the ages of eighteen and twenty-four steadily increased. By 1988 it had soared to triple-digit levels. From 88.1 per 100,000 in 1977, it increased to 98.2 in 1987 and to 143.4 in 1997. The highest rate during this twenty-year period was in 1993, at 187.1 per 100,000; the lowest was in 1984, 69.7.

Factors that identify people at higher than normal risk of homicide include most of the conditions encountered by blacks living in inner-city neighborhoods: living in POVERTY, dropping out of school, and using drugs and engaging in other types of criminal behavior. Moreover, escaping an inner-city environment does not guarantee complete cancellation of risk, since gang activity and the drug trade have invaded suburban and even rural neighborhoods as well.

Most violent attacks resulting in homicide have criminal motivation. The expansion of the drug trade in the United States has created an atmosphere of violent confrontation among traffickers similar to the gang violence of the Prohibition era. African American GANGS have been transformed into crime syndicates that attempt to control drug distribution. Many gang members are killed as a result of these criminal activities; disputes over drug sales result in the deaths of drug users as well as sellers.

In the absence of economic opportunity, many inner-city black youths have resorted to

Firearm Homicide Deaths per 100,000 People, 1995

	5-14 years old	15-24 years old	25-34 years old	35-44 years old	45-54 years old	55-64 years old	65-74 years old	75-84 years old	85 years and over
Male									
White	0.9	13.6	9.8	6.3	4.0	2.8	1.5	0.8	(–)
Black	4.1	121.0	80.7	38.3	24.6	15.9	10.8	(–)	(–)
Female									
White	0.4	2.2	2.3	1.8	1.2	0.8	0.7	0.8	(–)
Black	1.2	11.8	10.2	6.7	3.4	2.3	(–)	(–)	(–)

Source: U.S. National Center for Health Statistics.
Note: (–) Does not meet standard of reliability.

street crime, including muggings, car theft, and robberies. African Americans constitute a majority of those arrested for street robberies, and many offenders are found to be carrying handguns. The vast majority of robberies result in no injury to victims. However, nearly 10 percent of all homicides occur in the course of armed robberies.

Some homicides occur as the result of situational motivation, including sexual jealousy and real or imagined slights to the offender's ego. These types of homicide most often occur as the result of a quarrel with a family member or acquaintance. In nearly 50 percent of all black homicides, the murderer and the victim were acquainted.

Self-Destructive Behavior

The incidence of homicide among African Americans is related to the living conditions they endure, particularly the conditions that exist in the United States' inner-city neighborhoods. Meaningful economic opportunities are limited for most inner-city residents. They are severely limited for young black men, who experience a dramatically higher unemployment rate than their white counterparts.

As family ties with older male relatives and social ties with other residents who could serve as positive role models have deteriorated, many black male teenagers and young adults have turned to neighborhood gangs to provide them with a sense of community, stability, and power. As their hopes for improvement are frustrated, these inner-city residents may turn to alcohol or drugs for escape and become involved in criminal activities that express their contempt for their situation and their community.

Alienation and its resulting self-destructive behavior have been evident in the unemotional and seemingly random character of some violent crimes committed by young urban blacks. The media tend to focus public attention on violent and lurid crimes involving black offenders and white victims. Random violence and "sport violence" in particular were widely reported in the 1980's and 1990's. In the late 1980's for example, the media popularized the term "wilding" in its descriptions of the behavior of black youths who brutally assaulted a white female jogger in NEW YORK CITY's Central Park. Another widely publicized incident involved the homicide of a young white male tourist from Utah who was murdered in New York City when he resisted a robbery attempt against his family.

Little media attention has been focused on the much more pervasive problem of BLACK-ON-BLACK VIOLENCE and on how homicides related to this type of violence damage the social bonds within the African American community. Violent crime, including homicide, generally occurs within, not between, racial and ethnic groups. The primary reason is simply that criminals usually victimize people living or working nearby.

—*Judith Ann Warner*

See also: Crime and the criminal justice system; Substance abuse.

Suggested Readings:

Flowers, Ronald B. *Minorities and Criminality*. Westport, Conn.: Greenwood Press, 1988.

Free, Marvin D. *African Americans and the Criminal Justice System*. New York: Garland, 1996.

Gibbs, Jewelle T., ed. *Young, Black, and Male in America: An Endangered Species*. Dover, Mass.: Auburn House, 1988.

Jencks, Christopher. *Rethinking Social Policy: Race, Poverty, and the Underclass*. Cambridge, Mass.: Harvard University Press, 1992.

Pierce, H. B. "Blacks and Law Enforcement: Towards Police Brutality Reduction." *The Black Scholar* 17 (1986): 49-54.

Rose, H. M. "Can We Substantially Lower Homicide Risk in the Nation's Larger Black Communities?" In *Report of the Secretary's Task Force on Black and Minority Health*. Vol. 5. Washington, D.C.: Department of Health and Human Services, 1986.

Homosexuality: By the 1990's, the subject of African American homosexuality had received little public attention and had not yet been fully explored by scholars or the black community. African American gay men and lesbians come from all walks of life, from all classes, and from every occupational group. Their near invisibility, however, seemed to be the result of a general tendency on the part of white mainstream society to view the black community as a monolithic entity, thus failing to acknowledge its diversity. In addition, the slighting of the black lesbian experience grew out of the general lack of public attention given to the entire lesbian community.

Public ignorance of homosexuality within the African American community could be attributed mostly to the general perception that homosexuality itself was alien to the black experience and that discrimination on the basis of racial identity far outweighed the effects of discrimination based on sexual orientation. Nevertheless, a careful examination of the experiences of black gay men and lesbians reveals that they have been subjected to prejudice and misunderstanding as a minority within a minority. Assigned to MINORITY GROUP status by their racial heritage, black gays and lesbians have found that their sexual desires and behavior also classify them as a minority practicing an alternative lifestyle.

Social Strictures

As in white American society, homosexuality has been considered to be immoral within African American culture. Black churches, which have historically wielded enormous influence within the black community, continue to encourage strict adherence to the moral teachings of the Bible. In addition to these conservative religious values, other social pressures growing out of the slavery experience and its aftermath have contributed to homophobia in the black community.

Having struggled for so many years to assert their identity as human beings who deserved to be accorded equal rights and to be treated with respect, many African Americans have viewed black homosexuality as a betrayal of the image of black manhood, with black gay men seen as "feminizing" themselves to the point of relinquishing their male identity. Black women who have affirmed a lesbian identity have been seen as flouting conventional feminine roles as supportive wives and nurturing mothers. Even when the black community has extended some tolerance to black homosexuals, there has often been a strong sense that such tolerance will continue only so long as such individuals do not flaunt their identity in white society.

Homosexuality in the African American Community

Evidence of a homosexual subculture within the black community has generally been traced to the JAZZ nightclubs and ballrooms of HARLEM in the 1920's. Harlem clubs such as the Rockland Palace and the SAVOY BALLROOM staged popular drag balls in the 1920's that were attended by blacks as well as whites. The drag subculture of the era was depicted in a novel written by Blair Niles entitled *Strange Brother* (1931).

Other Harlem nightclubs featured popular performers such as Bessie SMITH and Gertrude "Ma" RAINEY, both of whom engaged in lesbian affairs. Entertainer Jackie "Moms" MABLEY launched her career as a stand-up COMIC who parodied the stereotype of the man-crazy woman in public while considering herself to be a lesbian in her private life. Another female entertainer who was more open about her lesbian identity was Gladys Bentley, who was known for her distinctively masculine behavior and attire and her open alliance with her white lesbian lover. During the McCarthy era, however, Bentley came under investigation for her ties to communist organizations and was forced to renounce her lesbianism.

The HARLEM RENAISSANCE movement of the 1920's and 1930's brought several gay and bisexual writers to prominence, including Wallace THURMAN, who wrote about intraracial prejudice in his first novel, *The Blacker the Berry* (1929), and presented a bitter chronicle of his relations with other black writers in his autobiographical second novel, *Infants of the Spring* (1932). Novelist and short-story writer Bruce Nugent was more open about his orientation. His 1926 story "Smoke, Lilies, and Jade" has been identified by some literary scholars as the first fictional account of the black homosexual experience. Poet Countée CULLEN wrote about homoerotic friendship in the poem "Tableau" but generally repressed such themes in his other works. According to biographers, there is evidence that Cullen's marriages—first to Yolande Du Bois and later to Ida Mae Robertson—allowed him to hide his homosexuality.

Other writers were more ambiguous about their sexual orientation. Because author Langston HUGHES was extremely guarded about his private life, the two-volume biography written by scholar Arnold RAMPERSAD contains no speculation about Hughes's alleged homosexuality. British filmmaker Isaac Julien, however, devoted his 1992 film *Looking for Langston* to exploring possible evidence of Hughes's homosexual leanings, particularly since Hughes and several other Harlem Renaissance writers were championed by prominent white literary critic Carl Van Vechten, who was himself gay.

Changing Attitudes

Three important milestones changed the public perception of homosexuals in American society. Two of these milestones involved the classification of homosexuality by the medical community. First, Dr. Alfred Kinsey released his reports on the sexual behavior of American men (published in 1948) and women (published in 1953). Kinsey's research objectively presented the first statistics on the subject of American homosexual behavior. Next, after a long and bitter internal debate, the American Psychiatric Association (APA) removed homosexuality from its official list of mental disorders in 1973, primarily as a result of new research findings and through the political efforts of gay liberation activists. A third important milestone that changed public perception of homosexuality was the police raid on the Stonewall Inn in NEW YORK CITY's Greenwich Village in June of 1969. In the street demonstrations that followed, gay men, drag queens, and lesbians from various social and economic backgrounds joined together to fight for their right to congregate and socialize in their own bars.

Visibility of Black Gays and Lesbians

In the 1960's, novelist James Baldwin was one of the first literary figures to write openly about the black gay experience. He explored themes of black homosexuality in works such as *Another Country* (1962) and *Tell Me How Long the Train's Been Gone* (1968); his 1956 novel *Giovanni's Room* had explored the lives of a white gay protagonist and his Italian lover. The repressive social climate that persuaded Baldwin to live as an expatriate in Europe also forced other black homosexuals to maintain their silence about their sexual orientation.

A Quaker and a pacifist who served as field secretary for the Congress of Racial Equality (CORE), Bayard Rustin was a leading civil rights activist who helped coordinate protests to enforce desegregation of public transportation and was a key organizer of the 1963 March on Washington. Although his arrest on a morals charge in 1953 threatened to make his homosexuality a matter of public record, Rustin did not choose to make his personal life known beyond his close circle of friends and associates.

After the Stonewall riots launched the gay liberation movement of the 1970's and 1980's, many gay men and lesbians were encouraged to be more candid about their homosexuality with family, friends, and colleagues. Even with the advent of the gay rights movement, however, African Americans' fight for acceptance as gays and lesbians has been a series of individual and highly personal struggles. Like white homosexuals, African American homosexuals do not constitute a monolithic group. Their social backgrounds range from middle class to lower class; they have attained various levels of education and wealth; some are religious, while others are atheists or agnostics. Some African American homosexuals wish only to disappear individually into the majority—the heterosexual world. These are considered "mainstream" gays and lesbians. At the other end of the spectrum are gay men and lesbians who enjoy flaunting their differences and openly identify with the homosexual subculture.

Many black gay men and lesbians have aligned themselves with white homosexuals to fight for gay and lesbian rights. At the same time, black gays and lesbians have had to face racism within the larger gay community. During the 1980's, African American lesbians and other lesbian women of color began to speak out about racism within the lesbian community. Just as Alice Walker and other black feminist writers had pointed out that black feminist concerns were being neglected within the

Novelist James Baldwin was one of the first African Americans to write openly about homosexuality. *(AP/ Wide World Photos)*

women's movement, writers such as Audre LORDE, Michelle CLIFF, and Barbara SMITH began to articulate their sense that the experiences of black lesbians were being overlooked by white lesbian activists. Gay activists such as documentary filmmaker Marlon T. RIGGS, writer Essex Hemphill, and public health activists Pat Richardson Norman and Phill Wilson began to take steps to educate the public about the realities of the black homosexual experience through films, books, and public policy.

In 1969 there were fifty lesbian and gay organizations in the United States; by 1995 there were more than twenty-five hundred. African American gays and lesbians have participated in many of these organizations and have been a visible presence at Gay Pride parades and marches celebrating the anniversary of the Stonewall raid. In 1978 the National Coalition of Black Lesbians and Gays was founded. Black gay men helped found the organization Black and White Men Together, which later became known as Men of All Colors Together. In his presidential campaigns of 1984 and 1988, Jesse JACKSON made a point of including gays and lesbians as part of his RAINBOW COALITION. The Black Gay and Lesbian Leadership Forum, which was founded in 1988, worked to organize a "Summit on Homosexuality in the Black Community" that was held in Atlanta in 1990. This summit helped persuade the NATIONAL ASSOCIATION FOR THE ADVANCEMENT OF COLORED PEOPLE (NAACP) to endorse the 1993 March on Washington held by gays, lesbians, and bisexuals.

Gay and Lesbian Literary Heritage

Building on the tradition of James Baldwin as well as themes of black homosexuality found in novels such as *The Color Purple* (1982) and *The Women of Brewster Place* (1982), many black gay and lesbian authors in the 1980's and 1990's found various outlets for expressing their ideas. Works by black gay novelists include Steven Corbin's *Fragments That Remain* (1993) and Larry Duplechan's *Eight Days a Week* (1985); important gay anthologies include *In the Life: A Black Gay Anthology* (1986), edited by Joseph Beam, and *Brother to Brother: New Writings by Black Gay Men* (1991), edited by Essex Hemphill.

E. Lynn Harris, a former computer salesman who is openly bisexual, used his own savings to publish his first novel, *Invisible Life* (1991), before signing a book deal with Doubleday in 1992. Noted lesbian poet Audre Lorde published a collection of speeches and essays entitled *Sister Outsider* (1984), as well as *The Cancer Journals* (1980) and her full-length autobiography *Zami: A New Spelling of My Name* (1982). Ann Allen Shockley has created positive Afrocentric images of lesbian identity in her works, which include the novel *Loving Her* (1974). Shockley has indicated in her works that African American lesbians can develop positive identities and have self-affirming sexual relationships with women from other cultural and class backgrounds.

It is unlikely that there will ever be an accurate count of gays and lesbians in the United States until the stigma associated with homosexuality is removed. In March, 1993, a New York Times/ABC News poll showed that 36 percent of Americans considered homosexuality "an acceptable alternative life style" and that 46 percent supported the legalization of homosexual relations between consenting adults. A majority of respondents—78 percent in fact—supported equal job opportunities for gays. Despite this growing tolerance, homophobia remains an enduring form of prejudice in the United States. Even when they have publicly asserted their homosexual identity, many black gays and lesbians continue to be marginalized within two other marginalized groups: the gay community and the larger black community.

—*Paul T. Lockman, Jr.*

See also: Class structure; Men; Women.

Suggested Readings:

Beam, Joseph, ed. *In the Life: A Black Gay Anthology*. Boston: Alyson, 1986.

Boykin, Keith. *One More River to Cross: Black and Gay in America*. New York: Anchor Books, 1996.

Brandt, Eric, ed. *Dangerous Liaisons: Blacks and Gays and the Struggle for Equality*. New York: New Press, 1999.

Garber, Eric. "T'aint Nobody's Business." *Advocate* (May 13, 1982): 12-13, 15.

Hawkeswood, William G., and Alex W. Costley. *One of the Children: Gay Black Men in Harlem*. Berkeley: University of California Press, 1996.

Hemphill, Essex, ed. *Brother to Brother: New Writings by Black Gay Men*. Boston: Alyson, 1991.

Keating, AnaLouise. "African-American Lesbian Literature." In *The Gay and Lesbian Literary Heritage*, edited by Claude J. Summers. New York: Henry Holt, 1995.

Pettiway, Leon E. *Honey, Honey, Miss Thang: Being Black, Gay, and on the Streets*. Philadelphia: Temple University Press, 1996.

Robert, J. R. *Black Lesbians*. Tallahassee, Fla.: Naiad Press, 1981.

Smith, Michael J., ed. *Black Men/White Men: A Gay Anthology*. San Francisco: Gay Sunshine Press, 1983.

Honky-tonk: Slang term for certain noisy taverns that featured boisterous MUSIC and for the style of music played there. In order to cope with the rowdy, high-spirited crowds that frequented these small nightclubs, the music that developed was energetic, rhythmic, and amplified. BOOGIE-WOOGIE music was often featured in honky-tonks, along with JAZZ and BLUES music. The word "honky-tonk" appeared in many song titles, including "Honky-tonk Train Blues" (1928).

Hood, James Walker (May 30, 1831, Kennet, Pennsylvania—1918): First black missionary to freed slaves in the South. Hood was also a temperance advocate, reconstructionist, CIVIL RIGHTS activist, and bishop of the AFRICAN METHODIST EPISCOPAL ZION CHURCH. Walker played a key role in making NORTH CAROLINA a center of the church. Among his publications is *One Hundred Years of the African Methodist Episcopal Zion Church: Or, the Centennial of African Methodism* (1895).

Hooker, John Lee (b. August 22, 1917?, Clarksdale, Mississippi): BLUES singer and guitarist. (Most sources agree on Hooker's August 22 birthdate, but years given for his birth vary between 1915 and 1920.) What is known about his early life is that he learned to sing in the choir of the AFRICAN METHODIST

John Lee Hooker in 1990. *(AP/Wide World Photos)*

Episcopal Church. Hooker's first exposure to the blues came from an older sister's boyfriend, 1940's recording artist Tony Hollins, who taught Hooker his signature piece, "Crawling King Snake." Hooker's unique "boogie" guitar style came from his stepfather, Will Moore, a musician of some local renown.

At fourteen, Hooker ran away to Memphis, Tennessee, where he worked as an usher in a Beale Street movie theater. His father, the Reverend William Hooker, quickly caught up with him and brought him back to Mississippi. By the age of seventeen, Hooker had moved to Cincinnati, Ohio, where he worked various day jobs while trying to break into the local music scene.

During World War II, Hooker was in Detroit, Michigan, still working odd jobs, when he was discovered playing at a house party by record store owner Elmer Barber. Barber introduced Hooker to record producer Bernie Besman, who secured him a recording deal. In 1948 Hooker released his first recording, the phenomenally successful "Boogie Chillen," backed with "Sally Mae" (named for a favorite aunt), for the Sensation label.

The success of "Boogie Chillen" moved Hooker to devote his full attention to his emerging career. Throughout the 1950's, Hooker recorded a number of sides for a number of companies under various aliases, including Texas Slim, Johnny Williams, John Lee Booker, and Birmingham Sam and His Magic Guitar, in order to maintain some control over his career without being held at the mercy of unscrupulous record companies, which often kept their artists enslaved through a long series of legal restraints.

By the 1960's, Hooker was being recognized by many of the young blues-influenced rock-and-roll musicians. Bands such as Canned Heat in the 1960's and Z. Z. Top in the 1970's based their sounds in large part on Hooker's unique boogie style. In 1989 Hooker recorded an album with an all-star lineup that included, among others, Carlos Santana, Bonnie Raitt, George Thorogood, Robert Cray, and harmonica player Charlie Musselwhite. Entitled *The Healer*, the album won Grammy Awards, W. C. Handy Awards, and the acclaim and adulation of blues fans around the world; it was one of the best-selling blues albums of all time.

Mr. Lucky, a 1991 release, featured Robert Cray as well as Rolling Stones guitarist Keith Richards, guitarists/singers Ry Cooder and Albert Collins, and others. It was equally well received, affording Hooker celebrity status and huge performance fees. Two more albums, *Chill Out* (1995) and *Don't Look Back* (1997, produced by longtime fan Van Morrison) were released in the 1990's, as were a number of compilations of old material. In 1997 Hooker also opened his own club in San Francisco, the Boom Boom Room. Hooker was inducted into the Rock and Roll Hall of Fame in 1990 and given a Blues Foundation lifetime achievement award in 1996. He continued to perform, though on a reduced basis, following an operation in 1994; Hooker was among the headlining acts, for example, at the 1999 Long Beach Blues Festival.

See also: Music.

Hooks, bell (Gloria Watkins, b. 1952, Hopkinsville, Kentucky): Scholar and feminist critic. Hooks acquired the moniker "black public intellectual" for her contributions as a feminist cultural critic and for her challenge to the domination of feminist studies by white women. Hooks is the author of numerous articles and books, virtually all of which concern how African Americans, especially women, are represented in American culture. She traces her lineage to feminist roots. She took her pen name, "bell hooks," from her outspoken great-grandmother, and she styles it in distinctive lowercase letters. She is the author of numerous articles and books, including *Ain't I a Woman: Black Women and Feminism* (1981), *Feminist Theory from Margin to Center* (1984), *Talking Back: Thinking Feminist, Thinking Black* (1989), *Yearning: Race, Gender, and Cultural Politics* (1990), and *Reel to Real: Race, Sex, and Class at the Movies* (1996). She published a poetry volume, *A Woman's Mourning Song*, in 1993.

Much of hooks's youth was spent reading aloud to illiterate members of her community and chafing under the authority exercised over her family by her father. Upon entering Stanford University in the early 1970's, she enrolled in women's studies classes and joined feminist reading groups. She encountered hostility from white feminists when she challenged their tendency to read and discuss the writings of white authors and critics exclusively. Hooks graduated from Stanford University in 1973 with a bachelor's degree in English. She attended the University of Wisconsin, Madison, where she received her M.A. degree in English in 1976. She was awarded the Ph.D. in English from the University of California at Santa Cruz in 1983. Her dissertation topic was "Toni MORRISON's Fiction: Keeping 'A Hold on Life.'" She published two books several years before she received her doctoral degree.

From 1976 to 1984, hooks served as an instructor or lecturer at several colleges and universities, including the University of Southern California, the University of California at Riverside, the University of California at Santa Cruz, Occidental College, and San Francisco State University. From 1985 to 1988, she was assistant professor of African and Afro-American studies and English at Yale University. In 1988 she accepted a post as associate professor of American literature and women's studies at Oberlin College. Hooks left Oberlin in 1994 to accept a position at City College of the City University of New York as Distinguished Professor of English.

One of the persistent emphases of hooks's work is its critique of much of institutionalized feminism in the light of its frequent disregard of questions of race and social class. Hooks is critical of feminists who do not promote radical change in American society and who disregard the interconnection of race, culture, and class issues. Her early writings argued that the feminist movement, in seeking to expose and protest oppression strictly in terms of gender, often dismissed social divisions among women in order to promote a notion of the universality of women's oppressed experience and a sense of a common bond among all women.

The notion of a common female oppression, hooks has argued, obscures the extent to which privileged white feminists have sought to preserve class interests rather than to bring about radical social change. The tendency of many feminists to accept unfulfilled, bored housewives as the symbols of women's oppression also brought hooks's criticism. She suggested that members of an employed underclass, working menial jobs for subsistence wages, experience a form of oppression that the feminist movement must acknowledge and study. She called for a broader feminist movement that would define and oppose all aspects of oppression. Her later writing, theoretically and philosophically astute yet lucid and accessible, covers a broad range of topics, including postmodernism, folk culture, and African American film.

The books that established hooks as a leading African American feminist were *Ain't I a Woman: Black Women and Feminism* (1981) and *Feminist Theory: From Margin to Center* (1984). Beginning in 1984 she analyzed books, films, and pop-culture icons, and her writing focused on race, gender, and representation issues. In *Black Looks: Race and Representation* (1992), hooks states that her purpose in writing is to "challenge and unsettle" her readers. She advocates a broad, multicultural feminist movement that will explore and oppose all types of oppression.

—*Updated by Yvonne Johnson*

See also: Black feminism; Class structure.

Benjamin Hooks (left) at a 1979 press conference also attended by—from left to right—Vernon Jordan, Coretta Scott King, Eddie N. Williams, and Bayard Rustin. (*AP/Wide World Photos*)

Hooks, Benjamin Lawson (b. January 31, 1925, Memphis, Tennessee): Civil rights leader. Hooks attended LeMoyne College in his hometown from 1941 to 1943, then transferred to Howard University, and finally to De Paul University in Chicago, where he received his law degree in 1948. Admitted to the Tennessee bar the same year, he maintained his individual practice until 1972. He served as a public defender from 1961 to 1964 and as a criminal judge of Shelby County, Tennessee, from 1966 to 1968.

Always an advocate of black capitalism, in 1955, while still in Memphis, Hooks cofounded and became the vice president of the Mutual Federal Savings and Loan Association of Memphis. He maintained his position on the board for fourteen years.

A World War II army veteran, Hooks was ordained to the ministry of the Baptist Church in 1956 and served as minister of the Middle Baptist Church in Memphis from 1956 to 1964. He became involved with the Civil Rights movement, eventually becoming a board member of the Southern Christian Leadership Conference (SCLC). He also served on the Memphis and Shelby County Human Relations Committee and on the Tennessee Council on Human Relations. In 1964 he moved to Detroit, Michigan, to become pastor of the Greater New Mount Moriah Baptist Church, a post he held until 1972.

In April of 1972, President Richard Nixon made Hooks the first African American to serve on the Federal Communications Commission. During his seven-year term, Hooks concerned himself with equal employment opportunities in the broadcasting industry.

In 1977 Hooks got his "job of a lifetime" when he became executive director of the National Association for the Advancement of Colored People (NAACP), a post he held for many years. In that position, he traveled nationally and internationally to promote the continuing civil rights crusade in the United States. In 1986 the NAACP rewarded him with the coveted Spingarn Medal.

Hoop Dreams (Fine Line, 1994): Documentary film directed by Steve James and originally slated for airing on the Public Broadcasting Service (PBS). The film depicts the basketball careers of Arthur Agee and William Gates, who begin the film as two fourteen-year-old boys from inner-city Chicago. As it follows the boys from junior high to college, the film examines their experiences on the basketball court and at home. Supported by their mothers, siblings, and friends, the young men enjoy exhilarating victories, yet also struggle with grades, troublesome fathers and coaches, parenthood, and their own broken dreams. The film probes the often-exploitive world of recruiting, as the young athletes are pursued by an elite suburban high school and several colleges. Many critics listed the documentary as the best film of 1994, but it failed to be nominated for an Academy Award as best documentary. The ensuing controversy helped bring the film to the attention of a wider audience and encouraged the Academy of Motion Picture Arts and Sciences to review their nominating procedures.

Hope, John (June 2, 1898, Augusta, Georgia—February 20, 1936, Atlanta, Georgia): Educator and university president. John Hope was the first president of the ATLANTA UNIVERSITY system, the first African American college consortium, founded in 1929. His mother was descended from slaves and his father was an affluent white man. Although he was denied his inheritance when his father died, Hope was able, through hard work and perseverance, to obtain a classical education. In 1890 he graduated with honors from Worcester Academy in Worcester, MASSACHUSETTS. He went on to attend Brown University in Providence, RHODE ISLAND, and delivered the class oration in 1894 when he received his bachelor of arts degree.

On the eve of his graduation from Brown University, a group of faculty members met with Hope and offered him a position on the Providence *Journal*, with the understanding that, with his light skin and blue eyes, he would "pass" as a white person. Hope refused this offer, moved to Nashville, TENNESSEE, and dedicated his life to improving educational opportunities for African Americans.

Hope taught at Roger Williams University in Nashville from 1894 to 1898. He joined the faculty at Atlanta Baptist College (later known as Morehouse College) in 1898 as a professor of classics, and in 1906 became the first African American president of the college. In 1929 Hope put together a plan designed to coordinate the six denominational colleges that competed for African American students in the Atlanta area—Atlanta University, Morehouse College, SPELMAN COLLEGE, Morris Brown College, Clark College, and Gammon Theological Seminary. By designating Morehouse and Spelman as undergraduate campuses, the plan allowed Atlanta University to become the first black university devoted only to graduate work. Under Hope's direction as president of Atlanta University, the six colleges shared faculty, resources, and a library. By pooling these resources, Hope was able to improve faculty salaries and attract quality teachers.

As a supporter of liberal arts EDUCATION, Hope stood in opposition to Booker T. WASHINGTON's philosophy of vocational and agricultural education. Hope's intellectual views matched those of W. E. B. DU BOIS, with whom he shared a warm friendship. Hope was the only college president to attend both the NIAGARA MOVEMENT meeting at Harpers Ferry in 1906 and the protest meeting in NEW YORK CITY that resulted in the founding of the NATIONAL ASSOCIATION FOR THE ADVANCEMENT OF COLORED PEOPLE (NAACP) in 1909.

In 1896 Hope married Lugenia Burns in CHICAGO, ILLINOIS. Together, they helped mold the African American social and intellectual community of Atlanta. Lugenia Hope taught physical education, reared two sons, and founded and directed the Neighborhood Union in Atlanta. John Hope supported his wife in all these endeavors.

John Hope served on many committees and councils dedicated to improving the lives of African Americans, and he was the recipient of many honors. Among these many honors, three were most representative of his life's work. In 1919 he was elected an alumni member of Phi Beta Kappa. In 1929 Hope received the Harmon Award for distinguished achievement in education. Hope went on to receive an honorary LL.D. degree from Brown University in 1935. When Hope died in 1936, funeral services were held in Morehouse Chapel, and his students served as pallbearers. Although Hope has received less attention than some of his contemporaries, his accomplishments as head of Atlanta University stand in testimony to his statesmanship and educational vision.

Hopkins, Claude Driskett (August 24, 1903, Alexandria, Virginia—February 19, 1984, New York, New York): JAZZ pianist, arranger, and composer. Reared in WASHINGTON, D.C., where his parents taught at HOWARD UNIVERSITY, Hopkins played the piano from the time he was seven years old. He studied piano and medicine at Howard, then went on to study at Washington Conservatory. He led his first band in the summer of 1924, in Atlantic City, NEW JERSEY. In 1925 he went to Europe to lead his own band for the Josephine BAKER revue, then toured Italy and Spain with his band in early 1926. Throughout the late 1920's, his band played venues such as the Roseland Ballroom, Asbury Park, and the Coconut Grove. His band continued to play throughout the 1930's, with long tenures at the Roseland Ballroom and the COTTON CLUB. The Claude Hopkins Orchestra appeared in several 1930's films. Hopkins formed a series of small bands throughout the late 1940's and early 1950's. Beginning in 1954, he made regular appearances with Henry "Red" Allen at the Metropole in NEW YORK CITY. He sat in regularly on recording sessions throughout the 1950's, and from 1960 through 1966 he led his own small group. He continued to play throughout the 1960's and 1970's.

See also: Music.

Hopkins, Lightnin' (March 15, 1912, Centerville, Texas—January 30, 1982, Houston, Texas): BLUES musician. Sam "Lightnin'" Hopkins's long career extended from country blues performances at plantations in East TEXAS to urban nightclubs, college folk festivals, international tours, and the stage of Carnegie Hall. Hopkins worked with his family in Texas cotton fields and learned to play guitar from his cousin Alger "Texas" Alexander and the itinerant bluesman Blind Lemon JEFFERSON. During his late teens, with friends such as guitarist Nathaniel Barnes, Hopkins began playing at country dances and parties in Texas and LOUISIANA. He devised an intricate guitar style involving jazz-like improvisations and cadenzas while developing a unique vocal approach, creating his own lyrics—often extemporaneously—rather than using traditional blues verses.

Hopkins settled in Houston and made his first recordings in 1946 for Los Angeles-based Aladdin Records. He and pianist Wilson "Thunder" Smith did not last as an act, but "Lightnin'," the nickname he used, remained with Hopkins. Between 1946 and 1955, he recorded almost two hundred sides for a number of labels, including Bill Quinn's Houston-based Gold Star Records. That company sold more than eighty thousand copies of Hopkins's "Baby Please Don't Go." Folklorist Mack McCormick was instrumental in introducing Hopkins to the college folk music audience in the late 1950's. Hopkins appeared in NEW YORK CITY's concert halls often in the next decade, including an appearance in 1960 in a Carnegie Hall show featuring Pete Seeger and Joan Baez. Later recordings showing his vast repertoire were released by Prestige, Folkways, and ABC Bluesville, as well as on European labels. He was the most frequently recorded blues artist of the post-World War II era. A documentary film, *The Blues According to Lightnin' Hopkins*, was made in 1968.

Unlike many other traditional bluesmen, Hopkins was not lost in impoverished obscurity. In 1979 he appeared again at Carnegie Hall. In Houston, after his death from cancer, several thousand fans stood quietly in line to pay their last respects.
See also: Music.

Hopkins, Pauline (1859, Portland, Maine—August 13, 1930, Boston, Massachusetts): Novelist, editor, and short story writer. Feminist and spokesperson for racial justice, Pauline Elizabeth Hopkins was one of the earliest African American writers to explore interracial relationships.

Hopkins began her literary career at fifteen, when she won a prize for an essay. After writing and appearing in a musical play, *Slaves Escape: Or, The Underground Railroad,* which was well received in BOSTON in 1880, she turned to editing and fiction writing. Many of her short stories and novels concerned SLAVERY and other efforts to oppress African Americans.

In *The Colored American*, a journal she edited, she wrote biographies of prominent African Americans and called for a black literary movement many years before the HARLEM RENAISSANCE occurred. Because some of her works focused on MISCEGENATION (*Of One Blood*, 1903, for example), she offended some of her readers. After she became ill in 1904, ownership of *The Colored American* passed into more conservative hands, and she was removed as editor. She then wrote for *Voice of the Negro*, another journal, but, aside from some articles and a booklet she later published herself, her literary career, which flourished between 1900 and 1904, was over. She lived in relative obscurity until her death on August 13, 1930, as a result of burns.

—*Thomas L. Erskine*

Suggested Readings:

Allen, Carol. *Black Women Intellectuals*. New York: Garland, 1998.

Gruesser, John Cullen, ed. *The Unruly Voice: Rediscovering Pauline Elizabeth Hopkins*. Urbana: University of Illinois Press, 1996.

Hopwood v. University of Texas: U.S. Court of Appeals, Fifth Circuit, AFFIRMATIVE ACTION case in 1996. The case involved a challenge to the legality of race-conscious admissions practices at the University of Texas Law School. In the 1978 BAKKE CASE (*Regents of the University of California v. Bakke*), the U.S. SUPREME COURT had upheld such practices as constitutional so long as no QUOTAS were employed. The equal protection clause of the FOURTEENTH AMENDMENT (1868) prohibits differential treatment of persons because of race unless such treatment is necessary to advance some compelling governmental purpose. Justice Lewis Powell argued in the *Bakke* case that racial preferences in admissions are justified when used to promote diversity in the student body.

Four white applicants to the University of Texas Law School, including Cheryl Hopwood, were denied admission in 1992. They sued on grounds that the admissions process constituted REVERSE DISCRIMINATION and violated their right of equal protection under the law.

The U.S. Court of Appeals, Fifth Circuit, stated that any use of racial classifications carries a heavy burden of justification, rejecting the promotion of student diversity as a sufficiently compelling reason. The court also disputed the law school's claim that its admissions process favoring African American and Mexican American applicants was justifiable as a means of overcoming the effects of past discrimination suffered historically by those minority groups in TEXAS's public education system. The court insisted that the law school could only seek to remedy past discrimination of its own doing.

The direct impact of the case was confined to the states of Texas, LOUISIANA, and MISSIS-

SIPPI, which are within the area of the U.S. Fifth Circuit Court. There racial preferences could no longer be employed by public educational institutions. The greater potential significance of the *Hopwood* decision lies in its holding that the *Bakke* decision is no longer controlling law.

—*Mario Morelli*

Horne, Lena (b. June 30, 1917, Brooklyn, New York): Actor and singer. On both sides of her family, Lena Mary Calhoun Horne was descended from members of the black American middle class dubbed the "TALENTED TENTH" by W. E. B. DU BOIS (who, as a young man, had been in love with Horne's grandmother). Her grandmother, Cora Catherine Calhoun, graduated from ATLANTA UNIVERSITY in 1881 and married Edwin Horne, who, like his wife, was an intellectual and an activist. Cora Horne was a founding member of the National Council of Colored Women. Lena lived in her grandmother's house long enough to absorb a discipline and commitment that stood her in good stead in years to come.

Lena Horne and Bill "Bojangles" Robinson in *Stormy Weather* (1943). *(Museum of Modern Art, Film Stills Archive)*

Her mother, Edna Scottron, a frustrated performer, married Edwin "Teddy" Horne. Although Teddy Horne's brother became a member of Franklin D. Roosevelt's "black cabinet," Teddy himself was something of a playboy. When Teddy and Edna divorced and went their separate ways, their daughter was often left with her grandparents in Brooklyn while her mother pursued her show-business ambitions. From time to time, Edna sent for Lena to live with her in the South or to stay with Edna's friends. In Brooklyn, Lena attended the Ethical Culture School (where songwriter Betty Comden was a classmate), the Girls High School, and a secretarial school. In her sojourns with her mother in the South, she attended segregated small-town schools.

Early Show Business Career

In 1933 Horne left school to perform as a dancer in the chorus line of Harlem's famed COTTON CLUB. As a sixteen-year-old chorus girl, Horne was carefully protected from the unwanted attentions of nightclub patrons by her mother. Because of her absences, a truant officer was sent by the school district to report on her whereabouts. After Edna Horne explained that the family was dependent on Lena's income and pleaded for lenience, the officer agreed simply to report Lena as missing. After two years at the Cotton Club, Lena auditioned as a singer with the Noble Sissle Society Orchestra in Philadelphia and went on the road with the band in 1936, accompanied by her mother and stepfather. Sissle's was the first African American band to play at Boston's Ritz-Carlton Hotel.

Teddy Horne introduced his daughter to Louis Jones, a twenty-seven-year-old gambling acquaintance and graduate of all-black West Virginia State College, during one of Lena's breaks from touring. At eighteen, Lena was an experienced performer who wanted to escape the drudgery of the road and the watchful eye of her mother. Jones dabbled in gambling as an escape from his job as a clerk in the Pittsburgh county coroner's office and saw in Lena the opportunity to gain a beautiful wife who would take care of his house and cater to his needs. Blind to his shortcomings, Horne married Jones and was soon pregnant with their first child, Gail Horne Jones.

Constantly in debt, the couple was supported financially by their parents. Frustrated by their dependence on others, Horne eagerly accepted her first film role only four months after her daughter was born in 1938. Traveling to Hollywood, Horne starred opposite Ralph Cooper in an all-black musical entitled *The Duke Is Tops* (1938). Filming of the musical was completed in ten days—and Horne was never paid for her performance in it. Horne returned to the East Coast and was reunited with her husband, but Jones was not happy with Horne's decision to continue a performing career; their son Edwin Fletcher "Teddy" Jones was born before the couple separated in 1939.

In New York, Horne recorded with Charlie Barnet's band while substituting for his white lead singer, and she recorded "Don't Take Your Love from Me" with Artie Shaw's band. Horne's big break, however, came when she was booked into Cafe Society Downtown, a famous cabaret in Greenwich Village. Club owner Barney Josephson thought Horne needed a fancier name and billed her as "Helena" Horne. Her success there led to a booking at a new Hollywood nightclub, the Trocadero. After she became a hit performer at the Trocadero, Horne was offered a contract by Metro-Goldwyn-Mayer (MGM) and became the first African American performer to sign a long-term contract with a major film studio.

Film Career

Horne's first film with MGM, *Panama Hattie* (1942), set the tone for her other film performances. She was introduced in a nightclub scene and sang "Just One of Those Things." The studio theorized that these scenes could be cut by southern theater managers without affecting the plot. The scenes, though, were often left intact, and southern audiences saw for the first time a black performer not cast as a butler or maid but as a gorgeous, glamorously dressed nightclub singer with a wonderful voice respectfully introduced as "Miss Lena Horne." Her inclusion in these films heightened filmgoers' perception of African American talent.

In 1942 Horne also starred in *Cabin in the Sky*, an all-black musical for MGM. This film performance was followed by a successful singing engagement at the Savoy-Plaza in New York. She then starred with Bill "Bojangles" Robinson in 1943's *Stormy Weather*, a landmark in black American films. Horne also appeared in *I Dood It* (1943), *Swing Fever* (1943), *Thousands Cheer* (1943), *Broadway Rhythm* (1944), *Two Girls and a Sailor* (1944), *Ziegfeld Follies* (1946), and *Till the Clouds Roll By* (1946).

During World War II, Horne was active with USO tours on American military bases. While enjoying these performances, Horne was offended by the segregation and racial prejudice she witnessed on these tours. She was particularly outraged by an incident at Fort Riley, Kansas, in which German prisoners of war were seated in front of black American servicemen at one of her performances. Horrified by this slight, Horne descended from the stage and walked down the aisle to perform directly in front of the black audience.

Afterward, Horne refused to accept Army funding and traveled to southern military camps using her own money. She also campaigned for better housing for Japanese Americans in California, especially for those returning from military service.

Long divorced from Louis Jones, Horne was secretly married to Lennie Hayton, a Jewish arranger-conductor employed by MGM, in Paris in 1947. They broke the news of their marriage in October of 1950 and left MGM to work in New York and Europe. Although her friendship with the outspoken black actor Paul Robeson, her membership in the Council on African Affairs and the Hollywood Independent Citizens Committee for the Arts, Sciences, and Professions, and her frank espousal of liberal causes were doubtless responsible for her blacklisting during the Joseph McCarthy era, Horne was still in demand for television and nightclub appearances. Ed Sullivan was particularly instrumental in removing her name from the television blacklist, and new audiences were exposed to her talent when she appeared on television. On Broadway, which ignored the blacklist, she starred in the successful musical *Jamaica* (1957) with Ricardo Montalban.

During World War II, Lena Horne posed for government propaganda pictures to encourage conservation of natural gas. *(National Archives)*

Later Years

In the 1960's, Horne was active in the Civil Rights movement. She participated in the March on Washington held on August 28, 1963, and performed at a Carnegie Hall benefit for the Student Nonviolent Coordinating Committee (SNCC) that same year. While many blacks believed her celebrity status had shielded Horne from the harsh effects of racial prejudice, Horne worked hard to dispel this myth and became active in various black women's organizations. The night before civil rights activist Medgar Evers was murdered, she had appeared at a rally with him, singing "This Little Light of Mine" and presenting Evers with a check from the National Association for the Advancement of Colored People (NAACP). In 1965 her autobiography, *Lena*, was published.

Horne's film career was revived when she was cast in a dramatic role as a black woman who falls in love and marries a white sheriff, played by Richard Widmark, in the film *Death of a Gunfighter* (1969). During the making of the film, she was reconciled with her son, from whom she had been separated for many years. Not long afterward, Teddy Jones died of kidney disease at the age of twenty-nine, just months after his grandfather Teddy Horne died. Lena experienced another great loss when Lennie Hayton died in 1971. She went into semiretirement, but later accepted a cameo role as Glinda the good witch in her son-in-law Sidney Lumet's film *The Wiz* (1978), a Hollywood version of the all-black hit Broadway musical based on *The Wizard of Oz*. In 1981 she returned triumphantly to Broadway in a one-woman show entitled *Lena Horne: The Lady and Her Music*. Although initially planned as a limited engagement, the production became the longest-running one-actor show in Broadway history.

In the 1980's, Horne received some of the highest honors possible for a performer, including a Tony Award, a New York Drama Critics Circle award, and a Kennedy Center award for lifetime achievement in the arts. In 1982 she received the NAACP's prestigious Spingarn Medal.

—*Katherine G. Lederer*

See also: Film; Music; Theater.

Suggested Readings:

Buckley, Gail L. *The Hornes: An American Family*. New York: Alfred A. Knopf, 1986.

Haskins, James, with Kathleen Benson. *Lena: A Personal and Professional Biography of Lena Horne*. New York: Stein and Day, 1984.

Horne, Lena. "Lena Horne Releases New Album After More Than a Decade, but Says, 'I Really Do Hate to Sing.'" Interview with Trudy S. Moore. *Jet*, June 20, 1994, 52-55.

Horne, Lena, and Richard Schickel. *Lena*. Garden City, N.Y.: Doubleday, 1965.

Howard, Brett. *Lena*. Los Angeles: Holloway House, 1981.

Horse, John (c. 1812, Florida—August 9, 1882, Mexico City, Mexico): Seminole Indian chief also known as Cavallo, Coheia, John Nikla, Gopher John, and Juan Caballo. The son of a Seminole father and a black mother, Horse fought against removal before cooperating with the U.S. Army to persuade others to participate in a relocation to Oklahoma from Florida that took place from 1838 to 1842. In 1849 Horse led an exodus of Seminole blacks to Mexico where, after several relocations, he obtained a land grant near Nacimiento. He married Susan July and had a son, Joe Coon; little else is known about Horse's personal life.

Horton, George Moses (c. 1797, Northampton County, North Carolina—c. 1883, Philadelphia, Pennsylvania?): Poet. Slave who taught himself to read and compose poetry. The self-taught Horton was the first American slave known to have protested bondage in verse and was the only slave to earn a significant income by selling his poems. In addition, Horton became the first African American to publish a book in the South. He has been described as the first African American professional man of letters.

Horton was born in Northampton County, North Carolina, on the small tobacco farm of his master, William Horton. He loved singing and listening to people read. With the help of his mother, some old, tattered spelling books, and the Bible, he learned to read and write. By the age of twenty, he used his weekends to walk eight miles to the University of North Carolina, where he would sell his poems to students for between twenty-five and fifty cents each. Many of his poems were also published in local newspapers.

By 1820 Horton had launched a career as a professional poet on the campus of North Carolina University. His literary efforts were encouraged by novelist Caroline Lee Hentz, North Carolina governor David L. Swain, and newspaperman Horace Greeley. With the goal of earning enough money to purchase his freedom, Horton published a collection of his poems in *The Hope of Liberty* in 1829. The profits, however, were not enough to pay for his freedom, and he remained a slave until after the Civil War. More than a hundred of his poems were published in *Naked Genius* in 1865.

—*Alvin K. Benson*

See also: Literature.

Horton, James Oliver (b. March 28, 1943, Newark, New Jersey): Author and history professor. Horton wrote several important books on the history of African Americans in the United States.

An advocate of American public history, Horton served as the historical adviser to several museums in the United States and abroad, including the Underground Railroad Freedom Center in Cincinnati, Ohio, and the National Civil Rights Museum in Memphis, Tennessee. He also served as the director of the African American Communities Project at the Smithsonian Institution's Museum of American History. Horton participated as a historical consultant in numerous film and video productions. During the late 1990's, Horton helped develop a film series on race in American history before the Civil War, helped produce a film on the Underground Railroad, and appeared on the public television series *Africans in America*.

Horton earned his Ph.D. in history from Brandeis University in 1973. With his wife, Lois Elaine Berry Horton, he wrote *Black Bostonians: Family Life and Community Struggle in the Antebellum North* (1979) and *In Hope of Liberty: Culture, Protest, and Community Among Northern Free Blacks, 1700-1860* (1997), which was nominated for a Pulitzer Prize. Horton also wrote *Free People of Color: Inside the African American Community* (1993). Horton and David Davis were the curators of a traveling exhibit, "Free at Last: A History of the Abolition of Slavery." Horton's academic positions include being a history professor at George Washington University.

—*Alvin K. Benson*

House music: Musical form that emerged from the dance clubs of New York City and Chicago in the early 1980's. House music pioneers included Larry Levans and Jesse Saunders. The genre drew from eclectic sources by producing long dance remixes of both well-known and obscure songs originally performed by soul, rock, and even folk musicians. These extended dance songs were merged into long interrupted sets that would be played in clubs.

The early mixers acknowledged diverse inspiration, ranging from Booker T. and the M.G.s to the German electronic band Kraftwerk and the lush harmonies of the Philadelphia International records produced by the Gamble and Huff studio team in the 1970's. The result was a unique form of dance music that could absorb almost any musical style.

Unlike hip-hop and rap, house music had no political edge, and the infrequent lyrics were usually simple celebrations of pleasure and sensuality. House music was similar to hip-hop, however, in that it soon grew in popularity beyond the boundaries of urban African Americans. The talented bass-and-drum team of Sly and Robbie, who contributed to several dance mixes in 1982 and 1983, won house music recognition beyond the original dance hall audience.

In the 1990's, house music was joined by the techno dance mix genre. The two are superficially similar, but techno relies more on electronically generated sounds. Its second decade saw house enter a nostalgic phase, with mixers turning to "old school" youthful ballads for their harmonies. Despite a lack of radio play, house remained popular and provided an example of African American music changing and adapting with the times.

—*Michael Polley*

Housing and Urban Development, Department of: Agency of the federal government. The Department of Housing and Urban Development (HUD) was created in 1965 as part of the executive branch of the federal government. HUD's head, the secretary of housing and urban development, is a member of the

Robert C. Weaver (left) with President Lyndon B. Johnson in September, 1965, shortly before Johnson named him the first secretary of HUD. *(AP/ Wide World Photos)*

president's cabinet. The first secretary of housing and urban development, an African American named Robert C. WEAVER, served under President Lyndon B. Johnson.

Among HUD's functions are providing grants to state and local governments for community development and providing housing grants; guaranteeing mortgages and home improvement loans under the Federal Housing Authority; funding local housing authorities to build, buy, and locate low-income housing and to bridge the gap between what low-income families can afford to pay and actual housing costs; making loans to private organizations that provide nonprofit housing to the elderly; providing grants for urban renewal; and, through the Government National Mortgage Association, insuring mortgage-backed securities.

The secretary of housing and urban development is appointed by the president and approved by the Senate. The secretary is assisted by an undersecretary, who is aided by the deputy undersecretary of field coordination and the deputy undersecretary for intergovernmental relations. There are also assistant secretaries on the staff, one for each of the following: fair housing and equal opportunity, administration, community planning and development, legislation and congressional relations, housing, policy development and research, housing for Native Americans, and public affairs.

When Jack Kemp was appointed secretary late in 1989, he took over an agency in the midst of scandal. Developers and consultants for developers, many of whom were former HUD employees, were making enormous profits from low-income housing. The Federal Housing Authority was losing money on defaulted mortgages and loans for its senior citizens' housing program. Agents were embezzling millions of dollars on HUD foreclosures. HUD, under former secretary Samuel R. Pierce, Jr., had been accused of widespread fraud, mismanagement, and political favoritism.

Kemp took steps to clean up HUD, but critics remained worried that it had lost much of its ability to provide low-income housing and funds for urban renewal. Whether its budget should be maintained, cut, or increased was constantly debated in Congress. The agency's budget went up and down; it was cut severely during the 1980's, then was increased again, from $12.8 billion in fiscal year 1989 to $24.8 billion in 1993 at the end of Kemp's tenure as HUD secretary. It was cut again to around $20 billion a few years later and increased again to about $25.5 billion in 1999.

The agency continued to provoke criticism and debate within the government in the 1990's, with advocates for the poor arguing that the agency was doing too little and with Republicans in Congress, on the other hand, wanting to abolish it altogether. Meanwhile, it became increasingly apparent that there was a severe shortage of low-income housing in the country. There were long waiting lists for public housing, and federal housing policies generally continued to give more assistance (subsidies and tax incentives) to the middle class and upper class than to the poor.

President Bill Clinton appointed Henry G. Cisneros secretary of HUD in 1993, and by the time of Cisneros's resignation in 1997, some progress had been made. Plans were under way to demolish many of the most decrepit of the nation's public housing units and to build new, less dense units and increase the number of rent vouchers available for low-income tenants. In the 1990's, HUD was partly responsible for overseeing about 1.4 million public housing units. Andrew M. Cuomo was appointed HUD secretary in 1997.
See also: Housing projects.

Housing discrimination: Discrimination in housing occurs whenever people are unable to buy or rent the housing they want because of their race, national origin, religion, or other personal characteristics. African Americans faced considerable discrimination in housing over the course of the twentieth century. There is evidence that this type of discrimination persists, although it has become less open than it was in the past. Many social scientists argue that housing discrimination is a major source of residential segregation in the United States.

Origins

Douglas S. Massey and Nancy A. Denton, authors of *American Apartheid: Segregation and the Making of the Underclass* (1993), have provided evidence that there was little overt housing discrimination in the United States before 1900. After the Civil War, most African Americans lived in the rural South, often working as sharecroppers or in other forms of hard, low-paying agricultural labor. When they did live in southern cities, they frequently lived near the whites who employed them. Those African Americans who lived in the North generally resided in the same poor neighborhoods as low-income whites.

Widespread discrimination in housing began in the early twentieth century, when blacks began to move out of the rural South to cities, particularly cities in the North. From 1906 through 1916, a series of crop diseases and floods led southern farmers to shift from producing crops such as cotton to growing food crops and raising livestock; both required less manual labor. At the same time that there was less need for farm workers in the South, the industrialization of northern cities created a demand for unskilled workers. World War I pushed this demand for workers even higher. The availability of jobs in the cities, the shortage of jobs in the countryside, and continuing racial oppression in the South all encouraged African Americans to move to cities, especially northern cities.

Whites frequently objected to the African American newcomers. Since the latter came from farms, were often extremely poor, and had little formal education, they were frequently seen as undesirable neighbors at best or even as threats. Rising racism forced African Americans to live in all-black neighborhoods, and whites began to devise strategies to keep nonwhites out of white residential areas. Sometimes these strategies involved violence: Massey and Denton report that fifty-eight black homes in white areas of Chicago were bombed between 1917 and 1921. Usually, however, violence was not needed to deny housing to nonwhites. If no white homeowners would sell or rent to African Americans, segregated neighborhoods could be maintained peacefully.

One of the techniques for enforcing RACIAL DISCRIMINATION in housing was the "neighborhood improvement association" or "property owners' association." White homeowners would band together in organizations of this kind in order to keep nonwhites from buying or renting homes. Neighborhood associations frequently used RESTRICTIVE COVENANTS to ma2ke sure that people practiced this type of discrimination. Restrictive covenants were contracts signed by property owners or by members of an association stating that property owners would not sell or rent to nonwhites. Discriminatory agreements of this kind became increasingly common in the United States until 1948, when the U.S. SUPREME COURT declared (in SHELLEY V. KRAEMER) that restrictive covenants could not be legally enforced. Despite the Supreme Court ruling, agreements among real estate agents and homeowners to keep minority members from white neighborhoods continued to exist in many parts of the country.

Discrimination and the Suburbs

After WORLD WAR II, the proportion of the American population living in the suburbs grew rapidly. The growth of the suburbs was encouraged by the U.S. government, which made mortgage loans available to new homeowners through the Federal Housing Administration (FHA) and the Veterans Administration (VA). These federal agencies guaranteed home loans made by banks and extended repayment periods so that new homeowners could enjoy comparatively low monthly payments.

Throughout the late 1940's, the FHA officially supported the use of restrictive covenants to maintain neighborhoods inhabited by single ethnic or racial groups. FHA policies continued to recommend these kinds of agreements until 1950, two years after the Supreme Court had declared that covenants could not be legally enforced. Throughout the 1950's, both the FHA and the VA disproportionately underwrote mortgages in the suburbs and in white areas, encouraging the trend toward white suburbs and black central cities.

During the 1950's and 1960's, the U.S. government engaged in a series of urban renewal projects that were intended to improve decaying cities. Low-income housing in the inner city was torn down, and the residents, who were most often African American, were resettled in newly built public housing. White resistance to black movement into the suburbs 2led public housing to be concentrated primarily in central city areas, reinforcing and creating dense concentrations of urban black POVERTY. In turn, the perception of African Americans as a poor, dependant population gave added fuel to white objections to minority movement into white neighborhoods.

During the 1970's, although the majority of African Americans continued to live in cities, blacks moved to the suburbs at an increasing rate. This trend did not result in the integration of most American suburbs, nor did it end housing discrimination. Instead, suburbs tended to become either white or black. One group of researchers looking at white opinions in 1976 found that 24 percent of whites reported that they would feel uncomfortable—and 7 percent said they would move—if their neighborhoods became only 8 percent black. Therefore, when a few African Americans moved into an area, many whites would begin to feel unsettled, and a small number would move out. This movement of whites would generally increase the minority percentage of the population. Since 24 percent of whites said they would move if their neighborhoods became more than 20 percent black, and 41 percent said they would move if their neighborhoods became more than 35 percent black, even the movement of a few minority members into a neighborhood could eventually lead to the departure of many white residents.

Such a "WHITE FLIGHT" would produce falling property values, as many homes were for sale at once. Therefore, housing discrimination in the suburbs often arose because of the desires of real estate agents and property owners to maintain market values of homes.

The Struggle Against Housing Discrimination

The year 1968 was a time of upheaval for racial relations in the United States. The assassination of Dr. Martin Luther KING, Jr., was followed by riots in major cities throughout the country. The Kerner Commission, appointed by the U.S. Senate to study the causes of the riots, reported that residential segregation was one of the chief sources of the unrest. These events helped push Congress to pass the CIVIL RIGHTS Act of 1968, also known as the Fair Housing Act. The Fair Housing Act outlawed most types of housing discrimination. It gave the power to enforce antidiscrimination policies to the Department of Housing and Urban Development (HUD). HUD, also in charge of most public housing in the United States, was responsible for investigating suspected housing discrimination and taking action against those who engaged in it.

Under this arrangement, people who attempted to buy or rent a home or apartment and believed that they had been discriminated against because of race, national origin, religion, sex, family status, or disability could call or write the Office of Fair Housing and Equal Opportunity at HUD to make a complaint. If HUD found that there was reason to believe that a landlord, real-estate agent, or property owner had engaged in illegal discrimination, the department could sue on behalf of those who were believed to have suffered discrimination or could even bring criminal charges against violators.

Discrimination with a Smile

Following the Fair Housing Act, discrimination became much less open, but it did not cease. Real-estate agents, mortgage lenders, and homeowners who wished to discriminate realized that they could be subject to legal penalties if they stated that they would not sell to nonwhites. Therefore, real estate agents may sometimes try to steer black clients toward housing in black areas without refusing to sell them property elsewhere. Sometimes those selling or renting houses and apartments will take telephone numbers of African Americans or other minorities and simply never call them back. If questioned, they can say they forgot or they lost the number.

This type of discrimination, nicknamed "discrimination with a smile," is difficult to prove. The most common way of establishing its occurrence is through audit studies. Audit studies involve sending whites and African Americans posing as home buyers or renters separately to real estate agents. By sending clients of different races but with similar incomes and assets to inquire about the same housing, agencies can determine whether discrimination is being practiced. Audit studies began in many cities around the United States in the late 1960's, usually carried out by local fair housing organizations. Audit studies have revealed continuing patterns of housing discrimination. In a review of audit studies carried out in Boston and Denver in the 1980's, John Yinger found that African American home seekers were shown only 54 of every 100 housing units shown to white home seekers. Similarly, in 1987, George Galster assembled reports from fair housing organizations in various parts of the United States and found that African Americans were likely to experience discrimination both in buying and in renting housing.

Redlining and Loan Discrimination

The term "redlining" refers to the reluctance of banks to make loans on homes in low-income African American neighborhoods. (Such areas are sometimes outlined in red on the maps used by lending agencies.) This practice means that new would-be homeowners cannot get mortgages to buy homes, and those who already own property cannot get loans to make improvements. As a result, the quality of the neighborhood goes down both because money is not available for repairs and improvements and because most residents are renters rather than owners. The end result is that members of minorities are denied the quality of housing enjoyed by whites.

The U.S. Congress passed the Home Mortgage Disclosure Act in 1975 in order to determine the extent to which mortgage lenders engage in housing discrimination through redlining. This act requires lending institutions to report amounts and numbers of loans made in particular neighborhoods. In 1977 Congress attempted to find a solution to redlining by passing the Community Reinvestment Act, which requires banks to devote some funds to loans in low-income neighborhoods. Although the act helped to improve some neighborhoods, it did not end discrimination in loans based on place of residence. A study in 1988 of mortgage lending in cities around the United States found that people buying in African American neighborhoods were denied mortgages more often than people buying in white neighborhoods.

Several investigations in the 1980's and 1990's revealed substantial continuing discrimination in home loans. Reporters for the *Atlanta Constitution* newspaper went through 10 million applications for loans made between 1983 and 1988. In their findings, published in 1989, they reported that 11 percent of white applicants were rejected, compared with 24 percent of African American applicants. The reporters also found that in many metropolitan areas the loan applications of low-income whites were rejected less often than the applications of high-income African Americans. In 1991 *The New York Times*, following an examination of information obtained from the U.S. Federal Reserve, reported that blacks at every income level showed higher rates of rejection for mortgage loans than whites.

Such studies report that, although significant gains have been made in the struggle against housing discrimination since the 1950's, and particularly since the Fair Housing Act of 1968, discrimination persists in subtle ways that are difficult to prove and eradicate.

—*Carl L. Bankston III*

See also: Housing and Urban Development, Department of (HUD); Housing projects; Kerner Report; Segregation and integration; Suburbanization; Urbanization.

Suggested Readings:

Farley, Reynolds, and Walter R. Allen. *The Color Line and the Quality of Life in America*. New York: Russell Sage, 1987.

Haar, Charles M. *Suburbs Under Siege: Race, Space, and Audacious Judges*. Princeton, N.J.: Princeton University Press, 1996.

Jackson, Kenneth T. *Crabgrass Frontier: The Suburbanization of the United States*. New York: Oxford University Press, 1987.

Kirp, David L., John P. Dwyer, and Larry A. Rosenthal. *Our Town: Race, Housing, and the Soul of Suburbia*. Piscataway, N.J.: Rutgers University Press, 1996.

Kivisto, Peter. "An Historical Review of Public Housing Policies and Their Impact on Minorities." In *Race, Ethnicity, and Housing in the United States*, edited by Jamshid Momeni. Westport, Conn.: Greenwood Press, 1986.

Massey, Douglas S., and Nancy A. Denton. *American Apartheid: Segregation and the Making of the Underclass*. Cambridge, Mass.: Harvard University Press, 1993.

Rasmussen, R. Kent. *Farewell to Jim Crow: The Rise and Fall of Segregation in America*. New York: Facts on File, 1997.

Yinger, John. *Cash in Your Face: The Cost of Racial and Ethnic Discrimination in Housing*.

Syracuse, N.Y.: Syracuse University Metropolitan Studies, 1993.

_______. "The Racial Dimension of Urban Housing Markets in the 1980's." In *Divided Neighborhoods: Changing Patterns of Racial Segregation*, edited by Gary A. Tobin. Newbury Park, Ca.: Sage Publications, 1987.

Housing projects: Housing funded by the government and intended for occupation by low-income families or individuals. The Public Works Administration built some low-cost housing in the 1930's to eliminate slum conditions. This effort might be considered the first set of housing projects. Plans called for African American management staffs and for reduced rents. By 1936 the government had spent $130 million in more than thirty cities. Black ARCHITECTS, contractors, and builders were hired to plan and construct many of these housing projects.

Over the next several decades, most public housing projects were segregated, constructed for all-black or all-white occupancy. Until 1962 the decision of whether to segregate public housing was left to the discretion of local housing authorities. Even when what was called urban renewal began around 1949, discrimination by private developers continued without much government interference. In December, 1972, the U.S. SUPREME COURT ruled that residents of racially segregated housing projects could sue to integrate the projects.

On August 1, 1968, President Lyndon B. Johnson signed the Housing and Urban Development Act. The act authorized more than $5 billion for a three-year program to provide 1.7 million units of new or rehabilitated housing for low-income families. A home ownership assistance program was to provide eligible low-income purchasers with interest-rate subsidies. Other subsidies assisted with construction or rehabilitation of rental and cooperative housing. The Department of Housing and Urban Development gave grants and direct loans to local housing authorities or authorized public agencies. It also aided in home purchases by allowing for transfer of ownership when tenants could obtain financing or when they had developed equity through performing maintenance.

President Gerald Ford signed the Housing and Community Redevelopment Act on August 22, 1974. It consolidated many of the housing programs that had proliferated since 1949. The act provided for block grants to local governments based on the population, degree of overcrowding, and degree of poverty within their jurisdiction. The grants could be used at community discretion to meet such needs as urban renewal, aid to displaced families, housing code enforcement, or provision of water and sewer facilities. The act also authorized a rent subsidy program of $1.23 billion. The intention of the act was to shift control of housing projects from the federal to the local level.

About one million black households lived in public or subsidized housing in 1980. That number was about one-fourth of all of the black households that were renters in that year.

See also: Housing discrimination.

Houston, Charles Hamilton (September 3, 1895, Washington, D.C.—April 20, 1950, Washington, D.C.): Attorney and educator. Charles Hamilton Houston was best known for his key role in school desegregation efforts. Dubbed the "First Mr. CIVIL RIGHTS," Houston influenced the legal careers of premier lawyers such as William H. HASTIE and U.S. SUPREME COURT Associate Justice Thurgood MARSHALL. Houston set the stage for dismantling Jim Crow segregation, entrusting completion of the task to his protégé, Thurgood Marshall.

Charles Houston (right) and Thurgood Marshall (left) worked with Donald Murray (center), whose case against the University of Maryland led to a landmark Supreme Court decision. *(Library of Congress)*

The son of William, a lawyer, and Mary Houston, a teacher, Houston received the benefits of a middle-class upbringing. Houston took advantage of these privileges by excelling academically. In 1911, at age fifteen, Houston graduated from Dunbar High School in WASHINGTON, D.C. He immediately entered Amherst College in MASSACHUSETTS, where he earned a bachelor of arts degree with honors four years later. Inducted into Phi Beta Kappa, Houston joined five other colleagues as class valedictorian. From 1917 until 1919, Houston served in the U.S. Army and became an officer in charge of leading segregated black units to fight in WORLD WAR I. His success in the Colored Officers' Training Camp at Fort Des Moines afforded him two notable leadership positions: first lieutenant in infantry and second lieutenant in artillery.

Eager to continue his studies, Houston entered Harvard Law School in 1919. Houston was a pioneer in many ways. He was the first African American selected as editor of the *Harvard Law Review*; in 1923, he was also the first African American to receive a Doctor of Juridical Science (J.D.) degree at Harvard. A year earlier, he graduated cum laude with an LL.B. degree. From 1923 to 1924, Houston studied civil law at the University of Madrid. In 1924 he was admitted to the District of Columbia bar. Initially, Houston practiced law with his father. Later he was a partner of Houston, Bryant and Gardner.

Designated associate professor and vice dean in 1929, Houston was responsible for the Howard Law School program. He was also an associate professor of law at Howard. In 1935 he left both positions to work for the NA-

TIONAL ASSOCIATION FOR THE ADVANCEMENT OF COLORED PEOPLE (NAACP). Appointed on a part-time basis, Houston initiated a legal effort to challenge unequal funding in public schools and discrimination in public transportation. Between 1935 and 1938, Houston served as the NAACP's first full-time paid special counsel.

The struggle to desegregate public schools was an arduous task. Yet, Houston repeatedly appeared before the U.S. Supreme Court, trying cases on the grounds that the FOURTEENTH AMENDMENT entitled all Americans to equal protection under the law. By visually documenting budget, pay, and environmental disparities between white and black schools in SOUTH CAROLINA, Houston provided the context used eventually to overturn PLESSY V. FERGUSON (1896). (This ruling established the constitutionality of the "SEPARATE BUT EQUAL" doctrine.) Seminal cases were *University of Maryland v. Murray* (1936), MISSOURI EX REL GAINES (1938), and *Steele v. Louisville & Nashville R.R.* (1944). As evidenced by the Supreme Court ruling in BROWN V. BOARD OF EDUCATION (1954), the contributions of Charles Hamilton Houston were instrumental in ending school segregation. Houston died from a heart ailment at age fifty-five.

See also: Civil rights and congressional legislation; Education; Jim Crow laws; Legal professions; Segregation and integration.

Houston, Whitney (b. August 9, 1963, Newark, New Jersey): Singer and actor. Gospel-trained musical artist who grew up singing in the church and who began topping the popular music charts with hits from her 1985 debut album, Houston is known for the exceptional range of her voice. Houston's inspiration and early singing coach was her mother, Cissy Houston, former member of a family gospel group and featured singer of the 1960's soul ensemble the Sweet Inspirations. Soul singer Aretha FRANKLIN also was a role model. At the age of eleven, Houston brought tears to the congregation of her NEW JERSEY church with a Sunday solo. At the age of fourteen, she joined her mother onstage at New York's Town Hall to sing a verse of "Tomorrow" from the musical *Annie*. While maintaining a B+ average in high school, Houston joined her mother in backing such singers as Lou Rawls. The statuesque young woman also became a FASHION model, appearing in *Vogue*, *Seventeen*, and *Cosmopolitan* magazines before graduating in 1981.

To advance her singing career, Houston recorded advertising jingles and sang on albums by the Neville Brothers and Paul Jabara. Her first album, *Whitney Houston* (1985), sold more than sixteen million copies. It

Whitney Houston (right) with her mother, soul singer Cissy Houston, at the American Music Awards in early 1987. *(AP/Wide World Photos)*

includes "Greatest Love of All," an assertion of inner strength and dignity, and "Saving All My Love for You," a melodic rock ballad that won Houston a Grammy Award as best female pop vocalist. Although some critics claimed that Houston tempered the full gospel power of her voice for conservative audiences, the album was a commercial success. Houston's popularity increased with videos, television appearances, and a national tour that culminated in sold-out performances at Carnegie Hall.

Houston won two National Music Awards early in 1986 and sang at the centennial celebration of the Statue of Liberty. Four singles from *Whitney* (1987), her second album, reached number one on the *Billboard* chart. A third album, *I'm Your Baby Tonight* (1991), has been heralded for its solid RHYTHM AND BLUES. In a 1988 benefit concert, Houston raised money for the UNITED NEGRO COLLEGE FUND (UNCF). In 1990 she received the UNCF's Frederick D. Patterson Award. She also donated proceeds from her early-1990's recording of "The Star Spangled Banner" to the Red Cross.

Whitney Houston performing at the White House in 1994 for U.S. president Bill Clinton and visiting South African president Nelson Mandela, a big fan of Houston. *(Reuters/Gary Cameron/Archive Photos)*

The 1990's ushered in many changes in Houston's life. Chief among them was her marriage to singer Bobby Brown in July, 1992. Houston and Brown had known each other for a few years, and their friendship had blossomed into a romance. The couple became parents of a daughter, Bobbi Kristina, born in 1993. Through the 1990's Houston and Brown's marriage frequently was rumored to be troubled, and tabloids reported that Brown had beaten her. Houston, in 1999 interviews, noted that the couple had had their troubles in the early years of their marriage, but she fervently insisted that Brown had never hit her and was not a womanizer.

Houston's professional career headed in new directions. Actor-director Kevin Costner approached her about costarring with him in the film *The Bodyguard*. Houston made her acting debut in the role of Rachel Marron, a popular singer who hires a bodyguard when she discovers that she is being stalked by a deranged fan. Released in 1992, the film was a box-office hit, taking in nearly $400 million worldwide by mid-1993. The film's success was boosted by its Grammy Award-winning sound track, featuring the hit single "I Will Always Love You," a remake of a song written by Dolly Parton.

Although motherhood placed some limits on her public appearances, Houston remained in the spotlight. In 1994 she became a key figure in a new advertising campaign launched by AT&T. That same year, Houston received an Image Award as Entertainer of the Year from the NATIONAL ASSOCIATION FOR THE ADVANCEMENT OF COLORED PEOPLE (NAACP). Houston faced a scare in 1995 when police arrested a Long Island resident on charges of stalking; she had secured a restraining order against a New Jersey man on similar charges in 1994. Both incidents grimly resembled the situation faced by her character in *The Bodyguard*.

The year 1995 saw the release of Houston's second film, an adaptation of Terry McMillan's 1992 best-selling novel *Waiting to Exhale*. Working under director Forest Whitaker as part of an ensemble cast, Houston played a single black woman living in ARIZONA who shares her problems with three other friends who face the challenges of finding true love in the 1990's. *Waiting to Exhale* was a box-office success, and its sound-track showcased Houston's vocal ability along with those of fellow pop singers Aretha Franklin, Chaka Khan, and Toni BRAXTON, among others. Her film and music career continued with the film *The Preacher's Wife* (1996), with Denzel WASHINGTON, and an all-star television production of a musical version of *Cinderella* (1997). Houston performed on *The Preacher's Wife* sound-track album and, in 1998, released the album *My Love Is Your Love*. In the 1990's Houston also became involved with a number of causes and funds, including her own Whitney Houston Foundation for Children, the UNITED NEGRO COLLEGE FUND, and the Children's Diabetes Fund.

—Updated by Wendy Sacket

See also: Film; Gospel music and spirituals; Image Awards; Soul music.

Houston, Texas: Biggest city in TEXAS, fourth-largest in the United States, and home to the country's fourth-largest African American community. In the 1990's Houston's black residents accounted for more than 26 percent of the city's 1.8 million population.

Houston's African American history began with the settlement of Harrisburg, which is now a part of the city, in 1823. The city of Houston itself was founded by J. K. and A. C. Allen in 1836 and was first known as Allen's Landing. During Houston's first fifty years it grew from a muddy town on Buffalo Bayou to a successful and prosperous railroad center, shipping rice, lumber, cattle, cotton, sugar, and other products of the region. After the CIVIL WAR ended in 1865, African Americans inundated the city, and it became informally known as the "black fraternal capital of Texas." Houston became the major hub for freedmen, and the city's Third Ward became the home to the largest number of African Americans in the city. The ward itself became a booming city-within-a-city for African Americans, the place to acquire a job or buy land.

Major changes occurred just before WORLD WAR I, when, between 1912 and 1914, the city's ship channel was dug. Houston became a deep-water port. The development of the Gulf Coast oil fields poured quick wealth into the community. Industries lined the channel, and jobs became plentiful. In 1940 Houston's African American population accounted for almost 25 percent of the city's 384,514 residents. During WORLD WAR II, war industries, especially shipbuilding, swelled the city even more, and several suburbs were brought into the metropolitan area. As Houston grew, its African American community grew.

Segregation was the norm prior to the CIVIL RIGHTS laws of the mid-1960's. Houston, however, escaped the major violence that erupted in other major cities during the 1960's. By the end of the 1960's, the inner part of the city no longer housed the majority of Houston's African Americans. The African American community expanded into all parts of the city as desegregation gradually opened new opportunities.

Concentrations of African Americans on Houston's East and South Sides, especially in the Third and Fourth Wards, made it possible for blacks to develop a political base. The first black U.S. congresswoman elected from Houston, Barbara Jordan, was elected in the early 1970's. Since the 1970's, many blacks from Houston have represented the business and political areas of the city's growth. The first black chief of police in Houston was Lee P. Brown, who went on to become the city's first black mayor.

—*Earl P. Andresen*

Howard University (Washington, D.C.): One of the most widely recognized and largest historically black educational institutions in the United States. The U.S. federal government's role of providing educational access to freed slaves started with the creation of the Freedmen's Bureau in 1865 and, through the bureau, the chartering of Howard University in 1867. Founded as a theological seminary for African American ministers and as a normal school, it was named for the commissioner of the Freedmen's Bureau, Oliver Otis Howard, who became its third president (1869-1874). The university's charter called for the education of all youth, and its first students were the white daughters of faculty members, but by 1900 the student body was almost 90 percent black. Its federal funding since its incipience may explain why a 1917 survey found that only two historically black institutions at that time—Howard and Fisk—offered true college-level instruction.

Howard has a strong liberal arts tradition. From its earliest days, Howard played a leadership role in the education of African Americans. Among its faculty and alumni are some of the finest black intellectual, artistic, and civic leaders, including Carter G. Woodson, Thurgood Marshall, Kenneth Clark, Stokely Carmichael, Amiri Baraka, and Toni Morrison. Howard's strong tradition of student activism can be traced to a 1925 student strike. Also important are the students' continued involvement in international affairs, their leading role in the Civil Rights movement, and their constant demands for shared governance.

By the early 1990's, Howard's two thousand faculty members and more than ten thousand students represented the greatest number of African American scholars at any single institution. A student body of which one-sixth was foreign attested the university's international reputation. Howard's eighteen schools and colleges offered more than seventy undergraduate and graduate degrees. Over the years, Howard produced a large percentage of the African American professionals in the fields of medicine and health sciences, engineering, religion, law, social work, and business.

Howard's facilities in 1992 included a television station, three art galleries, a teaching hospital, and the Moorland-Spingarn Research Center, the world's largest repository of materials relating to African American history and literature. The school had plans to expand its facilities beyond these impressive levels.

See also: Fisk University; Higher education; Historically black colleges; Howard University Medical School and Hospital.

Howard University Medical School and Hospital (Washington, D.C.): Oldest of the medical schools affiliated with historically black institutions. Along with Meharry Medical School, it has produced more than half of all the African American physicians in the United States.

The school and hospital had their beginnings after Reconstruction, emerging in an effort to meet the need for training of African American physicians. Racism and discriminatory practices prevented African Americans from attending already established medical schools. The Medical College of Howard University opened in 1868, utilizing the federally supported Freedman's Hospital in WASHINGTON, D.C., as its training facility. The founders of the medical college envisioned an institution that would provide instruction without regard to the race or gender of students. The medical college motto was Equal Rights and Knowledge for All. Until the early 1900's, most of the female physicians in Washington, D.C., both African American and white, were graduates of the Howard Medical College.

In 1907 the board of trustees officially changed the name, and the Howard Medical College became Howard Medical School. The Freedmen's Hospital officially became the school's teaching hospital in 1937, although it had served as the primary training facility since the founding of the medical college. The hospital remained under federal government control until 1960, at which point its management was transferred to HOWARD UNIVERSITY.

The Howard University Medical School and Hospital has an illustrious history. Born out of a need created by racism and JIM CROW LAWS, it has not escaped the ravages of racism. Racial distinctions surfaced in the Flexner Report of 1910, commissioned to determine the quality of the medical education at various schools. The report recommended that the school's mission should be to develop quality black physicians, whose duty it would be to settle in rural areas of the country and provide service there. It also concluded that the medical education of black physicians should stress principles of hygiene over academic medicine and research. This was clearly different from what was stressed and funded for white medical schools.

See also: Higher education; Historically black colleges; Howard University; Medicine.

Howlin' Wolf (Chester Arthur Burnett; June 10, 1910, West Point, Mississippi—January 10, 1976, Hines, Illinois): Chicago BLUES singer and harmonica player. Born Chester Arthur Burnett, he moved to the MISSISSIPPI Delta region in his early teens. There he heard blues singers Charley PATTON and Willie Brown. While traveling through ARKANSAS he met Sonny Boy WILLIAMSON (Rice Miller), who taught him how to play the harmonica. He made his first records, including "Moanin' at Midnight," at the Memphis Recording Service for Chicago's Chess Records with Ike Turner's Kings of Rhythm in 1950.

Howlin' Wolf during the early 1960's. *(Archive Photos)*

Although these sides were recorded in MEMPHIS, TENNESSEE, they helped define the aggressive, electric "CHICAGO BLUES" sound, and Howlin' Wolf himself would later move to CHICAGO. "Moanin' at Midnight," as well as subsequent records including "Smokestack Lightning," "Little Red Rooster," and "Spoonful," showed a unique vocal style, one which relied upon a tense, growling tone to convey a sinister effect. He recorded most of these songs, many of which were written by Willie Dixon, with his son, guitarist Hubert Sumlin.

Howlin' Wolf's performances were exceptionally physical affairs, with the singer regularly jumping wildly onstage and occasionally engaging in even more outrageous activities, including climbing up stage curtains. This wildness onstage served as an influence to rock performers of the 1960's, particularly white blues bands such as the Rolling Stones, Yardbirds, and Doors, whose singer Jim Morrison sometimes tried to capture the demonic sound of Wolf's vocals and who recorded some songs that Howlin' Wolf had popularized.

Howlin' Wolf remained popular through the 1960's, aided by the burst of popularity the blues saw among young whites during that decade. Particularly helpful were the Rolling Stones, who not only covered his music but also used their influence to get him on the television show *Shindig* in 1965. He continued to record throughout the 1960's, although some of his later records were novelty songs in which he made fun of his size and nickname, such as 1963's "Three Hundred Pounds of Joy." He also toured the United States, in addition to playing regularly in Chicago, throughout the 1960's and early 1970's. He played in concerts as late as November, 1975, even though he had had several heart attacks and had been undergoing dialysis treatment. Kidney damage eventually caused his death.

See also: Music.

Hughes, Langston (February 1, 1902, Joplin, Missouri—May 27, 1967, New York, New York): Poet. When James Mercer Langston Hughes was born, his father, James Hughes, embittered by racism in the United States, had already moved to MEXICO. His mother, Carrie Langston Hughes, left the baby with her mother, Mary Langston, and went to KANSAS looking for work. After a riot and lynching in Joplin in 1903, Mary Langston moved with her grandchild to Lawrence, Kansas, where she had friends.

Heritage

Langston Hughes was taught pride in his heritage from babyhood. Mary Langston's first husband was Lewis Sheridan Leary, a free African American killed in John Brown's raid on HARPERS FERRY. She later married Charles Langston, the brother of John Mercer LANGSTON, one of the most famous African Americans of the last quarter of the nineteenth century. When Lewis Leary was killed, a friend brought Mary Leary, pregnant with their child, his bullet-riddled, blood-stained shawl. She wore it and would later cover Langston Hughes with it for warmth on cold winter nights.

Carrie Hughes sent for Langston when he was of elementary school age, and they lived

Langston Hughes. *(Library of Congress)*

The Weary Blues

Langston Hughes published his poetry collection *The Weary Blues* in 1926. With its wide range of subject matter, the book illustrates Hughes's love for and devotion to black American life. The poems, in which Hughes made use of the blues style, celebrate black life in all of its forms, including dialect, heritage, spiritual growth, Harlem cabaret life, jazz and blues, sad and joyous moments, hope, and ties with Africa.

In the title poem, an old black man plays the blues on a battered piano, playing a "sad raggy tune" and making "that old piano moan." He sings:

I got the Weary Blues
And I can't be satisfied.
Got the Weary Blues
And can't be satisfied—
I ain't happy no mo'
And I wish that I had died.

together in Topeka, Kansas. When the school year began, he was denied admission to a white neighborhood school, the only school in the neighborhood; Carrie Hughes, however, convinced the principal to admit Langston to the white school.

Hughes's mother remarried and moved around a good deal. As a result, Hughes attended a number of schools. He graduated from grammar school in Lincoln, Illinois, and from high school in Cleveland, OHIO. After his high school graduation, he lived with his father in Mexico, where he wrote his first poem to be published; the poem, still one of his most famous, was "The Negro Speaks of Rivers."

In 1921 Hughes returned to the United States and attended Columbia University for a year; his poem "Theme for English B" recalls this time. Out of money, he left Columbia and in 1924 signed on as a seaman on the merchant ship *West Hesseltine*, which took him to Africa. He shipped out again, bound for Europe, jumped ship in Holland, and went to Paris. After returning to the United States, Hughes worked briefly for the scholar Carter G. WOODSON, who founded the JOURNAL OF NEGRO HISTORY.

Writing Career

Hughes's first volume of poetry, *The Weary Blues*, was published in 1926; his second, *Fine Clothes to the Jew*, was published in 1927. With financial help from a white patron, Charlotte Mason, he attended LINCOLN UNIVERSITY in PENNSYLVANIA and graduated in 1929. In 1930 and 1931, Hughes traveled to CUBA and HAITI, met and interviewed writers there, and translated some of their work into English. He can thus be credited with giving impetus to the literary Negritude movement.

Hughes then went to the Soviet Union, where he was supposed to write a film script. Financial backing for the film did not materialize, however, and Hughes supported himself for some months as a traveling correspondent for *Izvestia*. Back in the United States, he lived for a time in Carmel, CALIFORNIA, later a famous writers' colony. Through the 1930's, Hughes supported himself, his mother, and his younger half-brother by giving poetry readings around the country. During the Spanish Civil War, he went to Madrid as a war correspondent.

Though best known as a poet, Hughes did substantial work in other literary genres. His novels *Not Without Laughter* (1930) and *Tambourines to Glory* (1958) and his short-story collections, including *The Ways of White Folks* (1934) and *Laughing to Keep from Crying* (1952), testify to his abilities as a writer of prose fiction.

Hughes also made significant contributions to black American THEATER, writing several plays and helping to organize black theatrical companies. In 1935 he had been first excited and then disappointed by a Broadway production of his play *Mulatto*. He later founded the Harlem Suitcase Theatre and directed its production of his play *Don't You Want to Be Free?* in 1938.

The first volume of Hughes's autobiography, *The Big Sea*, was published in 1940. In 1943 he became a COLUMNIST for the CHICAGO DEFENDER, probably the most important African American newspaper in the country. Each column related an encounter between an educated narrator (Hughes) and "Simple," a Harlem working man who gave the narrator his views on black-white relationships, black American history, and politics and racism, all in the context of Simple's own daily life. Collected and published in several volumes, the Simple stories contain some hard truths, in the guise of humorous anecdotes, about the lives of black Americans in the United States before the period of the CIVIL RIGHTS movement.

At a time when the white world generally and the white publishing world specifically were not interested in African American culture or history, Hughes coedited such works as *A Pictorial History of the Negro in America* (1956) and *Black Magic: A Pictorial History of the Negro in American Entertainment* (1967). He continued to write excellent poetry, reflecting the tenor of the times, as evidenced by his *Montage of a Dream Deferred* (1951).

Later Years

Although in poor health in his later years, Hughes continued to write. His second autobiographical work, *I Wonder as I Wander*, was published in 1956; *Selected Poems of Langston Hughes* was published in 1959. In the brief years of the Kennedy administration, Hughes visited countries in Africa and Europe as a cultural emissary for the State Department. His last collection, *The Panther and the Lash: Or, Poems of Our Times* (1967), was published not long before his death in a Harlem hospital.

Langston Hughes was the most famous African American writer of his generation; his career spanned the period from the HARLEM RENAISSANCE of the 1920's to the Civil Rights movement of the 1960's. He was an influence on younger African American writers and on readers in every walk of life. Hughes expressed the aspirations and achievements of a people, chronicling their struggles with racism, their love of family and community, and their fight for a better world. In translating an African American musical art form, the BLUES, into the literary genre of poetry, moreover, he demonstrated the versatility and ability of BLACK ENGLISH to express all levels of thought and emotion.

—*Katherine G. Lederer*

See also: Autobiographies and memoirs; Brown, John; Literature; Negritude movement; Pan-Africanism.

Suggested Readings:

Berry, Faith. *Langston Hughes Before and Beyond Harlem*. Westport, Conn.: L. Hill, 1983.

Dace, Letitia, ed. *Langston Hughes: The Contemporary Reviews*. New York: Cambridge University Press, 1997.

Gates, Henry Louis, and Anthony Appiah, eds. *Langston Hughes: Critical Perspectives Past and Present*. New York: Amistad Press, 1993.

Haskins, James. *Always Movin' On: The Life of Langston Hughes*. Trenton, N.J.: Africa World Press, 1993.

Hughes, Langston. *The Big Sea: An Autobiography*. New York: Hill & Wang, 1963. Reprint. New York: Thunder's Mouth Press, 1986.

_______. *I Wonder As I Wander: An Autobiographical Journey*. New York: Hill & Wang, 1993.

_______. *Langston Hughes and the "Chicago Defender": Essays on Race, Politics, and Culture, 1942-1962*. Edited by Christopher C. De Santis. Urbana: University of Illinois Press, 1995.

McLaren, Joseph. *Langston Hughes: Folk Dramatist in the Protest Tradition, 1921-1943*. Westport, Conn.: Greenwood Press, 1997.

Rampersad, Arnold. *The Life of Langston Hughes*. 2 vols. New York: Oxford University Press, 1986, 1988.

Trotman, C. James, ed. *Langston Hughes: The Man, His Art, and His Continuing Influence*. New York: Garland, 1995.

Jazz singer Alberta Hunter performing on NBC's *Today Show* in early 1979. *(AP/Wide World Photos)*

Hulbert, Maurice "Hot Rod" (July 30, 1916, Helena, Arkansas—December 24, 1996, Towson, Maryland): Disc jockey and businessman. Hulbert worked at a number of radio stations, including Baltimore stations WWIN and WITH and Philadelphia's WHAT and WDAS. His greatest success as a disc jockey, however, came at station WDIA in MEMPHIS, TENNESSEE. He performed several roles at that station. He hosted a morning gospel program, an afternoon mellow music program, and an evening program called the *Sepia Swing Club*. It was in this evening work, in which he played RHYTHM AND BLUES, that he developed his fast-talking style that influenced many future disc jockeys and contributed to the unique character of African American radio.

See also: Music; Radio broadcasting.

Hunter, Alberta (April 1, 1895, Memphis, Tennessee—October 17, 1984, New York, New York): BLUES singer. Hunter was among the first African American women to record the blues, in the 1920's. She sang at churches and in local talent contests as a child. Her family moved to CHICAGO around 1907. Around 1913, she began singing in local cafes and nightclubs, then moved on to dinner theaters and cabarets. In 1920 she sang with Joseph "King" OLIVER at the Dreamland Cabaret in Chicago. The following year, she moved to New York and recorded with Fletcher Henderson for the Black Swan label. She then recorded her composition, "Down-Hearted Blues" (1922) for the Paramount label. In 1923 she replaced Bessie SMITH in the musical comedy, *How Come*, which had a lengthy tour. She also worked with cabaret singer Edith Wilson and, in 1924, recorded with Louis ARMSTRONG on the Gennett label. She recorded for various other labels, sometimes under the pseudonyms of Josephine Beatty (the name of her half-sister), May Alix, and Helen Roberts.

From the late 1920's to the mid-1930's, she spent much of her time in Europe. She appeared opposite Paul ROBESON in *Show Boat* in London in 1928 and was received enthusiastically on the nightclub and cabaret circuit throughout France. By the mid-1930's, she had sung in The Netherlands, Greece, Turkey, Egypt, Scotland, and Denmark. At the close of WORLD WAR II, she made USO tours to Europe, China, Burma, Africa, Korea, and India. In 1954 she retired from music to work as a practical nurse but occasionally accepted engagements (sometimes under pseudonyms).

She formally came out of retirement in 1977, and through the aid of television and radio appearances, commercials, and recordings, was discovered by a new generation of listeners. *See also:* Music.

Hunter-Gault, Charlayne (b. February 27, 1942, Due West, South Carolina): Broadcast journalist. Hunter-Gault became familiar to viewers of the *MacNeil/Lehrer Newshour*, a Public Broadcasting Service program, during the Persian Gulf War of 1991. In the field and dressed in combat clothes, she talked to ordinary soldiers as well as their officers.

Hunter-Gault was the first African American woman admitted to the University of Georgia. She was admitted by a court order, the result of a process lasting two years. During her two years at the university she was subjected to racist violence, including a student riot on the second night of her campus residence. She had selected the university because of her long-held ambition to become a journalist, but the campus newspaper was unreceptive to her talent. Instead, she worked on weekends for the *Atlanta Inquirer*, a newspaper founded by college students from around the state who were unhappy with CIVIL RIGHTS coverage in the mainstream newspapers.

After she graduated from the University of Georgia in 1963, she accepted a position at *The New Yorker*. In 1967 she won a Russell Sage Fellowship, enabling her to study at Washington University in St. Louis, MISSOURI. During her time in St. Louis, she served on the staff of *Trans-Action* magazine, which assigned her to cover the POOR PEOPLE'S CAMPAIGN in Washington, D.C. She soon joined the staff of WRC-TV, an NBC affiliate in Washington, D.C., and worked as an investigative reporter as well as an anchorwoman of local news broadcasts.

She relocated to NEW YORK CITY in 1968, where she worked for *The New York Times*, specializing in coverage of African American inner-city communities. Recognized by fellow journalists as an outstanding reporter with an extraordinary ability to communicate a situation's immediacy, she was given the *Times* Publishers Award in 1970 for an article she wrote about the life and death of a twelve-year-old heroin addict. She shared this award with fellow reporter Joseph Lelyveld. She went on, in 1974 and 1976, to receive two more

Charlayne Hunter-Gault (right) and Hamilton Holmes in 1961, when they were the first two African Americans admitted to the University of Georgia. *(AP/Wide World Photos)*

Publishers Awards for her stories about Paul Gibson, Jr., New York's first black deputy mayor, and for her stories on GHETTO crime and on the renaming of Harlem's Muslim Mosque for MALCOM X.

Hunter-Gault joined the *MacNeil/Lehrer NewsHour* (later the *NewsHour with Jim Lehrer*) on PBS in 1978 and went on to receive numerous awards recognizing her outstanding work in many areas, from the American invasion of Grenada to her series about apartheid in South Africa. She won a 1983 Emmy Award for her reporting from Grenada. She also published articles in *The New York Times Magazine* and *The New York Times Book Review, Saturday Review, Essence*, and *Vogue*, in addition to her writing for *The New Yorker*. In 1992 Hunter-Gault published her autobiography, *In My Place*. Hunter-Gault left the *NewsHour with Jim Lehrer* in 1997, after almost twenty years. She and her husband moved to South Africa, where she began reporting for National Public Radio (NPR).

See also: Black press; Print journalism; Television industry.

Hurston, Zora Neale (January 7, 1891, Eatonville, Florida—January 28, 1960, Fort Pierce, Florida): Novelist and anthropologist. Zora Neale Hurston was the most accomplished African American woman writing in the first half of the twentieth century. Her novels and FOLKLORE collections demonstrate her belief that black folk provided "the greatest cultural wealth of the continent," that folklore was the common person's art form, and that it derived from the "first wondering contact with natural law." Hurston's ability to capture this wonderment, to reproduce the sounds of folk speech, and to retell the imaginative stories of African Americans is the foundation of her talent as a writer of fiction. Living most of her life in obscurity, Hurston lived and wrote with confidence and an easy self-acceptance that have made her a favorite model for later generations of writers.

Upbringing and Influences

Zora Neale Hurston was born in Eatonville, FLORIDA, a self-governing all-black town that nurtured her sense of individuality. One of eight children, she was urged to "jump at de sun" by her mother, although her father feared that her audacious spirit would not be tolerated by white America. In *Dust Tracks on a Road: An Autobiography* (1942), Hurston describes the importance of Joe Clarke's general store, a repository of the rich African American oral tradition. There she heard black folk expressions and "lying" sessions—that is, exaggerated folk tales featuring talking animals such as Brer Rabbit, Brer Fox, and Buzzard—that she would later use in her finest writings.

Zora read widely, preferring adventure stories, Norse mythology, and the Greek myth of Hercules. Eatonville gave her a strong sense of herself, but she was also impatient with the confines of her small town.

> My soul was with the gods and my body in the village. People just would not act like gods. . . . Raking back yards and carrying out chamber-pots, were not the tasks of Thor. I wanted to be away from drabness and to stretch my limbs in some mighty struggle.

Zora's world fell apart at age thirteen when her mother died. Her stepmother had no use for her and her siblings, and Zora had to leave home. Passed from relative to relative, unable to attend school, and badly missing the close family environment she had grown up with, Zora was unhappy. She was also poor and had to work as a nanny and housekeeper, although she really wanted to read and dream. Tired of poverty and dependence, she hired on as a wardrobe girl for a young actor in a traveling troupe that performed Gilbert and Sullivan operettas. She was well-liked and, in turn, she enjoyed the camaraderie and adventure of traveling.

Participation in the Harlem Renaissance

Hurston began attending night school at Morgan Academy in BALTIMORE, MARYLAND, in 1917 and graduated in 1918. In the fall of 1918, she began attending HOWARD UNIVERSITY. While there, she wrote a story that caught the attention of Charles S. JOHNSON, the founder of *Opportunity* magazine, who sponsored literary contests and was instrumental in the development of the black arts movement of the 1920's known as the HARLEM RENAISSANCE. Johnson published her next two stories, "Drenched in Light" (1924) and "Spunk" (1925), and Hurston suddenly found herself among the Harlem Renaissance's prominent writers.

Both these stories and her play *Color Struck* (1926) were based on the folk life she had observed in Eatonville. During an age in which many African Americans felt that fitting into America meant showing that they could conform to middle-class values just as well as whites could, Hurston concentrated on the black masses and their values. Far from being ashamed of the lower classes, she knew that their expressions—black folklore, BLUES, and spirituals—represented a people who were healthy-minded and who had survived slavery through their own creative ingenuity.

Hurston's talent as a writer attracted the interest and friendship of several benefactors. Present at the *Opportunity* prize awards banquet were Fannie Hurst, a best-selling white author who befriended Hurston and hired her as a secretary, and Annie Nathan Meyer, who secured a scholarship for Hurston to attend Barnard College.

Anthropologist

Two other benefactors were instrumental in showing Hurston that the folk culture of Eatonville was of anthropological, as well as literary, interest. A paper she wrote at Barnard caught the attention of Franz Boas, the noted Columbia University anthropologist, with whom she was invited to study. He made her see that the Eatonville folklore was a continuation of African oral storytelling and urged her to return to the South to collect it. Another person who encouraged her in this regard was Charlotte Osgood Mason, nicknamed "Godmother" for her maternal characteristics and perhaps also because of her godlike behavior (she sat on a thronelike chair when her "godchildren" visited her). She was a wealthy white patron of the arts who was primarily interested in the preservation of "primitive" minority cultures—that is, cultures free of the civilized pretentions of modern life. She provided Hurston with money, a movie camera, and an automobile to use to go to the South to collect folklore. *Mules and Men* (1935), a masterful collection of southern black folktales, was the eventual result of this collecting effort.

Novelist

Although Hurston felt pressured to adapt her novels to a prescribed theme about the struggles against racism, she found such a theme a limitation. She chose instead to concentrate on those indigenous elements of black community life that survived without allowing racism to blight them.

Her first novel, *Jonah's Gourd Vine* (1934), is the story of a Baptist minister who delivers rich, metaphorical sermons but who upsets his congregation by following his own natural impulses and entering into adulterous relationships that his parishioners cannot reconcile with his role as minister. *Their Eyes Were Watching God* (1937), Hurston's masterpiece, explores a black woman's aspirations and frustrations as she struggles to become an autonomous human being. *Moses, Man of the Mountain* (1939) is an ambitious allegory about the "hoodoo man" Moses, who tries to

Zora Neale Hurston, the most accomplished female African American writer of the early twentieth century. *(Library of Congress)*

inspire in an enslaved people a group identity. To dispel the idea that black writers could only write of black subjects, she devoted her last novel, *Seraph on the Suwanee* (1948), to the subject of poor southern whites.

Richard WRIGHT criticized *Their Eyes Were Watching God* for its lack of protest against racial oppression. Hurston, however, disagreed with the attitudes of protestors, whom she grouped together in what she called "the sobbing school of Negrohood." In *Dust Tracks on a Road*, she insisted that individuals, black or white, ultimately had it in their power to determine their fates and that an appeal to racial specialness was the refuge of weakness. Believing that "skins were no measure of what was inside people," Hurston "began to laugh at both white and black who claimed special blessings on the basis of race." Although it was criticized—most notably by Arna BONTEMPS—her autobiography won the Anisfield-Wolf Award for its contribution to race relations.

Love and Marriage

With Hurston's devotion to both writing and collecting, she had little time for sustained relationships. She states in her autobiography that *Their Eyes Were Watching God* was written in HAITI in an attempt to come to terms with a love affair she had had with a college student in New York. She left him for the same reason that she had divorced her first husband, Herbert Sheen, in 1931. She felt that she must be free to pursue her career, and her relationships with men did not allot her that freedom. As she writes about her lover: "My work was one thing, and he was all of the rest"; to him, however, it was "all, or nothing." A second attempt at marriage in 1939, with Albert Price III, ended in divorce a year later.

Last Years

In 1948 Hurston was devastated when she was charged with molesting a ten-year-old boy, the son of a woman from whom she had rented an apartment in New York. Although she proved that she could not have committed the act because she was out of the country at the time, the story was sensationalized in the African American press with front-page headlines. Feeling betrayed, she wrote, "My race has seen fit to destroy me without reason."

After the 1948 publication of *Seraph on the Suwanee*, she never published another book. In her last decade, she worked as teacher, librarian, reporter, and maid. She also became active as a political conservative. In 1946 she supported the campaign of Republican Grant Reynolds against Adam Clayton Powell, Jr., in Harlem. Likewise, in the primary elections of 1950, she opposed the liberal Claude Pepper. In "I Saw Negro Votes Peddled" (1950), she attributed a lack of self-esteem to black complicity in vote-buying schemes perpetrated by the Pepper campaign. In 1954 she opposed the Brown v. Board of Education U.S. Supreme Court decision that ordered school desegregation. To her, again, it was a matter of self-respect: "How much satisfaction can I get from a court order for somebody to associate with me who does not wish me near them?"

After suffering a stroke in 1959, she died January 28, 1960, in a nursing home in Fort Pierce, Florida. She was buried in a grave that remained unmarked until the 1970's, when Alice Walker located it and erected a stone marker proclaiming Zora Neale Hurston to have been "A Genius of the South."

—*William L. Howard*

See also: Literature; Oral and family history.

Suggested Readings:

Carter-Sigglow, Janet. *Making Her Way with Thunder: A Reappraisal of Zora Neale Hurston's Narrative Art*. New York: Peter Lang, 1994.

Cronin, Gloria L., ed. *Critical Essays on Zora Neale Hurston*. New York: G.K. Hall, 1998.

Gates, Henry Louis, and Anthony Appiah, eds. *Zora Neale Hurston: Critical Perspectives Past and Present*. New York: Amistad Press, 1993.

Glassman, Steve, and Kathryn L. Seidel, eds. *Zora in Florida*. Orlando: University of Central Florida Press, 1991.

Harris, Trudier. *The Power of the Porch: The Storyteller's Craft in Zora Neale Hurston, Gloria Naylor, and Randall Kenan*. Athens: University of Georgia Press, 1996.

Hemenway, Robert E. *Zora Neale Hurston: A Literary Biography*. Urbana: University of Illinois Press, 1977.

Howard, Lillie P., ed. *Alice Walker and Zora Neale Hurston: The Common Bond*. Westport, Conn.: Greenwood Press, 1993.

Hurston, Zora Neale. *Dust Tracks on a Road: An Autobiography*. 2d ed. Urbana: University of Illinois Press, 1984.

_______. *Go Gator and Muddy the Water: Writings*. Edited by Pamela Bordelon. New York: W. W. Norton, 1999.

Lyons, Mary E. *Sorrow's Kitchen: The Life and Folklore of Zora Neale Hurston*. New York: Charles Scribner's Sons, 1990.

Meisenhelder, Susan E. *Hitting a Straight Lick with a Crooked Stick: Race and Gender in the Work of Zora Neale Hurston*. Tuscaloosa: University of Alabama Press, 1999.

Plant, Deborah G. *Every Tub Must Sit on Its Own Bottom: The Philosophy and Politics of Zora Neale Hurston*. Urbana: University of Illinois Press, 1995.

Hurt, "Mississippi" John (July 3, 1893, Teoc, Mississippi—November 2, 1966, Grenada, Mississippi): Blues singer, harmonica player, and guitarist. Hurt was one of three children of Isom Hurt and Mary Jan McCain. His earliest musical experiences were singing in the church. He taught himself to play the guitar and frequently sang at local parties, picnics, and dances, but much of his activity was as a laborer, farmer, and railroad worker. His earliest recordings were for the OKeh label in 1928. He recorded "Frankie," "Spike Driver Blues," and "Stack o'Lee Blues," among other works.

After recording only a few songs, Hurt apparently limited his performing to Mississippi. Until he was rediscovered in the early 1960's, he was largely unknown. He was far more popular during his brief reemergence, beginning in 1963, than he ever was during the 1920's. He was regarded not only as a bluesman but also as a preserver of a past era and tradition. To that end, he was featured at several folk festivals around the United States, including those in Philadelphia, New York, and Newport, RHODE ISLAND. He was also featured at several night clubs and on many university campuses, including Columbia, the University of Chicago, OBERLIN COLLEGE, and the University of Cincinnati. This led to several television and radio appearances, including the *Tonight Show* with Johnny Carson and radio tapings with folk singer Pete Seeger.

Hurt also rerecorded the songs that he originally recorded in 1928, as well as other songs in his large repertoire. They included "Avalon Blues," "Big Leg Blues," "Candy Man Blues," "Lazy Blues," "Nobody's Dirty Business," "Pera Lee," and "Sliding Delta." During his comeback, he recorded for the Library of Congress, Vanguard, and Piedmont labels. Four albums of his work were released between 1965 and 1972. In 1966 he suffered a fatal heart attack. His wife, Jessie, and fourteen of his children survived him.
See also: Music.

Hutton, Bobby James (1951, Oakland, California—April 6, 1968, Oakland, California): Member of the BLACK PANTHER PARTY for Self Defense. Hutton was one of the first Black Panthers. Along with Eldridge CLEAVER and other Panthers, he was caught in a shootout with Oakland police. As Cleaver and Hutton, choking with tear gas, emerged from a residence to surrender, the unarmed Hutton was shot to death. Hutton's death helped galvanize community support for the Black Panthers.

Hyers Sisters: (Anna Madhah Hyers, 1853, Sacramento, California—1930's, Sacramento, California; Emma Louise Hyers, 1855, Sacramento, California—1890's): Concert singers. Anna, a soprano, and Emma, a contralto, sang together in the well-known Hyers Sisters duo. After studying with their parents (their father was a tenor and their mother was a musician), Anna and Emma began to display serious musical talent when they studied voice and piano with German musician Hugo Sank. Later, they studied with Josephine D'Ormy and made their concert debut at the Metropolitan theater in Sacramento in 1867. After this successful concert, Samuel Hyers and his daughters toured other cities in CALIFORNIA and throughout the country. The *San Francisco Chronicle* praised Anna's performance of "Casta Diva," from Vincenzo Bellini's *Norma*, and other operatic arias. Emma was praised equally.

After further study, the sisters embarked on a national tour. In 1871 they sang at the Salt Lake Theater in Salt Lake City, UTAH, where they were joined by baritone Joseph Le Count. The Salt Lake audience was so appreciative that the group was asked to do a follow-up benefit performance. The group met similar praise on successive tour stops in CHICAGO and Cleveland. The success of these engagements led Samuel Hyers to enlarge his group to include tenor Wallace King, baritone John Luca, and accompanist A. C. Taylor.

With the added personnel, the group performed successfully in New York and, in 1872, in Boston, where they sang at the World Peace Jubilee with the FISK JUBILEE SINGERS. Other featured musicians who appeared with the group included violinist Claudio Jose Brindis de Salas, pianist Jacob Sawyer, and minstrel singer Sam Lucas.

In 1876 the Hyers Sisters Concert Company expanded its concert repertoire to include musical comedy and some light minstrel material, staging such works as *The African Princess*, *The Underground Railroad*, *Out of Bondage*, *Colored Aristocracy*, *Out of the Wilderness*, and *The Blackville Twins*. The group occasionally returned to the concert stage, until Emma died in the late 1890's. Anna sang operatic excerpts

with John H. Isham's Oriental America Company and traveled to Australia with the All-Star Afro-American Minstrels. She retired from the stage in 1902 and died sometime during the 1930's.
See also: Classical and operatic music; Minstrels.

Hyman, John Adams (July 23, 1840, near Warrenton, North Carolina—September 14, 1891, Washington, D.C.): U.S. representative from NORTH CAROLINA during RECONSTRUCTION. Born into SLAVERY, Hyman was employed by a jeweler named King, who taught him to read and write when Hyman was in his early twenties. The jeweler's actions stirred up controversy, and he was forced to sell Hyman to an ALABAMA slaveowner before leaving town. Having been sold numerous times, Hyman returned to to his Warrenton home in 1865 to become a farmer. He also began working for African American enfranchisement.

Hyman was a delegate to the REPUBLICAN PARTY's North Carolina state convention in 1867, where he was named to the party's state executive committee. Later that year, he was elected as a county delegate to the state constitutional convention to be held in 1868. Hyman was elected to the state senate in 1868 and lobbied among his black constituents for support of the new state constitution. In 1872 and 1874, he sought the Republican nomination for North Carolina'a Second District seat in Congress. Although defeated during his first attempt, Hyman received the nomination in 1874. He defeated his DEMOCRATIC PARTY opponent in the general election, becoming the first African American member of the House of Representatives from North Carolina. His victory was challenged, and he spent much of his term gathering evidence in his own defense.

Eventually, the challenger's claim was rejected, and Hyman became more active in Congress. He served on the House Committee on Manufactures. After an unsuccessful bid for renomination in 1876, he returned to his farm and opened a grocery and liquor store in Warrenton. Hyman served as special deputy collector of internal revenue for North Carolina's Fourth District from 1877 to 1878. He later moved to MARYLAND to work as a mail clerk's assistant. In 1889 he moved to WASHINGTON, D.C., to work in the seed dispensary of the federal Department of Agriculture.
See also: Congress members; Politics and government.

Hypertension: Medical problem common among African Americans. Also known as high blood pressure, and sometimes called the "silent killer" because it often exhibits no symptoms, high blood pressure strikes proportionately twice as many African Americans as whites. In 1986 more than 7.2 million African Americans were classified as being hypertensive, and half of all African Americans over the age of fifty had this disorder. High blood pressure is a major risk factor for cardiovascular disease, eye problems, and kidney disease. It can be fatal.

Blood pressure refers to how much work the heart does when pumping blood throughout the arteries in the body. Its measurement is expressed in two numbers: systolic pressure, which notes the thrust when the heart actually is beating, and diastolic pressure, the pressure when the heart is at rest between beats. It is generally agreed that a blood pressure of 140 (systolic pressure) over 100 (diastolic pressure) or above (also written as 140/100) is high.

For many years, doctors thought that differences in diet accounted for the high incidence of high blood pressure among African Americans. High salt intake, potassium deficiency, and overeating all have been associated with hypertension. All three factors have been observed in the eating habits of African

Americans. Doctors routinely recommend reduced salt intake, potassium supplements, weight loss programs, and exercise for their hypertensive patients. Medication is often prescribed to help people control their high blood pressure, especially when change in diet and exercise are not enough. Smoking also seems to aggravate high blood pressure.

Evidence is emerging that points to a strong connection between high blood pressure and stress. A study reported by the Johns Hopkins School of Medicine suggests that the stress related to long-term effects of POVERTY and discrimination increases the chances of hypertension. Consequently, many of the social, political, and economic realities African Americans face place them at higher risk for hypertension.

See also: Health; Health care professionals; Medicine.

I

Ice Cube (O'Shea Jackson; b. June 15, c. 1969, Los Angeles, California): Rap vocalist and actor. Born the son of middle-class parents who lived in South Central Los Angeles, Ice Cube became a founding member of N.W.A. (Niggaz with Attitude), the first nationally known gangsta rap group. After working with Andre "Dr. Dre" Young and Eric "Eazy-E" Wright on N.W.A.'s first album, *N.W.A. and the Posse* (1987), Ice Cube took time off to complete a one-year college program in drafting at the Phoenix Institute of Technology and received his degree in 1988.

Ice Cube achieved prominence as a rap artist as N.W.A.'s primary lyricist, and the fierceness of his work on N.W.A.'s album *Straight Outta Compton* (1989) gained nationwide attention. The raps on the two million-selling album contained some of the most graphic depictions of gang warfare and urban street life to be released on record thus far, and the antiauthority tone of the song "F— tha Police" led the Federal Bureau of Investigation (FBI) to write a letter to N.W.A.'s record company, Ruthless Records, stating that the law enforcement community "took exception" to the group's message. A fax campaign between local police forces on the group's concert tour route was interpreted by some observers as a form of censorship. Despite or because of the controversy, gangsta rap was an important new phenomenon in popular culture, and Ice Cube was its icon.

After leaving N.W.A. in 1990 over a royalty dispute, Ice Cube went on to a prolific career as a solo rap artist and film actor. His debut solo album, *AmeriKKKa's Most Wanted* (1990), continued in the tough gangsta tradition but included vocals by female rapper Yo-Yo on the song "It's a Man's World" as a counterpoint to Ice Cube's reputation as a sexist. Ice Cube went on to coproduce Yo-Yo's debut album, *Make Way for the Motherlode* (1991). Ice Cube's second album, *Death Certificate* (1991), was perhaps his most controversial release. Songs such as "Black Korea" prompted *Billboard* magazine and organizations such as the Simon Wiesenthal Center to condemn the album as racist and sexist.

Ice Cube released his next album, *The Predator* (1992), in the wake of the Rodney King verdicts and resulting civil disturbances in Los Angeles. The album juxtaposed fragments from the acquittal verdicts and Malcolm X speeches with protest raps such as "Now I Gotta Wet 'Cha," which condemns the police officers involved in the King beating and imagines revenge against them. The album entered *Billboard*'s rhythm and blues and

Ice Cube in early 1998. *(AP/Wide World Photos)*

pop charts at number one and went on to sell 1.5 million copies within the first month of its release. The album's great commercial success was accompanied by further accusations of racist and sexist lyrics and suggestion by some critics that Ice Cube's gangster rhetoric was wearing thin. *Lethal Injection* (1994) took a lighter tone with songs such as "Bop Gun (One Nation)," based on a funk song by George Clinton. Ice Cube released the compilation *Featuring . . . Ice Cube* in 1997 and *War and Peace, Vol. 1* in 1998.

Ice Cube's FILM career began with a role in 1991's *Boyz 'N the Hood* and continued with appearances in films such as *Trespass* (1992) and John Singleton's *Higher Learning* (1995). In addition to starring in *Friday* (1995), Ice Cube cowrote and coproduced the film; he also produced the film's sound-track album. In 1997 he appeared in *Dangerous Ground* and *Anaconda;* in 1998 he both directed and acted in *The Players Club;* in 1999 he costarred with George Clooney in *Three Kings.*

As a major media figure, Ice Cube became a national symbol of both rebellion and popular success. Backed by his "posse" of musicians, known as the Lynch Mob, Ice Cube created a reputation as one of rap's most violent, political, and starkly honest songwriter-performers. His controversial appeal sparked a lively debate about the relationship between social realism, popular culture, and black identity in America.

See also: Music.

Idaho: African Americans have played a small but important role in this state. The CENSUS OF THE UNITED STATES estimated that the 1997 African American population of Idaho was about 7,000, less than 1 percent of the state's total population.

1997 Population: 1,210,000
African American Population: 7,000
African American Percentage of Total: 0.58

Black people first came to Idaho to mine gold in 1860. In 1863, shortly after Idaho became a separate territory, influential European American miners in Boise County passed legislation outlawing black and Chinese immigration to the county. Similar bills failed in the territorial legislature two years later, so black miners continued to come. Some were very successful. A few African Americans homesteaded in northern Idaho, but most settled in the state's two largest cities, Boise and Pocatello. In 1910 Boise had 135 black residents, 1 percent of the population.

As happened in other states in the West, Idaho in 1867 passed laws preventing intermarriage. Economic opportunities were limited, a situation that continued into the twentieth century. In the early twentieth century, Idaho's African Americans worked in service industries and as laborers. As a result, few blacks came to the state and many left. The black population of 920 in 1920 had dropped to 595 by 1940.

During WORLD WAR II, African Americans came to work in new industries in the state. The black population continued to grow, increasing from 1,000 in 1950 to 3,370 in 1990. Most African Americans live in the Boise and Mountain Home areas, close to Idaho's largest Air Force base. In 1975 T. Les Purce of Pocatello became the first black MAYOR in the state.

—Jessie L. Embry

Illinois: In 1997 Illinois was the sixth most populous U.S. state and the home of the country's sixth largest African American population. Illinois's African American residents totaled an estimated 1.8 million, a little over 15 percent of the total population of the state. The majority of Illinois's black residents live in CHICAGO, but substantial African American communities are also found in Peoria, Rockford, Rock Island, East St. Louis, and other cities around the state.

Although Illinois was admitted to the union as a free state in 1818—slavery having been outlawed in the region by the Northwest Ordinance of 1787—the state was not a haven of freedom for African Americans during its early years.

By 1732 Illinois had been settled by 768 French Europeans and 445 African slaves. As the eighteenth century progressed and the United States achieved independence from Great Britain, increasing numbers of white Americans came to settle in Illinois, mostly from the slaveholding southern states. Laws passed in 1803 allowed "Indentured servitude" in Illinois, a thinly disguised form of SLAVERY. Meanwhile, the new state became hostile to the presence of FREE BLACKS. African Americans could hold neither citizenship nor many of the basic rights that went with it.

Laws passed in 1819 and 1829 prohibited African Americans from settling in the state without "certificates of freedom," without which they could be held as fugitive slaves. Property ownership by blacks was discouraged or prohibited, although a handful of early African Americans became wealthy or successful landowners despite the odds. Frank McWhorter, for example, bought his own freedom in KENTUCKY along with a tract of land. By the time of his arrival in Illinois around 1830, McWhorter had enough money to begin a series of land purchases that allowed him to establish the town of New Philadelphia in 1836.

The decisive abolition of slavery in Illinois, along with policies which discouraged settlement by free blacks, kept Illinois's African American population low until the CIVIL WAR. By 1860 Illinois's black population of about seventy-six hundred made up only about 5 percent of the state's population (which exceeded 1.7 million); fewer than one thousand blacks lived in Chicago.

However, during the years of American involvement in WORLD WAR I (1917-1919) and

1997 Population: 11,896,000
African American Population: 1,815,000
African American Percentage of Total: 15.26

after, many African Americans left the South and moved to industrial cities in the North. There were two reasons for this migration, often called the GREAT MIGRATION: First, the "JIM CROW" LAWS mandating strict segregation in the South made life in the South increasingly oppressive and even dangerous. Second, new economic opportunities were offered by the industrial cities in the Great Lakes states. African American populations began to grow in Illinois cities.

These African Americans were not always welcome in their new northern homes. In Chicago, for example, there was significant violence directed against black people during the recession of 1919; by 1930 the GREAT DEPRESSION had taken its toll on black businesses, and many African Americans lost their homes.

While WORLD WAR II brought better economic times, incidents of police brutality and HOUSING discrimination continued. Segregation in restaurants continued as well; the first lunch counter sit-in took place in Chicago in 1943, at a coffee shop named Jack Spratt's. As late as 1961, black people knew that they were expected to be out of the city limits of East Peoria by sundown or face possible violence. Chicago remained one of the most segregated cities in the United States. In 1966 Martin Luther KING, Jr., went to Chicago and led a number of marches against discrimination that brought violent reactions from whites. After King's death in 1968, riots on Chicago's West Side led to even more violent police repression. In 1969 Black Panther leader Fred HAMPTON was shot in his apartment by police and FBI agents.

By the 1980's and 1990's, however, the state's African Americans and organizations had begun to make their political presence felt. Jesse JACKSON founded OPERATION PUSH in Chicago in 1971, and he later contended for the national Democratic presidential nomination in 1984 and 1988. Harold WASHINGTON was elected as Chicago's first black mayor in 1983. In 1992 Illinois voters made Carol Moseley BRAUN the first black woman to be elected to the U.S. Senate. Roland Burris served for several years as comptroller of the state of Illinois, while Jesse White, in 1998, became Illinois' first black secretary of state.

—*Timothy C. Frazer*

Image Awards: Awards created by the NATIONAL ASSOCIATION FOR THE ADVANCEMENT OF COLORED PEOPLE (NAACP) for African American entertainers and writers who have succeeded in the entertainment business and have portrayed African Americans in a positive light.

The NAACP Image Awards are given annually to African American actors, writers, singers, and others who have succeeded in the fields of FILM, television, LITERATURE, and recording. In addition to honoring individual persons, the Image Awards honor organizations and projects that depict African Americans in a positive light. The first NAACP Image Awards ceremony was held on Octo-

Image Award Categories

Awards are made for most outstanding achievement in these forty-one categories:

Motion Pictures
Motion Picture
Actor in a Motion Picture
Actress in a Motion Picture
Supporting Actor in a Motion Picture
Supporting Actress in a Motion Picture

Youth Actor/Actress
Youth Actor/Actress

Television
Comedy Series
Actor in a Comedy Series
Actress in a Comedy Series
Supporting Actor in a Comedy Series
Supporting Actress in a Comedy Series
Drama Series
Actor in a Drama Series
Actress in a Drama Series
Supporting Actor in a Drama Series
Supporting Actress in a Drama Series
Television Movie/Miniseries/Dramatic Special
Actor in a Television Movie/Miniseries/dramatic Special
Actress in a Television Movie/Miniseries/Dramatic Special
Actor in a Daytime Drama Series
Actress in a Daytime Drama Series
Variety Series/Special
Performance in a Variety Series/Special
News, Talk or Information Series
News, Talk or Information Special
Youth or Children's Series/Special
Performance in a Youth or Children's Series/Special

Literary Work
Literary Work, Fiction
Literary Work, Nonfiction
Literary Work, Children's

Recording
New Artist
Male Artist
Female Artist
Duo or Group
Rap Artist
Jazz Artist
Gospel Artist—Traditional
Gospel Artist—Contemporary
Music Video
Song
Album

ber 22, 1962. Sammy Davis, Jr., was honored for his acting contributions and for laying the groundwork for many other African American entertainers. Davis was also credited with working to obtain equal employment opportunities for African American entertainers in Hollywood.

Suggestions for nominees are made by managers, record labels, and film studios and are submitted to the NAACP; from these submissions, final nominees are selected for the Image Awards' forty-one categories. Industry professionals and NAACP officials select the nominees for each category. Winners are chosen by the readers of The Crisis, the official publication of the NAACP, and the results are tabulated by accounting firms. As with a number of other awards ceremonies, no one except the accountants of these firms knows who the winners are until the envelopes are opened onstage.

Among the many prominent African American figures who have been honored by the Image Awards are Ella Fitzgerald, Whoopi Goldberg, and Stevie Wonder. Political figures and activists have also been honored. Since 1993 the Image Awards ceremony has been produced for telecast, with African American celebrities hosting the proceedings.

—*Carrie L. Fascia*

Actor Roscoe Lee Browne at the 1986 Image Awards ceremony. *(AP/Wide World Photos)*

Iman (Iman Abdumajid; b. 1955, Mogadishu, Somalia): Model. Best known by her first name, Iman became one of the highest paid models in the world. Born in Somalia, she was reared in neighboring Kenya and moved to New York City in 1976 at the invitation of photographer Peter Beard, who was convinced that she would do well as a fashion model. He had seen her picture at the house of Mirella Ricciardi, a photographer and mutual friend. Iman's career was boosted by various stories that said she was an unsophisticated village girl who was discovered by Beard while she was herding cattle or jumping out of the bush. On the contrary, Iman was the daughter of a gynecologist mother and a diplomat father. She studied at the University of Nairobi, took a degree in political science, and became fluent in five languages.

Unlike many African and African American models who had to go to Europe to become successful in the fashion industry, Iman's career soared immediately after she arrived in the United States. She initially signed with the Wilhelmina Modeling Agency, and her arrival in New York City was publicized by a twenty-minute documentary. She appeared on the cover of most major fashion magazines, including *Vogue*, British *Vogue*, and Italian *Vogue*, as well as on the covers of *Essence* and *Cosmopolitan* magazines. She modeled clothing and jewelry and was featured in the advertisements for a major cosmetics line. Iman's career expanded to include acting in television (*The Cosby Show*). She appeared in the films *Out of Africa* (1985), *The Hu-*

Somali-born model Iman in 1989. *(AP/Wide World Photos)*

man Factor (1979), and *No Way Out* (1987). She moved on to larger feature roles, appearing as a shape-changing alien in *Star Trek VI: The Undiscovered Country* (1991). As a business entrepreneur, she developed a line of African fabrics.

In 1982 Iman was in an automobile accident that threatened to end her modeling career. She suffered breaks in her collarbone, cheekbone, and three ribs. Her shoulder was also dislocated. She required five hours of surgery, from which she recovered fully. She had retired from high-fashion runway work by the early 1990's except for the rare project that caught her interest.

In 1992 Iman began actively promoting famine relief efforts in her native Somalia. She also became involved in other charity work in the 1990's, including work with the CHILDREN'S DEFENSE FUND. Iman married former National Basketball Association star Spencer Haywood, but they divorced. They had one child together, Zulekha. In 1992 Iman married British rock star David Bowie.

In 1994 Iman, a business partner, and a small group of investors launched a new line of "Iman" cosmetics, which were initially distributed through J. C. Penney stores. The line was designed primarily for African American, Asian, Hispanic, and Native American women. Iman subsequently worked out a licensing arrangement with the Ivax Corporation under which she retained creative control over the products and Ivax oversaw production and distribution. In 1997 the line's sales totaled about $30 million.

Imani Temple: Formal name of the African American Catholic Congregation, founded by George Augustus STALLINGS, Jr., in Washington, D.C., July 2, 1989. The temple takes its name from a Swahili word meaning "faith"; "Imani" is also the adopted name of the seventh and final cornerstone of the African American family holiday, KWANZAA (December 26-January 1), established by Maulana Ron KARENGA in 1966.

An African American priest of the ROMAN CATHOLIC archdiocese of WASHINGTON, D.C., George Stallings, Jr., believed that Cardinal James Hickey and the Roman Catholic Church under which he served were not sensitive enough to the spiritual needs of African Americans and that the documents of Vatican II (the second Vatican Council of Catholic bishops and the pope) allowed him to initiate new liturgical rites and ceremonies based on the African American cultural experience. Such an approach, he said, would satisfy the spiritual yearnings of African American Catholics. African American Catholics should be allowed to express themselves in worship in ways familiar to them—active joyous celebra-

The Reverend George A. Stallings (center) presiding over a service at the Imani Temple. *(© Roy Lewis Archives)*

tions of drumming, dancing, singing, and praying. Cardinal Hickey suspended Stallings as a priest of the Roman Catholic Church on July 4, 1989, for celebrating his rites of the Holy Mass for members of the Imani Temple.

Stallings's break with the Roman Catholic Church was formalized by a papal excommunication in February, 1990, after he consistently practiced his own brand of African American worship, which incorporated elements of both Catholism and African American celebrations such as Kwanzaa. The Imani Temple attracted thousands of worshipers and expanded from its Washington, D.C., headquarters to BALTIMORE, MARYLAND; PHILADELPHIA, PENNSYLVANIA; and Norfolk, VIRGINIA, in just a few years.

In May, 1990, Stallings was consecrated as the first bishop of the Imani Temple by six bishops from the Independent Old Catholic Churches of California in a ceremony in which African dances, gospel singing, and drumming were performed before a live audience of about one thousand. The six white bishops who consecrated Stallings to the office of bishop were themselves members of a Catholic church that had broken away from the Roman Catholic Church in the nineteenth century.

A new cathedral for the African American Catholic Congregation was dedicated in Washington, D.C., in 1994, with Stallings presiding as archbishop. In 1999 one of the church's leaders, Carlos E. Harvin, left to form his own religious organization. Differences had been growing between Stallings and Harvin in the 1990's.

Immersion schools: Schools offering an EDUCATION emphasizing African American culture and heritage. These schools are an innovation of the early 1990's, created in an attempt to combat high failure and dropout rates among African American students, particularly boys. The first schools of this type were organized in DETROIT, MICHIGAN, and Milwaukee, WISCONSIN. A 1991 court order stated that Detroit's three "male academies," as they were called, had to admit female students. Milwaukee opened an African American immersion school in September of 1991, using part of an elementary school that already was segregated by race. The school allowed girls to enroll to avoid legal challenges, and its first class was split roughly evenly between the sexes. NEW YORK CITY was considering special schools for male African Americans in 1991, and BALTIMORE, MARYLAND, had several classes in 1990 that were exclusively for male blacks.

Urban school districts with large black populations considered various approaches to combating high dropout and failure rates. Detroit, with a public school population that was 90 percent black, faced these problems to an exaggerated degree. Almost half of the city's male students dropped out before being graduated from high school. School officials wanted to intervene before high school. They designed the three "male academies," named for MALCOLM X, Marcus GARVEY, and Paul ROBESON, with extended hours, an emphasis on discipline, male role models in the classroom, and what has been called an Afrocentric curriculum. About twelve hundred students applied for the 560 openings in these academies.

The American Civil Liberties Union and the National Organization for Women Legal Defense and Education Fund sued the Detroit school board on behalf of a woman with three daughters in the city's public schools. An injunction issued on August 15, 1991, ruled that all-male public schools were unconstitutional, even though the city already had one school reserved for boys on an expulsion track and three for pregnant girls. Detroit's immersion schools, which became known as African-centered academies, were ordered to admit female students.

Debates concerning immersion schools focused on several topics. As in Detroit, the constitutionality and even the appropriateness of segregating schools by sex came into question. Some critics also saw segregation by race as a step backward, no matter what its goals. Finally, the Afrocentric curricula proposed by schools drew criticism. Scholars debated the precise definition of AFROCENTRICITY, or a focus on the African continent and African ideas, as well as debating the validity of Afrocentric scholarship, some of the results and conclusions of which have been questioned. Afrocentric curricula have as a goal placing the achievements of African people into proper perspective, with a side benefit of improving the esteem of black students. Questions arose concerning what that "proper" perspective is. Some educators argued that an Afrocentric perspective would be as detrimental as the more common Eurocentric one because it would contain the same sorts of biases.

Immigration and ethnic origins of African Americans: Several aspects of African American history make the African black unique among American minority groups. No other minority group has an immigration history that is even remotely similar. The large immigration flows that established blacks as the largest minority group in America occurred in the eighteenth and early nineteenth centuries and involved almost exclusively coerced migration by people being forced into SLAVERY. After the end of legal slavery in the 1860's, few additional African immigrants came to the United States. Meanwhile, large numbers of Europeans, Asians, and Latinos entered the country. Because of the structure of U.S. immigration legislation, it was not until after 1965 that any significant number of blacks migrated from other nations to the United States.

Areas of Origin

It is possible to determine the national, or ethnic, origin of fairly recent black immigrants to the United States, with the understanding that this relatively recent immigration has contributed very small numbers to the overall African American population. The growth of the black population has been unique in this respect. The African American population of the early 1990's numbered approximately 30 million people. If all black immigrants from 1900 to 1970 and their descendants are counted, they add up to only about one million people, or 3 percent of that total. Immigration from sub-Saharan AFRICA and the WEST INDIES during the twenty-year period from 1970 to 1990 provided 5 percent of the total, or 1.6 million people.

Although the African American population grew from 8.8 million in 1900 to 29.9 million in 1990, most of the growth is attributable to natural increase; immigration had little effect. The black population would have stood at about 27.5 million without any immigration at all. Almost 92 percent of the African American population in the 1990's consisted of descendants of individuals who initially reached the United States through the SLAVE TRADE. Of the 2.4 million individuals who represent the contribution of twentieth-century immigrants and their offspring to the African American population of the 1990's, two-thirds resulted from immigration between 1970 and 1990. Immigration for the period 1900 through 1950 produced black population increases ranging from 22,000 to 196,000 people. Increases attributable to immigration between 1960 and 1970 came to 266,000 (largely the result of mid-decade changes in migration laws) and jumped significantly to 834,000 for the period between 1970 and 1980 and to 774,000 for the period between 1980 and 1990.

Since 1978 reports containing detailed annual data from the U.S. Immigration and Naturalization Service (INS) have provided figures for immigrants to the United States by country of birth. While INS information is not categorized by immigrants' race, it is possible to calculate fairly accurate estimates of black migration flows by counting migrants from sub-Saharan Africa, excluding South Africa (because of the large proportion of white South African emigrants), and those from the predominantly black nations of the Caribbean. These data make it possible to examine the national origins of black immigrants who came to the United States between 1970 and 1980. These data also provide evidence that foreign-born blacks constitute a small but growing proportion of the African American population.

For each year from 1970 to 1990, there were constant increases in the absolute numbers of sub-Saharan African immigrants: 2,128 in 1970, 5,873 in 1976, 9,145 in 1982, and 28,016 in 1990. Nevertheless, the increases in the proportions of black Africans to all immigrants were modest (slightly less than 1 percent from 1970 to 1974, around 1 percent from 1975 to 1979, and about 2 percent from 1980 to 1990), because of increases in overall levels of immigration from 323,000 in 1970 to 1.5 million in 1990.

Immigration to the United States from the predominantly black West Indies involved much larger numbers of people during the same two-decade period: 45,069 in 1970, 61,322 in 1981, and 103,412 in 1990. These immigrants represented between 10 and 15 percent of all immigrants to the United States during this period, with the exception of 1989 and 1990, when black Caribbean migrants were only 7.1 and 6.7 percent of all immigrants, respectively. Overall, black migrants from Africa and the Caribbean combined represented 13 to 17 percent of all U.S. immigration from 1970 to 1988, decreasing to only about 8 percent in 1989 and 1990.

The growing presence of foreign-born blacks points out the importance of acknowledging ethnic diversity within the African American population. It should also be noted that there are important cultural differences among sub-Saharan African nations, as well as among

Top Five Countries of Origin of Black Immigration

Country	*1976*	*1981*	*1986*	*1991*	*1996*
Jamaica	11,100	23,569	19,595	23,828	19,089
Haiti	6,691	6,683	12,666	47,527	18,386
Guyana	4,497	6,743	10,367	11,666	9,489
Trinidad and Tobago	6,040	4,599	2,891	8,407	7,344
Nigeria	907	1,918	2,976	7,912	10,221

Source: U.S. Immigration and Naturalization Service.

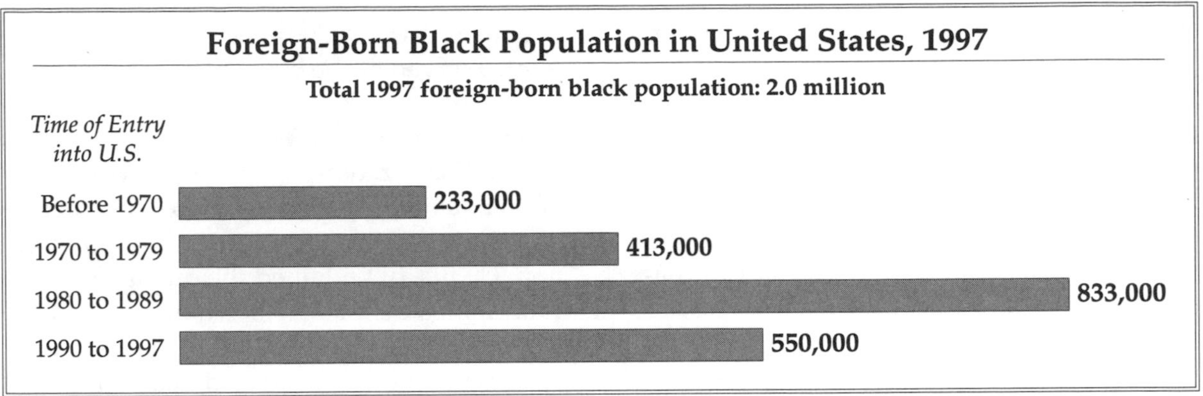

Source: U.S. Bureau of the Census.

predominantly black Caribbean nations—such as the BAHAMAS, HAITI, and JAMAICA. These differences include language, religion, levels of industrialization, urbanization, and technological development, and average educational attainment, among other factors. Such factors must be considered in order to avoid making stereotypical assumptions and broad generalizations about the cultural background of African Americans.

History of U.S. Immigration Laws

Reasons for the almost complete absence of blacks from immigration flows to the United States between the 1860's and mid-1960's can be easily understood by examining the historical development of U.S. immigration legislation. Until the last quarter of the nineteenth century, there were almost no restrictions on immigration to the United States.

By the time the Statue of Liberty was dedicated in 1886, U.S. immigration policy had changed through the passage of the first restrictive immigration legislation in Congress. The Immigration Acts of 1875, 1882, 1891, 1903, and 1917 prohibited "obnoxious" persons from entering the country. This designation applied to those who were destitute, suffered from various physical maladies, or were engaged in immoral activities. While these early laws were not targeted specifically at African Americans, there are laws dating from the same period that began the tradition of restricting the entry of immigrants based on their racial or national origin, a focus that underlay U.S. immigration policy from the late 1800's until 1965.

Because of growing concern over the presence of large numbers of Chinese immigrants (most of whom had been aggressively recruited to build railroads and work in mines), the U.S. government violated a recently signed treaty with the Chinese government in passing the Chinese Exclusion Act of 1882. This act and its amendments initially limited Chinese immigration and finally banned it altogether. It was not repealed until 1943. In 1907 the Japanese government signed the Gentlemen's Agreement which limited immigration from that country, and the Japanese Exclusion Act of 1924 eliminated it altogether.

Once racist and xenophobic sentiment had been successfully incorporated into national policy, there was a move to create comprehensive immigration restrictions based on racial and ethnic quotas. Most immigrants to the United States in the late 1800's were from western and northern Europe. By the turn of the century, immigration had increased to over a million people a year, nearly all from Europe, and over half of them were from southern and eastern European countries such as Italy, Poland, Russia, Greece, and Austria-Hungary. Although, in contemporary America, people of southern and eastern European ancestry are generally thought of as being white ethnics, in the early 1900's, each of these national origins was considered a separately identifiable racial category by many Americans, and discrimination against these immigrants was widespread.

In 1921 Congress passed the first law ever that limited the overall number of immigrants per year. In addition, within this limit of 350,000 total persons, there were restrictions based on national origin. The Quota Act of 1921, which was enacted with widespread public support, limited immigration to 3 percent of the population from any given foreign country in the United States as of the 1910 census. For example, there were 11,498 people in the United States in 1910 who had been born in Bulgaria. Therefore, 3 percent of that number, or 345, would be permitted to enter from Bulgaria each year. There was little attempt to disguise the fact that the 1910 census was used as the base because larger proportions of the U.S. foreign-born population was from western and northern Europe than in 1920.

After only three years, the Immigration Act of 1924 made national origin quotas permanent, and further restricted immigration to 2 percent of the ethnic groups in the country in 1890, when 70 percent of the foreign-born were from northern and western Europe. This act also barred Asians from immigration altogether, because naturalization legislation already prohibited Asian residents of the United States from becoming citizens. Finally, the National Origins Quota of 1929 was adopted, which established a Quota Board that was charged with taking the percentage of each national group in the United States in 1790 (the first census), calculating the contributions to those numbers of immigration since 1790, and using these data of very questionable quality to establish national origins quotas within an overall limit of 150,000 persons per year. These quotas served as the core of U.S. immigration policy for decades.

Following World War II, the Immigration and Nationalization Act of 1952, or McCarran-Walter Act, introduced a preference structure based on family reunification and occupational skills, but retained the quotas from the 1920's. President Harry S Truman vetoed the act, stating that the national origins quotas were patently racist and had been a national disgrace since their inception. Congress overrode his veto, but the end of racial immigration quotas clearly was at hand. President Dwight Eisenhower renewed the call for the abolition of these quotas, but little was actually accomplished until after President John Kennedy's death.

The most significant changes in U.S. immigration policy since the initiation of legal restrictions came in the form of the Immigration Act of 1965, commonly called the Kennedy-Johnson Act. This law was an enactment of suggestions for immigration reform make by President Kennedy in 1963. The old national origins quotas were eliminated (along with the "zero quotas" for Asians). Limits of 120,000 immigrants from the Western Hemisphere, and 170,000 from non-Western Hemisphere nations were established, with no more than 20,000 from any single country. Preference in admission was given to the relatives of U.S. citizens and legal residents, with parents considered to be outside of the numerical quotas.

The 1965 act has made a real difference in African American ethnicity. More than 75 percent of the 25 million immigrants to the United States since World War II have entered since this law was passed, and the new countries of origin have been in Asia, Latin America, the Caribbean, and Africa. Although black immigration flows seem quite small, they represent a significant increase over the pre-1965 levels. It is interesting to note that the sex, age, and educational characteristics of immigrants have changed very little from the time when almost all legal immigrants were European or Canadian. Only the racial composition has changed markedly.

Some observers predicted that the Immigration Act of 1990, which went into effect in October of 1991 and replaced the 1965 act, might increase levels of black immigration. This law raised the total annual limit to 700,000 immigrants and gave special consideration to "family reunification" and newly created immigrant categories, including "diversity immigrants." To counterbalance the enormous influx of Asians and Latin Americans that have been admitted since 1965, the INS began to issue diversity immigrant visas to citizens of countries in other regions that have experienced modest immigration flows in spite of the elimination of national origins quotas.

Controversies

The Immigration Act of 1965 was intended to eliminate racial bias and ethnic discrimination found in official U.S. immigration policy. Some observers have contended, however, that the emphasis on family reunification featured in that law and the 1990 act may inadvertently have perpetuated the continuation of racial inequities. The 1965 law reserved 74 percent of all visas for the adult relatives and extended family members of U.S. citizens and permanent resident aliens. The spouses and minor children of these new immigrants were allowed to enter without being counted within these numerical limits. In 1980 the proportion of such visas was raised to 80 percent. Some contend that family reunification amounts to a de facto continuation of national origins quotas, especially as it applies to black immigration.

Racial and ethnic groups that had benefited from the national origins quotas are much more likely to have living relatives in their homelands than groups who had been discriminated against for decades or generations. Blacks may suffer more than any other group in this respect because, as noted above, 92 percent of African Americans are descended from people indigenous to the U.S. population for a hundred years or more. In fact, Emanuel Celler, cosponsor of the 1965 act, stated during debate over the bill, "there will not be, comparatively, many Asians or Africans entering the country since the people of Africa and Asia have very few relatives here." Furthermore, researchers have claimed that Asians and Latin Americans, who have received most of the visas available since passage of the 1965 act, have created a phenomenon called "chain migration." Once large numbers of immigrants from Asian and Latin American countries were in the United States, their relatives back home received preference for admission. It is true that by the 1990's Latin America and Asia accounted for more than half of all legal immigration, and more than 80 percent of all new U.S. residents, if refugees and illegal entrants are included, while black African and Caribbean flows had increased only incrementally.

Another issue related to the admission of black foreign nationals for resettlement in America centers on U.S. refugee policy. Refugees are defined as people fleeing persecution at the hands of their governments, and they are eligible to apply for resettlement in the United States. In addition, since 1968, the United States has been a participant in the United Nations Protocol on Refugees, which states that foreign nationals already in the United States who were fleeing persecution are eligible for political asylum if they have a "well founded fear" of persecution if deported to their homeland. The differential treatment accorded asylum-seekers from Haiti and CUBA has generated some spirited discussion. In short, while tens of thousands of Haitians, who were fleeing the Duvalier regimes and the military junta that overthrew the Bertrand Aristide government, were deported or detained at sea and returned before reaching America, the U.S. government welcomed hundreds of thousands of Cubans fleeing Fidel Castro's Cuban regime.

The CONGRESSIONAL BLACK CAUCUS set up a task force to study the problem and concluded that refugee status should be accorded to the Haitian "boat people" in the name of humanitarianism and equitable application of the law. After failing to change the U.S. policy, the black congressional leaders joined prominent church leaders and the Voluntary Agencies Responsible for Refugees in stating publicly that racism was behind the differential treatment of Haitians and other asylum-seekers due to a reluctance on the part of the United States to admit large numbers of black refugees. Even as this controversy raged, the government announced that all Vietnamese and Laotians who reached safe haven would be considered refugees while those fleeing Haiti were subjected to case-by-case screening and deportation. Of the 341,180 refugees admitted to the United States from 1975 through 1979, not one was from Africa, and 24,061 African refugees were admitted from 1980 through 1990, compared with 1,448,976 from other parts of the world.

—*Jack Carter*

See also: Demography; Diaspora, African; Immigration and ethnic origins of African Canadians; Jamaica and Jamaican Americans; West Indies.

Suggested Readings:

Apraku, Kofi K. *African Emigres in the United States: A Missing Link in Africa's Social and Economic Development*. New York: Praeger, 1991.

Briggs, Vernon M., Jr., and Stephen Moore. *Still an Open Door? U.S. Immigration Policy and the American Economy*. Washington, D.C.: American University Press, 1994.

Edmonston, Barry, and Jeffrey S. Passel, eds. *Immigration and Ethnicity: The Integration of America's Newest Arrivals*. Washington, D.C.: Urban Institute Press, 1994.

Loescher, Gil. *Beyond Charity: International Cooperation and the Global Refugee Crisis*. New York: Oxford University Press, 1993.

Portes, Alejandro, and Ruben G. Rumbaut. *Immigrant America: A Portrait*. Berkeley: University of California Press, 1990.

Reimers, David M. *Still the Golden Door: The Third World Comes to America*. New York: Columbia University Press, 1985.

U.S. Department of Justice. *Statistical Yearbook of the Immigration and Naturalization Service*. Washington, D.C.: Immigration and Naturalization Service, 1979-1990.

Vickerman, Milton. *Crosscurrents: West Indian Immigrants and Race*. New York: Oxford University Press, 1999.

Immigration and ethnic origins of African Canadians: All persons of African descent in CANADA are either immigrants or descendants of immigrants. In the original colony of New France, there were some black slaves who lived and worked among the French-speaking population of soldiers and settlers. After the colony passed into British hands in the wake of the 1763 peace settlement, concluding the Seven Years' War, there were several waves of black immigration from the British colonies to the south. The first wave of immigrants consisted of slaves and freedmen who accompanied the white Loyalist refugees who fled the thirteen colonies during the AMERICAN REVOLUTION of the 1780's.

Another wave of immigrants consisted of slaves who fled the United States during the WAR OF 1812. During the 1850's, in the wake of the passage of the FUGITIVE SLAVE LAW, escaped slaves fled from the United States to Canada as their only hope of freedom. By the mid-1990's, native-born Canadians of African descent whose ancestors had come from the United States continued to predominate among African Canadians in Nova Scotia and persisted (in diminishing numbers) in southwestern Ontario, the site of pre-Civil War fugitive slave settlement.

From the late 1960's to the 1970's, however, it was immigration from overseas rather than from across the border that increased the size of the African Canadian population by at least 500 percent. According to population figures from 1986, 60 percent of all African Canadians were foreign born; the proportion of adult African Canadians who were foreign born was probably even greater. Surges in immigration were largely responsible for the growth of the African Canadian population of Toronto, Ontario, to 200,000—a figure that constituted between 7 and 9 percent of the total population of Toronto.

In 1986 the African Canadian population of Montreal, Quebec, stood at 90,000—a population built on the foundations of a community established by black American railway porters who settled in Montreal's Little Burgundy neighborhood during the 1920's. By 1986 African Canadians of recent immigrant background could be found in smaller numbers in Winnipeg and Vancouver in the west, and in Halifax in the Maritimes (where they were outnumbered by the larger native-born black community).

By the 1990's, however, the combined population of native-born and foreign-born people of African descent did not constitute as large a proportion of the total Canadian population as their African American brethren represented within the total American population. The African Canadian population was estimated at slightly more than 500,000 within a total Canadian population of 26,800,000. (Figures from the 1990 U.S. Census Bureau revealed that the African American population stood at 30,483,000 and constituted 12.1 percent of the total U.S. population.) Even among nonwhites, African Canadians were most likely outnumbered by Canadians of East Asian and South Asian ancestry.

Changing Immigration Policy

Traditionally, both English-speaking and French-speaking Canadians had seen themselves as transplanted Europeans within a country whose cultural traditions were perceived largely as an offshoot of Europe. For many years, Canadian immigration policy discouraged nonwhite immigration in favor of encouraging immigration from Great Britain and continental Europe.

In 1955 the Canadian government broke with tradition by devising a plan to import domestic workers from the West Indies into Canada. Some three hundred workers were imported each year. Most of these immigrants were women of African descent, often with high levels of educational achievement, who wanted to escape the poverty of their native islands. From the vantage point of the 1990's, such a policy could be criticized as reinforcing unfair racial and gender stereotypes in the eyes of white Canadians.

In the 1960's, when truly decisive changes in Canadian immigration law occurred, the country's economy was unusually prosperous and in need of more workers. Enlightened liberal opinion in Canada was beginning to frown on racially discriminatory immigration policies. As a result of its growing participation in United Nations peacekeeping operations, the Canadian government sought to improve its relations with Third World countries. In 1962 explicit color discrimination was removed from the immigration laws; further reforms came in 1967. After 1967 the Canadian government established immigration offices in West Indian countries in order to judge applications from those interested in immigrating to Canada. In deciding to accept or reject these applications, Canadian officials favored skilled workers. The liberalization of Canadian immigration rules came at the same time that Great Britain, Canada's former colonial overlord, was raising barriers against further immigration from the West Indies. Between 1905 and 1955, West Indian immigration to Canada had not exceeded 3,400; between 1967 and 1975, however, some 115,000 West Indians migrated to Canada.

With the worsening of the Canadian economy in the mid-1970's, there was a noticeable souring of white Canadian attitudes toward nonwhite immigrants. In 1975 the Green Paper proposed cutbacks in immigration. The Canadian government's sense of responsibility as a member of the international community, however, to some extent outweighed domestic political considerations. As late as the mid-1990's, Canada was especially generous in admitting refugees from war and dictatorship in the Third World. In 1994 Canadian politicians proposed modifications to the family reunification clause of the immigration law; these proposed changes were criticized as discriminatory in intent, particularly against West Indians.

Sources of Immigration

From the 1960's onward, immigrants from the British West Indies islands of JAMAICA, TRINIDAD, BARBADOS, St. Lucia, and Grenada were a major source of growth for the African Canadian population. Additional immigrants came from the South American country of Guyana, which had strong cultural links to the British West Indies. These countries had historically been plagued by a lack of employment opportunities for their oversized populations. Although the majority of these immigrants to Canada were of African descent, some 20 percent were people of South Asian descent (with origins in Bangladesh, India, Pakistan, and Sri Lanka). Within the nonwhite population of some West Indian nations, particularly Jamaica, there is a sharp distinction made between the black majority and the mulatto minority of mixed African and European descent.

By the mid-1990's, African Canadians of West Indian heritage were concentrated in the urban neighborhoods of Toronto and Montreal. In Toronto they were clustered along Eglinton Avenue within the city limits; pockets of settlement were found in Etobicoke and Scaraborough in the greater Toronto metropolitan area. Those who went to Montreal settled in several neighborhoods; one of these neighborhoods, Cote des Neiges, had a mixture of Asian and Latin American immigrants. In Montreal, African Canadians of West Indian heritage had a double minority status: They were nonwhites in a predominantly white city and were English-speaking residents of a predominantly French-speaking city. Like the white English-speaking population of Montreal, these African Canadians tended to oppose the Quebec separatist movement (if they were politically active at all).

Migration to Canada from the Republic of HAITI accelerated in the late 1960's, spurred on by political turmoil as well as by economic necessity. Haitian immigrants to Canada represented a wide ethnic and cultural spectrum, ranging from black rural peasants to wealthy members of the lighter-complexioned mulatto elite. Because most Haitian immigrants spoke either standard French or Haitian Creole (a French-based patois), many of them chose to settle in Montreal. Although some Haitians supported the white Quebec separatist movement, the common bond of language has not always been sufficient to bridge the racial gulf between black Haitian immigrants and Quebec's white French Canadian majority. In 1995 demographic estimates indicated that Haitians composed somewhere between one-third to one-half of Montreal's African Canadian population. Although there were no overwhelmingly Haitian neighborhoods in the city, Haitians did tend to concentrate in Montreal's north end.

By the mid-1990's, there were about 2,000 refugees from Cuba living in Canada, mostly in Toronto or in the Ottawa-Carleton metropolitan area. Although many of these refugees were whites of Spanish descent, at least some were of African or mixed Spanish and African descent.

The African Canadian population has also increased as the result of immigration from Africa itself. Some came to Canada through normal immigration channels from former British dependencies—Ghana, Kenya, Nigeria, Tanzania, Uganda, and Zimbabwe—and from former French dependencies such as Gabon and Mali. In the 1980's and 1990's, the Canadian government also admitted tens of thousands of refugees from African nations, including Rwandans and even some Ethiopian Jews (Falasha). By 1995 nearly 60,000 refugees from Somalia had settled in Canada; most of them were educated individuals from Somalia's well-to-do professional class. Approximately 30,000 of these Somali refugees settled in Toronto, with the rest distributed among cities such as Ottawa, Montreal, Edmonton, and Vancouver. With their Muslim faith and Arabic-influenced culture, these Somali refugees were separated somewhat from the Christian majority of African Canadians.

Problems of Economic Adjustment

During the 1980's and 1990's, certain white Canadians demanded that immigration be restricted. They complained that nonwhite immigrants relied excessively on the social services of the Canadian government, increased the country's unemployment problem, and contributed to an increase in violent crime. While there was some truth to these claims, anti-immigration proponents exaggerated their significance.

In the mid-1990's, the most publicized accusations of welfare parasitism were directed against Somali refugees. Some critics alleged that certain Somalis used welfare payments they received from the Canadian government to help finance warring political factions in their homeland. Articulate spokespeople for the community and liberal-minded white Canadians warned against the dangers of accepting stereotypes and jumping to conclusions. Because Somalis had arrived in Canada in large numbers only after 1985, it was premature to predict the formation of an intergenerational Somali-Canadian underclass based solely on 1995 welfare figures. The employment of Somalis in jobs as cab drivers, clerks, and storekeepers indicated that welfare dependency was not characteristic of the majority of Somali immigrants.

Although most immigrants from the Caribbean in the years after 1967 had established successful lives for themselves, there were, by

Somali women participating in a demonstration outside a Canadian immigration office. *(Dick Hemingway)*

West Indian participants in Canada's Caribana Festival. *(Dick Hemingway)*

the early 1990's, some ominous signs of socio-economic decline among Caribbean immigrants and their families living in large Canadian cities. Some observers pointed to lower skill levels among Caribbean immigrants as responsible for the decline. Those immigrants who were granted admission because of their skills often had higher educational qualifications than many white Canadians; these immigrants found professional success as physicians, lawyers, and journalists. The family reunification provisions of Canadian immigration law eventually lowered the average occupational and educational status of the immigrants over time. Some West Indians entered Canada as visitors or under temporary employment visas and stayed on illegally. Prejudice and discrimination on the part of white Canadians may also account for the declining economic status of some of Canada's Caribbean immigrants.

Haitians from the island's black peasant majority generally had more difficulty attaining economic success in Canada than members of Haiti's educated mulatto elite. Many Haitian immigrants in Montreal earned their living in factory jobs and as cab drivers; in the latter profession, they encountered hostility from white French Canadian competitors. Other Haitians began their own small businesses. In 1993, however, approximately 25 percent of all Haitians in Quebec were unemployed. The unemployment figure rose to 50 percent among young adult Haitians living in Quebec; that rate was much higher than that for Quebec youth as a whole and was exceeded only by the rate for young Jamaican-born immigrants.

In Toronto in the early 1990's, the Jane-Finch corridor and the Regent Park neighborhood—both heavily populated by African Canadians of British West Indian immigrant stock—were plagued by crime and social problems such as the illegal drug trade, chronic unemployment, impoverished families headed by single parents, and violent crime. In 1994 Toronto residents were horrified by two violent deaths: the random slaughter of a young Greek immigrant woman during the course of a robbery at a local cafe and the killing of a white Toronto police officer. In each case, the young man accused of committing the crime was a Jamaican-born immigrant.

Racial Violence and Police Brutality
Canadian government policy in the 1990's was strongly antiracist. Nevertheless, individual immigrants were often victims as well as perpetrators of violence. During the 1990's in Ottawa, a Grenada-born construction worker was assaulted by white youths while waiting at a traffic light. In July of 1991, white youths in Montreal started a fight with Somali refugee youths. Individuals of African descent born in Canada were also targets of racist assaults in the 1970's, 1980's, and 1990's.

Between 1978 and 1992, fourteen African Canadians were shot at by Toronto police. Of the four who were killed, at least two had been born in Jamaica. On May 4, 1992, anger over one of these incidents sparked a riot; although minor compared with incidents in the United States, the riot did result in property damage and some injuries. In the course of investigating charges of racism leveled against the Toronto police department, two government commissions established in 1989 and 1992, respectively, found evidence to support such charges. In Montreal in 1991, there was a public uproar over the killing of an unarmed, twenty-four-year-old father from St. Lucia by members of the largely white, French Canadian police force. In 1994 a retired Quebec judge issued a report condemning what he saw as the racism and brutality of the Montreal police force. In response to criticism from minority activists and independent investigators, police officials in Toronto and Montreal tried to increase the representation of racial minorities in their police forces.

Contributions by African Canadians
Although some immigrants did not achieve success and others experienced the sting of racial animosity and police brutality, many others received acclaim in their chosen professions. Jamaican-born Ben JOHNSON established a world record in the 100-meter dash at the 1988 Summer Olympics in Seoul, Korea, but found his victory negated after he tested positive for steroid use. In 1989 Haitian-born Bruny Surin became the premier runner in Canada, with a national record in the 100-meter event. Jamaican-born track star Donovan Bailey came to international attention with his 100-meter victories at the 1995 World Track and Field Championships and 1996 Olympic Games.

Immigrants of African descent have achieved notable success in the political arena. In local elections held in 1990, two Jamaican-born politicians were elected to serve in the Ontario Legislative Assembly: Alvin Curling and Zanana Akande. Akande was later named minister of community and social services in the Ontario provincial government. In October of 1993, Grenada-born Jean Augustine emerged victorious as a Liberal Party candidate and became the first African Canadian woman to be elected to the Canadian House of Commons. She was joined by Guyana-born Ovid Jackson, another Liberal candidate.

In the area of popular culture, several other African Canadians have achieved national recognition. West Indian-born Ivan Berry earned fame as the mogul of Canadian RAP music in 1990. On television, Haitian-born Anthony Kennedy secured his own talk show, which began broadcasting in 1993 in Quebec. In 1995 two Jamaican-born Canadians achieved fame as filmmakers who focused on the experience of poverty-stricken African Canadians living in Toronto: Clement Virgo with *Rude*, and Stephen Williams with *Soul Survivor*. Virgo's film received international attention when it was included as one of the films shown at the 1995 Cannes Film Festival.

An immigrant who arrived from BARBADOS in 1979, journalist Cecil Foster published two novels in Canada: *No Man in the House* (1992), a novel about the West Indian immigrant experience in Great Britain; and *Sleep On, Beloved* (1995), a novel exploring the challenges facing West Indian immigrants in Canada. Dany Laferriere, a Haitian-born novelist and essayist living in Quebec, released several works, including *How to Make Love to a Negro Without Getting Tired* (1985; later adapted to film in 1989), *An Aroma of Coffee* (1993), *Why Must a Black Writer Write About Sex* (1994), and *Dining with the Dictator* (1994), all of which were originally published in French.

In the British West Indies, people of African descent have constituted a majority population for many years. As a result, immigrants from these islands were more determined to break the longstanding barriers of discrimination that had hindered the achievements of many native-born African Canadians, who had become accustomed to their minority status. With the addition of West Indian-born physicians, lawyers, and other professionals, the black community in Canada had greater financial clout and became more vocal in their fight for equality. An example of a prominent immigrant civil rights activist is Jamaican-born Dudley Laws, who campaigned vigorously against racism and brutality directed at Canadians of African descent by the Toronto police force.

Despite these gains, the new diversity of the African Canadian community was something of a mixed blessing for the cause of racial equality in Canada. Although the black community stood up for the rights of Haitian-born immigrant taxi drivers, many Haitian immigrants were more interested in the political fate of their homeland than in Canadian politics. Somali refugees tended to hold themselves aloof from the black community as a whole and eschewed protests against police brutality. The very heterogeneity of the African Canadian population made it easy for white Canadians to stereotype their nonwhite neighbors as aliens deserving of mere toleration rather than as citizens deserving of equal rights.

—*Paul D. Mageli*

See also: Demography; Diaspora, African; Immigration and ethnic origins of African Americans; Racial violence and hatred.

Suggested Readings:

Avery, Donald H. "Immigration Policy and Social Trends Since 1952." In *Reluctant Host: Canada's Response to Immigrant Workers, 1896-1994*. Toronto, Canada: McClelland & Stewart, 1995.

Hamilton, Janice. "Exiles in a Cold Land: Montreal's Haitian Community Faces a Double Barrier of Prejudice." *Canadian Geographic* (December, 1990-January, 1991): 34-41.

Lazar, Barry, and Tamsin Douglas. "Black Montreal." In *Ethnic Montreal: A Complete Guide to the Many Faces and Cultures of Montreal*. Lincolnwood, Ill.: NTC, 1995.

McCarthy, Shawn. "Starting Over: Fleeing War and Chaos, Somali Refugees Struggle to Adjust to a New Life in Canada." *Canadian Geographic* (January/February, 1993): 68-75.

Megyery, Kathy, ed. *Ethno-Cultural Groups and Visible Minorities in Canadian Politics: The Question of Access*. Toronto, Canada: Dundurn Press, 1991.

Mercer, John. "Canadian Cities and Their Immigrants: New Realities." *Annals of the American Academy of Political and Social Science* 538 (March, 1995): 169-184.

Ramcharan, Subhas. *Racism: Nonwhites in Canada*. Toronto, Canada: Butterworths, 1982.

Saunders, Charles R. *Black and Bluenose: The Contemporary History of a Black Community*. East Lawrencetown, N.S.: Pottersfield, 1999.

Stoffman, Daniel. "Dispatch from Dixon (Somali Refugees)." *Toronto Life* (August, 1995): 40-47.

Walker, James W. St. G. *The West Indians in Canada*. Ottawa, Canada: Canadian Historical Association, 1984.

Income distribution: In 1997 the median incomes of all American families was $42,300. In other words, the incomes of half the families in the country were lower than this figure, and the incomes of the other half were higher. This median figure represented an increase of slightly more than $10,000 above the median for 1988. However, this increase did not benefit black and white families equally, as statistics for the period between 1988 and 1997 illustrate. In 1997 the average African American family—with a median income of $26,522—was markedly less well off than the average white American family, whose median income stood at $44,756.

Among married couples, median income was $36,840 for whites and $30,385 for blacks; among female-headed households, median income stood at $17,672 for whites and $10,687 for blacks. Between 1988 and 1997, the proportion of both whites and blacks who had yearly incomes of more than $34,999 increased, suggesting an increase in the size of the black middle class. The proportion of African Americans who earned yearly incomes of less than $10,000 peaked at 20.8 percent in 1990 and had decreased slightly to 18.9 percent by 1996.

Causes of Income Disparity

The disparity between the incomes of black and white Americans and the overall shift in income distribution are primarily the results of differences in occupation, employment patterns, education, and marital patterns. The economy of the United States grew steadily from World War II until 1973; this growth encouraged the continued Great Migration of blacks from the rural South to the industrial North. Migration improved the employment options that were available and created a shift in occupations for many African Americans.

Changes in the economy after 1973, however, did not improve the economic status of African Americans. Increased foreign competition faced by U.S. companies in the manufacturing and industrial sectors eroded many of the employment gains made by African Americans in the previous twenty-five years. Blacks were also affected by a shift in employment to industries in which they were underrepresented or in which employees received lower wages and fewer benefits. The economic status of blacks was further complicated by their dependence on part-time employment—resulting in their being paid for fewer hours during the year, on average, than whites.

Service Occupations

As of 1988, African Americans were disproportionately employed in lower-paying jobs, unprotected by tenure and seniority and more sensitive to fluctuations in the economy. Comprising 10.8 percent of the total American work force in 1996, blacks represented 17.6 percent of all U.S. employees in service occupations. These occupations encompassed such diverse workers as police officers, fire fighters, welfare aides, food service workers, nursing and dental aides, janitors, maids, beauticians, and transportation workers. Blacks also represented 15 percent of all the employed operators, fabricators, and laborers in the United States. These occupations included freight handlers, stock workers, material handlers, textile workers, pressing and sewing machine operators, motor vehicle operators, and laborers.

Professional Congresspersons; Employment

In 1996 blacks represented only 7.3 percent of all Americans employed in managerial or professional positions. This included individuals who were business managers, personnel managers, health managers, architects, engineers, natural scientists, math and computer scientists, physicians, dentists, nurses, therapists, librarians, teachers, counselors, economists, social workers, lawyers, and writers. African Americans were also underrepresented among precision production, craft, and repair workers. Only in the areas of technical sales and administrative support, where 10.5 percent of employees were African American, was the proportion of employed professionals comparable to the overall proportion of blacks in the labor force. This figure includes blacks engaged as health technologists and technicians, sales representatives, cashiers, secretaries, clerks, bank tellers, and insurance adjusters.

Unemployment and Wage Disparity

Occupations that employed a disproportionate number of African Americans paid less and had higher unemployment rates than other industries. In 1997 the overall U.S. unemployment rate stood at 4.9 percent; white unemployment stood at 4.2 percent, but black unemployment stood at 10.0 percent. During the same year, the median weekly salary for men was $579 ($30,108 per year); it was $431 for women ($22,412 per year). Unemployment in the service occupations stood at 6.7 percent in 1997, with a median weekly salary of $372 for men ($19,344 per year) and $282 for women ($14,664 per year). The unemployment rate for operators, fabricators, and laborers was 7.5 percent in 1997, with a median weekly salary of $436 for men ($22,672 per year) and $313 for women ($16,276 per year).

On the other hand, in 1997 there was a lower unemployment rate and a higher amount of reported earnings in the occupations that employed a lower-than-average number of African Americans. The unemployment rate for managers and professional workers was 2.0 percent in 1997; during the same year, the median weekly salary for men in these occupations was $875 ($45,500 per year), while it was $632 for women ($32,864 per year). The unemployment rate for those employed in the precision production, craft, and repair occupations stood at 4.8 percent. The reported median weekly salary was $569 for men ($29,588 per year) and $382 for women ($19,864 per year).

Gender Disparities

As illustrated by the wages cited above, women typically earn less per week than men in any given occupation. This fact, combined with the disproportionate number of female-headed households among African American families, contributes heavily to the difference in income between African Americans and whites. In 1988 women headed 9.2 percent of white families in the United States, while women headed around 30 percent of black families. By 1997 the percentage of white female-headed households had grown to 14.0 percent, while more than 47 percent of all African American families were headed by women.

Length of Employment

As of 1979, an African American male was expected to work on average 32.9 years; during those years, he would be expected to leave the labor force 3.9 times. A white American male was expected to work on average 39.8 years and to leave the labor force 3.6 times. An African American female was expected to work an average total of 27.4 years during her adult life and leave the labor force 5.4 times, while a white female was expected to work an average of 29.7 years and leave the labor force 5.4 times. African American men were expected to spend an average of 5 years unemployed and 11 years out of the labor force from age twenty to age sixty-five; white men were expected to spend an average of two years un-

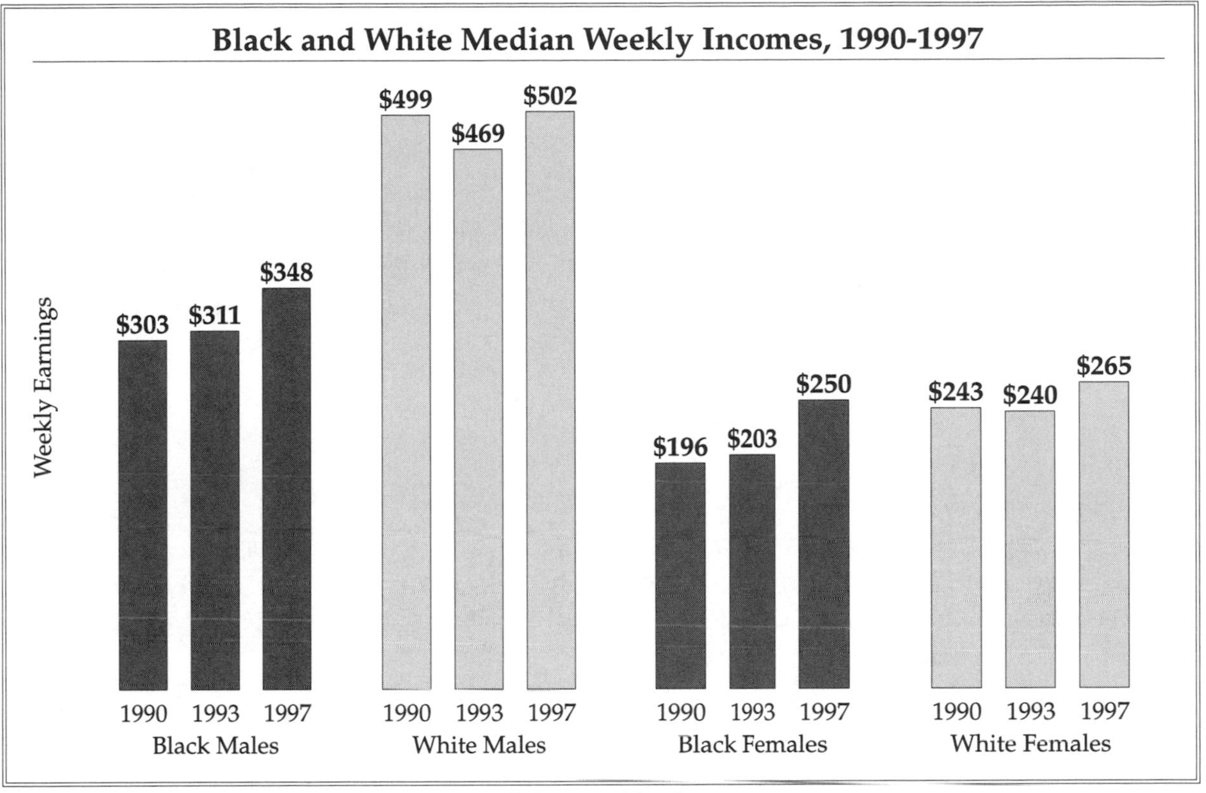

Source: Newsweek, June 7, 1999. Primary source, U.S. Bureau of the Census.
Note: Weekly wages for workers fifteen and older.

employed and seven years out of the labor force during the same age period.

Census data from the 1980's and 1990's suggest little change in these disparities. The percentage of adult blacks not in the labor force decreased slightly, from 39.0 percent in 1980 to 35.3 percent in 1997, a change which roughly paralleled the decrease in white nonparticipants (from 35.9 percent in 1980 to 32.5 percent in 1997). Figures from the 1990 census indicate that the rate of black participation in the work force remained constant at around 67 percent between 1980 and 1990 and would remain constant through 2006, while the participation rate for whites would increase slightly. In 1998 the percentage of blacks who had worked more that twenty years with the same employer (9.4) was roughly equal to the rate of whites working for the same employer in excess of twenty years (9.2 percent).

Impact of Education

Another factor influencing the distribution of income among blacks and whites in the United States is the increase in the percentage of college-educated African Americans. The percentage of blacks completing four or more years of college increased from 7.9 percent in 1980 to 14.7 percent in 1998. Although this increase did not match the increase in overall percentage of college-educated whites during this period (from 17.8 percent in 1980 to 25.0 percent in 1998), the suggested increase in actual numbers of blacks with college degrees is dramatic.

Because college graduates typically earn more per year than do those with less education, an increase in the proportion of black college graduates translates into an increase in the proportion of African Americans that earn higher salaries over the course of a year. In

1997 black men with four-year college degrees earned a mean yearly salary of $35,792, while black male high school graduates earned a mean yearly salary of $22,440. Black women with college degrees earned a mean yearly salary of $29,091, while those with high school diplomas earned a mean yearly salary of $15,789.

Lack of Income

While some of the disparity in the incomes of blacks and whites in the United States results from differences in occupations, education, and family status, some of the disparity is also explained by the percentage of workers who report no earnings. Regardless of age, African Americans have been more likely than whites to report no earnings in a given year. In 1984, 28 percent of African Americans and 9 percent of whites between the ages of twenty and twenty-four reported no earnings. For those between the ages of twenty-five and fifty-four, 16 percent of African Americans and 5 percent of whites reported no earnings. Furthermore, 42 percent of African Americans and 26 percent of whites between the ages of fifty-five and sixty-four reported no earnings, and 81 percent of African Americans and 78 percent of whites age sixty-five and older reported no earnings.

African Americans have made dramatic strides toward improving their economic status. Information from the 1990 census indicates that the number of affluent black families (with incomes greater than $50,000) rose from 266,000 in 1967 to nearly 2.5 million in 1989. College-educated black families in the 1990's are earning, on average, 93 percent of the incomes of comparable white families. While these statistics are encouraging, African Americans in general are still far from achieving economic parity with whites. The continued growth of the black middle class has created a broad economic gap that corresponds to the physical distance separating these newly affluent suburban residents from the millions of African Americans struggling to overcome POVERTY in declining inner-city neighborhoods.

—Llewellyn Cornelius
—Updated by Michael H. Burchett

See also: Black capitalism; Business and commerce; Demography; Employment and unemployment; Higher education; Organized labor; Public assistance programs; Single-parent households.

Suggested Readings:

Exter, Thomas G., and Cheryl Russell. *The Official Guide to American Incomes: The Demographics of Who Does and Who Doesn't Have Money, With a Special Section on Discretionary Income.* 2d ed. Ithaca, N.Y.: New Strategist, 1996.

Freeman, Richard B., Joshua Cohen, and Joel Rogers. *The New Inequality: Creating Solutions for Poor America.* Boston, Mass.: Beacon Press, 1999.

Jaynes, Gerald D., and Robin M. Williams, Jr., eds. *A Common Destiny: Blacks and American Society.* Washington, D.C.: National Academy Press, 1989.

Murray, Charles A. *Losing Ground: American Social Policy, 1950-1980.* New York: Basic Books, 1984.

Ryscavage, Paul. *Income Inequality in America: An Analysis of Trends.* Armonk, N.Y.: M. E. Sharpe, 1999.

U.S. Bureau of the Census. *Statistical Abstract of the United States.* Washington, D.C.: U.S. Government Printing Office, published annually.

Indentured servitude: System of bound labor in colonial America that included both Europeans and Africans. Many Europeans who wanted to start a new life in colonial British America could not afford the cost of transatlantic travel. A large number signed labor contracts, or "indentures," in exchange for passage across the ocean. Upon arriving in America, the indentured servant worked for a master for a set length of time, usually four to seven years. More than half of the Europeans who migrated to British America arrived as indentured servants.

Most servants hoped to establish their own farms after completing their service. However, the high death rates that marked life in most of colonial America during the early years of settlement meant that many servants did not survive their period of service. Those who survived discovered that the life of a servant was hard. Masters sought to maximize profits and usually provided only the minimum food and shelter necessary to ensure that the servant could continue to work.

For all their sufferings, however, indentured servants were not slaves. With the exception of convicts and young people who had been kidnapped in England, servants entered their condition voluntarily. They had contracts and could look forward to the day when they would be free from their master. Servants had some legal rights, and those with cruel masters could seek protection from the colonial courts. This remedy was not always effective, and some servants simply ran away from unreasonable and abusive masters.

In the seventeenth century a number of Africans were brought to the American colonies as indentured servants, and others who were brought as slaves were treated more as indentured servants. A historical study of Africans in the Chesapeake Bay area during the early decades of the seventeenth century, for example, indicates that their status is difficult to classify exactly. While they were brought to VIRGINIA as slaves, they worked with the European servants and often ran away with them. Also, some Africans later became free citizens, purchasing their freedom rather than surviving the length of their contract. Lacking a tradition of SLAVERY, the early English colonists blurred the lines between servitude and slavery during the settlement of the colonies.

This situation quickly changed. The growth of the Atlantic slave trade soon made it easier for colonists to obtain slaves. As mortality rates declined, purchasing a slave for life became a better investment than owning a servant's labor for only a limited term. In addition, the number of indentured servants declined. Word of the harsh working conditions in America and improving economic conditions in England led many poor workers to decide to remain at home. Finally, plantation owners grew concerned about the growing number of disaffected former servants in their midst, people who demanded equal privileges and access to economic opportunity. Slavery offered a convenient solution to the problem of social unrest. All these circumstances combined to produce slavery as a lifelong and hereditary condition from which there was little hope of reprieve.

—*Thomas Clarkin*

Suggested Readings:

Breen, T. H., and Stephen Innes. *"Myne Owne Ground": Race and Freedom on Virginia's Eastern Shore, 1640-1676*. New York: Oxford University Press, 1980.

Van der Zee, John. *Bound Over: Indentured Servitude and American Conscience*. New York: Simon and Schuster, 1985.

Independent schools: Schools that are operated privately, independently of most government controls. In a continued quest for quality schooling, thousands of African Americans committed to choice in education have placed their children in independent schools. More than four hundred such schools, 80 percent of which were owned and operated by and for African Americans, had been established throughout the United States by 1992, serving as an alternative to government schooling.

With an average enrollment of 130 students, these schools served approximately fifty-two thousand youngsters. The basic philosophy of the independent schools movement, inspired by Carter G. Woodson, is that African Americans should develop and carry out educational programs of their own in order to avoid miseducation.

African Americans have had their own independent schools for at least two centuries, including the African Free School in New York City, established in 1787. These schools were created to educate African Americans who were refused education in white institutions. Modern independent schools exist as an alternative to the public educational system, which many see as hindering the academic success of black children. The proliferation of these institutions, beginning in the early 1970's, came about as a consequence of parents' attempts to have some input into how their children were educated, and is linked to research movements which established that black children could be taught more effectively.

THE
HISTORY
OF THE
NEW-YORK
AFRICAN FREE-SCHOOLS,
FROM THEIR ESTABLISHMENT IN 1787,
TO THE PRESENT TIME;
EMBRACING A PERIOD OF MORE THAN
FORTY YEARS:
ALSO
A BRIEF ACCOUNT
OF THE
SUCCESSFUL LABORS,
OF THE
NEW-YORK MANUMISSION SOCIETY:
WITH
AN APPENDIX,
Containing Specimens of Original Composition, both in prose and verse, by several of the pupils; Pieces spoken at public examinations; an interesting Dialogue between Doctor Samuel L. Mitchill, of New-York, and a little black boy of ten years old and Lines illustrative of the Lancasterian system of instruction.

BY CHARLES C. ANDREWS,
TEACHER OF THE MALE SCHOOL.

New-York:
PRINTED BY MAHLON DAY,
NO. 376, PEARL-STREET.
....
1830.

Title page from a contemporary book on the New York African Free School. *(Library of Congress)*

A 1987 study found that independent schools were usually neighborhood schools, located in urban areas and serving children from their immediate vicinity. Racially homogeneous, they maintained an extended family atmosphere and charged moderate tuition. Half the schools were religious, the other half secular. Most received little or no support from governments, corporations, or foundations. Despite their limited resources, these schools attracted and retained qualified teachers committed to their educational philosophy. Academically, students at independent schools performed above national norms and were consistently ahead of their peers attending state schools. A 1990 nationwide survey of twenty-three hundred independent school students showed that 64 percent were above national norms in reading and 62 percent exceeded the norms in math. Success is attributed to the schools' high academic standards and students' motivation toward learning.

High academic expectations, effectiveness of administrators, genuine concern of teachers, and individual attention received by students are some of the factors explaining the success of independent schools. The schools offer a meaningful educational context for African American students, one which recognizes the impact of culture on the learning process. An important component of many programs is the central role played by African American culture, history, and values. Independent black institutions, a development within the independent schools movement, take a more radical approach by focusing exclusively on an Afrocentric curriculum.

Research indicates that, overall, these private institutions are positive forces in the education of African Americans. Concerns are raised, however, concerning whether independent schools are detrimentally elitist or segregationist. Some of the methods and ideas from the independent schools movement have made their way into public school systems.

See also: Afrocentricity; Education.

1997 Population: 5,864,000
African American Population: 484,000
African American Percentage of Total: 8.25

Indiana: Just north of Kentucky on the northern bank of the Ohio River, Indiana is a "border" state whose southern areas have traditionally been more southern than northern in their outlook. Evansville, Indiana, is the second-most southerly city in what was once referred to as the Old Northwest. Only Cairo, Illinois, is farther south geographically. Evansville lies far from the state capital of Indianapolis and, before modern transportation was available, was quite an insular community.

A large, industrious German population began to settle in Evansville during the 1830's. These Germans were as biased against African Americans as most of the indigenous population was. The jobs requiring skill in this part of the state were mostly held by whites. African Americans worked as servants for whites or held jobs as unskilled laborers. Nevertheless, Evansville attracted a substantial black population between 1865 and 1900. From a pre-Civil War high of 230 African American residents in the 1850 census, this population, which declined to ninety-six people in 1860, increased to 1,408 in 1870, 2,686 in 1880, 5,553 in 1890, and 7,405 in 1900, which represented one-eighth of the town's total population.

Rural schools in much of Indiana excluded African Americans in the 1860's, although such cities as Evansville, Indianapolis, South

Bend, and Gary offered them educational opportunities, usually in segregated facilities. The students who attended such schools were generally eager to learn. Those who were graduated from them often found opportunities to become teachers themselves.

In the 1870's, Indianapolis, which still practiced SEGREGATION in its elementary schools, had black students in its three local high schools. In 1927, however, the city opened the Crispus Attucks High School, a segregated facility that offered academic, technical, and manual training to African American students. All of the black students in Indianapolis were reassigned to the segregated facility when it opened.

It was not until 1949 that the Indiana State Legislature abolished segregation in the schools of the state. Until then, protests against segregation fell on deaf ears, at least officially. During the eighty years in which segregated schools were legal in Indiana, thirty-one of the State's ninety-two counties had segregated schools.

In the northern part of the state, particularly in the industrial city of Gary, which had a large black population, integration became a significant problem. The city designated some schools as transitional schools that were to move gradually from being segregated to being integrated. In doing so, however, district administrators selected their weakest schools as transitional schools, causing widespread complaints from parents of both races.

As early as the 1870's, both Evansville and Indianapolis, realizing the advantages of helping African Americans to become better educated, operated night schools for working-class adults, both white and African American. The latter, labeled "gray-headed scholars," flocked to these schools. The superintendents of both school districts acknowledged the African Americans' commitment to learning. Many of those who attended these night schools, most of them former slaves, were doing so to master the skills of basic literacy, of which they had been deprived under slavery.

—*R. Baird Shuman*

Infant mortality: Demographers have called the infant mortality rate the most sensitive index of the standard of living. It is generally held that a low infant mortality rate is indicative of a population's high per capita income, likelihood of adequate diet, advanced technology, and access to proper HEALTH care, including prenatal care.

The infant mortality rate is a calculation of the percentage of babies in a given population who do not survive their first year, but it means far more than that. The problem of infant mortality is certainly personal and distressing at one level, but beyond that level, infant mortality rates have the unique ability to uncover societal problems such as discrimination, lack of public EDUCATION, homelessness, domestic hunger, and POVERTY. Variations in infant mortality rates are indicative of relative differences in socioeconomic quality of life between groups, including the percentage of a population living below the poverty level.

Definitions

"Infant mortality" is an index that measures the number of babies who die before their first birthdays in a given year divided by the number of babies born in that year. Usually the rate is expressed based on a thousand live births. Infant death can be caused by a number of factors. More than 90 percent of infant deaths are the result of congenital anomalies (birth defects), sudden infant death syndrome (SIDS), complications of labor and delivery, slow fetal growth or birth trauma, and preventable causes such as infections, accidents, and HOMICIDE.

Because babies die from different causes, demographers divide infant death into two categories, neonatal mortality and postneonatal mortality. "Neonatal mortality" is the number of deaths to infants under twenty-eight days old in a given year divided by the number of births in that year. "Postneonatal mortality" is the number of deaths to infants from twenty-eight days old to one year of age in a given year divided by the number of births in that year. Both of these rates are also expressed based on a thousand live births. Deaths of infants less than twenty-eight days old are likely to be the result of indigenous causes related to low birth weight; roughly two-thirds of all infant deaths in the United States in the 1980's occurred during the neonatal period. Deaths to infants of more than twenty-eight days of age are likely to stem from exogenous causes related to poverty (poor nutrition, restricted access to health care, infectious diseases, and accidents). By the 1980's, only about one-third of U.S. infant deaths occurred in the postneonatal period.

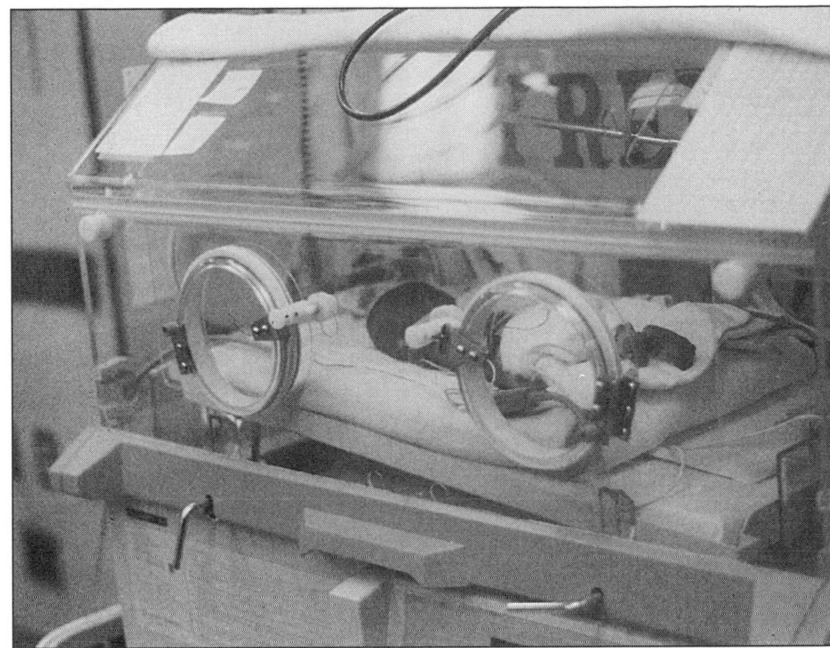

Infant mortality rates are based on the percentages of babies within defined groups who do not survive their first year of life. *(Betts Anderson/Unicorn Stock Photos)*

Low Birth Weight and Its Causes

The single factor most strongly associated with infant death at both the neonatal and postneonatal stages is low birth weight (defined as a birth weight of less than 5.5 pounds). Approximately 7 percent of all infants in the United States are born at low birth weight. These infants are forty times more likely to die than average-weight infants (approximately seven pounds). The risk of death for infants born at very low birth weight (less than 3.3 pounds) is two hundred times greater than the rate for average-weight infants. Demographers have discovered that low birth weight and, therefore, increased likelihood of infant death are caused by several factors: risks present before pregnancy, risks associated with pregnancy, and risks related to health care.

Risks present before pregnancy include medical risks of the mother, demographic risks, and behavioral and environmental risks. Medical risks to the mother can include multiple miscarriages, the birth of a previous low-birth-weight infant, diabetes, chronic high blood pressure, number of previous pregnancies (either zero or more than three), and low weight compared to height. Behavior such as smoking, alcohol or drug abuse, and poor nutrition can be associated with low birth weight. Demographic factors, including low socioeconomic status, low level of education, unmarried status, and race, are also associated with low-birth-weight infants. Second, the medical risks related to pregnancy associated with low-birth-weight infants include poor weight gain during pregnancy, fetal abnormalities (birth defects), some infectious diseases, brief interval between pregnancies, and multiple births. Finally, health care risks consist primarily of a lack of prenatal care.

Historical Shifts in Infant Mortality Rate

By the beginning of the twentieth century, the United States had an infant mortality rate of about one hundred deaths per one thousand births, a rate equivalent to the infant mortality rate in Third World nations in the 1990's. This rate fell rapidly from the turn of the century until World War II, leveled off through the 1960's, and declined rapidly again through the mid-1970's. Since that time, infant mortality has declined very slowly. Most of the reduction in infant mortality during the twentieth century has been caused by a decline in postneonatal mortality. Only since the mid-1970's has the improvement in the infant mortality rate in the United States occurred primarily for neonatal mortality, a result of improved technology in neonatal intensive-care units.

Even though the U.S. infant mortality rate dropped from about 100 deaths per 1,000 births at the beginning of the twentieth century to fewer than 9 deaths per 1,000 births in the 1990's, the rate for the United States as a whole does not compare favorably with the rates for the remainder of the developed world. By the early 1990's, the United States had slipped to approximately twentieth in its ranking. Nations such as Taiwan, Singapore, Hong Kong, and the Scandinavian countries all have lower infant mortality rates than the United States.

Rate Among African Americans

The Federal Children's Bureau reported in 1912 that there was a large discrepancy between the infant mortality rates of various

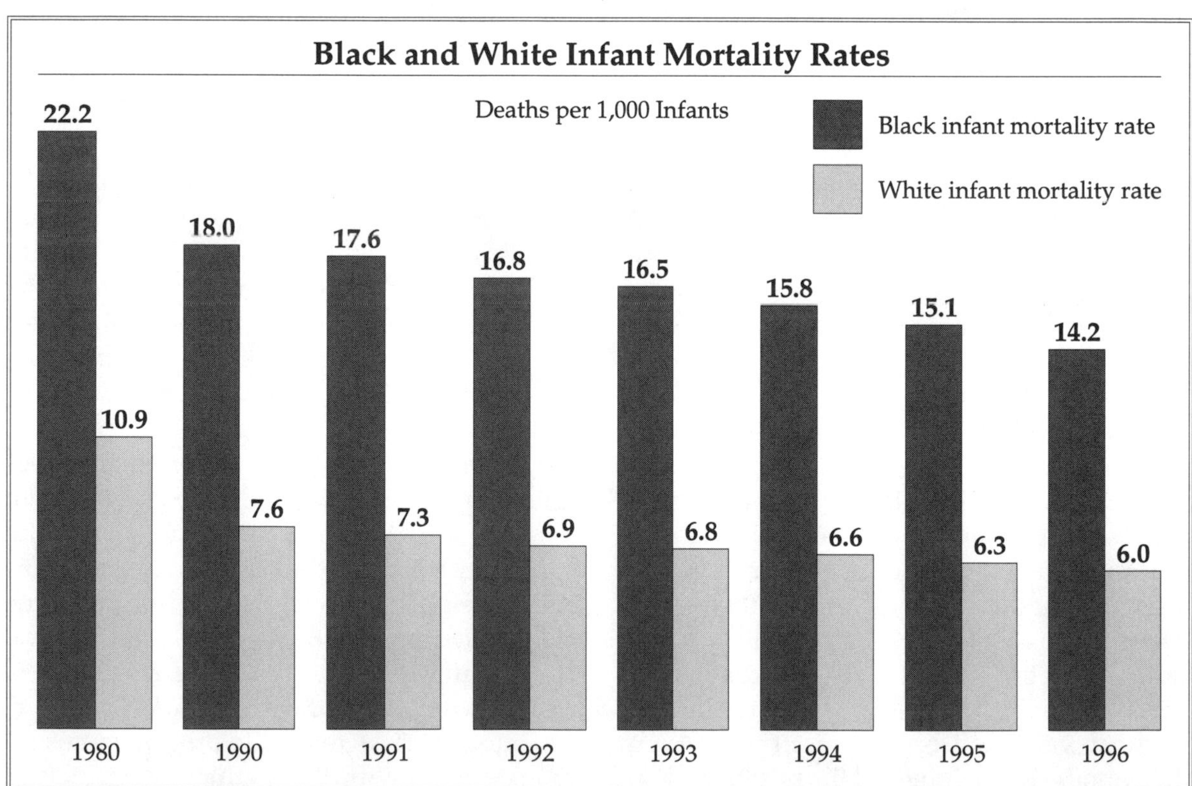

Source: Statistical Abstract of the United States, 1998.

subpopulations within the United States. Of special interest was the fact that the infant mortality rate within the African American community was more than twice the rate for the white population. Throughout the twentieth century, African American infant mortality rates fell as rapidly as, or more rapidly than, white infant mortality rates. By 1940 African American infant mortality had fallen to seventy-two deaths per one thousand births, compared with forty-three deaths per one thousand births in the white population. African American infant mortality fell much faster than the national rate until 1948. The rate fluctuated through the mid-1960's, and the gap between African American and white infant mortality rates increased. From approximately 1965 through the early 1990's, both African American and white infant mortality rates dropped at about the same pace; the discrepancy between subpopulations noted in 1912 is thus still evident in the 1990's.

Trends

African American babies die at approximately twice the rate of white babies in the United States. By the early 1990's, the African American infant mortality rate stood at eighteen deaths per one thousand births, compared with a white infant mortality rate of fewer than nine deaths per one thousand births. The discrepancy in infant mortality rates is one of the most telling differences between African Americans and whites, because it demonstrates the persistent gaps in living standards and health care between these population groups. Teenage mothers, unmarried women, and women with less education are at higher risk of having low-birth-weight babies; African American women are more likely than white women to have the characteristics associated with low-birth-weight babies.

Differences between African Americans and whites are complicated by other social factors, and race often works in combination with socioeconomic disadvantages. Poverty is also a major determinant of low birth weight and infant death; being born into poverty increases an infant's risk of death by 50 percent in both the neonatal and postneonatal periods. Research has shown that there continues to be an inverse relationship between infant mortality rate and socioeconomic status, and that this relationship persists across racial categories for both neonatal and postneonatal mortality.

One factor directly influencing infant mortality is access to health care; persons who are poor are less likely to have health insurance and are thus less able to obtain access to medical facilities and practitioners. As a result, they are also less likely to obtain health education or prenatal care. All of these factors are reflected in low levels of prenatal care, unhealthy behavior of mothers before and during pregnancy, and low birth weights. Within the African American community itself, too, there is variation in the infant mortality rate. Those in the middle class are likely to experience infant mortality rates similar to those of the white population, while those in the lower and working classes lag far behind.

—*John Marvin Pippert*

See also: Children; Demography; Hypertension; Medicine; Substance abuse; Teenage pregnancy.

Suggested Readings:

Dewart, Janet, ed. *The State of Black America 1991*. New York: National Urban League, 1991.

Farley, Reynolds, and Walter R. Allen. *The Color Line and the Quality of Life in America*. New York: Russell Sage Foundation, 1987.

Polednak, Anthony P. "Trends in US Urban Black Infant Mortality, by Degree of Residential Segregation." *The American Journal of Public Health* 86 (May, 1996): 723-726.

Turner, R. "Black-White Infant Mortality Differential Has Grown in Recent Decades and Will Persist into Next Century." *Fam-*

ily Planning Perspectives 27 (November/December, 1995): 267-268.

Weeks, John R. *Population: An Introduction to Concepts and Issues*. 5th ed. Belmont, Calif.: Wadsworth, 1992.

Wilson, William J. *The Truly Disadvantaged: The Inner City, the Underclass, and Public Policy*. Chicago: University of Chicago Press, 1987.

Ink Spots: Soul music group. The Ink Spots had nearly fifty hit songs, including eleven in the top ten. Members Orville Jones, Ivory Watson, Charles Fuqua, and Jerry Daniels (who was replaced by Bill Kenny in 1939) met while working as porters at the Paramount Theater in New York City. They were recording for the Victor label by 1935. In 1944 Jones died and was replaced by Herb Kenny (Bill's brother), and Watson was replaced by Billy Bowens.

The group's hits include "If I Didn't Care" and "Address Unknown" (1939), "We Three (My Echo, My Shadow, and Me)" (1940), and Duke Ellington's "Don't Get Around Much Anymore" (1946). The Ink Spots also sang with jazz great Ella Fitzgerald from 1944 to 1945 and appeared in the films *The Great American Broadcast* (1941) and *Pardon My Sarong* (1942). The group split in the 1950's. Charlie Fuqua and Bill Kenny each briefly led groups using the original group's name. Various groups used the name for the next several decades.

Innis, Roy (b. June 6, 1934, St. Croix, U.S. Virgin Islands): Civil rights leader. Innis (full name Roy Emile Alfredo Innis) moved to New York City at age twelve and attended school there. At City College of New York, he studied chemistry.

Innis became active in the Civil Rights movement during the early 1960's, joining the Congress of Racial Equality (CORE), which at that time had one of the largest mem-

Roy Innis campaigning for mayor of New York City in 1993. *(AP/Wide World Photos)*

berships among civil rights organizations. Innis continued working with CORE, and in 1965, he was elected chairman of the Harlem branch. In December, 1967, he became associate national director, and in 1968, he was named national director, succeeding Floyd McKissick, who took a leave of absence. Innis's position was challenged by some who questioned his leadership and accused him of making CORE a one-man operation. An attempt in the early 1980's to oust him failed, and he was named in 1981 as national chairman, the top position in CORE. Innis also coedited the *Manhattan Tribune*, a weekly tabloid covering Harlem and the Upper West Side of New York City, with William Haddad.

Because of his multidecade commitment to CORE, it is virtually impossible to separate Innis from the organization. To examine the development and changes of CORE is tantamount to examining Innis himself. As a civil rights organization, CORE is best known for its activities during the 1960's, when it participated in the FREEDOM RIDES and in the voter registration drives in the South in 1963 and 1964. During the mid-1960's, the membership of CORE included both African Americans and whites, so that many whites participated in the voter registration drives, which required hands-on experience. Whites as well as African Americans traveled from the North to stay in southern communities in MISSISSIPPI, LOUISIANA, ALABAMA, NORTH CAROLINA, SOUTH CAROLINA, and GEORGIA, where they lived with resident families and thus were able to gain access to people and areas ordinarily inaccessible.

As CORE's leader, Innis gradually began to advocate a policy that stressed separatism, pushing for more black-owned businesses and increasing authority in institutions. As a spokesman for the BLACK POWER MOVEMENT, he also advocated armed self-defense rather than nonviolence. Unlike most other civil rights leaders, he did not promote school integration, believing that separate institutions would serve African Americans best. Having lost financial support from whites and from a large number of African Americans who found separatism unacceptable, the influence and vitality of CORE diminished and its membership decreased from the seventy thousand claimed in the late 1960's.

Institute of the Black World: ATLANTA, GEORGIA, research center. The Institute of the Black World was established in 1969 as a community of African American scholars and activists who believe that African Americans need to control the definition of the African American past in order to master its future. The institute's major activities included research, analysis, and advocacy to foster self-understanding and self-determination for African Americans. Before it became an independent research center in 1969, the institute was a unit of the King Center in Atlanta. Among its concerns was examination of the EDUCATION of African Americans, with an eye to its efficacy as an instrument of social change and social equality. To this end, the institute published Lerone BENNETT's influential *The Challenge of Blackness* (1970), which addresses issues of teaching and racial identity.

Institutional racism: Term for racist attitudes and practices inherent in the foundation, development, and practices of the various institutions of society. Individuals within these institutions may not have any overt or intentional desire to behave in a racist manner. Institutional racism results from the unthinking continuation of past perspectives and injustices.

As one example, most aptitude and personality tests were designed so that the correct response is the one most often given or known by middle-class urban and suburban European Americans. As a result, rural, nonwhite, or lower-class individuals often respond in ways that are evaluated as abnormal or inferior. EDUCATION provides more examples of institutional racism. The basic perspectives of most public school curricula have not changed in several decades. For example, little is taught about the contributions to the United States or the world made by African Americans, women, or many other groups. As a result, many people see these groups as inferior, citing their lack of contributions as evidence of inferiority. In employment, what appears as meritocracy, or the distribution of employment opportunities based only on qualifications, often contains hidden elements of institutional racism, because all those competing have not had equal opportunities to acquire the qualifications.

Some theorists identify a special form of institutional racism called cultural racism. The assumed inherent superiority of certain values, according to the theory, results in negative evaluations of all behaviors not in line with those values. As a result, behaviors that are normal within one cultural setting are reinterpreted on the basis of the norms of another and, as a result, are attributed to "incorrect" and often negative motives. Cultural racism can be extremely subtle, as illustrated by the denotations and connotations of the words "black" or "dark" in the English language, or the label "flesh-toned" for products whose color approximates a white European skin tone.

See also: Employment and unemployment; Race, racism, and race relations.

Intellectuals and scholars: Throughout American history, African American intellectuals and scholars have faced particular disadvantages. These very disadvantages, however, may have made the African American scholarly and intellectual contribution to American society all the more valuable. Forced to overcome hardships and to define themselves in a society they could neither completely join nor leave, African American thinkers have been among the most insightful and creative analysts and artists in the United States.

Early African American Intellectuals

Enslavement did not prevent the emergence of black writers early in American history. Jupiter Hammon (1711-?), a slave living in New York, is generally believed to have been the first published black author in the United States. Another religious slave poet, Phillis WHEATLEY achieved even greater renown.

During the nineteenth century, prominent African American intellectuals were closely associated with the ABOLITIONIST MOVEMENT, the movement to abolish slavery. Frederick DOUGLASS was undoubtedly the best-known and most celebrated black intellectual of the slave period. In 1845, Douglass, an escaped, self-educated slave, published his *Narrative of the Life of Frederick Douglass*, an eloquent autobiography that called attention to the evils of SLAVERY. Douglass also founded the *North Star* newspaper and during the CIVIL WAR served as an adviser to President Abraham Lincoln.

W. E. B. Du Bois (left) with Spanish artist Pablo Picasso in Paris, where he was the U.S. delegate to the World Congress of Partisans of Peace in 1949. *(AP/Wide World Photos)*

Du Bois and Washington

W. E. B. DU BOIS and Booker T. WASHINGTON exemplified the two major trends in African American intellectual life following the Civil War. Washington stood for ACCOMMODATION, the strategy of adapting to life in the racially unequal United States for the sake of the gradual practical advancement of African Americans. Du Bois stood for opposition and defiance in the face of racial oppression.

Washington was born a slave in rural VIRGINIA. He enrolled in the HAMPTON INSTITUTE (Hampton Agricultural and Normal Insti-

(continued on page 1305)

Notable Nonfiction Books

Akbar, Na'im. *Visions for Black Men* (1991). Exploration of the plight of African American males growing up in a racist society, their transition from boyhood to manhood, and their self-knowledge and self-mastery. Akbar stresses the importance of education, self-evaluation, and self-definition in achieving effective change, as well as the positive role that parents can play by taking charge of their children's lives.

Baldwin, James. *The Fire Next Time* (1963). In two letters, one addressed to his nephew and the other to the American people, Baldwin presents his philosophy concerning black-white relations and expresses his dissatisfaction with the American inability to acknowledge and eradicate racial injustice. He believes that any identity founded on color superiority instead of genuine love is wrong, that Christianity brings about racism, and that the NATION OF ISLAM, whose followers believe that African Americans are God's chosen people and whites are devils, is destructive to all.

Baldwin, James. *Notes of a Native Son* (1955). Depiction of the painful reality facing African Americans and of one writer's search for his identity as a black man, an artist, and an American. Baldwin denounces the false portrayals of black life common in social protest novels and criticizes the United States' subtle evasion and distortion of racism. He believes that white Americans must acknowledge African Americans as full-fledged human beings.

Bernal, Martin. *Black Athena: The Afroasiatic Roots of Classical Civilization*, vols. 1-2 (1987-1991). A primary statement on AFROCENTRICITY, this book presents the theory that the roots of classical civilization actually lie in Afroasiatic cultures and that this fact has been ignored mainly because of racism. Volume 1 centers on the period between 1785 and 1850; volume 2 presents the archaeological and documentary evidence.

Carter, Stephen L. *Reflections of an Affirmative Action Baby* (1991). A law professor at Yale University and a two-time beneficiary of AFFIRMATIVE ACTION programs, CARTER presents his views on affirmative action. He doubts the effectiveness of affirmative action and is certain that it is no longer necessary, in part because of the growing black middle class. He also believes that special treatment of African Americans undermines their achievements and consequently diminishes their pride in their work.

Delany, Martin Robison. *The Condition, Elevation, Emigration, and Destiny of the Colored People of the United States Politically Considered* (1852). Writing in the early 1850's, DELANY responds to the situation created by the passage of the FUGITIVE SLAVE LAW in 1850, the conclusion by black leaders that it was racism that defined whites' reactions to African Americans, and the subsequent failure of moral suasion. He criticizes African Americans' heavy reliance on religion and calls for emigration to Central and South America as the only way blacks can elevate their condition.

Diop, Cheikh Anta. *Civilization or Barbarism: An Authentic Anthropology* (1991). Diop reexamines the African past and the contributions of black people to world history. He presents evidence that Egypt was a black, not white, civilization and explores the scientific contributions of black Egypt to Greece, arguing that Greek civilization was heavily influenced by Egyptian concepts.

Du Bois, W. E. B. *The Souls of Black Folk* (1903). Seminal work focusing on the situation of black people in the American South in the years following RECONSTRUCTION. The book scientifically analyzes their problems in an attempt to eradicate discrimination and bring about racial equality and justice. DU BOIS stresses the importance of intellectual achievement for African Americans, not only as a means of gaining leadership and power, but also as a weapon in their fight against prejudice.

Library of Congress

Historical Research Department of the Nation of Islam. *The Secret Relationship Between Jews and Blacks* (1991). Controversial work claiming that Jewish leaders and businesspeople played major roles in the African SLAVE TRADE and were themselves sub-

(continued)

stantial slave holders. Jewish scholars and some African American scholars acknowledged the existence of Jewish owners of SLAVE SHIPS and slaves but denied that there were many such persons. Other critics defended Jewish involvement as motivated by capitalism rather than racial prejudice. Some critics accused the NATION OF ISLAM of attempting to fuel misunderstandings and exacerbate already strained relations between the Jewish and African American communities.

Hooks, bell. *Remembered Rapture: The Writer at Work* (1999). Impassioned examination of writing, particularly the work of black female writers. Cultural critic Hooks interweaves autobiographical writing and essays on the power of words, influential black women writers, the publishing industry, and how race plays a role in a work's critical reception.

Jordan, June. *Technical Difficulties: African-American Notes on the State of the Union* (1992). Exploration of numerous cultural, economic, political, psychological, and social issues confronting African Americans and the ways they have responded to them. Jordan attempts to come to grips with the problem of synthesizing two American cultures—one dominant, the other marginalized. She calls for change, development, and understanding, but her invocation is couched in specifically African American terms.

King, Martin Luther, Jr. *The Papers of Martin Luther King, Jr.*, vols. 1-3 (1992-1997). The first volumes in a proposed fourteen-volume set to be published by the Martin Luther King, Jr., Papers Project, directed by Clayborne CARSON. This project aims to produce a definitive annotated edition of all of civil rights leader King's published work and much of his unpublished work. The first three volumes are subtitled *Called to Serve, January 1929-June 1951*; *Rediscovering Precious Values, July 1951-November 1955*; and *Birth of a New Age: December 1955-December 1956*.

Locke, Alain. *The New Negro: An Interpretation* (1925). Record of the life and culture of African Americans in the form of poetry, stories, and essays, four of which were written by Locke. LOCKE's collection traces the evolution of the black mind and spirit over the years through the interpretations of various authors, including Jean TOOMER, Zora Neale HURSTON, Claude MCKAY, Countée CULLEN, and Langston HUGHES.

Madhubuti, Haki R. *Black Men: Obsolete, Single, Dangerous? The Afrikan American Family in Transition* (1990). This exploration of the social, political, and economic conditions that led African Americans to their situation offers practical solutions to their hardships. MADHUBUTI compiled a list of two hundred books that he believes all African Americans should read. He also arranged a list of twelve secrets of life to help African Americans enjoy their blackhood and lead better lives.

Patterson, Orlando. *Slavery and Social Death: A Comparative Study* (1982). This study, which required more than fifteen years of historical and archival research, broadens the perspective of SLAVERY beyond the Americas, going back to its practice in ancient Rome and Greece. It deals with slavery and the issues of social death, dishonor, authority, power, property, natal alienation, and slavery's institutional process.

Steele, Shelby. *The Content of Our Character: A New Vision of Race in America* (1990). A CONSERVATIVE black, middle-class professor, STEELE criticizes African Americans for their inability to advance in the United States, for their exaggeration of racial issues in order to avoid competition with whites, for their promotions of black institutions and black pride, and for their tendency to identify with the poor among them. He also criticizes white racial attitudes, finds white guilt to be the only originator of the Civil Rights movement, and voices his disapproval of affirmative action programs. The book won the National Book Critics Circle Award in 1990.

Steele, Shelby. *A Dream Deferred: The Second Betrayal of Black Freedom in America* (1997). Steele attacks affirmative action, which he views as based on white assumptions of black inferiority. He argues that African Americans were betrayed first through the oppression of slavery and segregation and second through government preference programs that deny them pride in their accomplishments and thus their self-esteem.

Welsing, Frances Cress. *The Isis Papers: The Keys to the Colors* (1991). Examination of the issues of the global system of mass destruction (or white supremacy), the destruction of the black male (to ensure white genetic survival), and the genocide of nonwhites. The author believes that only by revealing the strategies and wrongdoings of white supremacists can peace be established and justice be restored, in the tradition of the Egyptian goddess Isis.

West, Cornel. *Race Matters* (1993). West argues that race still plays an important role in politics, economics, ethics, and spirituality. He analyzes nihilism in the black community, affirmative action, sexuality, Malcolm X, and relations between African Americans and Jews. He criticizes conservative blacks for ignoring the damaging effects of the image of blacks presented in advertising and mass media. West also offers solutions to some problems.

Jon Chase/Harvard News Service

tute), an industrial arts college founded by New England missionaries. In 1881 Washington became head of the Tuskegee Institute in Alabama, a public college intended primarily to train black teachers for black schools. Washington believed strongly in the idea of practical vocational training for African American students, arguing that this was the most realistic form of education for the children of slaves.

Du Bois, born in Great Barrington, Massachusetts, was a man of powerful intellect and strong passions. He graduated from Fisk University in 1888 and studied in Berlin from 1892 to 1894; there he came under the influence of German philosophy. In 1895, Du Bois received a Ph.D. from Harvard University. Du Bois bitterly rejected accomodationism. He was one of the founders of the National Association for the Advancement of Colored People (NAACP), and he established *The Crisis*, the official publication of the NAACP. By the end of his long life, Du Bois had become so alienated from the racially unequal United States that he embraced the Cold War rival of the United States, the Soviet Union. In the early 1960's he became a member of the Communist Party.

The First Half of Twentieth Century

By the 1920's and 1930's, there was a new generation of African Americans who had never known slavery by direct experience. Many in this generation lived in the cities of the North as a result of the Great Migration of African Americans from the rural South to the urban North that began with World War I. New York City's Harlem area became a center for music and art between the two world wars. Critics frequently trace the beginning of the literary side of the Harlem Renaissance to the appearance of author Jean Toomer's novel *Cane* (1923), which explored life among poorer urban African Americans. Other major figures of the Harlem Renaissance include poets Langston Hughes, Countée Cullen, and Claude McKay and anthropologist and novelist Zora Neale Hurston. Hurston's novel *Their Eyes Were Watching God* (1937) is widely praised as the finest fictional work of the Harlem Renaissance.

While New York provided a center for the somewhat Bohemian intellectuals of the Harlem Renaissance, Chicago became a home to prominent African American academic scholars in the 1930's and following decades. E. Franklin Frazier was a prominent sociologist. Frazier received his Ph.D. from the University of Chicago in 1931 and published a number of influential books, including *The Negro Family in America* (1939). Chair of the sociology department at Howard University from 1934 to 1959, Frazier was elected president of the American Sociological Association in 1948. St. Clair Drake (1911-1990) was another sociologist who studied at the University of Chicago. Together with Horace Cayton,

Drake published a classic study of African American life in Chicago, *Black Metropolis* (1946).

Novelists and Poets After World War II

The years between World War II and the peak of the Civil Rights movement in the 1960's saw the rise of major African American novelists who drew on their experiences as outsiders in their native land to create some of America's finest works of fiction. Richard Wright came from a poor family in Mississippi, educated himself by reading in public libraries, and moved to Chicago. His first novel, *Native Son* (1940), met critical and commercial success, as did his second work, *Black Boy* (1945).

Ralph Ellison was the son of a maid in Oklahoma who was educated at the Tuskegee Institute. Ellison's *Invisible Man* (1952) won the National Book Award. Although he did not publish another novel during his lifetime, Ellison's book of literary essays, *Shadow and Act* (1964), was highly praised. In 1999 Ellison's literary executor published a second novel, *Juneteenth*, put together from the novelist's notes and incomplete drafts.

Haki Madhubuti, seen here in 1987 with some of his company's books, founded the Third World Press in 1967 to make it easier for young African American writers to publish. *(AP/Wide World Photos)*

James Baldwin from Harlem, achieved renown with *Go Tell It on the Mountain* (1953). His *Notes of a Native Son* (1955) and *Nobody Knows My Name* (1961) dealt with racial problems in the United States. Following the angry essays in *The Fire Next Time* (1963), Baldwin became active in the Civil Rights movement and achieved recognition as a social critic.

The last decades of the twentieth century saw a flourishing of African American literature. Gwendolyn Brooks established her reputation as a poet during the 1940's and won the Pulitzer Prize for poetry in 1950. In 1968 she became poet laureate of Illinois. The poet Amiri Baraka was born as LeRoi Jones in New Jersey. He became active in the Beat movement of New York's Greenwich Village in the 1950's. He later turned to black nationalism and became involved in black theater and political activism.

Poet Maya Angelou came to wide public recognition with the publication of her autobiographical work *I Know Why the Caged Bird Sings* (1969). Her numerous other works won her nominations for the Pulitzer Prize and the National Book Award. In 1993, at the request of newly elected President Bill Clinton, Angelou read one of her poems at the presidential inauguration.

Ishmael Reed is known for his inventive, unconventional fiction and his essays on race and other social issues. In 1976 Reed founded the Before Columbus Foundation, an organization devoted to promoting literary cultural diversity. Alice Walker became one of the most celebrated novelists in America with the 1982 publication of *The Color Purple*. Walker's work concerned relations between men and women as well as race relations. Ohio-born Toni Morrison worked as an editor and a professor of English literature, as well as a novelist and essayist. Morrison wrote several highly successful novels, beginning with *The Bluest Eye* (1970). She won the Pulitzer Prize for the novel *Beloved* (1987) and received the Nobel Prize in Literature in 1993.

Academics and Social Critics

The topic of race in the United States has stimulated analyses and debates by African Americans inside and outside universities. Historian John Hope Franklin has often been referred to as the dean of African American historians because of his wide-ranging and influential books. Albert Murray, a literary and social critic who had attended Tuskegee with Ralph Ellison, taught at several universities before becoming an independent professional writer.

William Julius Wilson was considered one of America's preeminent sociologists beginning in the late 1970's. Wilson, who became president of the American Sociological Association, provoked controversy with his book *The Declining Significance of Race* (1978), which maintained that social class had become more important than race as an explanation of the disadvantages of many African Americans. African American Harvard sociologist Charles V. Willie was among those who challenged Wilson's theories.

During the decades of the 1970's and 1980's, a number of black intellectuals became critical both of black radicalism and of conventional racial liberalism. They were frequently referred to as "black conservatives," although several of them rejected the label. Economist Thomas Sowell, a staunch opponent of affirmative action, was the most influential and the most clearly conservative of these African American thinkers. Glenn Loury, another academic economist, was also critical of many liberal programs; unlike Sowell, however, Loury argued that the government should take action to overcome racial inequality. Shelby Steele, in *The Content of Our Character: A New Vision of Race in America* (1991), argued that many African Americans had adopted a view of themselves as victims and that they needed to concentrate on getting ahead by their own efforts.

—*Carl L. Bankston III*

See also: Autobiographies and memoirs; Higher education; Historiography; Literature; Science and technology.

Suggested Readings:

Banks, William M. *Black Intellectuals: Race and Responsibility in American Life*. New York: W. W. Norton, 1996.

Cruse, Harold. *The Crisis of the Negro Intellectual*. New York: Morrow, 1967.

Morrison, Toni. *Playing in the Dark: Whiteness and the Literary Imagination*. Cambridge, Mass.: Harvard University Press, 1992.

Posnock, Ross. *Color and Culture : Black Writers and the Making of the Modern Intellectual*. Cambridge, Mass.: Harvard University Press, 1998.

Wintz, Cary D., ed. *Black Writers Interpret the Harlem Renaissance*. New York: Garland, 1996.

Intelligence and achievement testing: The widespread use of intelligence testing began in World War I, when the U.S. Army began administering a test known as the "intelligence quotient" or "IQ" test to its new recruits. Within a few years, psychologists were using the new test to examine possible differences in intelligence among groups of people, in addition to differences among individuals. Princeton psychology professor Carl C. Brigham used data from the army's mental testing program to look at variations in intelligence between people of northern and western

Many critics have charged that standardized intelligence tests are culturally biased. *(James L. Shaffer)*

European heritage, descended from those who settled in the U.S. in earlier years, and the new waves of immigrants who were arriving from southern and eastern Europe. Brigham concluded that the new immigrants were less intelligent than the older white groups in the United States. He also found that black soldiers showed lower scores on the tests, and he attributed the group differences to variations in inherited mental capacities.

Through the years, descendants of the southern and eastern Europeans showed steadily rising scores on the IQ tests, raising questions about whether these really did measure inherited abilities. A black-white gap continued to appear in IQ testing, however, and some psychologists attributed this gap to inherited characteristics of the racial groups. In *The Testing of Negro Intelligence* (1966), Audrey M. Shuey reported results of 382 studies that used 80 different tests of intelligence. The average white score on these tests was 100 and the average black score was 85.

With the rise of the CIVIL RIGHTS movement in the 1960's, claims that whites tend to be more intelligent than African Americans became politically objectionable. As popular and academic awareness of racism in American life grew, the argument that mental ability is based on race appeared to be a justification for RACIAL PREJUDICE and discrimination. IQ tests also came to be seen increasingly as scientifically suspect. Because African Americans earned lower incomes than whites and had less access to educational resources, the test gap could be a result of black disadvantage rather than a result of black intellectual capabilities. Moreover, black and white Americans had cultures that were different in many respects. Therefore, some critics of IQ tests argued, intelligence tests really measured abilities to function mentally in a white cultural environment and were therefore biased against blacks.

The Race-I.Q. Controversy

By the late 1960's, claims of racial differences in intelligence seemed repulsive products of racism to many people. Therefore, a storm of controversy erupted in 1969 when educational psychologist Arthur Jensen published an article in the *Harvard Educational Review* in which he maintained that attempts to raise the educational level of black youngsters had failed because those youngsters had low average IQs. Jensen argued, further, that the black-white IQ gap was not a result of the social disadvantages of African Americans or a consequence of cultural bias in testing, but a matter of inherited racial differences in intelligence.

A few scientists and social commentators agreed with Jensen's position. Canadian psychologist J. Philippe Rushton and Richard Lynn, a professor of psychology at Ulster University in Northern Ireland, published numerous statistical studies arguing that IQ tests were valid measures of intelligence and that the racial gap could be attributed to biological characteristics. Most experts objected strongly to this line of argument, though. Biologist Stephen Jay Gould criticized IQ tests as measures of intelligence and challenged the view that intelligence is largely inherited. Psychologist Howard Gardner maintained that human mental abilities are too complex to be reduced to a single measure. He argued, instead, that there are many different types of intelligence; he called these "multiple intelligences."

The race-IQ controversy attracted renewed public attention in the 1990's, when Harvard psychologist Richard Herrnstein and social critic Charles Murray published *The Bell Curve: Intelligence and Class Structure in American Life* (1994). Herrnstein and Murray maintained that inherited intelligence was becoming increasingly important as a source of social inequality in American society. Pointing to racial and ethnic variations in IQ test scores, they claimed that variations in intellectual ability are the most likely reason for racial and ethnic inequality.

The work of Herrnstein and Murray stimulated a heated debate about intelligence and race in magazines, journals, and books. Philosopher Michael Levin carried the argument about a supposed connection between race and IQ much further than Herrnstein and Murray did. In a number of articles and in his book *Why Race Matters: Race Differences and What They Mean* (1997), Levin insisted that intelligence is largely inherited. He also claimed that there is a connection between intelligence and moral behavior. The less intelligent people are, in Levin's view, the more insensitive they are to the needs and desires of others and the more likely they are to engage in immoral or criminal behavior. Therefore, Levin maintained that the high rate of imprisonment of young African American men is not the consequence of an unjust society but the product of low average intelligence. Many of Levin's critics saw his argument as straightforward racism. Others pointed out that whites have lower average IQ scores than most Asian groups but that whites do not generally have higher rates of imprisonment than Asians do.

Achievement Tests

The development of achievement testing, like that of IQ testing, was motivated by the desire to classify people scientifically in order to fit them into an increasingly complex and bureaucratic society. While IQ testing was initially intended to assign new recruits to the military to appropriate tasks, achievement testing was developed to meet the needs of mass education. During the 1920's, Carl C. Brigham, who had earlier studied the IQs of ethnic groups, developed the Scholastic Aptitude Test (SAT) as an admission test for students applying to Princeton University. As a flood of students entered college in the years after World War II, standardized tests such as the SAT (later renamed the Scholastic Assessment Test) became increasingly important in judging college applicants.

In the primary grades, tests such as the California Achievement Test (CAT) became seen as a way of judging the success of students in learning required material. Some school districts instituted a policy of "tracking" students on the basis of their achievement test scores. Tracking means that students are placed into classes according to ability groups and are taught at different levels. Students who are in higher tracks are more likely to be seen as college-bound by their teachers and fellow students. The comparatively low achievement test scores of African Americans placed many of them in lower tracks and therefore limited their future academic progress. Many states established standardized achievement tests, such as LOUISIANA's Graduation Exit Examination (GEE), that students had to take and pass in order to obtain a high school diploma. African Americans have been heavily represented among those students whose graduations have been delayed by their test scores.

In the second half of the twentieth century, the growing weight placed on testing meant that a race gap in test scores would contribute to racial inequality. Achievement tests such as the SAT and the National Assessment of Educational Progress (NAEP) showed that throughout the 1970's and 1980's African American scores improved and the black-white gap narrowed but that African American scores continued to be significantly lower. In 1997 African Americans had average SAT scores of 857, compared with an average of 1052 for whites. The American College Test (ACT), the other major achievement test used for college entry, also showed a gap. African Americans had an average score of 17.1, compared with 21.7 for whites.

Some authorities have argued that achievement tests, like IQ tests, are culturally biased and are not true measures of educational achievement. From this point of view, the use of tests such as the SAT to determine entrance into college unfairly limits the chances of African Americans. Other authorities, such as sociologist Christopher Jencks, have argued that continued improvement in black test scores is essential in order for American society to move toward racial equality. Jencks pointed out that only 13.3 percent of African Americans who graduated from high school in 1982 earned college degrees, compared with 30 percent of whites. However, when African Americans and whites with equal test scores were compared, the black students were actually more likely to earn college degrees.

The use of achievement test scores to determine admission to college was one of the issues in the debate over affirmative action. Attempts by many colleges to increase their numbers of minority students meant that African American students were sometimes admitted to colleges that rejected white students with higher test scores. Those who objected to this practice maintained that the more qualified white students were suffering from reverse racial discrimination. Defenders of this type of AFFIRMATIVE ACTION, however, pointed out that colleges need students with qualities other than the particular ability to do well on standardized tests. Many commentators also pointed to evidence that achievement test results are not strongly related to later achievements in life, and they maintained that using test scores to limit the numbers of African American college graduates would deny a valuable source of talent to American society.

—*Carl L. Bankston III*

Suggested Readings:

Fischer, Claude S., et al. *Inequality by Design: Cracking the Bell Curve Myth*. Princeton, N.J.: Princeton University Press, 1996.

Gardner, Howard W. *Frames of Mind: The Theory of Multiple Intelligences*. New York: Basic Books, 1983.

Gould, Stephen J. *The Mismeasure of Man*. New York: W. W. Norton, 1981.

Herrnstein, Richard J., and Charles Murray. *The Bell Curve: Intelligence and Class Structure in American Life*. New York: Free Press, 1994.

Jencks, Christopher, and Meredith Phillips, eds. *The Black-White Test Score Gap*. Washington, D.C.: Brookings Institution Press, 1998.

Levin, Michael. *Why Race Matters*. New York: Praeger, 1997.

Mensh, Elaine, and Harry Mensh. *The IQ Mythology: Class, Race, Gender, and Inequality*. Carbondale, Ill.: Southern Illinois University Press, 1991.

Interracial marriage: Interracial marriage is a special case of exogamy, or marriage outside one's group. Although sociologists, anthropologists, and others have studied exogamy and endogamy (marriage within the group), few scholars have paid particular attention to marriage between members of different races. Most of these few are concerned primarily with American society.

One reason for this situation may be the difficulty in finding a definition for the term "race." Anthropologist Ashley Montagu and many others have argued that the concept of race has no biological or scientific validity. Humans are all, in a sense, mongrels. Moreover, physical anthropologists have traced the descent of all humankind to the same geographical area. Clearly, if there is no race, there can be no interracial marriage.

Race is a social concept based on consensus rather than science, and even a true consensus is lacking. For example, the racial categories listed on job application forms for the United States civil service and for other employers do not correspond to the categories formulated by anthropologists and other social scientists.

Reasons for Study

There are two main reasons why American social scientists have studied interracial marriage. First, the United States is one of a limited number of countries where different races have been living, if not side by side, at least within sight of each other over the course of several centuries. Although different races do cohabit and mix in several countries, including most countries of South and Central America, the United States and the Republic of South Africa are among the very few in which the concept of race became embodied in law.

Second, the culture of the United States seems to be obsessed, like few others, with the notion of race. Other nations and ethnic groups tend to be ethnocentric; taboos against marrying outside one's ethnic group (or "tribe") are common. These taboos should not be confused with racism or RACIAL PREJUDICE: In other countries, discrimination in this form is generally universal, applying equally against all outsiders and having little or nothing to do with skin color or complexion.

History

In most of the thirteen colonies, and later in the United States, taboos against exogamy, especially against marriage of black and white partners, were reflected in law. MISCEGENATION (marriage or cohabitation between a white person and a member of a different race) has taken place from the beginning. Although exceptional, there were cases of intermarriage between black and white indentured servants and, somewhat later, between indentured servants and slaves. This may be explained, in part, by the dearth of women in the colonies before 1750.

The first Africans reached VIRGINIA in 1619. SLAVERY and discriminatory legislation regarding miscegenation were introduced later. In 1662 Virginia set the fine for fornication by a white person with an African American at twice the amount for fornication with another white person. By 1691 all interracial liaisons had been prohibited. MARYLAND was quick to follow suit. Eventually, most states passed laws prohibiting intermarriage. By the nineteenth century, thirty-eight states had adopted such laws, the only exceptions being CONNECTICUT, ILLINOIS, MONTANA, NEW JERSEY, NEW YORK, VERMONT, WYOMING, and PENNSYLVANIA (where the law was repealed in 1780).

In 1913 twenty-eight states still had statutes banning marriage between black and white Americans. In some western states, miscegenation laws were probably aimed not so much against whites intermarrying with the few African Americans who lived there as against the intermarriage of whites with other ethnic groups, mainly Asian Americans.

Emancipation and the FOURTEENTH AMENDMENT had little immediate effect on laws against intermarriage. Only five states repealed these laws shortly thereafter. Laws against intermarriage remained on the books in most states. In FLORIDA, the practice of intermarriage was held to be "forever prohibited"; ALABAMA law specified that "the Legislature shall never pass any law to authorize or legalize any marriage between any white person and a Negro."

The punishment for intermarriage varied from state to state, with terms of imprisonment ranging up to ten years. In some cases, the punishment was the same as that for fornication, since the marriage itself was considered null and void. Despite the teachings of the QUAKERS regarding the abolition of slavery, the Pennsylvania law against intermarriage remained in effect until 1780. FREE BLACKS convicted of marrying whites could be sold into slavery.

In the twentieth century, laws against interracial marriage frequently were challenged. W. E. B. DU BOIS wrote on behalf of the NATIONAL ASSOCIATION FOR THE ADVANCEMENT OF COLORED PEOPLE (NAACP) against these laws. Nevertheless, in some states, conditions actually worsened; for example, in Virginia the penalty for intermarriage was increased as late as 1932. The usual response of the higher courts was that marriage was not a political institution, let alone a constitutional issue.

As a domestic issue, marriage was strictly within the jurisdiction of individual states. Courts also ruled that laws against intermarriage did not involve discrimination, since both black and white partners were punished equally. When the U.S. SUPREME COURT finally declared all such laws unconstitutional in 1967, laws banning racial intermarriage were still on the books in nineteen states, not all of which were in the South.

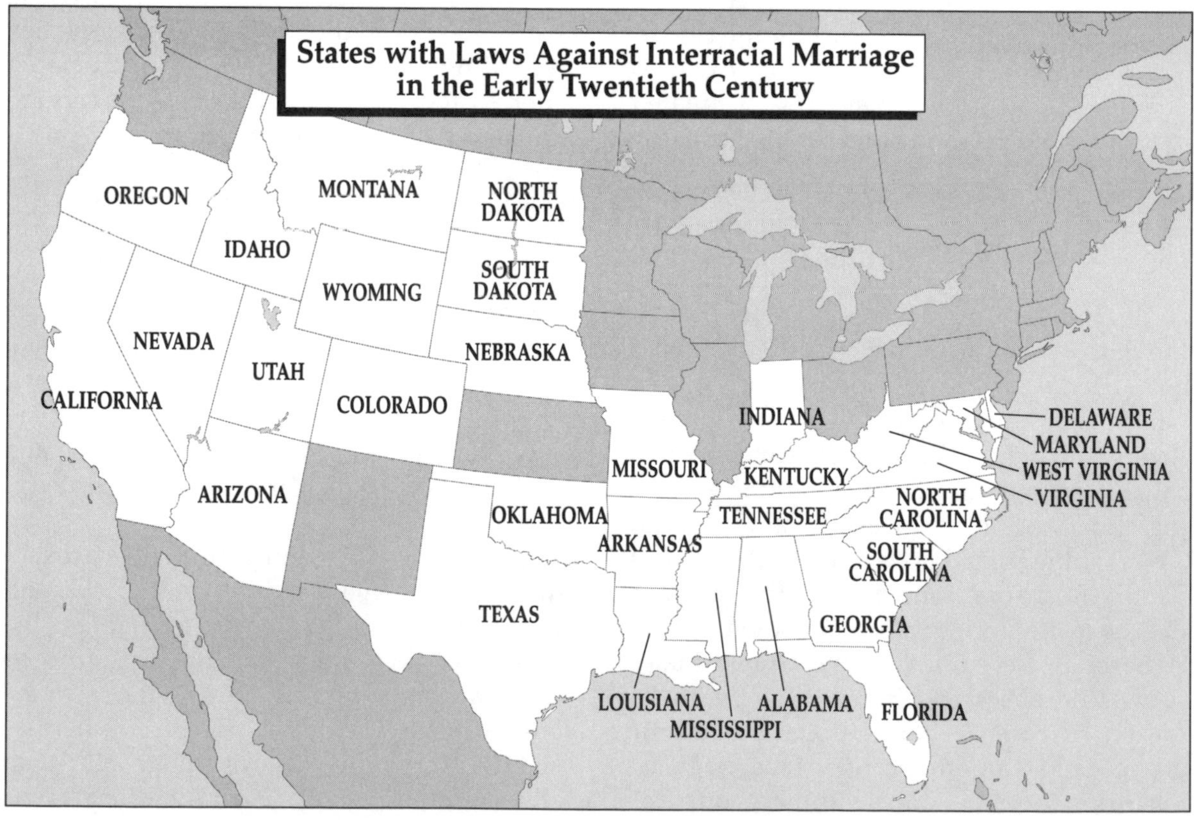

Effect of the Laws

If the intent of laws against intermarriage was to prevent miscegenation, they certainly were not effective. If their intent was to preserve the "purity of the white race," however, the laws were relatively successful, since the offspring of mixed unions were relegated into the black race. It has been estimated that four out of five African Americans have some white ancestry. In most southern states, it had never been a crime for a black woman to have a child by or to have sexual relations with a white man. Relations between black women and white men were common in some areas, especially in cities such as Charleston, SOUTH CAROLINA, and NEW ORLEANS, LOUISIANA.

Barbara McIntyre and Edward Cooper, an Oregon couple who ran a mail-order business called "People of Every Stripe" during the early 1990's. *(AP/Wide World Photos)*

Attitudes

Well into the twentieth century, most whites who expressed themselves on the subject continued to argue against intermarriage. When questioned by a reporter about his attitude toward intermarriage, for example, the only response President Harry S Truman could think of was the cliché, "Would you like your daughter to marry a Negro?" Most sociologists, claiming objectivity, merely insisted that intermarriage is best avoided because it forces the couple to face unusually difficult problems.

Some African American leaders, especially those described as black nationalists, preached the same prohibition. Point ten of Elijah MUHAMMAD's Muslim Program, which was for many years reprinted in most issues of the NATION OF ISLAM's *Final Call*, states: "We believe that intermarriage or race mixing should be prohibited." At a more secular level, Marcus GARVEY, who founded the UNIVERSAL NEGRO IMPROVEMENT ASSOCIATION (UNIA), taught similar doctrines. The statement of beliefs of the UNIA included a profession of faith "in the purity of the Negro race and purity of the White race." It also spoke "against miscegenation and race suicide." These leaders may have argued for racial purity and intolerance at least partly in response to white racism and intolerance, as a matter of racial pride. Others, both black and white, foreign and American, have argued in favor of ASSIMILATION. Social scientists have argued that in a society in which intermarriage, as distinct from miscegenation or concubinage, is predominant, racism is mild or minimal.

Trends

Although repeal of the laws against intermarriage modified the attitudes of a significant percentage of the white population, it did not open the floodgates of intermarriage. There is evidence that despite lingering prejudices and somewhat negative attitudes toward interracial marriage, the number of such marriages rose slowly but steadily in the United States.

According to records of the CENSUS OF THE UNITED STATES, only about 0.15 percent of all married couples consisted of black and white partners in 1970. The figure had risen to 0.34 percent by 1980 and to 0.41 percent by 1989. (This means that as of 1989 approximately 4 percent of married African Americans were married to a white person.) In 1998 the figure was about 0.60 percent—a four-fold increase over 1970.

Psychological evidence indicates gender differentiation in the acceptance or tolerance of mixed couples. Because of the continuing difference in status as determined by "race," black men and white women are more ready to accept a couple in which the man is black and the woman white. Black women and white men are more inclined to accept a couple in which the man is white and the woman is black. Black man-white woman married couples outnumbered black woman-white man couples almost three to one as of 1990; by the late 1990's there was a notably increased number of black woman-white man couples, and the ratio was slightly less than two to one.

The rise in interracial marriages may not reflect the evolution of more tolerant attitudes or changing values so much as the vastly greater opportunities to meet and intermingle socially, the partial integration of schools and workplaces, and increased migration and immigration. According to some surveys, there is a positive correlation between housing integration and exogamy.

Some evidence indicates that interracial marriages have at least the same chance of success as same-race marriages, in spite of the obvious cultural differences between partners. This situation may be the result of the additional effort the partners are willing to put into the relationship to make it work. Data regarding the offspring of interracial marriages are conflicting, but some studies indicate that children of mixed marriages, rather than viewing themselves as genetically victimized, tend to emphasize the positive side and do not experience excessive problems in adjustment.

—*Mario D. Fenyo*

See also: Biracial and mixed-race children; Ethnocentrism.

Suggested Readings:
Barron, Milton L., ed. *The Blending American: Patterns of Intermarriage*. Chicago: Quadrangle Books, 1972.
Henriques, Fernando. *Children of Conflict: A Study of Interracial Sex and Marriage*. New York: E. P. Dutton, 1975.
Kaeser, Gigi, and Peggy Gillespie. *Of Many Colors: Portraits of Multiracial Families*. Amherst: University of Massachusetts Press, 1997.
Nash, Gary B. *Forbidden Love: Secret History of Mixed Race America*, New York: Henry Holt, 1999.
Reuter, Edward Byron. *Race Mixture: Studies in Intermarriage and Miscegenation*. New York: Whittlesey House, 1931.
Stuart, Irving R., and Lawrence Edwin Abt, eds. *Interracial Marriage: Expectations and Realities*. New York: Grossman, 1973.
Washington, Joseph R., Jr. *Marriage in Black and White*. Boston: Beacon Press, 1971.

Inventors: Much attention and study has been devoted to the scientific achievements of such notable American inventors as Alexander Graham Bell, Thomas Edison, and Henry Ford. Few Americans realize that numerous African Americans have also made scientific discoveries that contributed significantly to the field of invention. Overcoming the disadvantages of prejudice, POVERTY, and poor EDUCATION, these black inventors were determined to use their knowledge of science to develop practical solutions to everyday problems.

Innovations in Whaling

Although he was born into SLAVERY in Richmond, VIRGINIA, Lewis TEMPLE made an important contribution to one of New England's

(continued on page 1316)

Notable Inventors

Alcorn, George Edward. *See main text entry.*

Baker, David (Apr. 2, 1881, Louisville, Ky.—?). While running the elevator service in the Board of Trade building in New Orleans, Louisiana, Baker invented scales to prevent elevator overloading. His other inventions include a sanitary cuspidor and a railway signaling device.

Banneker, Benjamin. *See main text entry.*

Beard, Andrew Jackson (1850, Eastlake, Ala.—1921?). Inventor of the jenny coupler, a mechanism that connected railcars automatically when they were pushed together, saving many railway workers from serious injuries. The invention, which Beard patented in 1897, earned him $50,000.

Blair, Henry C. (1804, Glenross, Md.—1860). The first African American to patent an invention (1834), Blair invented devices for planting corn and cotton.

Boone, Sarah. Inventor of the narrow wooden ironing board, with a padded covering and collapsible leg supports, which she patented in 1892.

Carruthers, George R. (b. Oct. 1, 1939, Cincinnati, Ohio). Astrophysicist at the Naval Research Laboratory, whose ultraviolet measurements branch Carruthers directed from 1980 to 1982, when he invented a lunar surface ultraviolet camera.

Carver, George Washington. *See main text entry.*

Crosthwait, David Nelson, Jr. (May 27, 1898, Nashville, Tenn.—Feb. 25, 1976, Michigan City, Ind.). Mechanical engineer, whose thirty-nine patents were primarily connected with heating and ventilating systems for power plants. His inventions include an automatic water feeder (1920), thermostat-setting apparatus (1928), and a vacuum pump (1930).

Evans, James Carmichael. *See main text entry.*

Ferrell, Frank J. (b. New York, 1800's). Ferrell's most important inventions involved improvements in valves for steam engines.

Forten, James. *See main text entry.*

Goode, Sarah E. Born a slave, Goode was the most important black female inventor of the nineteenth century. Her most noteworthy invention was a folding cabinet bed she patented in 1885.

Gourdine, Meredith C. *See main text entry.*

Hall, Lloyd Augustus (June 20, 1894, Elgin, Ill.—Jan. 2, 1971, Altadena, Calif.). Hall specialized in the preservation and processing of meat and bakery products. His discovery of curing salts had a great impact on the meat-packing industry.

Hillery, John Richard (Apr. 28, 1874, St. Mary's County, Md.—1940). Podiatrist who invented the tarsal arch support.

Jones, Frederick McKinley (May 17, 1892, Cincinnati, Ohio—Feb. 21, 1961, Minneapolis, Minn.). Versatile inventor whose many patents include a portable X-ray machine and a device for converting silent film projectors into sound projectors. His automatic refrigeration system revolutionized the trucking and railway industries.

Julian, Hubert Fauntleroy. *See main text entry.*

Julian, Percy Lavon. *See main text entry.*

Latimer, Lewis Howard. *See main text entry.*

Matzeliger, Jan Earnst. *See main text entry.*

McCoy, Elijah. *See main text entry.*

Morgan, Garrett Augustus. *See main text entry.*

Rhodes, J. B. Inventor of a home water closet, which he patented in 1899. By making indoor toilets practical, his invention eliminated the need for outhouses.

Richardson, W. H. (fl. 1800's). Inventor of a device, called a leveler, that kept baby carriages from tipping over. He patented the device in 1889.

(continued)

Rillieux, Norbert (1806, New Orleans, La.—Oct. 8, 1894, Paris, France). The son of a French man and an American slave woman, Rillieux was educated in Paris, where he became a teacher. He patented a vacuum evaporating pan, which was widely used in the sugar-refining industry, in 1846.

Louisiana State Museum

Robinson, Elbert R. Inventor of a railway trolley that used electric overhead wires to propel passenger cars. His patent was infringed on by two large corporations, and he lost control of it although he took his case to the U.S. SUPREME COURT.

Thrash, Dox (b. 1893, Griffin, Ga.). Painter and printmaker who coinvented the carborundum print process. Thrash worked for the Pennsylvania Federal Art Project. His own art work is represented in the National Archives.

Walker, C. J. *See main text entry.*

Woods, Granville T. *See main text entry.*

chief industries—whaling. After moving to New Bedford, MASSACHUSETTS, in 1829, Temple went to work as a blacksmith and owned his own forge. Much of his business was devoted to making and repairing the harpoons that whalers used to hunt and capture their prey. Temple created a special toggle bar that made it impossible for the harpoon to be dislodged during the wild chases that often occurred after the harpoon penetrated the whale's body. Although Temple never patented his invention, it was widely adopted and sold steadily, bringing Temple a comfortable income. Whaling experts hailed Temple's toggle as the most important invention in whaling history.

Advances in Shoemaking

Jan MATZELIGER was born in Dutch Guiana, where he began working in a government machine shop at the age of ten and became fascinated with the construction and operation of mechanical objects. As a young man, Matzeliger signed on as a merchant seaman and traveled abroad. Tired of life as a sailor, Matzeliger settled in Lynn, Massachusetts, one of the leading centers of shoe manufacturing in the United States. Once there, Matzeliger set to work devising a mechanical method of attaching shoe soles to the upper parts of shoes. The method of manually sewing these parts together, called hand lasting, was the slowest procedure in shoe manufacture. Matzeliger produced a shoe lasting machine that attached these parts automatically in one-tenth of the time necessary for hand lasting. This advance not only increased production but also cut the cost of production by 50 percent. Regrettably, the brilliant Matzeliger did not live to capitalize on his invention or enjoy its profits—hed ied of TUBERCULOSIS at the age of thirty-seven.

Contributions to the Railroad Industry

Two African Americans made significant contributions to the advancement of the American railroading industry. Elijah MCCOY was born to escaped slaves who found refuge in Colchester, Ontario, Canada. As a young man, McCoy traveled to Edinburgh, Scotland, where he served as an apprentice in mechanical engineering. Upon his return to the United States, McCoy had difficulty obtaining employment despite his advanced skills and education. Unable to secure a position as an engineer because of RACIAL PREJUDICE, he was hired to work as a railroad fireman. Although the job involved a great deal of hard labor, Mc-

Coy found time to become familiar with the mechanics of railroad engines.

As a result of his responsibilities in oiling locomotive engines, McCoy became interested in the problem of lubricating machines. In 1872 he patented an automatic machine lubricator designed specifically for steam engines. His later inventions included a device for lubricating locomotive engines and one for lubricating vehicular air brakes. During his lifetime McCoy held more than fifty patents, most of them for automatic lubricating devices. McCoy's inventions were so widely used that the purchasers of heavy-duty machinery would determine that a machine had automatic lubrications by asking, "Is it the real McCoy?" With this phrase, McCoy's name made its way into American slang as a synonym for excellence even though few know its connection with African American achievement.

Granville T. WOODS was another inventor who got his start as a railroad fireman-engineer, a job he held when he was sixteen years old. Later, Woods went to college and studied electrical technology. After starting his own electrical company, Woods became known as the "black Edison" and patented two devices related to telegraphy. The first, granted in 1885, was for a telegraphone, a device that allowed telegraphy operators to send messages vocally or in Morse code. The second, a synchronous multiplex railway telegraph patented in 1887, allowed messages to be transmitted between moving trains and railway stations. This device improved railroad safety by carrying warnings of dangerous obstacles, such as fallen trees or derailed trains, along railway tracks.

Some of Woods's other inventions included an improved steam boiler, a regulator for electric motors, a safe electric light dimmer, an overhead conducting system for electricity that led to the development of trolley cars, the "third rail" used to run subway trains in large cities, air brakes, electromagnetic brakes, and an automatic safety cut-off switch for electrical circuits. Many of his inventions were purchased by leaders in technology, such as the Bell Telephone Company, the General Electric Company, and the Westinghouse Corporation. Woods's record of scientific achievement and his prolific patent holdings have been matched by few inventors of any race.

Although Woods was compared with Thomas Edison, Lewis H. LATIMER was a black inventor who actually worked with Edison. Born in Massachusetts, Latimer began his career as an inventor by developing a water closet, or bathroom, for railroad cars that was patented in 1873. Later, he was employed as a draftsman for the U.S. Electric Lighting Company, where he invented new carbon filaments made from the cellulose of cotton thread and from bamboo slivers for incandescent light bulbs and improved the process for joining these filaments to the conducting wires in the bases of the light bulbs. These state-of-the-art developments contributed greatly to the commercialization of the light bulb. As a result of his accomplishments, Latimer was hired by the Edison Electric Light Company, the forerunner of the General Electric Company. Latimer's work as the only African American member of the Edison Pioneers—scientists who worked with Edison during his creative period—culminated in the authorship and publication of *Incandescent Electric Lighting* (1890), a book that became the standard guide for a generation of lighting ENGINEERS. Though most of the patents and proceeds from his inventions were held by his employers, Latimer continued to invent throughout his life, and one of his later inventions became a forerunner of the modern refrigerator.

Food Innovations

Joseph Lee was born in Boston, where he worked in a bakery as a young boy. Lee went on to work in the hotel and restaurant business and parlayed his business expertise to become the owner of a hotel. Reportedly, Lee began his career as an inventor because it bothered him to throw away large amounts of stale bread every day. His first invention, developed in 1895, was a machine that used stale bread to make bread crumbs. This machine led to the widespread use of bread crumbs in American cooking. Lee also developed and patented the first bread-making machine in 1900. The machine made bread ten times faster than it could be baked by hand. In addition to increasing bread production, the machine produced standard sized loaves of better quality in a more hygienic fashion. Lee's inventions contributed greatly to the growth of the American baking and food industry.

Improving Public Safety

Although he began his career as a tailor, Garrett A. Morgan achieved fame as a result of inventions that contributed to greater public safety. Born in Paris, KENTUCKY, Morgan moved to Cleveland and opened a tailoring business. Reportedly, Morgan's search for a method to prevent fabric from being scorched by overheated sewing machine needles led to the accidental invention of a hair straightening formula in 1913. The proceeds from sales of this straightener enabled Morgan to devote much of his life to scientific experimentation and invention.

Morgan's next invention, patented in 1914, was a canvas hood designed to protect the wearer from smoke and harmful fumes. Two tubes extending from the hood merged into one tube behind the wearer's back that ended near ground level. The tube end held a moist sponge designed to cool the air as it entered the tube and to trap any particles it contained. Another tube ran from the mouth of the wearer to a ball valve atop the hood. Exhalation raised the valve ball and allowed carbon dioxide to escape. Upon inhalation, the ball dropped back into place and prevented smoke from entering the lungs. Because of its simple design and great utility, Morgan's helmet-gas mask was widely used and earned for him a gold medal at an International Safety Exposition held in New York in 1914. In 1923 Morgan patented a traffic signal consisting of signs marked "Stop" and "Go" that were automatically raised or lowered at specific intervals. Morgan later sold the patent to this traffic signal for $40,000 to the General Electric Company, which replaced the signs with red, green, and yellow lights.

The achievements of these inventive African American scientists proved that ingenuity and creative problem-solving are not limited to privileged intellectuals of a particular race. Acceptance of their contributions may have been grudging at first, but African American inventors continued to pursue their dreams and became part of the rapid pace of technological innovation in the late twentieth century.

—*Sanford S. Singer*

See also: Science and technology.

Suggested Readings:

Aaseng, Nathan. *Black Inventors*. New York: Facts On File, 1997.

Carwell, Hattie. *Blacks in Science: Astrophysicist to Zoologist*. Hicksville, N.Y.: Exposition Press, 1977.

Chappell, Kevin. "How Black Inventors Changed America." *Ebony* (February, 1997): 40-45.

Haber, Louis. *Black Pioneers of Science and Invention*. New York: Harcourt, Brace & World, 1970.

Haskins, James. *Outward Dreams: Black Inventors and Their Inventions*. New York : Walker, 1991.

James, Portia P. *The Real McCoy: African American Invention and Innovation, 1619-1930*. Washington, D.C.: Smithsonian Institution Press, 1989.

Jenkins, Edward S. *To Fathom More: African American Scientists and Inventors*. Lanham, Md.: University Press of America, 1996.
"Modern Black Inventors." *Ebony* (October, 1998): 158-161.
Pizer, Vernon. *Shortchanged by History: America's Neglected Innovators*. New York: G. P. Putnam's Sons, 1979.
Sammons, Vivian O. *Blacks in Science and Medicine*. New York: Hemisphere, 1990.

Iowa: Iowa has always had a small black population. The first census, in 1850, listed 333 blacks, concentrated in the state's Mississippi River towns. The number of African Americans gradually increased in each census, reaching 19,692 in 1950. Blacks constituted less than 1 percent of the population until 1970, when the percentage increased to just over 1 percent. In 1997 the state's African American population was about 56,000, slightly under 2 percent of the total population.

The COMPROMISE OF 1850 excluded SLAVERY from the northern territory of the Louisiana Purchase. Consequently, Iowa never had slavery. The state did discriminate against blacks, however. The constitutional convention of 1844 attempted unsuccessfully to exclude blacks from residence in the state. The constitution of 1857 granted blacks legal standing in the courts and property rights but denied them the vote, the right to sit on juries, and membership in the General Assembly.

The franchise (the right to vote) was extended to the blacks by constitutional amendment in 1868. At the time, Iowa was one of only five states to enfranchise blacks (seven-

1997 Population: 2,852,000
African American Population: 56,000
African American Percentage of Total: 1.96

teen did not). At the same time, Iowa courts also admitted blacks to the public schools and universities.

During the GREAT MIGRATION north after 1910, blacks came to Iowa in limited numbers to work in the packing houses and factories. They settled primarily in a few urban areas, such as Des Moines and Waterloo. Segregation in housing became the norm during and after WORLD WAR I. Between the 1960's and 1990's, federal and state antidiscrimination laws and black activism reduced segregation in schools and employment, but they were less successful in reducing HOUSING DISCRIMINATION.

—*Robert D. Talbott*

Islam: Islam is the world's second largest RELIGION (behind Christianity), with an estimated number of followers of more than one billion in the mid-1990's. It flourishes in at least forty-eight countries, with approximately 285 million adherents in AFRICA, 670 million in Asia, 14 million in Europe, 1.4 million in Latin America, and 43 million in the former Soviet Union. It also has adherents in North America, where estimates of membership range from 3.4 million to 6 million in the United States alone. If the offshoot NATION OF ISLAM were to be included, that number might be nearly 8 million. Clearly, Islam appeals to a number of African Americans.

The Basics of Islam

The word "Islam" means "submission," and a Muslim is a person who submits to God, known by the name Allah in the Qur'an (or Koran), the scripture of Islam. Muslims believe that Allah created the world and created human beings to rule over it in submission to Allah. One way that Islam differs from Christianity is that, in Islam, humans are not born in a fallen state. Rather, their purpose in life is to worship and obey Allah. Hence, sin is basically unnatural. Still, humans do fall into disbelief and disobedience, from which they must extricate themselves by following the Five Pillars.

The Five Pillars of Islam begin with the confession of faith: "There is no God but Allah, and Muhammad is the Prophet of Allah." This confession points to the unwavering monotheism of Islam and to its belief that Allah revealed truth perfectly through Muhammad in the Qur'an. The other four pillars form the basis of Muslim religious life. Muslims offer prayer five times daily: dawn, midday, afternoon, evening, and night. These prayers consist of glorifying Allah and reciting passages from the Qur'an. Almsgiving (giving aid to the poor) is of two types: required giving of about 2.5 percent of one's worth annually, and charity giving above what is required. Muslims fast from dawn to dusk during the month of Ramadan, which can come at any time of the year since Islam follows a lunar calendar. Finally, Muslims are expected to make a pilgrimage to Mecca once in their lives if at all possible.

The Spread of Islam

The Prophet Muhammad lived from c. 571 to 632. During his life he unified most of the Arabian Peninsula around him and his new religion. Within ten years after his death, Islam had won over Syria, Iraq, and Egypt. In less than a century, it spread to Morocco, Spain, France, Turkey, and across Central Asia to India. It encountered Judaism, Christianity, Hinduism, and Buddhism along the way. Though those encounters were sometimes bloody, Islam presented itself as a moral force with a coherent doctrine and a system of government and law deserving respect from all. Muslim expansion continued as far east as China and as far south as sub-Saharan Africa. Islam spread sometimes as a military power, sometimes as a missionary religion, and sometimes as both. One consequence of its spread in Africa is that Islam can appeal to African Americans as an African religion.

During the 1960's, Malcolm X was the most famous and most widely heard spokesperson for Islam in the United States. *(AP/Wide World Photos)*

Migrations to America

Financial hardship in Syria, North Africa, and Arabia between 1900 and 1914 and in the Balkans, Anatolia, and Russia immediately after WORLD WAR I caused some Muslims to migrate to the United States. A search for education and economic prosperity continues to attract Muslims. Even earlier, however, had Muslims constituted an estimated 14 to 20 percent of the slaves brought from West Africa to the United States. Evangelized by Protestants (particularly BAPTISTS and METHODISTS), virtually all converted to Christianity. A few left narratives of their experiences written in Arabic script. Missionaries in GEORGIA and SOUTH CAROLINA noted that Muslim slaves identified Allah with the Christian God and Muhammad with Jesus, so a connection with Islam was often maintained. As late as the 1930's, descendants of those slaves recalled their grandparents facing eastward and praying five times daily.

The Ahmadiyya Mission

Muslim missionary followers of a reformer named Mirza Ghulam Ahmad came from India to the United States in 1920 for the purpose of converting Americans to Islam. They proselytized white and black Americans alike, hoping to end racial and ethnic separation among Muslims in America. Foreign missionaries, however, were less important to the development of Islam among African Americans than was their thinking about their own experience.

Pan-Africanism and Moorish Science

Toward the end of the nineteenth century, African American intellectuals began charging that white Americans and Europeans were turning Christianity into a "white man's religion." Edward Wilmot Blyden, sometimes called the "father of PAN-AFRICANISM," argued that Muslims in Africa had left the indigenous peoples masters of themselves and their homes, whereas Christians sought to dominate them. He concluded that as a religion for Africans everywhere, Islam was better than Christianity. Timothy Drew, better known as Noble Drew Ali, took up that theme and announced that Islam was the true religion of African Americans. In 1913 he founded the Moorish Science Temple in Newark, New Jersey, and taught that African Americans are not Negroes but "Asiatics" from Morocco. By his movement, he hoped to empower his followers to overcome racism and poverty. He died in 1929 under mysterious circumstances; his movement splintered but continued.

The Nation of Islam

In 1930 Wallace D. Fard (later known by other names, including Farrad Mohammed) appeared in Detroit, asserting that he had come from Mecca to acquaint African Americans with their true identity as Muslims from the "lost-found tribe of Shabbazz." He taught a program of self-knowledge by establishing an elementary and secondary school, a girls' training school, and a paramilitary group called the Fruit of Islam. Fard called his movement the Nation of Islam, though it and its successor movements are considered heretical or non-Muslim by many traditional believers. Members of the Nation of Islam are also known as Black Muslims.

After Fard's disappearance in 1934, he was succeeded by Elijah Poole, renamed Elijah Muhammad by Fard himself. Muhammad announced a program for African American advancement that consisted of Black Muslim-owned businesses coupled with observance of a strict ethical code and a refusal to participate in such civic functions as voting, saluting the American flag, or serving in the armed forces.

Boxing champion Muhammad Ali with members of Sisters of Islam at a Nation of Islam convention in 1966. *(AP/Wide World Photos)*

Malcolm Little, who became Malcolm X, became the chief spokesperson for Elijah Muhammad. He advocated black separatism and self-determination until he made a pilgrimage to Mecca and observed the racial diversity of Islam. He broke with Muhammad and established a new organization, the Muslim Mosque, shortly before he was assassinated.

Muhammad's movement divided again after his death in 1975. His son Warithuddin (Wallace Deen) Muhammad began moving the Nation of Islam toward orthodox Islam, as Malcolm X had wanted. He renamed the movement first the World Community of Islam in the West and then the American Muslim Mission. He also began admitting white members.

This new direction for African American Islam was repudiated by a number of members, in particular a large faction led by Louis FARRAKHAN. He broke with the American Muslim Mission and returned to the original separatist teachings of Elijah Muhammad. Farrakhan had become the most important spokesman for Black Muslims in the United States by the mid-1990's, filling auditoriums wherever he spoke. His separatist leanings, however, drew opposition from both white and black Americans, Muslims and non-Muslims.

Issues Facing Islam in the United States

This rift is evidence that the African American Muslim community is still seeking its way. From one perspective, the problem it faces is not new but is the same one that led African Americans out of predominantly white churches immediately after the CIVIL WAR. It involves whether and how African Americans can function as equals in a society they often perceive as racist. Between the end of the Civil War and 1880, African American Protestants left their churches wholesale, forming new bodies or joining with previously existing African American bodies.

Similarly, under the urging of Blyden and his successors, many African Americans (though by no means the majority) left Christianity behind as a "white religion" and joined Islam. Eventually they had to face whether to allow whites into their movement. The success of Muhammad's group may depend on how well it can achieve balance and whether a racially mixed group can effectively meet the needs of its African American constituency. The success of Farrakhan's organization may depend on how well it can intercede for African Americans from outside the political structure.

Another issue concerns the fact that the Nation of Islam is an American adaptation of Islam, so it must determine how to relate to the larger Muslim world, particularly that world's racial diversity. Likewise, other Muslims must decide whether to accept members of the Nation of Islam as authentic Muslims.

Finally, it should be noted that by the year 2000 Muslims had become so numerous in the United States were expected soon to outnumber the nation's Jewish population. With numbers come recognition and acceptance, so the religion of Islam is becoming more acceptable among the American people. That acceptance bodes well for African American Muslims of all persuasions. One symptom of (or perhaps a partial cause of) the improving image of Muslims in America is the popularity of growing numbers of African American sports figures, notably boxer Muhammad ALI and basketball player Kareem ABDUL-JABBAR, who enjoy high visibility and respect both because of their athletic ability and because of their Muslim religious faith.

—*Paul L. Redditt*

Suggested Readings:

Abu-Laban, Baha. "The Canadian Muslim Community: The Need for a New Survival Strategy." In *The Muslim Community in North America*, edited by Earle H. Waugh, Baha Abu-Laban, and Regula B. Quereshi. Edmonton: University of Alberta Press, 1983.

Barboza, Steven. *American Jihad: Islam After Malcolm X*. New York: Doubleday, 1996.

Elkholy, Abdo. *The Arab Moslems in the United States*. New Haven, Conn.: College and University Press, 1966.

Gardell, Mattias. *In the Name of Elijah Mohammad: Louis Farrakhan and the Nation of Islam*. Durham: Duke University Press, 1996.

Lee, Martha F. *The Nation of Islam: An American Millenarian Movement*. Lewiston, N.Y.: Mellon, 1980.

Lincoln, C. Eric. *The Black Muslims in America*. Boston: Beacon, 1961.

Lovell, Emily Kalled. "Islam in the United States: Past and Present." In *The Muslim Community in North America*, edited by Earle H. Waugh, Baha Abu-Laban, and Regula B. Quereshi. Edmonton: University of Alberta Press, 1983.

Marsh, Clifton E. *From Black Muslims to Muslims: The Resurrection, Transformation, and Change of the Lost-Found Nation of Islam in America, 1930-1964*. Lanham, Md.: Scarecrow Press, 1996.

Muhammad, Akbar. "Muslims in the United States." In *The Islamic Impact*, edited by Yvonne Yazbeck Haddad, Byron Haines, and Ellison Findley. Syracuse, N.Y.: University of Syracuse Press.

J

Jackson, George (September 23, 1941, Chicago, Illinois August 21, 1971, San Quentin, California): Martyr of the radical black prison movement. Jackson spent his last eleven years in prison, seven of them in solitary confinement. He became transformed into a black revolutionary. His writings include *Soledad Brother: The Prison Letters of George Jackson* (1970) and *Blood in My Eye* (1972). He was killed following a prison disturbance that resulted in the deaths of three prison guards and two inmates.

In 1960 Jackson was arrested for a gasoline station robbery in CALIFORNIA. Following a public defender's advice, he pled guilty and drew a severe sentence of one year to life. Embittered, Jackson proved to be a rebellious prisoner at Soledad and repeatedly was denied parole. Inspired by an older prisoner, W. L. Nolen, Jackson studied African American history, Marxism-Leninism, and BLACK NATIONALISM. Jackson's rebellious energy became channeled into political activity, and he began to write long letters to people outside the prison.

In 1969 Nolen organized protests over two arbitrary killings of African American prisoners, provoking prison authorities. Jackson's mentor and two others were murdered on January 13, 1970, by a guard later found innocent of wrongdoing. In retaliation, a guard was beaten to death. Jackson, along with two others, was accused of murder. They became known as the SOLEDAD BROTHERS and were transferred to San Quentin, a maximum security facility. Appointed as a field marshal in the BLACK PANTHER PARTY, Jackson dedicated himself to political agitation within his struggle to escape the gas chamber.

On August 7, 1970, Jackson's younger brother Jonathan conducted an armed attack on a Marin County, California, courthouse hearing, planning to take hostages to exchange for George Jackson and others. Authorities discovered the plan and had counterinsurgency specialists move in with high-powered weapons. Jonathan, two prisoners, and the judge were killed. A police infiltrator, it was later revealed, helped inspire the attack.

One year later, Jackson was shot fatally in the head while lying, already wounded, in a prison yard. He allegedly was attempting to escape following a violent confrontation with prison guards. In 1988 trial testimony disclosed that police authorities had created the 1971 prison disturbance as a pretext to silence the outspoken Jackson.

See also: Attica prison revolt; Davis, Angela.

Jackson, Janet (b. May 16, 1966, Gary, Indiana): Singer, dancer, and actor. The youngest member of the show business family that produced the Jackson 5 and solo singer Michael JACKSON, Jackson's career soared with the release of her third album and continued to advance with her personalized lyrics and songs that ranged from playful and seductive dance tunes to socially conscious tracks about POVERTY and other social problems.

Jackson first performed at the age of seven, singing and doing impressions in her family's nightclub act. In her teens, she acted in various television shows, including *Good Times*, *A New Kind of Family*, *Diff'rent Strokes*, and *Fame*, while making two albums of ballads and dance tunes. After graduation from high school in 1984, she eloped with musician James DeBarge. The marriage was annulled within a year.

Jackson then worked closely with coproducers James "Jimmy Jam" Harris and Terry

Janet Jackson played opposite Tupac Shakur in *Poetic Justice* in 1993. *(Museum of Modern Art, Film Stills Archive)*

Lewis to develop an album reflecting her experiences and expressing her independence. Released in 1986, *Control* was designed to reach into black households in the United States and speak directly to young African Americans. The hit album sold more than five million copies in the United States and three million copies abroad. Many of its songs, including "What Have You Done for Me Lately," also topped the singles record charts. Jackson won two American Music Awards in 1987.

Jackson's next album, *Janet Jackson's Rhythm Nation 1814* (1989), carried a message of racial harmony. With songs urging youth to avoid drugs and eliminate RACIAL PREJUDICE, the album sold eight million copies, and the *Rhythm Nation 1814* video won a Grammy Award. Jackson's 1990 world tour was nearly sold out. Featuring high-tech staging and smooth dancing, it strengthened her reputation as a performer who could project both sweetness and a streetwise attitude. In 1991 she won American Music Awards as best dance artist, best female pop-rock artist, and best female soul-RHYTHM-AND-BLUES artist. Jackson went on to release *Janet* in 1993 and *The Velvet Rope*—which reunited her with producers Jimmy Jam and Terry Lewis—in 1997. In the 1990's Jackson also returned to acting, appearing in films including *Poetic Justice* (1993).

In addition to performing and recording, Jackson donated money to the UNITED NEGRO COLLEGE FUND and to Cities in Schools, a dropout prevention program. She received the Humanitarian of the Year Award in 1991 for her support of the Make-a-Wish program for terminally ill children. She later donated a portion of the profits from her 1998 concert tour to the group America's Promise—the Alliance for Youth, a nonprofit children's mentoring program.

See also: Music.

Jackson, Jesse (b. October 8, 1941, Greenville, South Carolina): CIVIL RIGHTS activist and politician. While still young, Jesse Louis Jackson became one of the African American community's most important national spokesmen. His ancestors include black slaves, Cherokee Indians, and Irish plantation owners. His mother, Helen Burns, worked as a domestic and a cosmetologist; his father, who lived next door to his mother, was Noah Louis Robinson, a cotton grader who was married to another woman. Two years after Jesse was born, his mother married Charles H. Jackson, who adopted Jesse in 1957. In his later life, after he learned the circumstances of his birth, Jackson loved both Noah and Charles and claimed both as his fathers.

Youth and Education

Jackson grew up and attended public schools in Greenville, South Carolina, graduating from Sterling High School in 1959. He played baseball and basketball, but his greatest love among competitive sports was football; he became a star quarterback who led Sterling to a state football championship. Further, he found time to help his family financially. He worked part-time as a shoeshine boy, a golf caddy, a waiter, and a lumberyard hand. Active in his local Baptist church, he represented it at various Sunday-school conventions.

Because of his athletic ability, Jackson won a football scholarship to the University of Illinois; he hoped to become a star quarterback. Once he reached the campus, however, he was informed that all blacks on the team had to play line positions. After one unhappy year, he transferred to North Carolina Agricultural and Technical (A&T) State College in Greensboro; there, he starred as a quarterback while excelling academically in sociology and economics.

Student Activism

The North Carolina A&T students elected Jackson student body president in 1963, the same year that he became active in the civil rights crusade. He helped to organize picket lines and sit-ins at segregated restaurants, theaters, and hotels. He began receiving statewide recognition when merchants in downtown Greensboro began to integrate. Soon after he graduated in 1964, he joined the staff of North Carolina governor Terry Sanford. Jackson's major tasks included organizing and leading political clubs for young Democrats. Jackson, however, soon returned to his studies after winning a scholarship to the Chicago Theological Seminary, which he attended for two and a half years while also working part-time for Martin Luther King, Jr.'s Southern Christian Leadership Conference (SCLC).

It was also in 1964 that Jackson started his family. He married Jacqueline Lavinia Brown, whom he had met at North Carolina A&T. Over the years, they became the parents of five children—Santita, Jesse, Jr., Jonathan Luthur, Yusef DuBois, and Jacqueline Lavinia.

SCLC Involvement

In 1966 Jackson left the seminary and went to work full-time for the SCLC after King named him head of the Chicago branch of Operation Breadbasket, a movement that used boycotts and pickets to secure more services and better jobs for African Americans. Dynamic in his new position, Jackson had his greatest success when he launched a sixteen-week campaign against the A&P grocery chain; as a result of the boycott, A&P executives signed an agreement obligating the chain to employ 268 more blacks, including more African American store managers and warehouse foremen. Jackson's success in Chicago prompted King in 1967 to appoint his young follower the national director of Operation Breadbasket.

The Civil Rights movement suffered a near deathblow when James Earl Ray assassinated King in Memphis on April 4, 1968. Although Jackson was considered as a possible successor to the dead leader, most members of the SCLC believed that he was too young; further, members knew that King had already indicated his own personal choice, his longtime assistant Ralph Abernathy. Although Jackson remained with the SCLC for almost four more years, he apparently became unhappy with Abernathy's leadership. The Poor People's Campaign and March on Washington led by Abernathy failed, and Abernathy never exhibited the charisma and foresight for which King had become known. Without King, the Civil Rights movement fragmented.

Operation PUSH

In December, 1971, Jackson established Operation PUSH (People United to Save Humanity), an economic and political movement. By 1976 he had built PUSH into a national organization. That year, aided by a Ford Foundation grant, Jesse began his PUSH-Excel campaign; he toured inner-city schools across the United States, speaking out against drug abuse, vandalism, truancy, high dropout rates, and TEENAGE PREGNANCY. Within three years, nine major cities, including Chicago, LOS ANGELES, and NEW ORLEANS, had joined the Ford Foundation in underwriting PUSH-Excel. Kansas City Central High School was the site of one notable success: Absenteeism in the school's thirteen-hundred-member student body declined from an average of five hundred to two hundred per day.

By 1979 Jackson had become an unofficial international diplomat for the United States. That year, President Jimmy Carter approved Jackson's trip to South Africa, where he spoke to huge crowds, stressed black pride, and condemned apartheid. Next, he toured the Middle East, visiting Egypt, Syria, Israel, the West Bank, and Lebanon. In his speeches, he lobbied the United States and Israel, urging those countries to negotiate with the Palestine Liberation Organization (PLO). He came under criticism in both countries, however, when he embraced PLO leader Yasir Arafat and when he accepted money from the Arab League for Operation PUSH. Nevertheless, in the coming decades, Jackson continued his international travels, often going to crisis spots and pleading for peace and sanity. He intervened more than once to secure the release of hostages held by terrorists.

The 1984 Presidential Campaign

By early 1983, the liberal, reform-minded Jackson had had enough of the archconservatism of the Ronald Reagan era. Jackson decided to run for the presidency, hoping, at a minimum, to push the DEMOCRATIC PARTY to the left. In the fall, he took a leave of absence from PUSH, barnstormed the country, mounted a voter-registration drive, and again toured Europe, where he spoke to African American soldiers, discussed world hunger and disarmament, and reestablished himself as an international leader worried about worldwide problems. Back in the United States, in November, 1983, he announced his candidacy, promising to represent "poor and dispossessed" America. He wanted, he said, to create

Jesse Jackson (left) with Reagan administration attorney general William Smith during the early 1980's. *(AP/Wide World Photos)*

a "rainbow coalition" of all people who were "rejected . . . and despised." The phrase Rainbow Coalition was adopted by Jackson's campaign as a broad description of his supporters.

In his quest, Jackson had many natural assets. Standing six feet two inches tall, he was handsome in addition to being a spellbinding orator. Equally important, he showed great intellect and had strong analytical abilities. Nevertheless, Jackson's candidacy in 1984 did not fare well. First, many key African American leaders, including Andrew Young of Atlanta, Tom Bradley of Los Angeles, and Julian Bond of Georgia, endorsed Walter Mondale and refused to support Jackson because they feared that division in the Democratic Party would ensure Reagan's reelection. Further, Jackson had practically no budget and therefore could not advertise in mass media; instead, he tried to reach voters mainly through personal appearances. Many newsmen considered Jackson the most exciting candidate in an otherwise dull campaign and featured him prominently, but such coverage could not compete with the huge media budgets of the other candidates.

During the campaign, Jackson also made political blunders. In February, 1984, an African American newsman, Milton Coleman, reported that Jesse had anti-Semitic leanings and that he had referred to Jews as "Hymies" and to New York City as "Hymietown." Next, a major supporter of Jackson, Louis Farrakhan, the leader of the Nation of Islam, was perceived as having threatened the life of Coleman; Farrakhan also called Hitler a "great man" even if a wicked one. Later, Farrakhan called Judaism a "gutter" religion. Although Jackson eventually distanced himself from Farrakhan, his image suffered.

Jackson regained his momentum with a strong showing in five Democratic primaries (the "super Tuesday" primaries); he added to it when the New York primary was held. He had other strong showings, but it became increasingly clear that Mondale was emerging as the Democratic nominee. In part, the political system itself hindered Jackson's chances. As he pointed out later, he received 21 percent of the popular vote in the primaries, but at the nominating convention he had only 11 percent of the delegates. Nevertheless, Jackson proved a good loser; he endorsed Mondale and gave the convention a rousing speech.

The 1988 Presidential Campaign

From 1984 to 1988, Jackson continued his one-man freedom campaign nationally and internationally. Among other places, his tours took him back to the Middle East, to Africa, and to Western Europe. In 1988 he again campaigned for the Democratic presidential nomination. Indeed, he was the most significant opponent of the eventual nominee, Michael Dukakis; Jackson's presence in the Democratic field pushed other candidates toward more liberal reformist goals. Jackson accrued enough votes and delegates (twelve hundred) to go to the Democratic Convention as a force to be reckoned with. He used his leverage to demand changes to the party platform and a commitment to broadening the party's agenda. He also helped secure high-echelon positions in the party bureaucracy for African Americans, including the party chairmanship awarded to his campaign aide Ron Brown.

Activism in the 1990's

In 1990 Jackson was elected "shadow senator" of Washington, D.C., serving until 1996. Created by a 1980 ballot initiative, the position carries no budget, salary, floor privileges in Congress, or authority, but it afforded Jackson a forum to lobby for the federal district's statehood. The position also advanced his ability and his desire to remain in the political spotlight.

Bill Clinton's victory in the 1992 presidential campaign owed much to the endorsement

In January, 1999, Jesse Jackson (left) and Boeing chairman Phil Conduit announced they had reached a settlement in the class-action employment-discrimination suits brought against the giant aircraft manufacturer. *(AP/Wide World Photos)*

of Jackson, who helped generate support for Clinton among African American voters. Initially, however, relations between Clinton and Jackson were somewhat strained. At the national Rainbow Coalition leadership summit held in June of 1992, Clinton attacked certain comments made by rapper Sister SOULJAH regarding race relations. Observers saw Clinton's speech as part of an effort to demonstrate his independence from Jackson. Angered by the boldness and unexpectedness of the perceived affront, Jackson delayed his endorsement of Clinton and triggered rumors that he might announce his own candidacy. After weeks of speculation, Jackson announced that he would not enter the campaign, citing financial hardship and family stress. He eventually threw his support behind the Democratic ticket of Bill Clinton and Al Gore.

Jackson's activities generated headlines and controversy throughout the 1990's. He continued to serve as leader of the National Rainbow Coalition and to act as a roving ambassador, troubleshooter, and advocate for the poor and the dispossessed. He also wrote a weekly newspaper column. Beginning in 1992, he served as host of the political talk show *Both Sides with Jesse Jackson*, broadcast on CNN television. In 1996, on the eve of the Academy Awards ceremony, he protested racism in the film industry, noting that there was only one African American Oscar nominee that year.

That same year he also called for boycotts of corporations that practiced discrimination, notably Texaco and Mitsubishi; Texaco subsequently settled a discrimination suit for $176 million, and the Mitsubishi boycott ended in January, 1997, when the company announced plans to combat sexual and racial harassment aggressively. In 1997 Jackson established a project based in New York City to monitor and issue reports on corporate hiring and personnel practices regarding minorities and women. In early 1999 he helped prod Seattle aircraft manufacturer Boeing into reaching a $15 million class-action discrimination settlement.

In the mid-1990's Jackson devoted much of his time to the battle to keep AFFIRMATIVE ACTION programs in place. In 1995 he fought, unsuccessfully, to keep the University of California from banning affirmative action programs on its campuses. Soon another issue arose in CALIFORNIA: A statewide initiative banning affirmative action by the state government, Proposition 209, was put on the ballot in 1996. Voters passed the initiative despite the efforts of Jackson and many others. When it went into effect in 1997, Jackson led a protest march across the Golden Gate Bridge. (Opponents of Proposition 209 appealed to the U.S. SUPREME COURT, which refused to hear the case in November, 1997.)

Jackson announced in early 1999 that he would not run for the presidency in 2000. Little more than a month later, he made headlines when he met with Yugoslavian president Slobodan Milosevic.

Despite his accomplishments as a politician and activist, Jackson found his leadership role in the 1990's somewhat limited by certain liabilities. In view of his ties with Nation of Is/ *lam leader Louis Farrakhan, Jackson had difficulty in refuting charges that he shared or tolerated Farrakhan's anti-Semitic views. Also, unlike other black politicians who have advanced to the national stage after holding political office at the local level, Jackson appeared to have little interest in such endeavors. He sidestepped the opportunity to run for mayor of Chicago after the death of Harold WASHINGTON in 1987 and did not campaign for the post of mayor of Washington, D.C., after mayor Marion BARRY was convicted on drug charges in 1990. Nevertheless, Jackson continued to exhibit political prescience in his willingness to confront difficult issues. He was among the first to identify the problem posed by the flight of American jobs overseas, to address the critical issue of ACQUIRED IMMUNODEFICIENCY SYNDROME (AIDS) in the black community, and to confront the explosive issue of black-on-black crime.

—James Smallwood

—Updated by Shirley G. Kennedy

See also: Black-on-black violence; Clinton administration; Politics and government.

Suggested Readings:

Branch, Taylor. *Parting the Waters: America in The King Years, 1954-1963*. New York: Simon & Schuster, 1988.

________. *Pillar of Fire: America in the King Years, 1963-1965*. New York: Simon & Schuster, 1998.

Frady, Marshall. *Jesse: The Life and Pilgrimage of Jesse Jackson*. New York: Random House, 1996.

Garrow, David J., ed. *We Shall Overcome: The Civil Rights Movement in the United States in the 1950's and 1960's*. 3 vols. New York: Carlson, 1989.

Gibbons, Arnold. *Race, Politics and the White Media: The Jesse Jackson Campaigns*. Lanham, Md.: University Press of America, 1993.

Henry, Charles P. *Jesse Jackson: The Search for Common Ground*. Oakland, Calif.: Black Scholar Press, 1991.

Jackson, Jesse, and Elaine Landau. *Blacks in America: A Fight for Freedom*. New York: Julian Messner, 1973.

Kimball, Penn. *Keep Hope Alive!: Super Tuesday and Jesse Jackson's 1988 Campaign for the Presidency*. Washington, D.C.: Joint Center for Political and Economic Studies, 1992.

Powledge, Fred. *Free At Last? The Civil Rights Movement and the People Who Made It.* Boston: Little, Brown, 1991.

Stanford, Karin L. *Beyond the Boundaries: Reverend Jesse Jackson in International Affairs.* Albany: State University of New York Press, 1997.

Jackson, Jesse, Jr. (b. March 11, 1965, Greenville, South Carolina): Attorney, activist, and Illinois politician. The eldest son of the famous Jesse Jackson, Jesse Jackson, Jr., inherited a taste for politics. After attending St. Albans prep school in Washington, D.C., he graduated magna cum laude from North Carolina A&T University before earning his master's degree in divinity from the Chicago Theological Seminary and a law degree from the University of Illinois.

Known to friends and family as "Junior," the younger Jackson demonstrated his own commitment to activism by spending his twenty-first birthday in a Washington, D.C., jail after being arrested during an antiapartheid protest. Described as more soft-spoken and methodical than his visionary and charismatic father, Jackson was appointed to serve as national field director for the Rainbow Coalition in 1993; he also served as secretary of the black caucus of the Democratic Party National Committee.

Congressman Jesse Jackson, Jr., in early 1996. *(AP/Wide World Photos)*

After Illinois congressman Mel Reynolds resigned in August of 1995 in the wake of his conviction on sexual misconduct charges, Jackson announced his intention to campaign in the Democratic primary to fill Reynolds's unexpired term. Although he was reared in Chicago, Jackson did not establish residency in the district until 1995 and was considered by some observers to be a political upstart riding on the strength of his father's political influence. After a tough campaign in which he appealed for support among previously unregistered young voters, the younger Jackson won the Democratic primary and went on to secure a landslide victory in the special congressional election held on December 12.

Jackson, Joseph Harrison (September 11, 1900, Rudyard, Mississippi—August 18, 1990): Religious leader. Jackson served as president of the National Baptist Convention from 1953 to 1982. He received his B.A. and honorary Doctor of Divinity degrees from Jackson College in Mississippi, his Bachelor of Divinity from Colgate-Rochester Divinity School in 1932, and an M.A. from Creighton University in 1933. He pastored Baptist churches in Mississippi, Nebraska, and Philadelphia, Pennsylvania, before being called to the historic Olivet Baptist Church in Chicago in 1941. Jackson served on the foreign mission board and was a member of the executive committee of the Baptist World Alliance (London). As president of the National Baptist

Convention, he inaugurated land-use programs in Liberia and financed Baptist missions in Africa. His missionary concerns are reflected in his book *A Voyage to West Africa and Some Reflections on Modern Missions* (1936).

Jackson is best known for his conservative political and social views and for his disagreements with Martin Luther KING, Jr. These disagreements concerned means rather than ends. He did not oppose CIVIL RIGHTS for African Americans, but he did oppose the practice of civil disobedience. He suggested that African Americans should use the courts to obtain their goals. Jackson was one of the instigators of a schism that resulted in the formation of the Progressive Baptists in 1961. Among his books are *The Eternal Flame: The Story of a Preaching Mission in Russia* (1956), *Many but One: The Ecumenics of Charity* (1964), and his influential *A Story of Christian Activism: The History of the National Baptist Convention, U.S.A., Inc.* (1980).

Gospel singer Mahalia Jackson performing at the Imperial Palace in Tokyo, Japan, in 1971. *(AP/Wide World Photos)*

Jackson, Mahalia (October 26, 1911, New Orleans, Louisiana—January 27, 1972, Evergreen Park, Illinois): GOSPEL MUSIC singer. Popularly known as the Queen of Gospel Song, Jackson was the daughter of a preacher who also worked as a barber and a stevedore. Although she admired BLUES singer Bessie SMITH, Jackson's deeply religious parents would permit nothing but religious music in their home. When Jackson was four, her mother died. Jackson sang in her father's church choir until age sixteen, when she moved to CHICAGO to live with her aunt. As a member of the Greater Salem Baptist Church in Chicago, Jackson became the lead singer in the choir. She saved enough money working as a hotel maid to open her own beauty shop. At an early age, however, she had vowed to God that she would devote her life to a ministry of song.

Her professional career began to take root during her seven-year tenure as a member of the Johnson Singers, a gospel quintet. She recorded her first song in 1934, "God Gonna Separate the Wheat from the Tares." Striking out on her own in 1941 as a soloist, Jackson recorded her first hit record in 1945, "Move on Up a Little Higher." It sold eight million copies and made her famous in Europe and America. Moving onto the tour circuit, she held concerts throughout the United States and in Europe. She recorded a number of other hit songs, among which were "Upper Room," "Even Me," and "Silent Night," and hit albums such as *Bless This House* and *Sweet Little Jesus Boy*.

Jackson started a radio show on CBS in 1954, becoming the first gospel singer to be so featured. She was prominent in the CIVIL RIGHTS movement of the 1960's, inspiring many with her song "We Shall Overcome." She was featured in films, including *Imitation of Life* (1959) and *The Best Man* (1964). Books written about Jackson include an autobiography, *Movin' on*

Up (1966), written with Evan McLeod Wylie; *Mahalia Jackson Cooks Soul* (1970); and *Just Mahalia, Baby* (1975) by Laurraine Goreau.

Jackson, Maynard, Jr. (b. March 23, 1938, Dallas, Texas): GEORGIA politician. Maynard Holbrook Jackson, Jr., was the first African American MAYOR of ATLANTA, GEORGIA. His 1973 election made him the first black mayor of any major southeastern city in the United States. He received the B.A. degree in 1956 from Morehouse College and the LL.D. degree with honors in 1964 from the North Carolina Central University School of Law. He was the youngest person to become mayor of Atlanta as well as the youngest mayor of a major American city.

Jackson was admitted to the Georgia bar in 1965. He worked as an attorney for a legal services center from 1967 to 1969 and founded a law partnership in 1970. In 1969 he was elected vice mayor of Atlanta. He ran for the office of U.S. senator from Georgia in 1968 against longtime incumbent Herman Talmadge and gained national attention by losing by only a small margin. His successful campaign for mayor in 1973 represented a new political empowerment for African Americans in the South's primary business and economic urban area. Jackson was the transitional figure between dominance of moderate white political leadership and the newer era of black power in Atlanta's political institutions.

Jackson served two consecutive four-year terms as mayor. He practiced law for eight years and was reelected to the mayor's position in 1989. His substantial win, with 79 percent of the votes, was significant partly because Atlanta's population was only 67 percent African American. Although the white business establishment had been critical of Jackson's commitments to minority business programs during his first terms, he was characterized as cooperative by both white corporate executives and by black civic leaders in the term beginning in 1990. He successfully continued and extended the previous political alliances between the corporate and African American communities.

Jackson's political goals centered on making urban government responsive to the citizenry. He considered the citizen/customer as the top priority, as would progressive businesses. He emphasized citizen safety, health, and employment opportunity, issues that appealed to a broad spectrum of the population. He was particularly committed to improving city departments' response time to individual and group needs and complaints. His administrative style was marked by compassionate but businesslike management.

Jackson, Michael (b. August 29, 1958, Gary, Indiana): Singer, songwriter, and dancer. As the self-proclaimed King of Pop, Michael Joseph Jackson adopted a wide variety of musical styles that ranged from bouncy MOTOWN dance tracks and lush ballads to the funk-style rhythms of the New Jack Swing of the 1990's. As a solo performer he combined a highly energetic dancing style with an enigmatic and sexually ambiguous stage persona. Jackson also insisted on controlling all aspects of his performing career.

Michael Jackson was born in Gary, Indiana, a predominantly African American industrial city. His father, Joe, had earlier played in a BLUES group but had left the MUSIC business to provide for his nine children. At the age of five, the diminutive and irresistibly cute Michael was chosen to front the Jackson 5, the family band that included his older brothers Jackie, Jermaine, Tito, and Marlon. They had started out singing Ray CHARLES tunes around the house after school, but soon they were working clubs, Michael performing dances inspired by African American superstars James BROWN and Sammy DAVIS, Jr.

Michael Jackson (center) performing with the Jackson 5 on *The Sonny and Cher Comedy Hour* in 1972. *(AP/Wide World Photos)*

Jackson 5 Success

The Jackson 5 and Diana Ross and the SUPREMES both performed at a 1968 benefit concert for Muigwithania, a local black pride organization headed by Richard HATCHER, who was then campaigning to be Gary's first African American mayor. Ross was so impressed by the Jackson 5's performance that she had Berry GORDY, Jr., sign them to his African American record label Motown.

The group's rowdy "I Want You Back" (1969) was described by rock critic Dave Marsh as "the greatest debut single of any act since the fifties" and "certainly the greatest record ever made by a singer who had yet to reach puberty" (Michael was eleven at the time of the record's release). The next two singles, "ABC" (basically a rewrite of the chorus of "I Want You Back") and "The Love You Save," also hit number one; thus, the Jackson 5 became the first rock group to have their first three singles reach the top of the charts. These songs were driven by exciting rhythm tracks, and Michael's vocals were charged with adolescent energy and honed to a fine edge by years of live performance. The fourth single, "I'll Be There," was a change of pace: a slow song. It also became their fourth number-one song and Motown's biggest-selling single up to that time.

The Jacksons and Early Solo Career

While still singing on hit songs for the Jackson 5, Michael released his first solo album, *Got to Be There* (1972), which yielded three top-ten songs, including the ballad title track and the lively "Rockin' Robin." He later topped the pop charts with the unlikely song "Ben," about a boy and his rat. In 1972 the Jackson 5 received commendations from the Senate and the House of Representatives for their "Contributions to American Youth" and the positive role models they provided for children of all races.

After more hit records, Michael and most of his brothers moved from Motown to Epic Records. Jermaine stayed behind for a solo career; Michael's younger brother Randy, who had toured with the Jackson troupe beginning in 1973, moved with his brothers to Epic. Because Motown claimed ownership of the trademark name "Jackson 5," the group was renamed "The Jacksons." Epic insisted that the Jacksons' first two albums, *The Jacksons* (1976) and *Goin' Places* (1977), be produced by the Philadelphia hit-making team of Gamble and Huff. Compared with the Jacksons' earlier efforts, these albums were relative failures. Next, Michael tried his hand at acting, playing the Scarecrow in *The Wiz* (1978), a film version of the hit Broadway black musical based on *The Wizard of Oz* (1939). The film was unsuccessful, however, as was its sound track album.

The Jacksons recovered from these fiascoes with the release of the *Destiny* album (1978), which was the first album on which Epic Records allowed the brothers to write and produce their own material. The single "Shake Your Body (Down to the Ground)," written by Michael and Randy, sold more than two million copies. When an extended dance remix was made of this song (one of the first such remixes), conservative Epic executives had many reservations, but when it was released, it achieved immense popularity in dance clubs and on the radio.

Superstardom

In 1979 Michael Jackson established himself as a solo star with his album *Off the Wall*, produced by Quincy JONES. The album sold seven million copies and yielded two number-one songs, "Don't Stop 'Til You Get Enough" and "Rock with You," plus two additional top-ten songs, "She's out of My Life" and the title cut. "She's out of My Life" was a sad, lonely ballad featuring an emotional vocal performance.

The next Jacksons album, *Triumph* (1980), lived up to its name, and most of the victories with fans and critics belonged to Michael. After touring with his brothers, Michael began work with Quincy Jones on a new solo album, *Thriller* (1982). *Thriller* was a genuine phenomenon: Album sales soared, eventually passing the forty-million mark, after Jackson's appearance on the *Motown 25* television special on May 16, 1983. Wearing a glittering white sequined glove on his right hand and a black fedora, Jackson electrified the audience by BREAK DANCING to the insistent beat and pulsing bass of the song "Billie Jean."

Jackson was no longer the pint-sized leader of the Jackson 5, as most of the public remembered him; suddenly, he had become a rock icon of the 1980's. The video for "Billie Jean," featuring Jackson shadowed by a private detective who is not mentioned in the lyrics but who personifies the song's claustrophobic mood, broke the "color barrier" on cable music channel MTV. This all-music-video cable channel had shown videos by white artists almost exclusively. MTV programmed the *Thriller* videos only after a huge buildup of public demand and a boycott threat from Columbia Records. The thirteen-minute-long video for the song "Thriller," directed by John Landis, featured the voice of horror-film star Vincent Price, dancing zombies and ghouls, and Jackson himself turning into a werewolf.

Awards and Acclaim

The *Thriller* album yielded an unstoppable onslaught of top-ten singles, including not only the number-one songs "Billie Jean" and "Beat It" (which combined the dance-funk genre with the heavy-metal guitar of Eddie Van Halen) but also "The Girl Is Mine," a duet with Paul McCartney, "Wanna Be Startin' Somethin'," "P.Y.T. (Pretty Young Thing)," and "Human Nature." In 1983 *Cash Box* magazine lavished Jackson with awards for being the top male artist, top male singles artist, top black male artist, and top black male singles artist and for having the top pop single ("Billie Jean"), top pop album (*Thriller*), top black single ("Billie Jean"), and top black album (*Thriller*).

Next, Jackson reluctantly went with his brothers on the "Victory Tour," which began in Kansas City on July 6, 1984. Fans in sold-out arenas and coliseums paid thirty dollars for tickets but saw only a ninety-minute show that featured disappointingly little of Jackson's solo work.

Late in 1985, Jackson and Lionel Richie cowrote "We Are the World" as part of a benefit project directed toward famine relief in Ethiopia. The project was undertaken in emulation of an effort by a group known as Band Aid that had made the successful benefit recording "Do They Know It's Christmas?" on which a number of primarily British musicians sang. "We Are the World," which was released under the umbrella name U.S.A. for Africa, featured a multiracial cast that included African American music legends Ray Charles, Stevie Wonder, Smokey Robinson, and Dionne Warwick along with newer stars James Ingram, Lionel Richie, and Jackson himself.

More Successful Albums

Jackson's next album was *Bad* (1987), which sold 25 million copies worldwide and spawned a record five number-one songs. After the *Bad* tour, during which Jackson sang and danced before 4.4 million people in fifteen countries, Jackson announced that he was forsaking life on the road. He did not intend to tour again, but instead planned to continue expanding into videos and film. In 1988 he released his ninety-four-minute *Moonwalker* video, a montage of various songs and dances, highlighted by the spooky "Smooth Criminal."

In March, 1991, Jackson announced a deal with Sony, which owned Columbia Pictures, that would allow him to make feature-length films, theatrical shorts, and television programs, in addition to six new albums on a new label, Nation Records. This deal, which involved close to one billion dollars, was the biggest in music history at the time. Later that year, Jackson released his next album, *Dangerous* (1991), which debuted at number one and was preceded by the music video for the song "Black or White." Although the song carried a message of racial harmony, the original version of the video drew heavy criticism for scenes showing Jackson smashing a car.

Michael Jackson performing in Southern California in 1988. *(AP/Wide World Photos)*

The release of *Dangerous* prompted Jackson to launch a spectacular world tour to support sales of the record. In 1992 he continued his commitment to charitable causes by establishing the Heal the World Foundation to promote greater awareness of child abuse and other issues related to children. Jackson performed during the spectacular halftime event at Super Bowl XXVII in January of 1993, garnered public sympathy for his eccentricities during an interview with Oprah WINFREY aired on prime-time television, and marked the debut of his new MJJ/Epic record label by releasing the sound track to the film *Free Willy* later in June. Also in 1993, he was given a Living Legend Grammy Award.

Controversy in the 1990's

Jackson's desire for privacy concerning his personal life was shattered in August of 1993, when tabloid headlines publicized allegations that he had molested a young boy who had visited Jackson at his Neverland estate north of Santa Barbara, CALIFORNIA. The LOS ANGELES Police Department and Santa Barbara law enforcement officials began an investigation into possible criminal charges at the same time that a civil suit was filed against Jackson by the family of the alleged thirteen-year-old victim. After collapsing during a concert in Singapore in November, Jackson canceled the remainder of his lucrative overseas *Dangerous* tour and released a statement claiming that he was suffering from an addiction to prescription painkillers. Disturbed by the wave of negative publicity, executives at Pepsi ended the company's ten-year endorsement deal with Jackson.

Hoping to avoid protracted public exposure of his private life, Jackson instructed his lawyers to reach a settlement with his teenage accuser in exchange for dropping the civil case. Although the exact terms of the January, 1994, agreement were never revealed, news stories reported that the settlement was in excess of $10 million. In August of that year, Jackson again made headlines when his publicist confirmed that Jackson had married Lisa Marie Presley, the twenty-six-year-old daughter of the late Elvis Presley. Jackson and his wife appeared on the MTV Music Awards in 1994 and collaborated on a few of the new songs included in Jackson's long-awaited greatest hits collection, *HIStory: Past, Present and Future, Book I*, a double album that was released in June of 1995.

The couple drew more attention for themselves that same month when they appeared together in an interview with journalist Diane Sawyer that was televised on the ABC newsmagazine *Prime Time Live*. Although the interview did little to clarify the details of Jackson's relationship with Presley, it did serve to publicize Jackson's new album, which had begun to draw criticism for the perceived anti-Semitism found in the lyrics to the single "They Don't Care About Us." Jackson issued an apology for the lyrics, saying that he had meant no harm, but some of his fans were disturbed by the anger and profanity found on the double album.

Jackson continued to be in the public eye. In December of 1995, he collapsed during a rehearsal for a concert slated to be aired on the HBO cable channel and was rushed to a NEW YORK CITY hospital. Diagnosed with severe dehydration brought on by a bout with the flu, Jackson remained hospitalized for five days. In February of 1996, Jackson angered officials in Brazil, who were unhappy over his decision to film a music video for "They Don't Care About Us" that depicted the plight of impoverished children living in the slums of Rio de Janeiro. Jackson did secure permission to film the video, which was directed by Spike LEE. Also in February, Lisa Marie Presley announced that she had filed for divorce after twenty months of marriage to Jackson, citing irreconcilable differences. Presley's announcement generated little surprise and fueled rumors that the couple's marriage had been part of a public relations campaign to defuse the intense criticism that had been directed at Jackson. The couple divorced in August.

In November, 1996, Jackson announced that he was going to be a father; the mother of the child was Debbie Rowe, a longtime friend and the assistant to a dermatologist who had been treating Jackson for about fifteen years. Jackson and Rowe married later that month, and their son, Prince, was born in February, 1997. A daughter, Paris, was born to Jackson and his wife in April, 1998. His second marriage proved to be short-lived. In October, 1999, Rowe filed for divorce.

In 1997 the Jackson 5 were inducted into the Rock and Roll Hall of Fame and Jackson released *Blood on the Dance Floor: HIStory in the Mix*. In December of 1998, the Recording Industry of America (RIAA) reported that Jackson's *Thriller* was the biggest-selling album of all time.

—*Frank Wu*
—*Updated by Wendy Sacket*

See also: Jackson, Janet.

Suggested Readings:

Andersen, Christopher P. *Michael Jackson: Unauthorized*. New York: Simon & Schuster, 1994.

Brown, Geoff. *Michael Jackson, Body and Soul: An Illustrated Biography*. New York: Beaufort Books, 1984.

Grant, Adrian. *Michael Jackson: The Visual Documentary*. New York: Omnibus Press, 1994.

Jackson, Michael. *Moonwalk*. New York: Doubleday, 1988.

Marsh, Dave. *Trapped: Michael Jackson and the Crossover Dream*. New York: Bantam Books, 1985.

Regan, Stewart. *Michael Jackson*. New York: Greenwich House, 1984.

Terry, Carol D. *Sequins and Shades: The Michael Jackson Reference Guide*. Ann Arbor, Mich.: Pierian Press, 1987.

Jackson, Samuel L. (b. December 21, 1948, Atlanta, Georgia): Actor. A graduate of Morehouse College, Jackson gained extensive stage experience, appearing with the Negro Ensemble Company and the New York Shakespeare Festival. Working with Lloyd Richards, Jackson starred in the Yale Repertory Theatre's premieres of August Wilson's *The Piano Lesson* (1987) and *Two Trains Running* (1990). Jackson's commitment to the theater eventually led him to help found the Atlanta-based Just Us Theatre Company.

Jackson was cast in film director Spike Lee's *School Daze* (1988). Lee was impressed with Jackson's talent and began working closely with him on subsequent film projects. Jackson's roles in *Do the Right Thing* (1989), *Mo' Better Blues* (1990), and *Jungle Fever* (1991) brought him to the attention of Hollywood directors. The jury of the Cannes Film Festival was so impressed by Jackson's work in *Jungle Fever* that they created a best supporting actor award to recognize his contribution to the film.

Although some critics were less impressed with Jackson's small supporting role in the blockbuster film *Jurassic Park* (1993), dismissing it as journeyman work, Jackson provided a welcome voice of calm rationality and conscience in his part as a computer control room administrator trying to cope with the potentially dangerous whims of a wealthy theme park entrepreneur.

Jackson's ability to endow even minor roles with an individual persona was important to his success as an actor in comedies such as *National Lampoon's Loaded Weapon I* (1993) as well as gritty dramas such as *Fresh* (1994). His role as a hit man in screenwriter-director Quentin Tarentino's *Pulp Fiction* (1994) provided Jackson a wider scope for his talent. Jackson's teaming with John Travolta heightened the film's dramatic impact and underscored the script's peculiar sense of humor—as when Jackson's character recites a passage from the

Samuel L. Jackson (right) with Bruce Willis, with whom he made *Die Hard with a Vengeance* in 1995. *(AP/Wide World Photos)*

Bible's book of Ecclesiastes before killing his victims.

In a role that ran counter to the usual pairing of male characters in action-adventure films, Jackson served as an unwilling savior in *Die Hard: With a Vengeance* (1995), helping Bruce Willis's character survive on the streets of HARLEM while protesting the crazed car chases and other outrageous tactics Willis's character engages in to stop a mad bomber. Jackson remained busy and in demand through the 1990's, appearing in *Jackie Brown* (1997) with Pam GRIER, *Out of Sight* (1998), *The Negotiator* (1998), *Star Wars Episode One: The Phantom Menace* (1999), and *Deep Blue Sea* (1999).
See also: Lee, Spike; Wilson, August.

Jackson, Shirley Ann (b. August 5, 1946, Washington, D.C.): PHYSICIST and political appointee. The daughter of Beatrice and George Jackson, Shirley Jackson attended Roosevelt High School in WASHINGTON, D.C., where she graduated as valedictorian in 1964. After high school, she attended the Massachusetts Institute of Technology (MIT), where she earned a bachelor of science degree in physics in 1968. Upon completing her undergraduate degree, Jackson began work on a doctoral degree in physics. Directed by James Young, the first tenured African American physics professor at MIT, Jackson's research focused on theoretical elementary particle physics. When Jackson completed her doctoral studies in 1973, she became the first black woman to receive a Ph.D. at MIT.

As a student and as an alumnae, Jackson's activism helped increase the number of black graduate students, many of whom went on to finish doctoral degrees. Jackson continues her support as a member of the board of trustees at MIT. She also served as a vice president of the MIT Alumni Association and helped with three other MIT visiting committees.

Upon receiving her Ph.D., Jackson took a job at the Fermi National Accelerator Laboratory in Illinois, working as a resident associate theoretical physicist between 1973 and 1976. From 1974 to 1975, Jackson also took a position as a visiting science associate at the European Organization for Nuclear Research (CERN) in Geneva, Switzerland, where she worked on theories pertaining to strongly interacting elementary particles. In 1976 Jackson began work at AT&T Bell Laboratories in Murray Hill, New Jersey. Her research there involved topics based on theoretical material sciences, her specialty being solid or condensed state physics.

Jackson received many scholarships, fellowships, and awards, including an award from the Ford Foundation for Advanced Study Fellowship (1971-1973) and a Martin Marietta Corp. Fellowship (1972-1973). In

Physicist Shirley Ann Jackson in 1997. *(U.S. Nuclear Regulatory Commission)*

1985 Jackson was selected as "Woman of the Year" by the Lenape Professional and Business Women; in November of 1986, she was named a fellow of the American Physical Society. In 1981 Jackson was featured in the "exceptional black scientists" poster series sponsored by CIBA-GEIGY, a pharmaceutical company. In recognition of her scientific expertise, President Bill Clinton appointed her to serve as chair of the Nuclear Regulatory Commission in 1995.

Jackson also became an active member of a number of organizations, including the Iota chapter of Delta Sigma Theta sorority (she served as its president for a time), Sigma Xi (an academic honor society), the American Physical Society, the American Association for the Advancement of Science, and the National Society of Black Physicists. She was elected to serve as the president of the National Society of Black Physicists in 1980-1982.

Jacob, John Edward (b. December 16, 1934, Trout, Louisiana): CIVIL RIGHTS activist and president of the NATIONAL URBAN LEAGUE. Jacob grew up in HOUSTON, TEXAS. After receiving his undergraduate and master's degrees from HOWARD UNIVERSITY, he became a social worker for the Department of Public Welfare in BALTIMORE, MARYLAND, in the early 1960's. Jacob began his career with the National Urban League in 1965 as director of education and youth incentives at the WASHINGTON, D.C., Urban League. Recognized for his commitment and administrative skills, he rose through the ranks of the civil rights organization, serving as acting executive director and president of the Washington, D.C., chapter and as executive director of the San Diego Urban League. In 1979 he became executive vice president of the national office of the Urban League. In 1982 he succeeded Vernon JORDAN, Jr., as the organization's president and remained in that post until 1994.

Under Jacob's leadership in the 1980's, the league concentrated on four priority issues: pregnancy among African American teenagers, poor households headed by single women, crime in the black community, and voter education and registration. Jacob repeatedly spoke out against the Reagan administration's budget cuts. In 1982 he launched the league's TEENAGE PREGNANCY prevention program, and in 1985, he promoted the "Male Responsibility Campaign" for responsible sexual behavior among black teenage boys. Jacob also headed a national EDUCATION program designed to raise student test scores through tutoring, counseling, and mentoring.

In the face of what he termed "the new reality of racial hostility," Jacob called for sweeping urban renewal and a global outlook for the 1990's. He advocated a "Marshall Plan for America," a proposal for injecting money into inner cities to reinvigorate the economy, provide jobs and training, and make the United States more globally competitive. He also urged African Americans to unite with other ethnic groups in political activism.

As an effective civil rights leader, Jacob helped African Americans become better employed, better educated, and better positioned in the American economy. His efforts contributed to the ongoing strength of the National Urban League, which survived long after similar civil rights groups dissolved. In 1989 Jacob was recipient of the United Way of America's National Professional Leadership Award. In addition to his work with the National Urban League, Jacob served on the board of trustees of Howard University as chairman and was also on the boards of several nonprofit organizations that promoted economic development and African American leadership.

Jamaica and Jamaican Americans: Caribbean island located 100 miles south of CUBA. The island's population of 2.5 million is approximately 90 percent African and African European. Through much of the twentieth century, Jamaicans have immigrated to North America in search of economic opportunity. By the late 1990's more than 500,000 people of Jamaican origin were living in the United States and Canada.

Jamaican History

Jamaica has a long and conflict-filled history. Spanish conquistadores decimated the native Arawaks in the early 1500's through the introduction of SLAVERY and epidemic diseases. The British navy wrested the largely depopulated island from Spain in 1655. As part of the British Empire, Jamaica soon became a center for the production of sugar cane based on African slave labor. By the early 1800's the slave population numbered over 300,000.

The island's African population established a long record of resistance to slavery that laid the foundations for the independent nation of Jamaica. Runaway slaves, known as MAROONS, found refuge in mountainous terrain. They established their own Maroon communities and waged a guerrilla struggle against British planters and colonial officials. In 1831 Samuel Sharpe, an educated domestic slave and lay minister, led a bloody uprising against slavery. Sharpe's revolt failed, but it added to the pressure for the abolition of slavery.

The colonial government abolished slavery in 1834, but many African Jamaicans nevertheless opposed British-dominated colonial rule. An anticolonial revolt, the 1865 Morant's Bay Rebellion, ended in brutal repression by

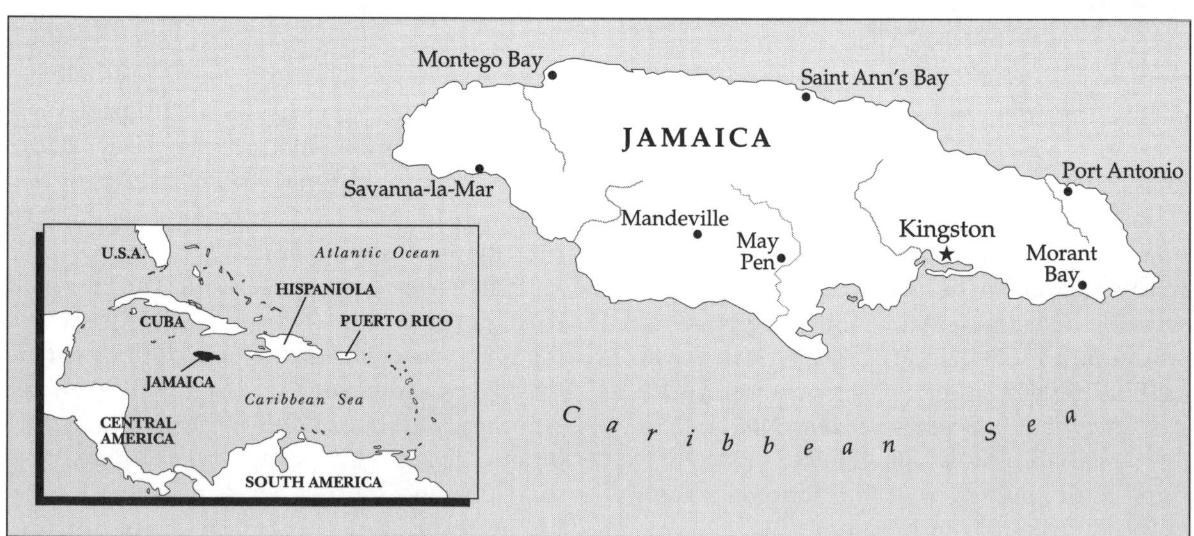

Jamaicans harvesting bananas around 1900; a century later, bananas were still a mainstay of the island economy. *(Library of Congress)*

Governor Edward Eyre. Eyre ordered the executions of nearly four hundred African Jamaicans. The London government removed Eyre from office and restructured the colonial administration, but Jamaica's African population still had no voice in the island's government. Seven decades later, the islandwide strike of 1938 led by Alexander Bustamante and Norman Manley pushed the colonial government to open the political system to Africans. Under the leadership of Bustamante and Manley, Jamaica gained its independence in 1962.

Modern Jamaica

With numerous hills and mountains, Jamaica's tropical landscape has much to offer the tourist, but these same characteristics pose challenges for the farmer and merchant. Jamaica's fragile economy is built on tourism, bauxite mining, and productive banana and coffee lands, but the island often faces high rates of inflation and unemployment. Jamaica has seen a shift from the predominantly socialist policies under Prime Minister Michael Manley (1975-1980) to more reliance on free enterprise in Manley's second government (1989-1992) and the administration of Prime Minister Percival Patterson, which began in 1992. Although Jamaican political campaigns are hard fought and sometimes violent, the island has a free and articulate press in which opponents debate issues such as the merits of socialism and free enterprise.

Religion and music have been important in Jamaican culture since the colonial era. Opponents of slavery such as Samuel Sharpe drew inspiration from Baptist and METHODIST teachings. The majority of Jamaicans are Protestants, while approximately one-third belong to Afro-Caribbean religious movements including the Rastafarians. Bob Marley, a RASTAFARIAN, gained an international audience for Jamaica's REGGAE music as an expression of African consciousness.

Jamaicans in North America

The movement of Jamaicans to North America began in significant numbers in the early twentieth century. By 1930 the United States had approximately 100,000 immigrants from the British Caribbean, most of whom were Jamaican. The second wave of immigration reached the United States and Canada in the 1960's. By 1990 435,000 documented (legal) immigrants from Jamaica lived in the United States, with many of them in the Northeast—especially NEW YORK CITY. Jamaicans also formed a large part of the 115,000 West Indians who settled in Canada in this period, mostly in the Toronto area.

Jamaican prime minister Norman Manley addressing a meeting of AfriCare. *(© Roy Lewis Archives)*

Jamaican Americans confront the same racial barriers that burden other African Americans in the United States and Canada. In addition, temporary residents must fend for themselves and earn money for their families back in Jamaica without the advantage of U.S. or Canadian citizenship. Jamaican immigrants struggle to find remunerative employment in large cities. Typical lower-income jobs include domestic service and menial work in the restaurant industry, but many Jamaicans have become successful merchants in large urban ethnic communities.

Some Jamaicans have attained success in the highly competitive environment of North America, while others have not been so fortunate. Marcus GARVEY, a Jamaican immigrant, attracted a large following among African Americans in the United States in the 1920's with his combination of BLACK NATIONALISM with business entrepreneurship. Hounded by intensive government investigations and charges of fraud, however, Garvey was deported back to Jamaica.

Other Jamaicans had more positive experiences. Harry BELAFONTE was born in New York City to a Jamaican mother; he grew up on the island, where he received his early schooling. Belafonte achieved fame in the New York theater and in films, and his live performances and recordings of calypso songs gave that Caribbean folk music international popularity in the 1950's and 1960's. Belafonte was also a CIVIL RIGHTS activist in these years. Two Jamaican Canadian athletes, Ben JOHNSON and Donovan Bailey, received acclaim in the 1980's and 1990's for their performances in Olympic track competition. Johnson's 1988 records were disallowed, however, when he was found guilty of steroid use; however, Bailey won the 100 meter dash in world-record time of 9.84 seconds at the 1996 Olympics in Atlanta.

Colin POWELL rose through the ranks of the U.S. Army to become chairman of the Joint Chiefs of Staff (1989-1993). The son of Jamaican immigrants in New York City, Powell in 1991 organized and supervised U.S. and allied forces in Operation Desert Storm (the Persian Gulf War), the offensive that expelled the occupying Iraqi army from Kuwait.

Jamaican Influence

Although a small island, Jamaica has had a comparatively large influence in the Caribbean and North America through the accomplishments of outstanding individuals in the popular arts, political and military affairs, and sports. The island nation continues to struggle for an improved standard of living for its people, but its shortcomings in economic development have contributed to the stream of immigrants to North America.

—*John A. Britton*

See also: Immigration and ethnic origins of African Americans; Immigration and ethnic origins of African Canadians; West Indian heritage; West Indies.

Suggested Readings:
Bakan, Abigail. *Ideological and Class Conflict in Jamaica*. Montreal: McGill-Queen's University Press, 1990.
Floyd, Barry. *Jamaica: An Island Microcosm*. New York: St. Martin's Press, 1979.
Foner, Nancy. *New Immigrants in New York*. New York: Columbia University Press, 1987.

James, Daniel "Chappie" (February 11, 1920, Pensacola, Florida—February 25, 1978, Colorado Springs, Colorado): MILITARY officer. The first African American to attain four-star general rank in the armed forces, James was appointed to command the North American Air Defense Command in 1975. Prior to this appointment, James had had a distinguished Air Force career, flying numerous combat missions in the Korean and Vietnam wars. Shortly after his retirement in 1978, James died of a heart attack.

A former Tuskegee Airman, Daniel James was the first African American to become a four-star general in the Air Force. *(U.S. Air Force)*

James, Etta (Jamesetta Hawkins; b. January 25, 1938, Los Angeles, California): Singer. James grew up singing in church choirs. She also spent time in San Bernardino, CALIFORNIA, with her great aunt. She played with the children next door, who had records of Lightnin' HOPKINS and Smokey Hoggs.

At the age of fifteen, James sang with the Peaches, a female group whose other members were older than her. She demanded an audition for the trio from Johnny Otis, an influential musician in the RHYTHM-AND-BLUES scene in Los ANGELES. In 1954 Otis recorded the Peaches with his band, a group of the most popular rhythm-and-blues musicians in the area. During the recording session, Richard Berry, impressed by James's singing, devoted much of the time to duets with James and Otis. "Roll with Me, Henry," a tune cowritten by James and Otis and later retitled "The Wallflower," came out of that session. It reached number two on the rhythm-and-blues charts in 1955.

James became part of an older crowd of well-respected musicians such as Berry, the Cadets, Johnny Watson, and the Flames. Many of her songs were written by Berry and backed by the Cadets. Her singles included "Good Rockin' Daddy," "I'm a Fool," and "Hey Henry," in the 1950's rock-and-roll style. "Strange Things Happening" echoed her gospel roots.

James developed a heroin addiction in the 1960's and cut back on her recording. When she returned to music in the mid-1970's, her style had matured and moved closer to her gospel roots as she dug deeper into a 1960's soul sound. Her later work is a fusion of gospel and rock and roll. James's voice is full and

Etta James in 1988. *(AP/Wide World Photos)*

passionate as well as highly controlled, and her singing sometimes transforms into a deep growling that rises into shouts. She did not have any major hit records after the 1960's, but she remained an active and popular concert performer through the 1990's. In 1994 James released an album of songs first made popular by one of her idols, Billie Holiday, *Mystery Lady: Songs of Billie Holiday*, for which she won a Grammy Award for Best Jazz Vocal Performance; in 1995 she released *Time After Time*. James was inducted into the Rock and Roll Hall of Fame in 1993.

See also: Gospel music and spirituals; Jazz; Soul music.

Jazz: Musical genre that incorporates improvisation, swing, phrasing, and articulation into single individual performances. Although improvisation is one of the salient features of jazz, its use alone does not make musicians jazz performers. In addition to improvisation, swing, phrasing, and articulation, jazz musicians must develop both individual sounds and approaches that will distinguish their styles from those of other performers of the same genre. Hence, true jazz musicians espouse diversity within continuity, a characteristic that separates jazz from music of the European tradition.

Origins

No single place or date of origin can be cited for jazz. It is logical, however, to assume that its origins back to the antebellum period, as improvisation, swing, phrasing, and articulation were staples of African American musical practice during this period. Jazz is a musical genre born and nurtured in African American culture, yet it is laden with transformed and reinterpreted African (particularly West African) musical concepts. Among the transformed and reinterpreted African concepts retained in jazz, especially the earlier styles, are

Legendary jazz musician Louis Armstrong during his youth.

the teaching of improvisation through an oral rather than written tradition, the use of call-and-response, the bending of tones to emphasize emotion and meaning, and the use of African performance techniques.

Although no reliable or valid evidence exists to prove the time and place of the origins of jazz, most jazz scholars agree that NEW ORLEANS, LOUISIANA, has always been an important center of jazz activity. In the history of jazz, New Orleans is interesting for myriad reasons. Remnants of African culture survived in the musical practices of Congo Square (a place where blacks gathered to play music) until the late nineteenth century, and the development of and support for early jazz was inextricably linked to the cultural activities of African Americans. Specifically, many early New Orleans jazz musicians were also members of brass bands, and these bands were hired to perform for both business advertisements and funeral processions. Early New Orleans jazz greats such as Louis ARMSTRONG, Buddy BOLDEN, William "Bunk" JOHNSON, and Edward "Kid" ORY are among the musicians who played in brass bands. Among the most famous brass bands were the Excelsior Brass Band (1880-1931), the Onward Brass Band (1885-1930), the Reliance Brass Band (1892-1918), and the Tuxedo Brass Band (1917-1925).

The opening of Storyville, a legal red-light district, was also important to the development of New Orleans jazz, because the area provided permanent employment for many musicians. The New Orleans style featured pianists such as Jelly Roll MORTON (whose repertoire consisted of BLUES, rags, and jazz tunes) with five- and seven-man groups. A five-man group commonly included cornet, clarinet, trombone, drums, and sousaphone, and a second cornet and either banjo or guitar were added to form a seven-man group. The cornet played the melody; the clarinet played obbligato parts and harmony above melody and occasionally doubled the melody. The

Pianist Jelly Roll Morton. *(National Archives)*

trombone would outline the harmony and play glissandi; the sousaphone would play "um-pah" parts, and the drums would play rhythm. The second cornet would play countermelodies while the banjo or guitar strummed chords. The horn players were known as the "front line" and were expected to improvise whenever necessary. Before the closing of Storyville in 1917, an exodus of New Orleans players to other cities, especially CHICAGO, had begun.

By 1922 Baby and Johnny DODDS, Johnny St. Cyr, Joe "King" OLIVER, and Kid Ory were performing in Chicago; this was also the year that Louis Armstrong accepted an invitation to join King Oliver in Chicago. With the influx of New Orleans players to Chicago, a debate ensued concerning whether there was a Chicago-style jazz or simply a New Orleans jazz in Chicago. Both styles existed.

The Chicago style was led by Bix Beiderbecke, the Austin High Gang, Bud Freeman, and Muggsy Spainer. The Chicago style espoused a 2/4 rhythmic feel, the use of tenor saxophone and guitar, and a smooth blending of ensemble and improvisational style. This was exemplified in the music of Beiderbecke. As a style, New Orleans jazz continued to advocate the same characteristics that it had featured in New Orleans, including the same role and function of the instruments, the use of a banjo and clarinet, and mostly flat-four rhythm.

Swing

Although both Chicago and New Orleans jazz styles continued to proliferate in the 1920's, a new style called "swing" also emerged. The origin of swing can be traced to a 1926 recording by Fletcher Henderson entitled "The Stampede." Henderson and Don REDMAN originated the musical formula of swing, which featured unison melodic lines played either by a section or the entire band, often backed by call-and-response patterns, as well as excellent soloists. By the time Benny Goodman was crowned King of Swing in 1935, Henderson had become his chief arranger. Even though Goodman credited Henderson, the general public never accepted either Henderson or Redman as a "King of Swing." After Henderson sold Goodman more than thirty compositions for his 1935 band, other white bands began to hire African American arranger/composers. Tommy and Jimmy Dorsey hired Sy Oliver, and Paul Whiteman hired Redman, to name two. It should be noted that although Benny Goodman was not the inventor of swing, he was an excellent musician and a humanitarian; he gave Billie HOLIDAY her first recording opportunity, and he was one of the first white band directors to hire African American musicians, including Charlie CHRISTIAN, Teddy WILSON, Mildred Bailey, Lionel HAMPTON, and Charlie Shavers. Several other swing bands were also popular in the 1930's, including those of Jimmie LUNCEFORD, Charlie Johnson, Luis Russell, and William "Chick" WEBB.

Count BASIE and Duke ELLINGTON were the most successful of the swing band musicians; their bands were active from the late 1920's and early 1930's until their deaths. (Basie died in 1984 and Ellington in 1974.) Basie spent many years in Kansas City before moving to NEW YORK CITY. He featured a blues-based style that espoused short motifs, shout brass choruses, dynamic contrast, swing writing, and outstanding soloists.

Count Basie in 1950. *(AP/Wide World Photos)*

Unlike Basie, Ellington advocated an eclectic style that encompassed everything from romantic ballads such as "Prelude to a

Kiss" and "Sophisticated Lady" to a book of compositions based on world music cultures, including "Caravan," "Liberian Suite," and "Latin American Suite." Ellington also composed a book of concert compositions, for example *Black, Brown, and Beige, Suite Thursday,* and *Reminiscing in Tempo,* a book of concertos written for his musicians. In addition, he composed a book of sacred concerts. Ellington composed the majority of compositions played by his band. One of the famous exceptions was "Take the A Train," Ellington's theme song, which was written by Billy STRAYHORN. (The band's first theme song was "East St. Louis Toodle-Oo.")

Bebop

Although swing bands enjoyed great popularity among the general public, some musicians became frustrated with the clichéd musical phrases and entertainment appeal of the music. A return to small groups and emphasis on improvisation and creativity became the hue and cry of musicians such as Dizzy GILLESPIE, Thelonious MONK, Charlie PARKER, and Max ROACH. The return to small-group jazz was in full force by the late 1930's, hastened by the experiments taking place at after-hours clubs such as MINTON'S PLAYHOUSE in HARLEM. The new style was called BEBOP (or simply "bop") and evolved amid the strong African American consciousness that had existed in Harlem since Marcus GARVEY's back-to-Africa movement.

Bebop was performed primarily by quartets, quintets, and sextets, which, in most cases, featured drums, piano, bass, alto or tenor saxophone, and trumpet; it was common to employ both alto and tenor saxophones in a sextet. Among the most salient musical features were disjunct melodies, compositions based on the contrafact (especially "I Got Rhythm," "What Is This Thing Called Love," and "Cherokee"), and use of high-hat cymbal, polyrhythms, and walking bass lines. In addition to Gillespie, Monk, Parker, and Roach, musicians such as Fats NAVARRO, Earl "Bud" Powell, and Charles MINGUS were also exponents of bebop.

After Parker's death in 1955, a move to continue and expand bebop evolved. In addition to emphasizing combos, the music also emphasized the aforementioned bebop concepts, along with pianists playing hornlike melodic lines, evenly articulated phrases, and the feeling of an accented fourth beat as a unifying device. Among the most important exponents of "hard bop" were Clifford Brown, Sonny Rollins, Richie Powell, and Billy Taylor. The hard-bop continuum led to "free jazz" in the late 1950's, with Ornette COLEMAN, John COLTRANE, and Cecil Taylor as its leading exponents. Both Coltrane and Taylor often featured tonal and atonal compositions or sections within a composition, with no predetermined melodies or harmonies. Some pieces were composed spontaneously. Coleman's music was predicated on a theory he called "harmolodics," which espoused the simultaneous sounding of a specific melody or theme. He also theorized that melodies or themes could be sounded simultaneously in different tonalities, that all notes were equally important, and that tonal centers were irrelevant.

Later Movements

"Third stream," a style inspired by Gunther Schuller, lies between jazz and classical music. It embodies elements of both and evolved in the 1950's with the Modern Jazz Quartet (featuring Connie Kay, John Lewis, Percy Heath, and Milt Jackson) as its foremost exponents. This style closely parallels "cool" jazz, a style that dates to Miles DAVIS's 1949 recording *Birth of the Cool* and that is based on soft dynamics, ballads, chamber-music groups, straight tone quality, and the use of French horns, oboes, and bassoons. In addition to Davis, other leading exponents of cool jazz have included Chet Baker, Dave Brubeck, and Stan Getz.

(continued on page 1360)

Notable Male Jazz Musicians

Adderley, Cannonball. *See main text entry.*

Adderley, Nat (Nov. 25, 1931, Tampa, Fla.—Jan. 2, 2000, Lakeland, Fla.). Trumpeter and cornetist. Nathaniel Adderley was the brother of Julian "Cannonball" ADDERLEY. He worked with his brother's group from 1955 to 1975, then led his own ensemble. He also performed with Lionel HAMPTON, J. J. Johnson, and Woody Herman. Among Adderley's well-known compositions are "Work Song," "Jive Samba," and "Shout Up a Morning." His recordings include *Work Song* (1960), *Hummin'* (1976), *On the Move* (1982), and *Mercy, Mercy, Mercy* (1995).

Albright, Gerald (b. Aug. 30, 1957, Los Angeles, Calif.). Saxophonist. Albright was influenced by Maceo Parker of the James Brown group. Albright worked with Cab CALLOWAY, Anita Baker, Les McCann, Marlena Shaw, Patrice Rushen, Janet JACKSON, and Rick James, as well as the TEMPTATIONS and Third World. His recordings include *Just Between Us* (1987), *Bermuda Nights* (1988), *Live at Birdland West* (1991), and *Live to Love* (1997).

Ammons, Albert. *See main text entry.*

Anderson, Cat. *See main text entry.*

Armstrong, Louis. *See main text entry.*

Baker, David (b. Dec. 21, 1931, Indianapolis, Ind.). Educator, musician, conductor, and composer. A Dizzy GILLESPIE Scholarship enabled Baker to attend the School of Jazz in Lenox, Massachusetts, in 1959. The author of many books and compositions of music, Baker also toured with Quincy JONES and performed with various orchestras. He headed the jazz program of the School of Music at Indiana University in Bloomington.

Barefield, Eddie (Dec. 12, 1909, Scandia, Iowa—Jan. 4, 1991, New York, N.Y.). Clarinetist and saxophonist. Edward Emmanuel Barefield performed on alto and tenor saxophones, as well as on clarinet. During the 1930's, he worked with Bighorn Young, Don REDMAN, Fletcher Henderson, and Cab Calloway. The 1940's included associations with legendary musical artists such as Benny CARTER, Ella FITZGERALD, and Duke ELLINGTON. Barefield also was active in films, including *The Swinging Kid* (1935), which starred Al Jolson, and *Every Day's a Holiday* (1937), with Louis ARMSTRONG. In 1968 Barefield worked on the film *The Night They Raided Minsky's*.

Basie, Count. *See main text entry.*

Bechet, Sidney. *See main text entry.*

Benson, George (b. Mar. 22, 1943, Pittsburgh, Pa.). Guitarist and singer. As a child, Benson was exposed to his stepfather's collection of Benny Goodman recordings, which featured innovative guitarist Charlie CHRISTIAN. During the 1960's and early 1970's, he recorded only instrumental jazz pieces. In 1976 he combined jazz vocals with guitar and produced the highly successful album *Breezin'*, receiving three Grammy Awards. With his brand of easygoing jazz fusion, Benson continued to be very popular, while at the same time criticized by jazz purists. He collaborated with such artists as Earl Klugh, James Moody, Patti Austin, and the Count BASIE Orchestra. Benson released *That's Right* in 1996 and *Masquerade Is Over* in 1999.

Blake, Eubie. *See main text entry.*

Blakey, Art. *See main text entry.*

Blythe, Arthur (b. July 5, 1940, Los Angeles, Calif.). Alto saxophonist and composer. Blythe studied saxophone with Kirtland Bradford and worked with Horace Tapscott, Chico Hamilton, Gil Evans, Jack DeJohnette, Julius Hemphill, and Lester Bowie. He performed in a variety of styles, including BEBOP and freer forms. In 1984 he formed a group known as the Leaders. His recordings include *The Grip* (1977), *In the Tradition* (1979), *Illusions* (1980), and *Night Song* (1997).

Bolden, Buddy. *See main text entry.*

Brown, Clifford "Brownie" (Oct. 30, 1930, Wilmington, Del.—June 26, 1956, Pennsylvania). Trumpeter. Brown began the study of music at age thirteen, in his high school band. At Delaware State College and Maryland State College, he began to earn a reputation as a formidable jazz musician. He learned and mastered the modern jazz idiom in college jazz bands and in brief excursions to Philadelphia, where he played with musicians such as Fats Navarro, Dizzy Gillespie, and Charlie PARKER. During the 1950's, he was one of the premier trumpeters; he achieved his greatest fame through his work with drummer Max ROACH in the Brown/Roach Quintet. He played with that group until he was killed in an automobile accident in 1956. The Brown/Roach Quintet had a profound and lasting influence on the development of bebop.

Brown, Marion (b. Sept. 8, 1935, Atlanta, Ga.). Alto saxophone player. Brown was influenced by and played with John COLTRANE, Archie Shepp, and Sun Ra while living in New York City from 1962 to 1967. With a bebop background, Brown reinterpreted jazz standards and created new forms through his own compositions. *Live in Japan* was released in 1999.

Brown, Oscar, Jr. (b. Oct. 10, 1926, Chicago, Ill.). Vocalist and songwriter. Brown performed mostly in nightclub and theater settings. His compositions include songs for *We Insist! Freedom Now Suite* (1960), a recording by Max Roach. Brown wrote lyrics for Nat Adderley and Miles DAVIS, among others. He also hosted a television program, *Jazz Scene USA* (1962). As a leader, he recorded *Sin and Soul* (1960) and appeared in the British production *Wham! Bam! Thank You Ma'am* (1963). He released *Then and Now* in 1995.

Brown, Ray (b. Oct. 13, 1926, Philadelphia, Pa.). Bassist. Brown's musical education began at age eight, when he took piano lessons and memorized the recordings of Fats WALLER. In his high school band, he took up the bass and came to be influenced by the playing of Jimmy Blanton. Brown moved to New York City in 1945, where his fame was to come through his participation in many of the early recording sessions of Dizzy Gillespie, Charlie Parker, and Bud Powell that established the foundation for the jazz revolution known as bebop. He went on to lead his own band, primarily backing his wife, singer Ella Fitzgerald. During the 1950's and early 1960's, Brown was a bassist with the Oscar PETERSON Trio.

AP/Wide World Photos

After the late 1960's, he worked as a freelance performer and producer. In 1999 he released *Christmas Songs with Ray Brown*.

Byas, Don. *See main text entry.*

Byrd, Donald (b. Dec. 9, 1932, Detroit, Mich.). Trumpet and flügelhorn player. Byrd earned a master's degree in music education from the Manhattan School of Music and a law degree from North Carolina Central University (1976). During the 1950's, he was associated with musicians such as Art BLAKEY, Max Roach, Sonny ROLLINS, Arthur Taylor, Lou Donaldson, George Wallington, Pepper Adams, and John Coltrane. In 1955 Byrd joined Art Blakey's Jazz Messengers. Byrd recorded on roughly sixty albums between 1955 and 1958. He later taught at Rutgers University, HAMPTON INSTITUTE, and HOWARD UNIVERSITY while continuing his recording career. From 1968 to 1972, Byrd was director of the Howard University Jazz Institute. He formed the commercially successful vocal group the Blackbyrds. During the 1990's, he taught at Queen's College in New York City.

Callender, Red (Mar. 6, 1918, Haynesville, Va.—Mar. 8, 1992, Saugus, Calif.). String bass and tuba player. Called "Red" because of his red hair, George Callender is known not only for his own great musical talent but also as the man who taught Charles MINGUS to play the bass. Callender showed a musical talent from a young age. He went on to work with such legendary artists as Louis Armstrong, Nat "King" COLE, Erroll GARNER, and Johnny Otis. Callender was one of the first black musicians to break the color barrier in Hollywood, performing in such films as *I Dood It!* (1943), *New Orleans* (1947, with Louis Armstrong), and *St. Louis Blues* (1958). His autobiography, *Unfinished Dream: The Musical World of Red Callender*, was published in 1985.

Calloway, Cab. *See main text entry.*

Carney, Harry (Apr. 1, 1910, Boston, Mass.—Oct. 8, 1974, New York, N.Y.). Baritone saxophonist. Howell "Harry" Carney was a member of the Duke Ellington Orchestra for more than forty years. He played clarinet as well as alto saxophone and was the preeminent jazz baritone saxophonist of his era. In 1926 he made his first recordings with Duke Ellington and His Kentucky Club Orchestra. In col-

(continued)

laboration with Ellington, he composed "Rockin' in Rhythm" (1931) and "Cotton Club Stomp" (1943). Carney also recorded with Benny Goodman, Lionel Hampton, and others. He can be heard as a leader on *Harry Carney with Strings* (1954) and on a 1980's compilation, *Harry Carney: Rare Dates Without the Duke, 1944/49* (1982).

Carter, Benny. *See main text entry.*

Carter, James (b. Jan. 3, 1969, Detroit, Mich.). Saxophonist and composer. Carter started playing the saxophone when he was eleven. In 1986 he played with Wynton MARSALIS. Carter also played with the Charles Mingus Big Band, the Lincoln Center Jazz Orchestra, and Julius Hemphill. Although the tenor saxophone is his primary instrument, he became adept at most reed instruments. Carter also is comfortable playing any jazz style, including DIXIELAND and free form. His recordings include *JC on the Set* (1993), *Jurassic Classics* (1994), and *In Carterian Fashion* (1998).

Carter, Ron. *See main text entry.*

Christian, Charlie. *See main text entry.*

Clarke, Stanley (b. June 31, 1951, Philadelphia, Pa.). Bassist. Performing on both acoustic and electric bass, Clarke worked with Horace Silver, Pharaoh Sanders, Art Blakey, Stan Getz, Dexter GORDON, and Joe Henderson. He was part of the Return to Forever group led by Chick Corea in the early 1970's. Beginning in 1977, Clarke led his own ensemble that produced a top twenty hit, "Sweet Baby" (1981), with George Duke. Recordings include *Children of Forever* (1972), *The Clarke/Duke Project II* (1983), *Rite of Strings* (1995), and *At the Movies* (1995).

Cole, Nat "King." *See main text entry.*

Coleman, Ornette. *See main text entry.*

Coltrane, John. *See main text entry.*

Daniels, Billy (William Boone; Sept. 12, 1915, Jacksonville, Fla.—Oct. 7, 1988, Los Angeles, Calif.). Vocalist. Daniels performed with Erskine Hawkins and Cab Calloway. He also appeared in the films *When You're Smiling* (1950) and *Rainbow Round My Shoulder* (1951) and in the black stage productions *Hello, Dolly!* (1975), *Golden Boy* (1964), and *Bubbling Brown Sugar* (1977). His recordings include *When You're Smiling* (1950), which contained his theme song, "That Old Black Magic," and *The Magic of Billy Daniels* (1978).

Daniels, Jimmy (c. 1908, Laredo, Tex.—June 29, 1984, New York, N.Y.). Singer. From 1939 to 1943, Daniels owned a HARLEM supper club which featured his own singing. After completion of military service in WORLD WAR II, he returned to club singing. In New York City clubs such as Bon Soir and Little Casino, and also in Paris, London, and Monaco, Daniels developed loyal followings for his interpretations of the works of Cole Porter, George and Ira Gershwin, and Richard Rodgers and Lorenz Hart.

Davis, Miles. *See main text entry.*

Dixon, Charlie (c. 1898, Jersey City, N.J.—Dec. 6, 1940, New York, N.Y.). Banjoist, arranger, and composer. Charles Edward Dixon grew up in New Jersey and played jazz in clubs in New York City and in Boston before becoming a regular performer with Sam Wooding at New York's Nest Club in 1922. He joined Fletcher Henderson's band in January of 1924. Dixon left Henderson's group in 1928 to lead a band that accompanied dancer Cora LaRedd. Although he no longer performed with Henderson, Dixon continued to arrange jazz charts for Henderson's band and arranged the piece "Harlem Congo" (1937) for Chick Webb.

Dodds, Johnny. *See main text entry.*

Durham, Eddie. *See main text entry.*

Eckstine, Billy. *See main text entry.*

Eldridge, Roy. *See main text entry.*

Ellington, Duke. *See main text entry.*

Ellington, Mercer (Mar. 11, 1919, Washington, D.C.—Feb. 8, 1996, Copenhagen, Denmark). Trumpet player, composer, and arranger; son of legendary jazz composer Duke Ellington. His first composition, "Pigeons and Peppers," was recorded by his father when Mercer was eighteen years old. He attended Columbia University and the Juilliard School of Music. In addition to leading his own band, he worked with such musicians as Dizzy Gillespie, Charles Mingus, and Carmen McRae. Upon Duke Ellington's death in 1974, Mercer took over as conductor of his father's orchestra. In the early 1980's, he conducted the Broadway musical *Sophisticated Ladies*, a showcase for Duke Ellington songs. The younger Ellington's compositions include "Things Ain't What They Used to Be," "Jumpin' Punkins" (written with his father), "Moon Mist," and "Blue Serge."

Europe, James Reese. *See main text entry.*

Farmer, Art (Aug. 21, 1928, Council Bluffs, Iowa—Oct. 4, 1999, New York, N. Y.). Trumpeter and flügelhornist. Farmer had gained a considerable reputation by the early 1950's. He joined such other musicians as trumpeter Clifford Brown, trombonist Jimmy Cleveland, and singer Annie Ross in a band led by vibraphonist Lionel Hampton. Farmer then formed a group with saxophonist Gigi Gryce. After performing with pianist Horace Silver and saxophonist Gerry Mulligan, in 1959 Farmer became coleader, with Benny Golson, of the Jazztet, which remained together until 1962. Farmer and Golson reconstituted the sextet in the 1980's. In the 1960's, Farmer began playing the flügelhorn almost exclusively. He quickly became the most proficient jazz flügelhorn player. Later in the 1960's, Farmer expatriated himself to Austria and became active in European music circles only occasionally returning to the United States. In the late 1980's, he recorded a series of albums for Contemporary Records.

Foster, George Murphy "Pops." *See main text entry.*

Gaillard, Bulee "Slim" (Jan. 1, 1916, Detroit, Mich.—Feb. 26, 1991, London, England). Singer, guitarist, and pianist. Gaillard was a popular performer as part of a duo, first with drummer Leroy "Slam" Stewart in the late 1930's and then with drummer Tiny Brown. He specialized in a kind of nonsense or scat singing and hit his peak with the creation of "Opera in Vout" in 1946. In 1989 the British Broadcasting Corporation (BBC) did a four-part series on his career.

Garner, Erroll Louis. *See main text entry.*

Gillespie, Dizzy. *See main text entry.*

Gordon, Dexter. *See main text entry.*

Hampton, Lionel. *See main text entry.*

Hancock, Herbie. *See main text entry.*

Handy, John Richard, III (b. Feb. 3, 1933, Dallas, Tex.). Primarily an alto saxophonist, Handy also performed on clarinet, flute, and tenor saxophone. As a self-taught clarinetist, he became known for his saxophone virtuosity and solo abilities in the upper register of the instrument. Playing with Charles Mingus's group in the late 1950's, Handy was part of the recordings *Jazz Portraits* (1959) and *Mingus ah um* (1959). He also recorded as a bandleader in the late 1950's, producing *In the Vernacular* (1959). He reunited with the Mingus band in 1964 and formed another ensemble of his own. After Mingus's death, Handy joined the Mingus Dynasty ensemble in 1979 and returned to his primary jazz style. He joined the group Bebop and Beyond in the early 1980's.

AP/Wide World Photos

Hartman, Johnny (1922, Chicago, Ill.—1983). Ballad-oriented singer. After military service in World War II, Hartman sang with Earl Hines, Dizzy Gillespie, and Errol Garner. In the early 1960's, he made a critically acclaimed and popularly received album with John Coltrane.

Hawkins, Coleman. *See main text entry.*

Hawkins, Erskine (July 26, 1914, Birmingham, Ala.—Nov. 11, 1993, Willingboro, N.J.). Trumpeter and bandleader. From the late 1930's to the mid-1950's, Hawkins's band played long engagements at the Savoy Ballroom in Harlem. The band recorded and made frequent radio broadcasts, becoming one of the most popular bands in the United States. Its recording of "Tuxedo Junction" (1939), for which Hawkins shares composition credit, is cited often as a classic swing performance.

Heath, Jimmy (b. Oct. 25, 1926, Philadelphia, Pa.). Saxophonist, flutist, composer, and educator. James Edward Heath worked with Philadelphia-based bands during the mid-1940's. After working with

(continued)

Dizzy Gillespie's big band in 1947, he met Charlie "Bird" Parker in Philadelphia in 1948. Soon nicknamed "Little Bird," Heath organized his own Philadelphia-based big band. In 1960 he began his career as an educator, teaching for the Jazzmobile Workshop, and performed with trumpeter Art Farmer. In 1975 he formed, with his brothers bassist Percy Heath and percussionist Albert "Tootie" Heath, a band called the Heath Brothers. The Heath Brothers recorded seven albums. One, *Live at the Public Theatre* (1979), was nominated for a Grammy Award in 1980.

Henderson, Fletcher "Smack" (Dec. 18, 1897, Cuthbert, Ga.—Dec. 29, 1952, New York, N.Y.). Arranger, pianist, and bandleader. Henderson is generally recognized as the first jazz musician to use written arrangements. His orchestral arrangements, particularly those for Benny Goodman's band in the 1930's, were important contributions to the new swing sound.

Henderson, Joe (b. April 24, 1937, Lima, Ohio). Tenor saxophonist. Henderson first gained recognition in the early 1960's when he played with trumpeter Kenny Dorham. He went on to play with Horace Silver's quintet and Herbie HANCOCK's band. Although influenced by John Coltrane, Henderson developed his own distinctive sound. While his solos can be fiery, there is an almost mournful sound to his ballad playing. His 1992 release *Lush Life: The Music of Billy Strayhorn* was a huge success. He followed up *Lush Life* with other acclaimed releases, including *So Near, So Far (Musings for Miles)* (1993), *Double Rainbow: The Music of Antonio Carlos Jobim* (1995), and *Porgy and Bess* (1997).

Hines, Earl "Fatha." *See main text entry.*

Hodges, Johnny. *See main text entry.*

Hopkins, Claude Driskett. *See main text entry.*

Jackson, Milt (Jan. 1, 1923, Detroit, Mich.—Oct. 9, 1999, New York, N.Y.). Vibraphonist. Jackson played the guitar and piano from the age of seven before settling on the vibraphone in his teens. In 1945 he had an opportunity to move to New York City and play with Dizzy Gillespie. His reputation firmly established, Jackson played with many of the modern jazz greats throughout the late 1940's. His greatest fame came in his helping to establish, in 1952, the Modern Jazz Quartet, perhaps the greatest popularizer of post-swing era jazz. In early 1999, he released *Explosive* with the Clayton-Hamilton Jazz Orchestra.

Jamal, Ahmad (Fritz Jones, b. July 2, 1930, Pittsburgh, Pa.). Pianist. Jamal began playing professionally at the age of eleven. He left high school in the late 1940's to join trumpeter George Hudson's orchestra. Jamal played with Hudson until 1951, when he formed his first trio, the Three Strings. He changed his name from Fritz Jones to Ahmad Jamal upon his conversion to Islam in the early 1950's. Jamal's first album, *Ahmad Jamal at the Pershing*, came out in 1958. Critics and fellow musicians such as Miles Davis admired Jamal's spare but fluid and elegant style. Recordings include *Ahmad Jamal at the Blackhawk* (1961), *At the Top—Poinciana Revisited* (1968), *Jamal Plays Jamal* (1974), *Ahmad Jamal Live at Bubba's* (1981), and *Nature* (1998).

Jarreau, Al (b. Mar. 12, 1940, Milwaukee, Wis.). Singer. Jarreau grew up singing street-corner material and the songs of his major influences, Sarah Vaughan, Billy Eckstine, and Jon Hendricks. By the late 1960's he had moved to Los Angeles, where he was discovered by Warner Bros. Records. His 1975 recording *We Got By* and his 1978 live album *Look at the Rainbow* both sold well overseas. In 1978 he broke through in the United States, winning Grammy Awards as best jazz vocalist in 1978 and 1979. The blockbuster 1981 album *Breaking Away* followed, with its hit single "We're in This Love Together." Jarreau released solo recordings and collaborations with saxophonist David Sanborn, keyboardist/producer Bob James, bassist Stanley Clarke, and others. He released *Tribute to Bill Withers* in 1998.

Jaxon, Frankie "Half-Pint" (b. Feb. 3, 1895, Montgomery, Ala.). Singer and composer. Jaxon grew up in Kansas City, where he began to sing in local clubs around age fifteen. From 1914 to 1926, he alternated between performing at the Paradise Cafe in Atlantic City, New Jersey, and at the Sunset Cafe in Chicago. After 1926, he settled permanently in Chicago. He performed intermittently until 1941 when, dissatisfied with the insecurities of the entertainment industry, he took a job in government.

Johnson, Budd. *See main text entry.*

Johnson, Bunk. *See main text entry.*

Johnson, James P. *See main text entry.*

Johnson, James Louis "J. J." (b. Jan. 22, 1924, Indianapolis, Ind.). Trombonist, composer, and arranger. James Louis Johnson is credited with perfecting the modern jazz trombone style. After playing with the Benny Carter band and Count Basie Orchestra, Johnson recorded as a bandleader, producing *Mad Bebop* (1946), *Boneology* (1947), and *Blue Mode* (1949). In 1954 Johnson collaborated with Kai Winding, forming a trombone duo and recording *Jay and Kai* (1954). As a composer, Johnson produced *Jazz Suite for Brass* (1956). Combining composing and performance, Johnson was associated in the 1960's with Miles Davis, Clark Terry, and Sonny Stitt. His move to Los Angeles in 1970 led to his writing for film and television. In 1980 he recorded *Concepts in Blue*. Working with Wayne Shorter, he released *Heroes* in 1999.

AP/Wide World Photos

Jones, Elvin (b. Sept. 9, 1927, Pontiac, Mich.). Drummer. A member of a musical family which included brothers Thad and Hank, Jones performed in ensembles in the Detroit area during the 1940's. Jones, along with Kenny Clarke, Art Blakey, and Max Roach, contributed to innovations in jazz percussion. By 1956 Jones had migrated to New York City, where he worked with artists such as Harry Edison, Bud Powell, Stan Getz, Sonny Rollins, and Donald Byrd. From 1960 to 1966, Jones was a principal member of the John Coltrane Quartet. His polyrhythmic percussion style became a hallmark of the group's sound. Jones developed as a leader during the early 1960's, recording *Illuminations* (1963) and *Heavy Sounds* (1968). In 1982 he joined with saxophonist Dave Liebman to produce *Earth Jones*. During the 1990's, Jones regularly led and appeared with ensembles in major jazz venues. In 1998 he released *At This Point in Time*.

Jones, Hank. *See main text entry.*

Jordan, Stanley (b. July 31, 1959, Chicago, Ill.). Electric guitarist. Jordan played in local rock and roll groups in his early teens and won an award at the Reno Jazz Festival in 1976. He graduated from Princeton University in 1981, having studied electronic music, theory, and composition, and went on to play with Dizzy Gillespie and Benny Carter. His performance at the Kool Jazz Festival in 1984 brought him acclaim, as did his appearance at the 1985 Montreux International Jazz Festival. His second album, *Magic Touch*, was produced by Al di Meola and released in 1985 to great success. Jordan's approach to jazz electric guitar—tapping the strings with both hands, allowing him to play two independent lines at the same time—was unprecedented. He released *Live in New York* in 1998.

Kirk, Rahsaan Roland. *See main text entry.*

Klugh, Earl (b. Dec. 16, 1954, Detroit, Mich.). Acoustic guitarist. Klugh studied both piano and guitar while growing up, playing guitar from the age of ten. He began touring with George Benson in the early 1970's, played on Benson's 1971 album *White Rabbit*, and in 1973 joined Benson's group. After playing guitar with Return to Forever on a U.S. tour in 1974, Klugh stopped touring to focus on his own projects and to record as a sideman. His 1979 album, *One on One*, recorded with Bob James, received a Grammy Award that year. Klugh's early style was influenced by guitarists such as Chet Atkins and George Van Eps, but he later moved to a more fluid style that combined elements of melodic mainstream jazz and rhythm and blues.

AP/Wide World Photos

Lateef, Yusef (William Evans; b. Oct. 9, 1920, Chattanooga, Tenn.). Multi-instrumentalist and composer. Although Lateef is known primarily as a tenor saxophonist, he also took up flute, oboe, bassoon, and Asian and African instruments, becoming adept at the "pneumatic" flute and various bamboo flutes. He became known for his work as a leader of small groups. He also worked with Kenny Burrell and, after 1959, with Charles Mingus, Cannonball Adderley, and Donald Byrd. He produced *Suite 16* (1970), which contained "Symphonic Blues Suite," composed for quartet and orchestra with improvisa-

(continued)

tional sections, as well as *In a Temple Garden* (1979). During the 1980's, he lived in Nigeria. From this experience came *In Nigeria* (1983). In 1998 he released *Nine Bagatelles.*

Lewis, Ramsey (b. May 27, 1935, Chicago, Ill.). Pianist. Lewis began playing jazz piano with a trio he formed in the mid-1950's. The trio achieved local recognition through its engagements in Chicago and on the road. The group was relatively unnoticed until it recorded a single, "The In Crowd" (1965), which sold in the millions of copies. From relative obscurity, and on the basis of only a few recordings, the group became one of the most popular jazz combos in the United States. Perhaps because of his sudden major commercial success Lewis may not have received his due as a composer and performer. He attempted to bridge the gap between popular, or "commercial," music and the more arcane approach of modern jazz. He released *Appassionata* in 1999.

Lunceford, Jimmie. *See main text entry.*

Marsalis, Branford (b. Aug. 26, 1960, Breaux Bridge, La.). Soprano and tenor saxophonist. Marsalis represents the 1980's neotraditional jazz movement. He is the brother of trumpeter Wynton MARSALIS. He toured with the big bands of Art Blakey and Lionel Hampton, and then toured with the Clark Terry orchestra in 1981 and with Wynton Marsalis's quintet in 1982. With Wynton as leader, Branford Marsalis performed on *Wynton Marsalis* (1981) and *Black Codes (from the Underground)* (1985). During the mid-1980's, he was associated with Miles Davis, Dizzy Gillespie, and Herbie Hancock. In 1983 Marsalis recorded *Scenes in the City* , his first album as a leader. He recorded *Royal Garden Blues* (1986), then his first classical album, *Romances for Saxophone* (1986). In 1985 Marsalis joined rock performer Sting and performed on the recording *Dream of the Blue Turtles.* In 1992 Marsalis was chosen as music director and arranger for NBC-TV's *The Tonight Show with Jay Leno.* He left the show in 1994 to pursue his own projects. In 1999 he released *Requiem.*

© Roy Lewis Archives

Marsalis, Wynton. *See main text entry.*

McCann, Les (b. Sept. 23, 1935, Lexington, Ky.). Pianist and singer. Lester Coleman McCann learned to play the tuba and drums as a youngster but was mostly self taught when it came to piano. After winning a Navy talent contest as a singer in 1956, he appeared on *The Ed Sullivan Show.* In 1958 he moved to California and began leading his own jazz trio. He released two albums in 1960, *Les McCann Plays the Truth* and *The Shout.* Both albums were successful, and their GOSPEL MUSIC-tinged flavor influenced other young musicians. McCann performed with Eddie Harris at the 1969 Montreux International Jazz Festival. In the 1970's, McCann began to experiment with electric piano and keyboards, and he eventually focused more on rhythm and blues and SOUL MUSIC rather than jazz. Although he suffered a stroke in 1995, he battled back and began playing again.

McGriff, Jimmy (b. Apr. 3, 1936, Philadelphia, Pa.). Organist. Originally a bassist, McGriff was inspired by Jimmy Smith to become a jazz organist. He had commercial success at his first recording session as leader, with "I've Got a Woman" (1963). He recorded frequently, usually as a leader but also as a sideman, as with drummer Buddy Rich in 1974. He released *The Dream Team* in 1996 and *Straight Up* in 1998.

Mingus, Charles. *See main text entry.*

Monk, Thelonious. *See main text entry.*

Montgomery, Wes (Mar. 6, 1925, Indianapolis, Ind.—June 15, 1968, Indianapolis, Ind.). Guitarist. Montgomery played with the Lionel Hampton band before joining his two brothers, Buddy and Monk, in a band. He went on to release a number of influential albums of his own. Famous for his unique style of plucking his guitar with his thumb, Montgomery influenced many other jazz greats with his personalized style of swing and improvisation.

Moody, James (b. Feb. 26, 1925, Savannah, Ga.). Saxophonist and flute player. A multi-instrumentalist, Moody primarily plays alto and tenor saxophones and flute. He also sings. Most famous for his 1949 recording of "I'm in the Mood for Love," he played irregularly with trumpeter Dizzy Gillespie beginning in the 1940's. He released *Moody Plays Mancini* in 1997 and *Moody's Blues* in 1999.

Morgan, Lee. *See main text entry.*

Morton, Benny. *See main text entry.*

Morton, Jelly Roll. *See main text entry.*

Moten, Bennie. *See main text entry.*

Navarro, Fats. *See main text entry.*

Noone, Jimmie. *See main text entry.*

Oliver, King. *See main text entry.*

Oliver, Sy. *See main text entry.*

Ory, Kid. *See main text entry.*

Page, Hot Lips. *See main text entry.*

Parker, Charlie "Bird." *See main text entry.*

Peterson, Oscar. *See main text entry.*

Powell, Bud (Sept. 27, 1924, New York, N.Y.—July 31, 1966, New York, N.Y.). Pianist. Bebop artist Earl "Bud" Powell played with trumpeter Dizzy Gillespie, saxophonist Charlie Parker, and drummer Max Roach. An innovative, emotional pianist, Powell was a pioneer who successfully transferred the sounds of the guitar and other string instruments to the keyboard.

Redman, Don. *See main text entry.*

Roach, Max. *See main text entry.*

Rollins, Sonny. *See main text entry.*

Rushing, Jimmy. *See main text entry.*

Sampson, Edgar "the Lamb" (Aug. 31, 1907, New York, N.Y.—Jan. 16, 1973, Englewood, N.J.). Alto saxophone and violin player, arranger, and composer. He played with Duke ELLINGTON for a season before moving on, in 1926, to play with Arthur Gibbs. Sampson worked with the Charlie Johnson Band, then joined Fletcher Henderson from 1931 to 1932. He played with Chick WEBB from 1934 to 1936, when he left to be a freelance arranger. After a brief stint as musical director for Ella FITZGERALD, he resumed regular playing, leading his own band in New York City from 1949 to 1951. He arranged for several Latin-flavored bands in the 1950's.

Shepp, Archie (b. May 24, 1937, Ft. Lauderdale, Fla.). Tenor saxophonist and playwright. Raised in Philadelphia, he recorded his first record in 1960 with Cecil Taylor. Shepp was one of the first jazz musicians to incorporate social themes into his music, which included songs containing poetry about MALCOLM X. His musical sound was strongly influenced by the styles of John Coltrane and Sonny Rollins.

Short, Bobby (b. Sept. 15, 1926, Danville, Ill.). Singer and pianist. Short's public image is most often associated with the sophisticated Cafe Society of New York. More than two decades of cabaret singing and piano playing at the Carlyle Hotel in New York City reflect his early years, when he performed with such jazz figures as pianists Art TATUM and Nat "King" Cole. He is considered an important interpreter of Cole Porter and the more obscure songs of Richard Rodgers and Lorenz Hart. In 1999 he released *You're the Top: The Love Songs of Cole Porter.*

Shorter, Wayne. *See main text entry.*

Silver, Horace (b. Sept. 2, 1928, Norwalk, Conn.). Pianist and composer. Silver, the son of a Cape Verde Islander, played in the Stan Getz quintet and performed in drummer Art Blakey's Jazz Messengers in the early 1950's before forming his own quintet in 1956. Silver's gospel-inspired harmonies and emotion-filled melodies formed the basis of the funk style of jazz that influenced such later musicians as Herbie Hancock and Chick Corea. He released *Jazz Has a Sense of Humor* in 1999.

Sissle, Noble (July 10, 1889, Indianapolis, Ind.—Dec. 17, 1975, Tampa, Fla.). Composer and bandleader. With fellow composer Eubie BLAKE, Sissle wrote and directed the highly successful all-African American musicals *Shuffle Along* (1921) and *Chocolate Dandies* (1924). He also toured widely for nearly half a century with his own bands, which featured such outstanding musicians as Sidney Bechet and Tommy Ladnier.

Smith, Jimmy (b. Dec. 8, 1925, Norristown, Pa.). Organist. Beginning in the mid-1950's, Smith became one of the most popular and acclaimed jazz organ-

(continued)

ists. He influenced many other players, including Jimmy McGRIFF and Joey DeFrancesco, and recorded frequently. In 1999 he released *Groovin' at Small's Paradise*.

Smith, Willie "the Lion." *See main text entry.*

Spand, Charlie. Pianist in the barrelhouse tradition in the 1920's and 1930's. Although a number of his lyrics refer to his southern upbringing, Spand lived in Detroit for most of his career, cutting twenty-four sides, including the moderately successful "Soon This Morning" for Paramount Records in 1929. Additionally, he recorded several critically acclaimed piano and guitar duets with period recording star Blind Blake (Arthur Phelps). A fluent pianist who was technically sound while not overly flashy, Spand was a highly sought session musician and a major influence on subsequent generations of BLUES pianists.

St. Cyr, Johnny (Apr. 17, 1890, New Orleans, La.—June 17, 1966, Los Angeles, Calif.). Early Dixieland banjoist and guitarist. In his native New Orleans, and in Chicago, California, and elsewhere, John Alexander St. Cyr performed and recorded with such famous jazzmen as King OLIVER, Louis Armstrong, Earl "Fatha" HINES, and Jelly Roll MORTON. St. Cyr was a highly regarded ensemble player rather than a soloist.

Stitt, Sonny. *See main text entry.*

Strayhorn, Billy. *See main text entry.*

Tatum, Art, Jr. *See main text entry.*

Taylor, Billy (b. July 24, 1921, Greenville, N.C.). Pianist. William "Billy" Taylor developed careers as a pianist, composer, arranger, conductor, author, and educator. He was reared in Washington, D.C. Migrating to New York City in the 1940's, he secured an engagement with the legendary Ben WEBSTER. Taylor also worked with Dizzy Gillespie, Charlie Parker, Machito, and Don Redman. During the 1950's, he performed with Billie HOLIDAY, Oscar Pettiford, and Roy ELDRIDGE, and formed his own trio. In the 1960's and 1970's, Taylor hosted jazz programs for WLIB and WNEW radio in New York and served as general manager for WLIB, a black-owned station. During the 1980's, he hosted *Jazz Alive* for National Public Radio. Taylor is known for his expressive and technically masterful piano renditions, revealing the influences of Nat "King" Cole and Art Tatum.

Tyner, McCoy. *See main text entry.*

Waller, Fats. *See main text entry.*

Washington, Grover, Jr. (Dec. 12, 1943, Buffalo, N.Y.—Dec. 19, 1999, New York, N.Y.). Saxophonist. In 1971 Washington fronted his own recording group, resulting in his debut album, *Inner City Blues*. Reviewers praised his virtuoso saxophone work. Washington became much in demand on the jazz concert circuit. Recognized as one of the leading reed players in the world of jazz, he attempted to break out of conventional jazz molds through increasing experimentation and use of forms such as rock and rhythm and blues. For his efforts, he was awarded a Grammy Award for best jazz fusion performance in 1981. Washington's musical career encompassed roles as composer, producer, sound-track artist, and video performer as well as instrumentalist. He released *Soulful Strut* in 1996.

Webb, Chick. *See main text entry.*

Webster, Ben. *See main text entry.*

Williams, Joe (Dec. 12, 1918, Cordele, Ga.—Mar. 29, 1999, Las Vegas, Nev.). Singer. Williams is best known for his years with the Count Basie band (1954-1961). His first Basie recording session resulted in the hit "All Right, Okay, You Win" (1955). His album *Nothin' but the Blues* won a Grammy Award in 1984.

Williams, Stanley R. "Fess" (Apr. 10, 1894, Danville, Ky.—Dec. 17, 1975, New York, N.Y.). Clarinetist and bandleader. After graduation from TUSKEGEE INSTITUTE in 1914, Williams taught music for several years in Kentucky public schools, where he received his nickname, an abbreviation of "professor." From 1919 to the mid-1940's, Williams regularly led dance bands. His Royal Flush Orchestra played long engagements in New York City's Harlem neighborhood and attracted a national following through recordings, tours, and radio broadcasts.

Wilson, Teddy. *See main text entry.*

Young, Lester. *See main text entry.*

Notable Female Jazz Musicians

Allen, Geri (b. June 12, 1957, Pontiac, Mich.). Pianist and composer. Allen earned a degree in jazz studies at HOWARD UNIVERSITY, then moved to New York City, where she studied with BEBOP pianist Kenny Barron. During the early 1980's, she played with Oliver Lake and Steve Coleman. She released her first album, *The Printmakers*, in 1985. Capable of playing both bebop and free jazz and blessed with the ability to meld melody with expressive improvisational style, she released albums including *Twylight* (1989), *Maroons* (1992), *Twenty One* (1994), and *Gathering* (1998).

Anderson, Ivie (July 10, 1904, Gilroy, Calif.—Dec. 28, 1949, Los Angeles, Calif.). Singer. Anderson was the featured vocalist (1931-1942) in Duke ELLINGTON's orchestra during its rise to worldwide prominence in the swing era. The warmth, elegance, and lyricism of Anderson's singing were important contributions to the orchestra's musical appeal.

Armstrong, Lillian Hardin. *See main text entry.*

Carn, Jean (b. 1948?). Carn began singing at the age of fifteen. She met her husband, Doug Carn, while performing in weekend jazz sessions. They moved to Hollywood shortly after their marriage and eventually produced their debut album. After moving to New York City, the couple recorded *Spirit of the New Land* and *Revelations* before they separated in 1973. Carn then became a solo vocalist with the Duke Ellington orchestra. While performing in New York, she met Norman Connors, who helped produce her solo albums. She toured with Connors and Earth, Wind, and Fire. Her first solo album was released in 1977 and contained the hit single "Free Love." Other albums include *Happy to Be with You* and *When I Find You Love*. She had another hit with "Valentine Love."

Carter, Betty. *See main text entry.*

Coltrane, Alice. *See main text entry.*

Crawford, Randy (b. 1952, Macon, Ga.). Singer. Performing regularly at a Cincinnati, Ohio, nightclub by the time she was fifteen years old, Crawford developed a searing vocal talent that was clear from an early age. She soon made her way to New York City via St. Tropez, France. In addition to appearing as a guest artist on other people's records, Crawford has released several albums on her own, including *Everything Must Change*, *Miss Randy Crawford*, *Raw Silk*, *Now We May Begin* (which contained her first solo hit, "One Day I'll Fly Away"), *Secret Combination*, and *Windsong*. She also collaborated with George Benson and Quincy JONES. In 1998 she released *Every Kind of Mood*.

Fitzgerald, Ella. *See main text entry.*

Holiday, Billie. *See main text entry.*

Horn, Shirley (b. 1934, Washington, D.C.). Singer, pianist, and bandleader. After studying at Howard University, Horn formed a trio in 1954. During the 1960's, she established her reputation as a top jazz pianist through her recordings with musicians such as Miles DAVIS, Quincy JONES, Hank JONES, and Kenny Burrell. She released a tribute to Davis, *I Remember Miles*, in 1998.

McRae, Carmen. *See main text entry.*

Phillips, Esther (Esther Mae Jones; Dec. 23, 1935, Galveston, Tex.—Aug. 7, 1984, Los Angeles, Calif.). Singer. Phillips started singing in the church and, by age fifteen, had won an amateur contest in Los Angeles. She went on to record her first number-one hit song, "Little Ester," in 1950. She sang BLUES, jazz, RHYTHM AND BLUES, SOUL, pop, and country and western music. Like singer Ray CHARLES, Phillips successfully merged soul music with jazz and country.

Reeves, Dianne (b. 1956?, Detroit, Mich.). Vocalist. With the encouragement of her mother and stepfather, Reeves was discovered by jazz trumpeter Clark Terry at a music educators' festival in Chicago when she was seventeen years old. Terry invited her to sing with his group. In the mid-1970's, Reeves moved to Los Angeles, eventually joining a Latin jazz-rock group called Caldera. She later toured as principal vocalist with Sergio Mendes and in 1983 began a two-and-a-half-year stint performing with Harry BELAFONTE. Reeves's own work was influenced heavily by the Brazilian, African, Caribbean, and Third World musical influences she encountered while singing with Mendes and Belafonte. In

(continued)

1988 she released *Dianne Reeves* on Blue Note Records. The album topped the jazz charts for eleven weeks. In 1999 she released *Bridges*.

Richmond, June (July 9, 1915, Chicago, Ill.—Aug. 14, 1962, Gothenburg, Sweden). Singer. Richmond was one of the great big-band singers during the swing era. She performed with Andy Kirk and Twelve Clouds of Joy, a big band from Kansas City. Like all the other major female big-band singers of this era, including Ella FITZGERALD, Billie HOLIDAY, Lena HORNE, and Ivie Anderson, Richmond performed all over the United States. After moving to Paris in 1954, she continued to perform widely in Europe.

Scott, Hazel. *See main text entry.*

Shaw, Marlena (b. New Rochelle, N.Y.). Singer. Shaw has performed jazz, easy-listening, and soul music in her career. She made her stage debut at the APOLLO THEATER at the age of ten. After marrying and starting a family, she began singing in a New York City lounge in 1963. Shaw also sang with the Count BASIE Orchestra, and in 1972 she became the first female artist to be signed to Blue Note Records, where she spent the next five years cutting an album per year. She had a rhythm-and-blues hit single in 1976 with "It's Better than Walking Out." In 1989 she performed with Joe Williams at Carnegie Hall.

Sullivan, Maxine. *See main text entry.*

Vaughan, Sarah. *See main text entry.*

Washington, Dinah (Ruth Lee Jones; Aug. 29, 1924, Tuscaloosa, Ala.—Dec. 14, 1963, Detroit, Mich.). Singer. Known as the "Mother of Soul," Washington influenced many artists, including the "Queen of Soul," Aretha FRANKLIN. Washington first sang GOSPEL MUSIC in church, later joining the Lionel HAMPTON band as lead singer in 1943.

Williams, Mary Lou. *See main text entry.*

Wilson, Cassandra (b. Dec. 4, 1955, Jackson, Miss.). After establishing herself as a vocalist in the 1970's, Wilson moved to New York City in 1982, where she worked with Abbey LINCOLN, Dave Holland, and Steve Coleman. Her 1993 blues-flavored recording *Blue Light 'Til Dawn* was a significant boost to her career. She continued to stretch herself with such releases as *New Moon Daughter* (1995) and *Traveling Miles* (1999). Blessed with a distinctive voice, Wilson proved willing to take chances.

Wilson, Nancy (b. Feb. 20, 1937, Chillicothe, Ohio). Singer. Discovered by bandleader and saxophonist Julian "Cannonball" ADDERLEY during a performance in 1959 in Columbus, Ohio, Wilson subsequently was signed by Capitol Records. Capitol released her first hit record, "Guess Who I Saw Yesterday," shortly thereafter. With a string of recordings and performances since the late 1950's, Wilson also heads, along with her husband and manager, Kenny Dennis, Wil-Den Enterprises, an organization that manages and publishes the works of entertainers in various media. In 1995 she released *Spotlight On*.

Beginning with "funky style" jazz, a style that espoused a return to the blues and gospel roots of jazz that was led by the Jazz Crusaders, Ramsey Lewis, Horace Silver, and Stanley Turrentine, an eclectic jazz genre inspired by Miles Davis and known as "fusion" evolved. Spin-off groups that emanated from Davis's band—including John McLaughlin's Mahavishnu Orchestra, Weather Report (co-led by Josef Zawinul and Wayne Shorter), Herbie Hancock's Head Hunters, and Tony Williams's Lifetime—developed a jazz-rock-soul genre that emerged in the late 1960's. Jazz-rock fusion used electronic instruments and devices, multilayered rhythmic ostinatos (repeating patterns played by percussion, bass, and keyboard), solo and group improvisation, modal scales, and high volume levels.

Simultaneously, the jazz-soul movement, led by Julian "Cannonball" ADDERLEY, advocated emotion and meaning, drawing heavily upon blues and gospel musical elements in its style. While fusion continued, a cadre of musicians, including Donald Harrison and Wynton MARSALIS, championed a return to nonfusion

(continued on page 1362)

Notable Jazz Groups

Blackbyrds. Members of this singing group got together while attending Howard University, where they were engaged by trumpet player Donald Byrd. Byrd helped the group record its first single, "Walking in Rhythm," and album, *Flying Start*, while its members were still in school. Byrd's work with the Blackbyrds produced the kind of crossover music that he could not accomplish on his own. Three of the five Byrd-produced Blackbyrds albums went gold. The group eventually grew away from Byrd and turned to George Duke to produce its sixth album, *Better Days* (1980). The group stopped recording in the 1980's, and the members went on to work on other projects. Byrd re-formed the Blackbyrds in 1994.

Jazz Crusaders. Later known as the Crusaders (1971), the group was formed at the beginning of the 1950's in Houston, Texas. The Jazz Crusaders underwent a variety of transitions during their history, emerging as the exponent of a jazz-rock-soul-funk fusion in the 1970's. The three mainstays and founders were pianist Joe Sample, drummer Stix Hooper, and saxophonist Wilton Felder. In the 1950's, the ensemble expanded with the inclusion of trombonist Wayne Henderson, bassist Henry Wilson, and flutist Hubert Laws. The Jazz Crusaders became a popular and frequently recorded group. With their transition to jazz fusion during the 1970's, the Crusaders began to perform in the jazz-funk style, including elements of soul and rock and utilizing electric instruments. Henderson and Hooper departed, leaving Sample, Felder, and new members Ndugu on drums, Larry Carlton on electric guitar, and Max Bennett on electric bass.

Joshua Redman Quartet. Jazz quartet formed by saxophonist Joshua Redman that featured some of the most outstanding young players in the jazz world in the 1990's. Son of saxophonist Dewey Redman, Joshua Redman earned top honors in the Thelonious Monk International Jazz Saxophone Competition in 1991. His first album, *Joshua Redman*, was released in March of 1993 and reached number three on the jazz charts. For his third album, *Mood Swing* (1994), Redman recorded with prominent young musicians including twenty-one-year-old bass virtuoso Christian McBride. (Chris Thomas filled the bass position after McBride left to form his own group.) In 1995 the group released a double live album that received favorable reviews. *Freedom in the Groove* was released in 1996 and *Timeless Tales (For Changing Times)* was released in 1998.

Mingus Dynasty. Group established in 1979 to play the music and continue the spirit of bassist and composer Charles Mingus. Composed originally mostly of musicians who had played with Mingus—pianist Don Pullen and drummer Dannie Richmond, among others—the group underwent numerous changes in personnel before disbanding in 1991.

Modern Jazz Quartet. Prominent combo formed in 1952. Organized by pianist John Lewis, the quartet emerged during an era when big band music no longer dominated jazz. Musicians associated with Dizzy Gillespie formed the group, with Lewis serving as its music director. The group played regularly until 1974 and had brief reunions afterward, releasing *Celebration* in 1992 and *In Concert* in 1996. One of the group's founding members, vibraphonist Milt Jackson, died in 1999.

Take 6. Gospel-oriented, a cappella vocal group known for its mixture of jazz chord structures, gospel lyrics, and masterful vocalization techniques. Take 6 was formed in Huntsville, Alabama, in 1980. The group performed in local churches. Soon original members Claude V. McKnight, Mark Kibble, and Mervyn Warren were joined by Cedric Dent, David Thomas, and Alvin "Vinnie" Chea. The group signed with Warner Bros. in 1987. It also signed with Reunion Records, a gospel label, in order to saturate both the pop and the gospel markets. The group's first album, *Take 6* (1988), brought critical acclaim from the gospel and jazz communities. The group continued to record during the 1990's, releasing such albums as *Brothers* (1996), *So Cool* (1998), and *We Wish You a Merry Christmas* (1999).

Reprise Records

World Saxophone Quartet. Group founded in 1976 by David Murray. This revolutionary all-saxophone

(continued)

group has included from the beginning Murray, Oliver Lake, Julius Hemphill, and Hamiet Bluiett. Among the group's recordings is a 1986 album of compositions associated with Duke ELLINGTON and composed by Ellington or Billy STRAYHORN. In 1993 Hemphill left the group and was replaced by various saxophone players, including Arthur Blythe. The group released *Selim Sevad: A Tribute to Miles Davis* in 1998 and *M'Bizo* in 1999. Murray also established a solo career.

traditional jazz, a movement that seemed appropriate and necessary to counteract the commercial bent of some fusion jazz recordings. In addition to fusion, a conscious attempt to incorporate world music instruments and concepts began to receive substantial attention. These influences can be heard in the styles of Stan Getz, Tito Puente, Airto Moriera, and selected recordings of Ravi Shankar.

During the 1980's, Marsalis became a prominent jazz figure. Considered a neotraditionalist, he was very vocal in his support of jazz as he defined it. Along with a number of other black jazz musicians who came upon the scene in the 1980's, Marsalis became known as one of the "young lions." These musicians were neotraditionalists who played the hard bop style of jazz that was popular during the late 1950's and early 1960's. In general, the neotraditionalists frowned upon the use of electronic instruments commonly found in jazz fusion and disapproved of the dissonant sound of free jazz. In addition to Marsalis, some of the most notable young lions include trumpeters Roy Hargrove and Terence Blanchard, pianists Marcus Roberts and Mulgrew Miller, and bassist Christian McBride.

In 1987 Marsalis became head of the new jazz program at New York City's Lincoln Center for the Performing Arts. Under the direction of trumpeter Jon Faddis, a jazz program also was started at Carnegie Hall in 1993. In 1997 Marsalis's *Blood on the Field* became the first nonclassical work to receive a Pulitzer Prize in music.

While the young lions narrowly defined what jazz meant to them, there were other highly accomplished black jazz musicians who stretched the boundaries of jazz, including pianist Geri Allen, violinist Regina Carter, vocalist Cassandra Wilson, and saxophonists Joshua Redman, David Murray, and James Carter. In 1992 veteran tenor saxophonist Joe Henderson scored a huge hit with his release of *Lush Life*. He continued to release quality work throughout the 1990's. Most jazz styles can be heard at various venues throughout the world, including hard bop, cool, free jazz, and swing. At the 1998 Texaco New York Jazz Festival, both bop and free jazz were featured. George Lewis, Roscoe Mitchell, Oliver Lake, Dwight Andrews, and others performed at the tenth National Black Arts Festival in Atlanta, Georgia, in 1998.

—Eddie S. Meadows

—Updated by Jeffry Jensen

See also: Chicago jazz; Dixieland jazz; Gospel music and spirituals; Ragtime; Soul music.

Suggested Readings:

Buerkle, Jack V., and Danny Barker. *Bourbon Street Black: The New Orleans Black Jazzman*. New York: Oxford University Press, 1973.

Gourse, Leslie. *Wynton Marsalis: Skain's Domain, a Biography*. New York: Schirmer Books, 1999.

Kofsky, Frank. *Black Music, White Business: Illuminating the History and Political Economy of Jazz*. New York: Pathfinder, 1998.

Oliphant, Dave, ed. *The Bebop Revolution in Words and Music*. Austin: University of Texas at Austin, 1994.

O'Meally, Robert G., ed. *The Jazz Cadence of American Culture*. New York: Columbia University Press, 1998.

Rosenthal, David. *Hard Bop: Jazz and Black Music, 1955-1965*. New York: Oxford University Press, 1992.

Schuller, Gunther. *Early Jazz: Its Roots and Musical Development*. Vol. 1 in *The History of Jazz*. New York: Oxford University Press, 1968.

_______. *The Swing Era: The Development of Jazz, 1930-1945*. Vol. 2 in *The History of Jazz*. New York: Oxford University Press, 1989.

Shipton, Alyn. *Groovin' High: The Life of Dizzy Gillespie*. New York: Oxford University Press, 1999.

Tirro, Frank. *Jazz: A History*. New York: W. W. Norton, 1977.

Jefferson, "Blind" Lemon (July 11, 1897, Couchman, Texas—December, 1929, or December, 1930, Chicago, Illinois): BLUES singer and guitarist. Jefferson was one of seven children. His parents, Alec and Classie Jefferson, were farmers. Although there are conflicting sources, he apparently had some limited sight as a child, which he eventually lost. One of his sisters was also a musician. As a child, Jefferson worked singing on the streets and at occasional parties, as well as in juke joints, barrelhouses, saloons, and similar settings in various northern TEXAS towns, mostly in the DALLAS area. He traveled as far south as Galveston, Texas. In 1917 he came in contact with and musically influenced Huddie "LEADBELLY" Ledbetter in Dallas.

During the early 1920's, he was an itinerant musician traveling mostly in the South, singing in MISSISSIPPI, ALABAMA, GEORGIA, NORTH CAROLINA, and VIRGINIA. During this period, he married Roberta Jefferson and had at least one child. His son Miles Jefferson also became a musician.

Jefferson eventually went to CHICAGO, where he played in brothels, in small clubs, and at house rent parties. In 1926 he made his first known recordings, which were sacred songs rather than blues, for the Paramount label. Later, he recorded many of the blues songs for which he is best remembered, including "Long Lonesome Blues," "Shuckin' Sugar Blues," "Jack O'Diamond Blues," "Black Snake Moan," and "Match Box Blues." He also recorded for the OKeh label (1927) in Atlanta and again for Paramount (1929). Some of those recorded works were "Bed Springs Blues," "Corina Blues," "Deceitful Brownskin Blues," "Eagle Eyed Blues," "Gone Dead on You Blues," "One Dime Blues," "Pneumonia Blues," "Prison Cell Blues," "Rabbit Foot Blues," "Tin Cup Blues," and "Wartime Blues."

Jefferson reportedly died of exposure on a Chicago street in December of 1929 or 1930. He was buried in Wortham, Texas, and a marker was placed on his grave in 1967. Jefferson was, with the possible exception of Charley PATTON, the most influential of the early bluesmen. His vocality (high falsetto, with raspy, taut, nasalized sound) became the standard for many of his contemporaries and later blues musicians. His guitar playing techniques were also imitated widely from his many recordings.

See also: Music.

Jeffries, Leonard (b. January 19, 1937, Newark, New Jersey): Educator. Leonard Jeffries' controversial academic career focused on changing the way that the history of black people—both Africans and the African diaspora—is taught. Jeffries was chair of Afro-American Studies at the City College of New York, head of black studies at San Jose State College in CALIFORNIA, and vice president of the African Heritage Studies Association, which was launched informally at the 1968 convention of the African Studies Association. Its stated goal was to reconstruct African history along Afrocentric lines, to unite black scholars intellectually, and to distribute information on establishing and evaluating African and black studies programs.

Leonard Jeffries speaking at a press conference at New York City College in early 1992. *(AP/Wide World Photos)*

Some of Jeffries' writings support "MELANIN THEORY," claiming that white people are biologically inferior to black people. White people, according to his reasoning, suffer from an inadequate supply of melanin, making them unable to function as effectively as people with darker skin. White people perpetrate a large number of crimes and atrocities because the genetic makeup of white people was deformed during the Ice Age, he argues, while black genes were enhanced by "the value system of the sun."

Through much of his career, Jeffries served as chair of the Black Studies Department (earlier the Afro-American Studies Department) at the City College of the City University of New York (CUNY). In July of 1991, he gave a speech at a black cultural festival held in Albany, New York. The speech, which focused on the need for African-centered education, stated that white historians have worked to strip Africa of its significance and place in the world. The speech was later aired on a state-run cable television channel.

In the speech, Jeffries stated that Jews and the Italian Mafia in Hollywood had conspired to denigrate the image of African Americans in FILM. He also alluded to the role of rich Jews who participated in the SLAVE TRADE and referred to one of his colleagues as the "head Jew" at City College. Politicians, Jewish leaders, and other community leaders criticized Jeffries' speech as anti-Semitic and racist and lobbied for the removal of Jeffries from his post as department chair. Jeffries and his supporters responded by saying that his academic freedom and First Amendment rights to free speech were being attacked.

In October of 1991, Bernard W. Harleston, president of City College, recommended that Jeffries be reappointed as department chair for a probationary period of eight months instead of the customary three-year period. His recommendation was approved by the CUNY Board of Trustees on October 28, and the university promised to investigate allegations that Jeffries had made threats against a Harvard University journalism student. In March of 1992, the board officially dismissed Jeffries as department chair. (His appointment as a tenured full professor was not affected.)

Jeffries responded to his dismissal by suing the university, seeking reinstatement and compensatory damages. In May of 1993, a federal grand jury found that the university had violated Jeffries' First Amendment rights and awarded him $400,000 in damages. A federal judge later reinstated Jeffries as chair (in August, 1993) but reduced the amount of the award to $360,000. On appeal, the U.S. Second Circuit Court of Appeals upheld Jeffries' reinstatement but threw out the award for damages. After he was reinstated, Jeffries' term as department chair expired in June of 1995; he was succeeded by Moyibi J. Amoda, a

Nigerian-born political scientist who had been on the City College faculty for more than twenty years.

In 1996 City College eliminated the departmental status of four ethnic studies departments, including black studies, making them "programs" instead. Jeffries was assigned to the faculty of the school's political science department.

—*Updated by Kwame Nantambu*

See also: African heritage; Afrocentricity; Diaspora, African.

Jehovah's Witnesses: RELIGION founded by Charles Taze Russell in 1872 near Pittsburgh, PENNSYLVANIA. Jehovah's Witnesses believe in an imminent battle of good and evil, an Armageddon after which 144,000 faithful followers will rule with Christ. Members follow a strict code of behavior that includes door-to-door proselytizing and recruitment of new members. Historically, African Americans have composed about 20 to 30 percent of the members of the Jehovah's Witnesses. With a membership of more than five million worldwide, Jehovah's Witnesses continues to grow, and its African American membership continues to increase.

In the 1950's and 1960's, both the Jehovah's Witnesses' publications, *The Watchtower* and *Awake!*, virtually ignored the church's African American following. Both publications are illustrated with drawings, and early editions of *Awake!* included only a handful of illustrations depicting black people. In early editions of *The Watchtower*, blacks were illustrated as African or Caribbean natives dressed in traditional costume. In those years African Americans were not prohibited from joining the Jehovah's Witnesses, but neither were they directly encouraged.

By the late twentieth century, many African Americans were devoted Jehovah's Witnesses despite the fact that members were prohibited from joining any other organizations, including such secular groups as the NATIONAL ASSOCIATION FOR THE ADVANCEMENT OF COLORED PEOPLE (NAACP). Leaders of the Jehovah's Witnesses are chosen by a group of church officials, and African Americans are largely absent from the congregation's leadership. *The Watchtower*, the organization's leading publication, is published by the Watchtower Bible and Tract Society, headquartered in Brooklyn, New York. African Americans have held positions with this society, although not in leadership roles.

—*Carrie L. Fascia*

Jemison, Mae C. (b. October 17, 1956, Decatur, Alabama): First black female astronaut. Jemison earned her B.S. in chemical engineering at Stanford University (1977) and her M.D. at Cornell University Medical School (1981). She served as a Peace Corps staff physician in Sierra Leone and oversaw a medical program for volunteers in LIBERIA before practicing as a physician in the United States from 1985 to 1987. Jemison's first space flight took place in September of 1992, when she served on the crew of the space shuttle *Endeavor*. Jemison left the astronaut program in 1993 and accepted a teaching position at Dartmouth College.

See also: Aviators and astronauts.

Jenifer, Franklyn Green (b. March 26, 1939, Washington, D.C.): Educator. Fourth African American and first alumnus to head HOWARD UNIVERSITY. Jenifer received his B.S. and M.S. degrees from Howard in 1962 and 1965, in microbiology. Until 1970 Jenifer worked as a plant virologist with the U.S. Department of Agriculture's laboratory in plant virology in Beltsville, Maryland. He was an assistant professor of biology at Rutgers University in 1970, associate in 1971, and full professor in 1976.

He chaired that department from 1976 to 1977 and was associate provost of Rutgers's Newark Campus from 1977 to 1979. From 1979 to 1986, Jenifer was vice chancellor of the New Jersey Department of Higher Education in Trenton and is remembered for supporting the system's research efforts in science and technology. Until 1991 he was chancellor of the Massachusetts Board of Regents of Higher Education, responsible for twenty-seven public colleges and universities and 180,000 students.

As a member of many educational, scientific, and corporate organizations, Jenifer served on boards of directors for the American Council on Education, the Woods Hole Oceanographic Institution, the Public Broadcasting Service, the Massachusetts Higher Education Assistance Corporation, and the Council for Aid to Education. Jenifer also chaired the American Association for the Advancement of Science's National Council for Science and Technology Education and contributed to the State's Task Force for Minority Achievement in Higher Education, the Committee on Educational Equality, and the American Council on Education's Commission on Women in Higher Education.

Jenifer took office as president of Howard University at a time when the university was facing some of its toughest financial and administrative challenges, but he used his wealth of managerial and academic experiences to inspire unity on campus and hope and faith in the school's financial and academic future. He acted as a strong advocate of education for African Americans at the highest possible level. During the *United States v. Mabus* case in 1991, he urged the U.S. Supreme Court to act expeditiously to preserve and strengthen historically black colleges. Jenifer resigned the presidency of Howard in 1994 to become president of the University of Texas at Dallas.

See also: Higher education.

Jet: Digest-sized weekly news magazine published by the Johnson Publishing Company. After its debut in 1951, it quickly became the top-selling magazine covering black news.

John H. Johnson, *Jet*'s founder, based the magazine's format on *Quick*, then a million-selling publication from *Look* magazine's publisher that had a large black readership. Johnson chose the title *Jet* because of two connotations: speed (the magazine could be read quickly) and color (a dark velvet-black). Each issue provided summary coverage of national and international black news, arranged in categories such as education, business, entertainment, health, black history, sports, society, children, and "Beauty of the Week."

Jet provided in-depth coverage of the Civil Rights movement. In his autobiography, Johnson recalled, "We told the story. More to the point, we were a part of a story that cannot be recalled or told without referring to the pages of *Ebony* and *Jet* and the two million photographs in our archives." Among the many events of significance to African Americans covered in *Jet* were Rosa Parks's refusal to move to the back of a Montgomery, Alabama, bus in 1955; the signing of the Civil Rights Act of 1960; the five-day Selma to Montgomery march, led by Martin Luther King, Jr., in Alabama in 1965; Nelson Mandela's victory in South Africa's first all-race election in 1994; and the Million Man March in 1995.

By 1969 *Jet* was among the top twenty magazines in sales in the United States. It is considered an authoritative source of information on African American life and events.

—*Glenn Ellen Starr Stilling*

See also: Black press; *Ebony*.

Jewish Americans and African Americans: The relationship between African Americans and Jewish Americans is coeval with the history of the United States. In 1621 Elias Legardo came to VIRGINIA on the *Abigail*, the first Jewish person to arrive in the colony; shortly before, the first Africans had arrived. Indeed, the presence of Africans in North America helped to ensure that the Jewish community would not be the primary recipient of bigotry, the role Jews had played traditionally in Europe. Similarly, it was recognized that reducing bigotry against African Americans would also help to reduce anti-Semitism. Recognition of this fact helped to ensure that many Jewish Americans played prominent roles in the African American struggle for equality. This was notably the case during the time when the abolition of SLAVERY was an important issue.

Yet this is only part of the picture. Jewish Americans were viewed as "white" and thus shared in a certain racial privilege. Moreover, anti-Semitism in Europe was stoked in part because those who were Jewish were barred from high-ranking roles in feudal societies; they were consigned to then less-reputable tasks associated with nascent capitalism. The "Merchant of Venice" stereotype perpetuated by William Shakespeare of Jewish people as heavily involved with commerce was a partial product of the reality of this feudal anti-Semitic bias. Hence, there were a number of Jewish Americans involved in the slave trade, which was considered an acceptable form of commerce in the antebellum South. Moreover, a prominent leader of the Confederacy, Judah Benjamin, was also a prominent leader of the Jewish community. This point-counterpoint of Jewish abolitionists and Jewish slave-traders has marked the black-Jewish relationship in the United States. Similarly, Jewish Americans were not the prime recipients of bigotry—they helped to fund the AMERICAN REVOLUTION and were beneficiaries of the First Amendment prohibition against a state religion—but anti-Semitism continued to persist, despite the relatively small number of Jews in the country.

The Black-Jewish Alliance

A new stage was marked in the black-Jewish relationship when Julius Rosenwald, the president of Sears, Roebuck, and Company from 1910 to 1925, began his philanthropy aimed at funding the education of African Americans. At the time, the Jewish population of the United States was growing, fueled by waves of immigration from Eastern Europe. The poverty, modes of dress, and customs of many immigrants were looked at askance by some, which fueled anti-Semitism. Rosenwald was of the opinion that racism and anti-Semitism had a similar root and that efforts to improve the plight of African Americans would have a salutary impact on Jewish Americans.

This notion of common origin of these prime forms of bigotry received a boost in 1915 when Leo Frank, a Jewish American in GEORGIA, was subjected to a punishment traditionally reserved for African Americans: He was lynched as a direct result of bias.

The founding of the NATIONAL ASSOCIATION FOR THE ADVANCEMENT OF COLORED PEOPLE (NAACP) on February 12, 1909, the centennial of the birth of Abraham Lincoln, was evidence of what came to be called a "black-Jewish alliance." W. E. B. DU BOIS was the most prominent African American leader of this CIVIL RIGHTS organization, which was founded by an assortment of socialists and liberals that included many Jews.

Over the years, black and Jewish attorneys fought side by side in the courts to overturn JIM CROW LAWS. Du Bois worked closely with Franz Boas of Columbia University, an anthropologist who was one of the earliest advocates of the equality of races. Melville HERSKOVITS, another Jewish anthropologist, also worked closely with leading African American scholars in his effort to demonstrate the historical cultural similarities between Africans and African Americans and the equality of the races generally. By the same token, approximately a decade later the Communist Party-USA was founded, and from the beginning had a significant percentage of Jewish Americans and African Americans in its leadership. It is understandable why those who have been subjected to radical forms of bias would be attracted to radical remedies of their plight; nevertheless, this association of Jewish Americans and African Americans with militance and radicalism served to reinforce preexisting bigotries.

World War II was a turning point in the decline of racism and anti-Semitism. The rise of Nazism suggested the debacle that would occur if bias were not checked. Ironically, a number of concentration camps with Jewish prisoners were liberated by segregated African American battalions. Moreover, the onset of the Cold War meant that the United States had difficulty winning hearts and minds by charging the Soviet Union with human rights violations when Jim Crow laws and other forms of prejudice were allowed to exist in the United States. The resultant erosion of Jim Crow also meant an erosion of anti-Semitism. This facilitated the entry of many Jewish Americans, particularly men, into elite circles of society, including the major universities and professions. Yet the price to be paid for this victory was an erosion of the influence of Jewish and black radicals—figures such as Herbert Aptheker and Du Bois—in their respective communities. The result was the rise of narrow nationalism and neoconservatism in both communities, a development that set the stage for a later crisis in black-Jewish relations.

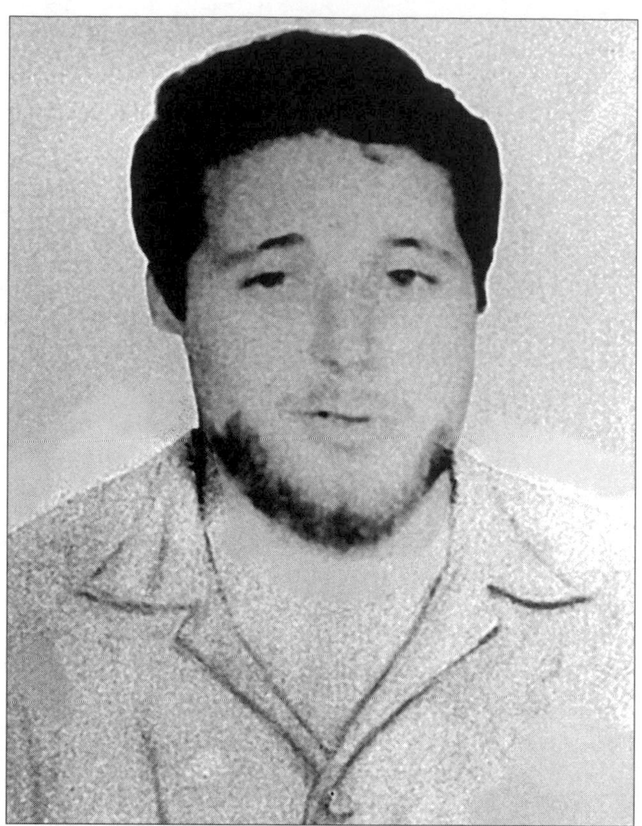
Michael Schwerner, one of the two Jewish civil rights workers killed in Mississippi in 1964. *(AP/Wide World Photos)*

Strains in Black-Jewish Relations

The first evidence of the crisis erupted with the Suez War of 1956. Many Jewish Americans supported Israel, while many African Americans sympathized instinctively with the underdog African nation of Egypt. This brewing crisis erupted again in 1967 with the Six-Day War. This time, the Student Nonviolent Coordinating Committee (SNCC), a major civil rights group, not only supported the Arab states but also denounced what it perceived as Israeli aggression. Stung, many Jewish organizations and individuals retaliated by cutting funding to SNCC and other civil rights organizations.

Yet at the same time that Israel was disrupting relations between American blacks and Jews, a number of Jewish Americans were continuing to play prominent roles in the struggle against Jim Crow. In 1964, when three civil rights workers were murdered in Mississippi, two were Jewish—Andrew Schwerner and Michael Goodman—and one, James Chaney, was African American. Polls continued to show that the Jewish community was more friendly toward the Civil Rights movement than other white Americans were. Jewish lawyers including William Kunstler and Arthur Kinoy acted as attorneys for the Civil Rights movement; Jack Greenberg served as an aide to Thurgood MARSHALL as he led NAACP litigation victories against Jim Crow.

Nevertheless, there were real problems in the heralded alliance, though it could be argued that the issues were more regional than national. For example, a disproportionate percentage of the Jewish population resided in NEW YORK CITY, which also happened to hold the largest African American population in the country. In New York, African Americans often confronted Jewish Americans as tenant to landlord or customer to shopkeeper. In Harlem and Bedford-Stuyvesant, these mercantile relationships often boiled over, and in a society where class consciousness was not high, such tensions often were expressed in racial and religious terms. Similarly, during the controversial teachers' strike in New York City in 1968, a proposal for community control of schools promulgated mostly by African Americans was opposed by a teachers' union led and heavily populated by Jewish Americans. Still, the concentration of the news media in New York City and the fury of such conflicts often obscured the fact that black-Jewish tensions may have been more a subset of a regional conflict than a national pattern.

Even when tensions erupted during the ousting of Andrew YOUNG from his post as U.S. ambassador to the United Nations in 1979, a New York flavor was evident. Young, a prominent black, resigned under pressure after having conducted an unauthorized meeting with representatives of the Palestine Liberation Organization, an act that sparked a furor in leading Jewish organizations. A headline in the *New York Post* stoked anger on both sides by suggesting that these organizations, infuriated with the Young meeting, had demanded his ouster.

Controversy Regarding Affirmative Action

It was difficult to say, however, that the conflict over AFFIRMATIVE ACTION was a regional issue. Many Jewish organizations were of the opinion that measures to include African Americans, other minorities, and nonminority women at all levels of society could harm Jewish interests, in part because quotas could be involved in the implementation of such measures. African Americans countered by pointing out that nonminority women—especially Jewish women—were probably the most significant beneficiaries of affirmative action and that, in any case, the quotas of old, which had been designed to exclude Jews, could not be compared with goals and timetables that were designed to include those previously beyond the pale. Nevertheless, the rise of neoconservatism and the prominent role played in this movement by Jewish intellectuals hostile to affirmative action complicated the alliance.

In any event, black-Jewish relations continued to be centered in New York City. At City College of New York in 1991, a Jewish professor charged that blacks were racially inferior, while an African American professor singled out the Jewish role in the slave trade and in perpetuating the negative images of minorities flowing from Hollywood. In Crown Heights, Brooklyn, the accidental killing of a black youth, Gavin Cato, by a Jewish motorist in 1991 led to the retaliatory slaying of a Jewish rabbinical student and a spate of racial-religious rioting.

A Decaying Alliance

Yet, whether a regional phenomenon or not, it is apparent that the alliance of old is fraying. This is in part a class question: Although many Jewish Americans have moved up to the elite levels of U.S. society, few African Americans have, and the groups' interests thus often conflict. It is in part ideological, in that the erosion of radical influence in both communities has facilitated the rise of neoconservatism among

Jews and narrow nationalism among blacks. It is partly religious, in that most African Americans are Christians or are influenced by ISLAM, and some have accepted the ancient biases of these religions against Judaism. Lastly, it is partly racial, in that Jewish Americans continue to enjoy a measure of "white privilege" that African Americans constantly challenge. Whatever the case, the rise of politicians such as David Duke is a reminder that racism and anti-Semitism have similar roots and that an allied struggle against both may be necessary to eradicate either.

—*Gerald Horne*

See also: Race, racism, and race relations; Racial discrimination; Racial prejudice; Racial violence and hatred; Religion.

Suggested Readings:

Finkelstein, Norman H. *Heeding the Call: Jewish Voices in America's Civil Rights Struggle*. Philadelphia: Jewish Publication Society, 1997.

Franklin, V. P., et al., eds. *African Americans and Jews in the Twentieth Century: Studies in Convergence and Conflict*. Columbia: University of Missouri Press, 1998.

Friedman, Murray. *What Went Wrong: The Creation and Collapse of the Black-Jewish Alliance*. New York: Free Press, 1995.

Friedman, Saul S. *Jews and the American Slave Trade*. New Brunswick, N.J.: Transaction, 1998.

Horowitz, Irving L. *Daydreams and Nightmares: Reflections on a Harlem Childhood*. Jackson: University Press of Mississippi, 1990.

Kaufman, Jonathan. *Broken Alliance: The Turbulent Times Between Blacks and Jews in America*. New York: Charles Scribner's Sons, 1988.

Levine, Hillel, and Lawrence Harmon. *The Death of an American Jewish Community: A Tragedy of Good Intentions*. New York: Free Press, 1992.

Phillips, William M., Jr. *An Illustrious Alliance: The African American and Jewish American Communities*. New York: Greenwood Press, 1991.

Weisbord, Robert G., and Richard Kazarian, Jr. *Israel in the Black American Perspective*. Westport, Conn.: Greenwood Press, 1985.

Jim Crow laws: Racially discriminatory statutes enacted by southern states after the CIVIL WAR ended in 1865. Also known as jimcrowism, the term "Jim Crow" developed into a late nineteenth-century synonym for segregation that endured well into the twentieth century.

The term's origins go back to a prewar minstrel character developed by the white entertainer Thomas D. Rice . More a caricature than

Contemporary caricature of T. D. Rice's Jim Crow character. *(Arkent Archive)*

Typical "Jim Crow" sign of the past. *(Library of Congress)*

a character, Rice's "Jim Crow" was a comic buffoon. Slow, misshapen, and dense, he was created to be humiliated and laughed at by white audiences. After the war, the name "Jim Crow" became a white stereotype of African Americans generally.

With the abolition of SLAVERY after the Civil War, the governments of the defeated Confederate states moved quickly to enact discriminatory laws that would reassert some of the white control over African Americans that had ended with slavery. Known as BLACK CODES, these laws restricted the rights of former slaves to own property, choose their employers, travel freely, and vote. The federal government overturned the black codes during the period of RECONSTRUCTION, which lasted from 1866 to 1877. Afterward, however, the South's reconstituted state governments imposed new discriminatory laws, including many that segregated public accommodations, conveyances, housing, and schools.

During the twentieth century African Americans increasingly referred to segregated institutions as "Jim Crow." After federal CIVIL RIGHTS legislation began sweeping away legally enforced segregation during the Civil Rights movement era, Jim Crow became a relic of the past.

—*Christopher E. Kent*

Job Opportunities in the Business Sector program: Federal government effort to find jobs for the disadvantaged. The Job Opportunities in the Business Sector (JOBS) program was launched in 1967. President Lyndon B. Johnson called together members of the National Alliance of Businessmen to work with the U.S. Department of Labor in finding ways to employ the jobless, especially those from minoritsy and disadvantaged groups. By 1970 about eighty thousand people had been hired in connection with the program.

The JOBS program was designed to make direct payments to organizations, both for-profit and nonprofit, that provided training and counseling for the targeted workers. The program's goal was to enable employers to hire and train in entry-level jobs disadvantaged individuals who otherwise would not have found employment. Upgrading of current employees who were members of targeted groups also was encouraged.

Black enrollment in the JOBS program fell, between 1971 and 1973, from 43 percent to 26 percent of those in the program. This decrease was a result in part of an emphasis by President Richard M. Nixon and his administration on helping groups other than disadvantaged minorities. For fiscal 1974, the program was allocated about $60 million, with the allocation rising to about $90 million for 1975.

See also: Employment and unemployment; Johnson administration; Nixon administration.

Jockeys: Black jockeys were major participants in early organized horse racing. A horse named Aristides won the first Kentucky Derby in 1875. His jockey was Oliver Lewis, an African American. All but two of the jockeys in that first Derby were African Americans.

Southern slaveowners interested in horses often built tracks on which to race their animals against other planters' horses. Slave blacksmiths shod the horses; slaves fed, watered, exercised, and trained them; and slaves rode them in the races. After the Civil War, African American involvement in the sport continued. Two years after Lewis, Billy Walker, riding Baden Baden, won the Derby. In 1882 Babe Hurd won it on Apollo.

Perhaps the most famous African American jockey was Isaac Murphy, who first won the Derby as Buchanan's rider in 1884. Murphy won two more Derbys, as the jockey on Riley in 1890 and as Kingman's rider in 1891. Other African American winning jockeys were

A former slave, Billy Walker rode Baden Baden to victory in the 1877 Kentucky Derby. *(AP/Wide World Photos)*

Notable Jockeys

Lewis, Oliver. Lewis won the first running of the Kentucky Derby in 1875, on a horse named Aristides. He later became a trainer in Lexington, Kentucky.

Long, James (b. 1954, New York, N.Y.). Long was the first African American jockey to win a race at the Saratoga Springs track in New York, in 1974. One of the few black jockeys active at the time, Long dropped out of school in the eleventh grade to pursue his career as a jockey.

McCurdy, Robert C. (b. 1941, Atlantic City, N.J.). McCurdy was one of the relatively few black jockeys active in the 1960's. In 1963, he was the leading jockey at the Garden State Park fall meet, winning thirty races. He won more than a hundred races in total that year. He had his first winner in 1962 and retired in 1964 to run a liquor store—which an active jockey would not be allowed to do. His career earnings exceeded one million dollars, and he rode more than three thousand mounts to a total of 264 wins.

Murphy, Isaac. *See main text entry.*

White, Cheryl (b. 1954, Rome, Ohio). On June 15, 1971, White rode her first mount in an organized race and became the first recognized female jockey.

Winkfield, Jimmy. Winkfield was victorious in consecutive Kentucky Derbys, with His Eminence in 1901 and Alan-a-Dale in 1902. He continued his career in France, becoming a successful jockey and trainer there.

Enoch "Babe" Henderson on Joe Cotton (1885); Isaac Lewis on Montrose (1887); Alfie Clayton on Azra (1892); J. (Soup) Perkins on Halma (1895); Willie Simms, who won the Derby twice, on Ben Brush in 1896 and Plaudit in 1898; and Jimmy Winkfield, on His Eminence in 1901 and Alan-a-Dale in 1902.

African American jockeys were just as successful at other race courses. In 1891 Monk Overton, riding at CHICAGO's Washington Park, won the first six races. Sixteen years later, another African American jockey, Jimmy Lee, won all six races at Churchill Downs. As racial violence and animosity spread in the United States, black jockeys all but disappeared from racing, just as African Americans were excluded from other professional sports. Jackie ROBINSON's success with BASEBALL's Brooklyn Dodgers in 1947 led to a gradual reintegration of African Americans into the sporting world, including horse racing. Nevertheless, black jockeys made no particular impact on the sport through the rest of the twentieth century.

John Henry myth: The subject of songs, stories, poems, and paintings, John Henry is a mythical cultural hero. He is celebrated as the "steel-driving man" who competed against and defeated the newly invented automatic steam drill in the nineteenth century.

During the 1870's, construction of the Chesapeake & Ohio Railroad in WEST VIRGINIA required laborers, many of them African Americans, to lay track and to cut tunnels through the Appalachian Mountains. The work was demanding, dangerous, and slow. To speed construction, the railroad company brought in a steam drill for tunneling and laying track.

The manual way of laying track involved numbers of two-man teams, one member of which drove in steel spikes with a sledgehammer. According to the story, John Henry, one of the black drivers, stood up for himself and his coworkers by challenging the steam drill to a steel-driving race. In many versions, the competition occurred at the 1.25-mile long Big Bend Tunnel, which was dug in 1872. Many drivers used ten-pound hammers, but John Henry was so strong that he could wield a twenty-pound hammer in each hand, a fact that allowed him to defeat the machine. Having beaten the machine, John Henry died from exhaustion, still holding a hammer in his hand.

Because such inventions as the steam drill placed laborers such as John Henry at risk of losing their jobs, his victory over technology, not simply his dying, is emphasized in music, literature, and art. Most versions of the John Henry myth stress his awareness of his fate as an infant, his physical strength, his test and

Paul Robeson in a 1940 stage production of Roark Bradford's *John Henry. (AP/Wide World Photos)*

success against the steam drill, and his death. Some versions also emphasize women's love for John Henry, so that the story takes on sexual connotations.

Scholars have attempted to determine whether there is any factual basis for the John Henry story but have been unable to find consistent evidence that it is based on a real person or event. Nevertheless, both the conflict played out between man and machine and the pervasiveness of the John Henry myth itself remain integral parts of American culture.

—Kevin Eyster

Johns, Vernon (April 22, 1892, Darlington Heights, Virginia—June 11, 1965, Washington, D.C.): Minister. An intellectually gifted and iconoclastic minister, Vernon Napoleon Johns combined liberal social gospel theology with strong messages of racial equality and economic self-sufficiency.

Born near Farmville, VIRGINIA, to former slaves, Johns attended Virginia Theological Seminary and College and graduated with a B.D. from OBERLIN COLLEGE, where he had persuaded the dean to admit him by translating works from German and Greek. He enrolled in the Graduate School of Theology at the University of Chicago and was ordained a BAPTIST minister in 1918. In the 1920's he pastored at several Baptist churches, and in 1926 his "Transfigured Moments" became the first selection by an African American minister to be included in the well-known yearly collection *Best Sermons*. From 1929 to 1934 he was president of Virginia Theological Seminary and College.

Never one to settle anywhere for long, Johns was an itinerant lecturer/preacher at colleges and Baptist churches and a part-time farmer for much of the remainder of his life. From 1947 to 1952 he preceded Martin Luther KING, Jr., as the pastor of Dexter Avenue Baptist Church in MONTGOMERY, ALABAMA. There he antagonized local whites by delivering sermons such as "It's Safe to Murder Negroes in Montgomery" and "When the Rapist Is White." He also offended his black middle-class congregation with sermons such as "Mud Is Basic" and by peddling produce outside the church after Sunday services. Johns was director of the Maryland Baptist Center from 1953 to 1960.

—Richard W. Leeman

Johnson, Ben (b. December 30, 1961, Falmouth, Jamaica): Sprinter. Born in JAMAICA, Benjamin Sinclair Johnson, Jr., emigrated to Canada with his family in 1976. Johnson's mother worked more than one job in order to earn enough money to allow her sons to train as sprinters. Ben's older brother Edward took him to train at the Toronto Optimist Club when Ben was fifteen years old. Eager to compete as a sprinter, Ben entered a Black Heritage track meet three days after his first training run. Although he competed in shoes that lacked cleats and had placed his starting blocks the wrong way, Johnson finished his first 100-meter competition in eleven seconds flat.

Ben and his brother trained with Canadian coach Charlie Francis, a former world-class athlete who built a TRACK AND FIELD program around a group of Jamaican-born sprinters. Edward Johnson accepted a track scholarship to attend Lamar University in TEXAS, but Ben turned down American scholarships in order to keep training with Francis. Johnson became legendary in Canadian track circles for his determination to practice and maintain a regimen of weight training. After securing sponsorship from corporations such as Mazda, Timex, and Adidas, Johnson began earning sufficient income from track meets to help his family move from Toronto's Little Jamaica neighborhood to a large suburban home.

Johnson earned international fame at the 1987 World Track and Field Championships held at Rome, Italy, where he edged out American sprinter Carl Lewis to finish the 100-meter event with a world record time of 9.83 seconds. Johnson's record surpassed the record of 9.93 seconds set by American Calvin Smith in 1983 at the U.S. Olympic Committee Sports Festival held in Colorado Springs. Johnson's victory was the first gold medal won by a Canadian at a world championship track meet in fifty-five years, and it brought attention to the growing number of black athletes competing for Canada.

Johnson finished first in the 100-meter event at the 1988 Summer Olympics in Seoul, Korea, with a world-record time of 9.79 seconds. Post-race drug screening revealed that Johnson tested positive for banned substances. He was disqualified, his record was disallowed, and second-place finisher Carl Lewis was awarded the gold medal. Johnson's world records in the 100-meter event and indoor 60-meter event were also declared invalid, and charges against him were upheld in a special hearing held in Canadian courts. Although he was allowed to compete at the 1992 Summer Olympic Games, Johnson was banned from the sport for life after testing positive again for steroid use in 1993.

See also: Canadian blacks; Jamaica and Jamaican Americans.

Johnson, Budd (December 14, 1910, Dallas, Texas—October 20, 1984, Kansas City, Missouri): Tenor saxophonist, composer, and arranger. The younger brother of trombonist Keg Johnson, Albert J. "Budd" Johnson received his first music instruction from his father, who was an organ and cornet player. Johnson was privileged to study next with Booker T. Washington's daughter, Portia Pittman. At this time, Johnson played the piano, but he soon tried playing drums and became involved with a touring show. Before long, Johnson switched to tenor saxophone and began playing in bands that toured Texas. In 1929 he joined Terrence Holder's band, Twelve Clouds of Joy, which also worked throughout Texas. The band later was taken over by Jesse Stone, and it expanded its touring area into Missouri. Johnson next played under the leadership of George E. Lee, until 1931. In 1932 Johnson moved to Chicago, Illinois, where he envisioned himself playing with some of the great names in jazz.

Johnson first played with Clarence Shaw at the Grand Terrace in Chicago. Within a relatively short period of time he got a chance to play with Louis Armstrong. Johnson stayed with Armstrong until Armstrong's band broke up in the summer of 1933. During 1934, he alternated between Jesse Stone's Cyclones and Earl Hines's band. Starting in 1935, Johnson began an almost continuous relationship with Earl Hines's band which lasted until 1942. He became Hines's musical director in 1938 and was responsible for producing a number of innovative big band pieces. Johnson gained eminence among younger musicians for his bold and forward-looking approach to jazz arrangements and compositions. During the 1940's, he did arrangements for Billy Eckstine, Woody Herman, Buddy Rich, and many others. Johnson remained active as a saxophonist by playing for Eckstine, Dizzy Gillespie, Sy Oliver, and others.

By the 1950's, Johnson was leading his own small groups. He also arranged and produced some early rock and roll records. While continuing to do freelance arranging and playing, Johnson played with Benny Goodman during 1956 and 1957, Gil Evans in 1959, Quincy Jones during 1959 and 1961, and Count Basie during 1961 and 1962. He played again with Hines, intermittently throughout the late 1960's. In 1969 Johnson formed the JPJ Quartet, which included Bill Pemberton on string bass, Oliver Jackson on drums, and Dill Jones on piano. The quartet remained together until 1975. Throughout the 1970's and into the early

1980's, Johnson taught at a number of universities and played at several international jazz festivals. Johnson was an important arranger and composer whose best work combined the swing sound with a BEBOP flavor. He was also a very gifted saxophonist whose heartfelt yet restrained style delivered a solid impact.
See also: Chicago jazz.

Johnson, Bunk (December 27, 1879, New Orleans, Louisiana—July 7, 1949, New Iberia, Louisiana): Cornetist and trumpeter. William Geary "Bunk" Johnson was one of the JAZZ world's most colorful and controversial figures. He began his career after demanding an audition with the legendary yet unstable cornetist Buddy Bolden, who was impressed by the youngster's arrogance. In turn, Johnson became the only link to the unrecorded Bolden, playing in the style of his mentor.

As a teenager, Johnson moved to Storyville, the NEW ORLEANS red-light district. Its honky-tonks and nightlife made Storyville an important part of the emerging world of jazz. It was in Storyville that Johnson was exposed to the sounds of Buddy Bolden, pianist Ferdinand "Jelly Roll" MORTON, and other performers who established New Orleans as the jazz capital of the world.

After his stint as second cornetist in Bolden's Olympia Band, Johnson wandered about the United States, playing sporadically with a number of bands and teaching music through a Works Progress Administration program. Eventually he faded into obscurity. In 1942, however, he was rediscovered by jazz enthusiasts William Russell and Frederick Ramsey, Jr., and became a focal point of the New Orleans jazz revival of the 1940's.

Along with many of his contemporaries, Johnson began recording and performing for countless fans who sought answers to the origins of the music. True to his nickname, Johnson usually had a story to tell. He had become a master of hyperbole, telling impossible stories and boasting of excesses. In many ways, Johnson's return to prominence served to divide the jazz world into camps of either pro or anti-Bunk Johnson.

When he was not playing the role of unreliable historian, Johnson continued to provide ample evidence of his music skills. In 1945 some much-needed dental work afforded Johnson the opportunity to resume his recording career. He also played a number of dates with clarinetist Sidney BECHET, which brought them both some critical acclaim. In 1948 Bunk Johnson suffered a stroke from which he never recovered fully.
See also: Music.

Johnson, Charles Richard (b. April 23, 1948, Evanston, Illinois): Writer and artist. A master storyteller with published works in a variety of genres, Johnson helped expand the boundaries of African American LITERATURE. Weaving together a unique combination of African American themes, traditional folktales, and key ideas from philosophy and Eastern religion, he produced award-winning novels, short stories, screenplays, literary studies, and drawings that reflect the black experience and affirm human goodness in a complex world.

Artistic from an early age, Johnson published his first drawing at age seventeen, under the guidance of cartoonist and writer Lawrence Lariar. Johnson sold more than one thousand drawings to magazines and eventually published two books of drawings, *Black Humor* (1970) and *Half-Past Nation Time* (1972). He studied journalism at Southern Illinois University in Carbondale and graduated in 1971. He wrote and aired episodes of *Charlie's Pad*, a 1970-1971 how-to television show on cartooning. Johnson continued to write for television while exploring other media. His teleplays include *Charlie Smith and the Fritter Tree* (1978); *Booker* (1984, cowritten with John

Author Charles R. Johnson receiving the National Book Award for *Middle Passage* in 1990. *(AP/Wide World Photos)*

Allmann), a dramatization of Booker T. Washington's struggle for education, which won four awards; and *Me, Myself, Maybe* (1982).

After earning his master's degree from Southern Illinois University in 1973, Johnson undertook three years of doctoral work at the State University of New York at Stony Brook while writing novels. His novels, known for their vivid imagery, mystery, allegory, and sometimes humor, usually deal with the personal journeys and rites of passage of African American protagonists. They include *Faith and the Good Thing* (1974), written under the tutelage of writer John Gardner, *Oxherding Tale* (1982), a philosophical slave narrative that was given the 1983 Governor's Award for Literature, and *Middle Passage* (1990), a portrait of a mystical African tribe of Zen sorcerers that earned Johnson a National Book Award. Johnson had already won critical acclaim for tales about this tribe in *The Sorcerer's Apprentice* (1986), a collection of short stories examining prejudice and cultural assimilation.

In the late 1970's, Johnson began teaching at the University of Washington and serving as fiction editor of the *Seattle Review.* He was director of the university's creative writing program from 1987 to 1990. During that time, he published his first work of literary criticism, *Being and Race: Black Writing Since 1970* (1988). In 1990 he was awarded an endowed chair, the first Pollock Professorship in Creative Writing at the University of Washington.

Johnson's novel *Dreamer* was published in 1998; a collection entitled *I Call Myself an Artist: Writings by and About Charles Johnson,* edited by Rudolph P. Byrd, and *Africans in America: America's Journey Through Slavery,* cowritten with Patricia Smith and based on a television series produced for Boston Public Broadcasting Service station WGBH, were published in 1999.

Johnson, Charles S. (July 24, 1893, Bristol, Virginia—October 27, 1956, Louisville, Kentucky): Scholar, educator, and sociologist. His father, the Reverend Charles Henry Johnson, was an emancipated slave whose former master drilled him in Latin, Greek, and Hebrew, and in English and American literature. Johnson's mother, Winifred Branch Johnson, wove spirituals and work songs into hymns.

Johnson attended Wayland Academy, a division of Virginia Union University in Richmond. He graduated from Virginia Union as valedictorian and earned his doctorate on a fellowship at the University of Chicago. In Chicago, he formed a close association with sociologist Robert E. Park, from whom he developed an objective, scientific attitude toward race relations. Park was president of the Chicago branch of the National Urban League.

Johnson, a man with many talents, served in various capacities. He was director of research and records (1917-1919) of the Chicago Urban League. While he was associate executive director of the Chicago Commission on Race Relations, he developed a classic study, *The Negro in Chicago: A Study of Race Relations and a Race Riot* (1922). Johnson moved to NEW YORK CITY in 1921 to become the director of the Department of Research and Investigations for the Urban League. In 1923 he assumed the editorship of the Urban League's magazine, *Opportunity: A Journal of Negro Life*.

In 1928 Johnson left the National Urban League to become chair of the social science department at FISK UNIVERSITY. He did most of his social science writings there. In 1946 he became the first African American president of Fisk, which he developed into an outstanding university.

Johnson served on many committees that were appointed by presidents of the United States from Herbert Hoover to Dwight D. Eisenhower. He was the recipient of several honorary degrees and one of the most influential African Americans in the nation, upon whose counsel many foundations and philanthropic enterprises relied.

See also: Race, racism, and race relations; Washington, Booker T.

Johnson, Eddie Bernice (b. December 3, 1935, Waco, Texas): Nurse and TEXAS politician. Johnson grew up in Waco, Texas, and left home to attend college in Indiana. After earning her nursing degree from St. Mary's College of Notre Dame in 1955, she returned to Texas and worked for sixteen years as a psychiatric nurse at the Veterans Administration Hospital in Dallas. During this time, she earned a second nursing degree from Texas Christian University in 1967. In 1972 she launched her political career when she ran as a Democratic candidate for a seat in the Texas House of Representatives. Although labeled as an underdog, Johnson won a landslide victory on her way to becoming the first African American woman elected by the citizens of Dallas to hold public office.

During her term in the state legislature, Johnson earned a master's degree in public administration from Southern Methodist University. Her political skills came to the attention of President Jimmy Carter, who appointed Johnson to serve as a regional director of the Department of Health, Education, and Welfare (HEW) in 1977. She left office in 1981 to launch her own business. In 1986 she won election to the Texas State Senate. During her six years in the state senate, Johnson focused attention on EDUCATION and improved access to health care. A tenacious fighter against racial injustice, Johnson worked hard on behalf of her constituents. She chaired the reapportionment committee that was responsible for establishing three new federal congressional districts based on population figures for Texas established in the 1990 U.S. census.

Among the new districts created by her committee was the Thirtieth District, with a population that was 50 percent African American and 17 percent Hispanic. After she announced her candidacy for this newly created congressional district, Johnson was criticized by opponents who accused her of political opportunism. Declaring her intention of providing political representation for a strong minority district without diminishing the political base of neighboring districts, Johnson campaigned on the basis of her demonstrated commitment to public service. Voters in the new district gave Johnson a landslide victory over her opponent, and she became one of fifteen African American members of 1993 freshmen legislators in Congress (including Senator Carol Moseley BRAUN). She was named the CONGRESSIONAL BLACK CAUCUS whip (later the group's secretary) and was appointed to serve on the Science, Space, and Technology

Committee and the Public Works and Transportation Committee. Johnson was reelected in 1995, 1997, and 1999.
See also: Carter administration; Congress members; Politics and government; Redistricting.

Johnson, Fenton (May 7, 1888, Chicago, Illinois—September 17, 1958, Chicago, Illinois): Poet. Johnson was educated in CHICAGO's public schools and attended Northwestern University and the University of Chicago. Although Johnson wrote in diverse literary forms, he is best known for his poetry. Much of his poetry focuses on racial injustices and, at the same time, depicts the positive aspects of African American life. His poetry was heavily influenced by the urban realism of Carl Sandburg and the gloomy pessimism of Edgar Lee Masters.
See also: Literature.

Johnson, George Ellis (b. June 16, 1927, Richton, Mississippi): Business executive. Johnson founded Johnson Products Company, involved in hair care and cosmetics, in 1954 and incorporated it in 1957. In 1971 it became the first company owned by an African American to be listed on a major stock exchange, the American Stock Exchange.

Johnson was an entrepreneur from an early age. His family moved to CHICAGO, ILLINOIS, when he was very young. He soon began selling old newspapers and milk and soda bottles. When he was nine years old, his mother had a shoe-shine box built for him. He would walk more than thirty blocks to the downtown area to secure customers. He left school in the eleventh grade and worked as a lab assistant at Fuller Products Company from 1945 to 1948, when he became a production chemist. He supported a wife and two children, so for a while had to work a second job as a hotel busboy. S. B. FULLER, the company's owner, proved to be an inspirational example of black entrepreneurship for Johnson, who chose to go into partnership with a black barber. A finance company turned down his request for a $250 business loan. He applied for a loan of the same amount from a different branch of the company, this time stating that he wanted the money to take his wife on a vacation. The second request was granted, allowing him to start Johnson Products Company.

George Ellis Johnson.

His bad experiences with the financial world led Johnson to help organize the Independence Bank in 1964. The bank later named him as chair of its board of directors. He established the George E. Johnson Foundation in 1969 to give assistance to civic and welfare organizations worldwide. His George E. Johnson Educational Fund, endowed by him in 1972 with a million dollars, had by 1985 awarded more than five hundred business education scholarships to low-income students.

When his company went public, Johnson sold 17 percent of it for nearly eight million dollars but stayed on as president and chief executive officer. In 1975 the company controlled about 60 percent of the black hair care market, but the Federal Trade Commission required it to put notices on its Ultra Sheen hair relaxer containers noting that the product contained lye. Johnson had never patented his product because he did not want to face the delays involved in the process. Other companies had copied his product, but none was forced to put warning labels on its product. By 1980 the Johnson Products Company's market share had fallen to 40 percent. The company opened a factory in Lagos, Nigeria, in 1980 and planned to market a range of products in Africa. Ultra Sheen soon became the generic name used in Nigeria for hair straightening products.

EBONY magazine gave Johnson its American Black Achievement Award in 1978. Johnson was named to the boards of directors of numerous major companies, including Commonwealth Edison Company. He also served on the board of the Chicago Urban League.
See also: Business and commerce.

Johnson, Georgia (September 10, 1886, Atlanta, Georgia—May 14, 1966, Washington, D.C.): Poet, dramatist, and composer. Johnson was educated in Atlanta's public schools, ATLANTA UNIVERSITY, HOWARD UNIVERSITY, and the Oberlin Conservatory of Music. She is best known for her four volumes of poems and numerous poems appearing in periodicals. The content of her poetry is varied, ranging from universal themes, such as love, nature, dreams, and loneliness, to social protest.

Johnson, Henry (1897, Winston-Salem, North Carolina—July 2, 1929, Washington, D.C.): MILITARY hero. Johnson served in the 369th Infantry Division (formerly the Fifteenth New York Infantry), the first black regiment to fight in WORLD WAR I. It engaged a German regiment at Champagne, on the Rhine River. Johnson took on a German patrol unit singlehandedly after his four comrades on the guard had been wounded. Johnson, although wounded himself, rescued a captured member of his company, confiscated German equipment, and killed and wounded several German soldiers with the three bullets in his rifle, his bolo knife, and the rifle itself after he had emptied it. For his heroics, France honored him with its Croix de Guerre. Johnson was the first American to win the Croix de Guerre in World War I. Although the United States did not honor Johnson with a medal, the Army recognized his valor by promoting him from private to sergeant. Before the regiment left Europe, France recognized the entire 369th Infantry Division with a separate Croix de Guerre.

Johnson, Jack (March 31, 1878, Galveston, Texas—June 10, 1946, Raleigh, North Carolina): Boxer. John Arthur "Jack" Johnson was one of the greatest—and most controversial—prizefighters in history. Further, his career meant much to African Americans, who had little to celebrate in the early twentieth century, a time when segregation and discrimination had reduced them to third-class citizenship.

Early Career

Johnson began his BOXING career early; as a youth he fought bouts in the Galveston area. He and his opponents engaged in "battle royals," in which five or more black youngsters would climb into a ring and engage in a brawl; at the end of a bout, a predominantly white crowd would toss pennies and nickels into the ring. Because racial attitudes discouraged interracial matches, Johnson fought only other African American youngsters. Money he earned in battle royals did not give him a living wage nor allow him to help support his parents, so he took work as a porter and later became a barber's helper. By the time he matured, Jack had become a muscular dockworker who weighed slightly more than 180 pounds and stood more than six feet tall. He never gave up boxing, and by 1897 he was fighting opponents one-on-one in various clubs in the Houston-Galveston area. He won most of his bouts with a defensive, counterpunching style.

By 1901 Johnson had proven that he was the best black boxer in eastern TEXAS; in search of bigger purses, he went to CALIFORNIA, which had become a national center for boxing. Soon, he was fighting local boxers in the Bakersfield area and was working as a sparring partner for Kid Carter of Oakland. Later, he fought in CHICAGO and in various East Coast cities. When he returned to California, he brought a solid reputation as a fighter with him. In 1902 Johnson fought his first match with a white man, Jack Jeffries, the brother of the reigning world heavyweight champion, Jim Jeffries. Jim Jeffries could only watch as his brother was knocked out by the African American boxer.

Cross-Country Tours

Soon, Johnson began another Chicago-East Coast tour, a successful one in which he won all his bouts. After his return to California, he soon contracted to fight "Denver" Ed Martin, who held the "Negro" heavyweight title. In the 1903 match, Johnson bested Martin in a twenty-round decision. Now a 195-pound bundle of muscle, Johnson demanded, but did not get, a title fight with Jim Jeffries, who said that he would retire rather than fight a "Negro." Other leading white heavyweights such as Bob Fitzsimmons and Marvin Hart also dodged the black champion. In early 1904, however, Hart's manager relented when promised a large gate by promoters of a Johnson-Hart interracial fight. Although Johnson's defensive style kept him in the match for twenty rounds, he was disqualified by the referee, who ruled that he was not aggressive enough.

Johnson again set out on a cross-country tour. Back on the East Coast from 1904 to 1907, he fought many bouts against both black and white boxers, including at least one European. He also toured, putting on boxing exhibitions with his friend Joe Jeannette. Then, in 1907, on the advice of promoters, he went to Australia, a world boxing center. There he fought both white and black Australians, and by the time he returned to California, he had gained an international reputation. White champions had an increasingly difficult and more embarrassing time ducking him.

Drive to the Championship

In 1907 in PHILADELPHIA, Johnson met the white boxer Bob Fitzsimmons—who at different times had held the crowns in the middleweight, light heavyweight, and heavyweight divisions. Facing a forty-four-year-old boxer who was fighting because he was poverty-stricken, Johnson won the match in the second round. Then, after Johnson won yet more bouts on the West Coast, he demanded a championship fight with the white Canadian Tommy Burns, who had taken the crown in 1906. Just as white sportswriters were finally intervening with Burns, asking him to "play fair" and fight Johnson, the Canadian suddenly left the country, fighting in England, Ireland, and France. Johnson was a step behind Burns, though, and finally caught him in Australia, where promoters made Burns a financial offer that he could not refuse.

According to writer Jack London, who personally watched the fight on December 26, 1908, in Sydney, Johnson humiliated Burns, hitting him at will and taunting him with each blow. Long denied a chance to fight for the white heavyweight crown, Johnson seemed to toy with the Canadian, who at the end of thirteen rounds was covered with blood. Yet Burns would not quit; police entered the ring in the fourteenth round to end the match.

The white world was astounded by Johnson's victory, because of prevailing beliefs that black people were inferior, mentally and physically, to whites. Even Burns had become a victim of that theory; he believed the myth that blacks had hard heads but weak stomachs. Burns thus concentrated on hitting Johnson with body punches while Johnson laughed at him. Additionally, while Johnson was crafty and quick, he—like all blacks—was believed to have little physical durability; if the fight really got tough, Johnson was expected to quit.

Jack Johnson, the first African American world heavyweight boxing champion. *(Arkent Archive)*

Johnson's Image

Johnson had adopted the persona of what one of his biographers later called "The Bad Nigger"; the mature Johnson never played "Sambo" for whites. Indeed, he was arrogant; his self-esteem and ego were available for everyone to see both in and out of the ring. He played the sporting-man image to the hilt. He wore wild clothes, replete with clashing colors, and he was never seen without an assortment of flashy hats, canes, and jewelry. Johnson consorted with gamblers and prostitutes, some of whom were white. Moreover, three of his four wives were white; Johnson thus broke the most sacred of white society's taboos.

Seeing his arrogance, his "uppity" behavior, many whites began a campaign to find a "Great White Hope" who could take the championship away from Johnson. Most blacks applauded Johnson and his antics; he became a hero to the African American community. His very life disproved theories about white supremacy.

From day one of Johnson's reign as champion, some whites searched frantically for a way to annul his accomplishments. The first white challenger was Stanley Ketchel, a former middleweight champion. Although Ketchel managed at one point to put Johnson on the canvas, Johnson won with a knockout in the twelfth round. Next, Jim Jeffries, the former heavyweight champion, came out of retirement to face Johnson, who bested him in fifteen rounds; after the fight, several white RACE RIOTS occurred. Johnson successfully defended his title until 1915.

Career in Decline

Given Johnson's apparent indestructibility, some whites tried to "divorce" Johnson from the championship. In 1913 in California, promoters held a "White Heavyweight's Championship," and Luthur McCarty emerged with the new crown; yet the world knew

McCarty was a counterfeit and dismissed his victory. Anti-Johnsonians were not beaten, however; they searched the law until they found a way to attack him. In 1910 Congress had passed the Mann Act, which forbade men from transporting women across state lines for "immoral purposes." Congress had apparently intended the law to strike at organized prostitution, but the loose wording of the Mann Act allowed authorities to prosecute any individual who crossed a state line with any woman who was not his wife. In 1913 Johnson was tried under the Mann Act, convicted, and sentenced to one year in prison; he fled to France, where authorities refused requests to extradite him.

Johnson and his second wife, Lucille Cameron, settled in Paris, where Johnson continued to fight, but the French people had little interest in boxing. By 1915 Johnson was suffering financial troubles, so he agreed to go to CUBA to fight the up-and-coming Jess Wilard. At thirty-seven years of age, Johnson was finally bested by a man who was half a foot taller and at least twenty pounds heavier. Many white Americans rejoiced; a white hope had finally won.

Even after the loss of his title, Johnson continued to live the only life he knew. He fought in France, England, Spain, and MEXICO. He also performed exhibitions demonstrating his strength; for a time, he traveled with a circus. In the end, Johnson was forced to return home because he alienated authorities in host countries; in 1920 he reentered the United States, where he began serving his prison term. In the last quarter of his life, Johnson continued to make his living from public appearances based on his past notoriety; he remained the sporting man, loving flashy clothes, wild women, and fast cars.

Johnson's life became the subject of a Broadway play, *The Great White Hope*, in which James Earl JONES won a Tony Award in 1969 for his portrayal of Johnson. Jones also earned an Oscar nomination for his reprisal of the role in the film adaptation of the play the following year.

—James Smallwood

See also: Ali, Muhammad; Louis, Joe; Robinson, Jackie; Sports.

Suggested Readings:

Batchelor, Denzil. *Jack Johnson and His Times*. London: Phoenix Sports Books, 1956.

Bennett, Lerone, Jr. "Jack Johnson and the Great White Hope." *Ebony* (April, 1994): 86-93.

Deardorff, Donald L., II. "World Boxing Champion Jack Johnson, Contemptuous and Irritating, Taunted Whites." *St. Louis Journalism Review* 26 (October, 1995): 8-10.

Gilmore, Al-Tony. *Bad Nigger: The National Impact of Jack Johnson*. Port Washington, N.Y.: Kennikat Press, 1975.

Roberts, Randy. *Papa Jack: Jack Johnson and the Era of White Hopes*. New York: Free Press, 1983.

Johnson, James P. (February 1, 1894, New Brunswick, New Jersey—November 17, 1955, New York, New York): Composer and piano player. Considered to be one of the leading exponents of New York stride piano, James Price Johnson is credited with some two hundred compositions. Johnson was a major influence on JAZZ pianists of his era and afterward, having influenced Duke ELLINGTON and Art TATUM.

In 1908 the Johnson family moved to NEW YORK CITY, where Johnson was exposed to a variety of musical influences. He received formal training in the European classical tradition from Bruto Giannini and was exposed to BLUES songs and ragtime pianists Abba Labba (Richard McLean) and Eubie BLAKE. Johnson, who recorded with Bessie SMITH, Perry BRADFORD, and numerous other artists during the 1920's, performed in New York venues such as Barron's nightclub and Drake's Dance Hall.

Known for his participation in cutting sessions during which pianists competed for supremacy, Johnson, described as "the father of stride piano," became part of a select group of New York stride pianists that included Fats WALLER and Willie "the Lion" SMITH.

Johnson's compositions included "The Harlem Strut" (1921) and "Carolina Shout" (1921). Johnson also wrote for the Broadway stage during the 1920's, composing his first musical, *Runnin' Wild,* in 1923. Out of this musical emerged "The Charleston," which became identified with the dance craze of the era. Johnson also began writing longer compositions such as "Yamekraw," a piano rhapsody that William Grant STILL brought to Carnegie Hall in 1927. Fats Waller was a key collaborator with Johnson, having performed as soloist in the premiere of "Yamekraw." Waller and Johnson composed the Broadway revue *Keep Shufflin'* (1928). During the 1930's, Johnson continued to write longer compositions, producing "Harlem Symphony" (1932), "Jasmine" (1934), a piano concerto, and "Symphony in Brown" (1935). He also recorded *Jingles* (1930) and *You've Got to be Modernistic* (1930).

Collaborating with Langston HUGHES, Johnson wrote the music for "De Organizer," a one-act blues opera which was performed at Carnegie Hall in 1940. During the 1940's, Johnson, who participated in the radio series *This Is Jazz* (1947), suffered health problems, culminating in a number of strokes that caused his retirement from music in 1951.

Johnson, James Weldon (June 17, 1871, Jacksonville, Florida—June 26, 1938, Wiscasset, Maine): Novelist, poet, songwriter, journalist, teacher, attorney, CIVIL RIGHTS activist, and diplomat. James Weldon Johnson was one of the most influential and respected African Americans of the early twentieth century. If he stood in the formidable shadows of Booker T. WASHINGTON and W. E. B. DU BOIS, he nevertheless contributed in numerous and important ways to the development of African American culture before, during, and beyond the HARLEM RENAISSANCE.

Early Life and Careers

James William Johnson (he changed his middle name to Weldon in 1913) was born in Jacksonville, FLORIDA, to James Johnson, a headwaiter at a resort hotel, and Helen Dillet Johnson, a schoolteacher at Stanton School, the local school for black students. As a boy, Johnson was largely shielded from the racism that he would be forced to confront throughout his adult life. Johnson's parents instilled in him and in his brother, John Rosamond JOHNSON, a deep sense of racial pride as well as an appreciation of LITERATURE and of music; the brothers were avid readers and proficient pianists at an early age. After graduating from Stanton School in 1887, Johnson enrolled in preparatory school at ATLANTA UNIVERSITY, earning his college degree in 1894. He returned to Jacksonville to become principal of Stanton School. He founded the short-lived *Daily American*, a weekly newspaper. In 1896 he embarked on yet another career path, that of law, under the tutelage of a local attorney. Despite the opposition of a racist lawyer on the examining panel for his bar examination, Johnson passed and was admitted to the Florida bar in 1898.

Musical Collaborations

In the years that followed, however, he devoted his energies not to law but to poetry and music. With his brother and Bob Cole, Johnson collaborated on a number of musical compositions, the most famous of which is "Lift Every Voice and Sing" (1901), composed in celebration of Abraham Lincoln's birthday. Johnson wrote the lyrics to the song, which was later adopted by the NATIONAL ASSOCIATION FOR THE ADVANCEMENT OF COLORED PEOPLE

(NAACP) and which became known as the "Negro national anthem." Johnson's musical collaborations were so successful that in 1902 he left his position at Stanton School and moved to NEW YORK CITY to pursue a career in music with his brother and Cole. The trio scored a major hit with "Under the Bamboo Tree" (1902), which was used in the popular stage musical *Sally in Our Alley*. In 1905 their popularity brought them a six-week engagement at a London theater.

The year before the London engagement, Johnson had joined a black political organization that lobbied for President Theodore Roosevelt in the election of 1904. Johnson collaborated with his brother and Cole on two campaign songs for the successful Roosevelt campaign. At the suggestion of Roosevelt political supporters, Johnson, who was fluent in Spanish, applied for foreign-service positions, and in 1906 Roosevelt appointed him U.S. consul at Puerto Cabello, Venezuela. Three years later, Johnson took charge of the U.S. consulate at Corinto, Nicaragua. In 1910 he married Grace Neil, and in 1913 he resigned from the foreign service and returned to New York City. Shortly thereafter, he became contributing editor to the NEW YORK AGE, an influential black weekly. During his nine years with the *Age* (1914-1923), Johnson wrote several hundred editorial essays on a wide variety of social, political, and literary topics of concern to the black community.

When Johnson first published *The Autobiography of an Ex-Coloured Man* anonymously in 1912, many readers thought it was a real autobiography. *(Arkent Archive)*

Novelist

While stationed in Corinto, Johnson published his only novel, *The Autobiography of an Ex-Coloured Man* (1912); it is his most famous work and is considered a landmark in African American literature. The novel—which was first published anonymously and which many readers believed was an actual autobiography—is the story of an illegitimate son of a southern white man and his mulatto mistress. Because he is light-skinned, the book's unnamed narrator does not discover that he is a "nigger" until a racist grade school teacher separates him from white students in the class. Following the death of his mother, whom his father had abandoned, the narrator travels in the North, South, and Europe, his journey a symbolic exploration of race relations in the United States.

Like the mulatto characters who preceded and would follow him in American fiction—for example, the fair-skinned heroine of Frances E. W. Harper's *Iola Leroy* (1892) and the self-hating Joe Christmas of William Faulkner's *Light in August* (1932)—Johnson's protagonist must struggle with his racial identity and decide whether to reject or embrace his African American racial heritage. At first, the narrator determines to be a great and famous "coloured man," but after witnessing the horror of LYNCHING, he decides to pass for white and turns his back on the struggle for racial justice. That decision, however, leaves the "ex-coloured man" spiritually unfulfilled and guilt-ridden. Despite its artistry and compelling scenes, *The Autobiography of an Ex-Coloured Man* was virtually ignored by the literary establishment and the reading public until 1927, during the Harlem Renaissance, when it was reissued with an admiring introduction by the influential white critic and novelist Carl Van Vechten.

Poet

While working on the novel, Johnson, who had begun writing poetry in college, was composing poems, including "Fifty Years." Commemorating the fiftieth anniversary of the signing of the EMANCIPATION PROCLAMATION, the poem praises the spiritual strength of African Americans and stresses their patriotism and their contributions to the building of the nation. In 1917 Johnson published *Fifty Years and Other Poems*, with a laudatory introduction by the Columbia University professor and critic Brander Matthews. (During his early days in New York, Johnson had taken courses in dramatic literature from Matthews, who recognized Johnson's talents and encouraged him to write his novel and poetry.) The several dozen poems and jingles in the collection include a number of dialect verses and cover a wide variety of subjects and moods, but their form is conventional.

James Weldon Johnson, perhaps the most versatilely talented civil rights leader of the early twentieth century. *(Library of Congress)*

In his next volume of poetry, *God's Trombones: Seven Negro Sermons in Verse* (1927), Johnson experimented with free verse as he sought to capture the style and rhythms of African American preachers' sermons. Most critics consider these poems superior to those of the earlier volume. In addition to his own poetry, Johnson performed a major service to African American literature by editing *The Book of American Negro Poetry* (1922; revised and enlarged in 1931), *The Book of American Negro Spirituals* (1925), and *The Second Book of American Negro Spirituals* (1926). His prefatory essay to the first edition of *The Book of American Negro Poetry*, in which he argues that the music and folktales of African Americans are the most distinctively American contributions to world art, is a seminal work of African American literary criticism.

Johnson produced another volume of poetry, *St. Peter Relates an Incident: Selected Poems*, in 1935, but most of his literary work during the 1930's was in nonfiction genres: *Black Manhattan* (1930), a history of blacks in New York City; *Along This Way* (1933), his autobiography; and *Negro Americans, What Now?* (1934), an analysis of the problems facing African Americans and suggestions for solving those problems.

Civil Rights Activist

Unlike the ambivalent narrator of *The Autobiography of an Ex-Coloured Man*, Johnson himself was throughout his life deeply committed to the civil rights struggle. In addition to his literary activities on behalf of his race, he was a major force in the NAACP. Johnson joined the organization in 1916 and in 1920 was elected its head, the first African American to hold that position. Under Johnson's leadership, the NAACP agitated for civil rights. Johnson was particularly active in the campaign against lynching, but his lobbying of Congress to pass an antilynching bill was futile. In 1930 Johnson resigned his NAACP post to become a professor of creative literature and writing at FISK UNIVERSITY, where he remained until a 1938 car accident brought his remarkable life to a close.

Often referred to as the "elder statesman" of the Harlem Renaissance, Johnson influenced many of the younger black writers of that era and such later ones as James BALDWIN and Ralph ELLISON. In 1971 special issues of *Phylon* and THE CRISIS honored the centennial anniversary of his birth.

—*Lawrence J. Oliver*

Suggested Readings:

Bruce, Dickson D., Jr. *Black American Writing from the Nadir.* Baton Rouge: Louisiana State University Press, 1989.

Fleming, Robert E. *James Weldon Johnson.* Boston: Twayne, 1987.

________. *James Weldon Johnson and Arna Bontemps: A Reference Guide.* Boston: G. K. Hall, 1978.

Levy, Eugene. *James Weldon Johnson: Black Leader, Black Voice.* Chicago: University of Chicago Press, 1973.

Price, Kenneth M., and Lawrence J. Oliver, eds. *Critical Essays on James Weldon Johnson.* New York: G. K. Hall, 1997.

Stepto, Robert B. *Behind the Veil: A Study of Afro-American Narrative.* Urbana: University of Illinois Press, 1979.

Wilson, Sondra K., ed. *In Search of Democracy: The NAACP Writings of James Weldon Johnson, Walter White, and Roy Wilkins (1920-1977).* New York: Oxford University, 1999.

Johnson, John H. (b. January 19, 1918, Arkansas City, Arkansas): Business executive. John Harold Johnson founded the JOHNSON PUBLISHING COMPANY, which produces EBONY, JET, and other magazines. He became involved in a number of other business ventures as well; his interests combined to give him a net worth estimated at more than $150 million in the 1990's.

Johnson's mother, Gertrude, took him to live in CHICAGO, ILLINOIS, in 1933, because there were no high schools in his Arkansas City birthplace for black children. Chicago was the destination for many black migrants at the time and was viewed as offering the best opportunities for African Americans. Johnson took the eighth grade twice in Arkansas City because the family could not afford to move by the time he was ready to advance into high school. Mrs. Johnson worked occasionally as a domestic in Chicago, but for two years she was unable to keep her family off welfare. At the time of his high school graduation, Johnson abandoned the name of Johnny, by which he was known, and chose John Harold.

Johnson approached Harry Pace, the president of Supreme Life Insurance Company, after one of Pace's speeches. Pace, impressed with Johnson, offered him a part-time job at the company so that he would be able to afford college. Johnson attended Northwestern University and the University of Chicago but dropped out because he preferred the business environment at Supreme. He edited the company's monthly newspaper and briefed

Pace, an African American accused of being out of touch with the black community, on the news events that he read about in newspapers and magazines.

This experience convinced Johnson of the need for a black general interest magazine, even though previous similar ventures had failed. Pace allowed Johnson to use a company mailing list to solicit prepaid subscribers, but he still needed money for postage. He borrowed $500, using his mother's furniture as collateral. *Negro Digest*, the first product of Johnson Publishing Company, premiered on November 1, 1942. Using a technique that he would implement for other products later, Johnson bought copies of the magazine from newsstands to convince distributors that there was demand for it and that they should promote it.

By the end of 1943, *Negro Digest* had a monthly circulation of fifty thousand. An October, 1943, column by Eleanor Roosevelt for the recurring feature "If I Were a Negro" helped push circulation to one hundred thousand. Johnson launched *Ebony* in November of 1945 and *Jet*, a pocket-sized weekly news summary, in November of 1951. In that year, he became the first African American to be recognized by the U.S. Junior Chamber of Commerce as one of the ten outstanding men of the year.

Johnson began branching into other business fields. He began Beauty Star Cosmetics as a mail-order firm in 1946. After his magazines became more successful, he wanted to let the cosmetics line die, believing it was not respectable. Orders continued even after he stopped advertising, so he gave the line new life as Supreme Beauty Products in 1960. Fashion Fair Cosmetics, taking its name from the Ebony Fashion Fair that toured the United States, was launched in 1973 as an upscale line providing products specifically for black women. Johnson ventured into hardcover book publishing in 1962 with *Before the Mayflower: A History of the Negro in America, 1619-1962*, by Lerone BENNETT, Jr., a historian and senior editor at *Ebony*. Johnson bought WJPC, an AM radio station, in 1973 and followed it with other radio acquisitions. *Negro Digest* was discontinued in 1951, but several new titles took its place. *Ebony Man*, a FASHION and lifestyle magazine, was launched in 1985.

At one time, Johnson was criticized for the heavy focus on entertainment in *Ebony*. He argued that the features drew readers, who only then would investigate the serious issues also covered in the magazine, and he also led the magazine to greater attention to issues. The Magazine Publishers of America named him as Publisher of the Year in 1972. He was inducted into the Black Press Hall of Fame in 1987.

In 1971 Johnson was elected to the board of Twentieth Century-Fox. This led to appointments to numerous other boards of directors. In 1974 he was elected chairman and chief executive officer of Supreme Life Insurance Company, his old employer. He also became the company's largest stockholder.

Johnson also was active in politics. In 1957 he was a member of a press team that accompanied Vice President Richard Nixon on a tour of nine African countries. President John F. Kennedy named Johnson as special ambassador to the independence ceremonies of the Ivory Coast in 1961, and President Lyndon B. Johnson made him a delegate to the independence ceremony in Kenya in 1963 as well as naming him to the National Selective Service Commission.

Johnson published his autobiography, *Succeeding Against the Odds*, in 1989, with the assistance of Lerone Bennett, Jr. In that book, he describes his business and personal life, touching on plans to have his daughter, Linda Johnson Rice, succeed him. He made her president and chief operating officer of Johnson Publishing Company.

See also: Black press; Business and commerce.

Johnson, J. Rosamond (August 11, 1873, Jacksonville, Florida—November 11, 1954, New York, New York): Composer and performer. John Rosamond Johnson was the second son of James and Helen Johnson, and brother to James Weldon JOHNSON. His mother taught him to play the piano at an early age. After Johnson completed his formal education in Jacksonville, he went to the New England Conservatory of Music in Boston, where he studied with Charles Dennée, Dietrich Strong, George Whiting, and Carl Riessman, among others. He also studied privately with Samuel Coleridge-Taylor in London. In 1896 he went to NEW YORK CITY, where he was a member of the cast of John Isham's *In Oriental America*. He returned to Jacksonville in 1897 to serve as a public school teacher, and later as music supervisor, until 1908.

He began in 1899 to set to music texts by his brother, James Weldon Johnson. This collaboration produced several works, among which are the opera *Toloso* and the song "Lift Every Voice and Sing" (1901). In 1901 both brothers teamed up with William Cole, a singer, dancer, writer, and actor. The trio successfully wrote and produced musical comedies and songs. Among these are *The Shoo-Fly Regiment* (1906) and *The Red Moon* (1908), written for all-black casts. Under a three-year contract signed with Joseph W. Stein, the Johnson brothers and Cole wrote many songs, including "The Maiden with the Dreamy Eyes," "The Maid of Timbuctu," "My Castle on the Nile," "Under the Bamboo Tree," and "Oh, Didn't He Ramble." These songs were performed by such leading singers as Anna Held, Lillian Russell, Bert WILLIAMS, Marie Cahill, George Primrose, and Fay Templeton. The brothers and Cole also signed another contract, with Klaw and Erlanger, that led to the production of *Sleeping Beauty and the Beast* (1901) and *Humpty Dumpty* (1904) as Broadway musicals.

In 1906 James left the trio to become the U.S. consul in Venezuela. Rosamond and Cole

Composer J. Rosamond Johnson in 1939. *(AP/Wide World Photos)*

established a vaudeville act that toured the United States until Cole died in 1911. In 1912 Johnson collaborated with Charles Hart in London and produced *Come Over Here*. After his marriage to Nora Ethel Floyd in London, Johnson returned to the United States to assume the directorship of the Music School Settlement for Colored People in HARLEM in 1914. After serving in the armed forces, he teamed up with Taylor Gordon in vaudeville acts in the 1920's. He remained active as a performer in George Gershwin's *Porgy and Bess* productions between 1935 and 1942. He also took roles in *Blackbirds* (1939), *Mamba's Daughters* (1939), and *Cabin in the Sky* (1940).

In addition to his performances, Johnson served as music editor for several publishers. He collaborated with his brother in two publications: *The Book of American Negro Spirituals* (1925) and *The Second Book of Negro Spirituals* (1926). He also published two collections, *Shout Songs* (1936) and *Rolling Along in Song* (1937).

Johnson, Judy (October 20, 1900, Snow Hill, Maryland—June 15, 1989, Wilmington, Delaware): BASEBALL player. William Julius "Judy" Johnson, the son of William and Annie Johnson, began his baseball career with black amateur and semiprofessional teams in PENNSYLVANIA. In 1921 Johnson signed to play with the Philadelphia Hilldales, one of the top NEGRO LEAGUE BASEBALL teams of the time. An outstanding defensive third baseman and a powerful hitter, Johnson led the Hilldales to Eastern Colored League pennants in 1923, 1924, and 1925 and to victory in the 1925 Negro League World Series. Johnson also played for the Pittsburgh Homestead Grays and the Pittsburgh Crawfords before retiring as a player in 1936.

In the 1950's, after the breaking of the major league color line, Johnson began a career as a scout and instructor with the Philadelphia Athletics and, later, the Philadelphia Phillies. In 1973 Johnson retired from baseball; two years later, he was inducted into the National Baseball Hall of Fame.

Johnson, Katherine G. (b. 1918, West Virginia): Physicist and space scientist. Johnson worked with the National Aeronautics and Space Administration with teams that tracked manned and unmanned orbital missions. She was a pioneer in new navigation techniques to determine more practical ways of tracking space missions. Her work involved analysis of data from the lunar missions.
See also: Physicists.

Johnson, Lonnie (February 8, 1889, New Orleans, Louisiana—June 18, 1970, Toronto, Canada): BLUES musician. Johnson's father led a string orchestra and trained all of his thirteen children to play stringed instruments in the musical group. Alonzo "Lonnie" Johnson first mastered the violin, then the guitar, bass, and piano. He did not sing at that time.

He and his brother James "Steady Roll" Johnson played together in various restaurants until U.S. Navy officials shut down the NEW ORLEANS, LOUISIANA, district known as Storyville in 1917. Johnson went to England with a touring group. When he came back to New Orleans in 1918, he discovered that his entire family, except for his brother James, had died in the 1918 influenza epidemic.

For some time thereafter, he played on Mississippi River riverboats, such as the *Capitol*, with Fate Marable. He and his brother James lived in St. Louis, MISSOURI, where they worked day jobs. Learning of a blues contest at a local theater, with a first prize of a recording contract with OKeh records, Johnson entered and sang for the first time. He won, and in January, 1926, his first record was issued, "Mr. Johnson's Blues" and "Falling Rain Blues."

Johnson performed on the RKO and Theatre Owners Booking Association (TOBA) circuits. Johnson thought of himself as an instrumental performer rather than a singer, and he worked as a studio musician for OKeh records. In that role, he played with Louis ARMSTRONG's Hot Five ("I'm Not Rough" and "Hotter than That") and Duke ELLINGTON ("The Mooche" and "Hot and Bothered"). He also toured with the Bessie SMITH show.

In 1939 his Bluebird (RCA Victor) recording, "I'm a Jelly Roll Baker," was a RHYTHM-AND-BLUES hit. Cincinnati's King Records released his "Tomorrow Night" in 1947, and it was something of a "crossover" hit, popular with white listeners as well as with African Americans. Johnson's self-accompaniment on a twelve-string acoustic guitar influenced younger blues guitarists, and he is credited with popularizing the single-line countermelody to the vocal among performers such as Big Bill BROONZY and B. B. KING.

In subsequent years, Johnson worked in CHICAGO, ILLINOIS, HOUSTON, TEXAS, and other cities, usually in between "day jobs." After a brief career revival in the early 1960's at folk festivals in the United States and England, he moved to Canada. He was hit by a car in 1969, never recovered his health, and died of a stroke in 1970. Johnson's formative New Orleans experience and his knowledge of East Texas bluesmen such as Blind Lemon JEFFERSON and T-Bone WALKER made his sound quite different from that associated with Delta and Kansas City blues.

Johnson, Magic (b. August 14, 1959, Lansing, Michigan): Professional BASKETBALL player. Earvin "Magic" Johnson, Jr., represents one of the revolutions in the game of basketball. He, possibly more than any other player in the history of the game, brought flexibility to player roles and positions. Enthusiasm born of love for the game, unprecedented skill at the point guard position, and the deep social implications surrounding his retirement give Johnson's life the qualities of a legend.

Award-Winning Career

Johnson grew up in a working-class MICHIGAN home. His father was a body worker in an auto plant and did many odd jobs to augment the family income. Johnson gives credit to his father for guidance on many levels, from general work ethic and business sense to specific points in the fundamentals of basketball. At Everett High School notoriety first came to the six-foot, eight-inch guard. As he led Everett to the 1977 Michigan state championship, Johnson became a local hero to area youth, who already were pretending to be Johnson in their playground games.

During his two-year college career at Michigan State University, Johnson received All-Big-Ten and All-American honors. He led the Spartans to the national championship in 1979. The Los Angeles Lakers chose Johnson as the first pick of the 1979 National Basketball Association (NBA) draft. His impact was immediate. The Lakers were transformed from a slow-down, half-court team to the fast-break, running team that would win five NBA championships in the 1980's. After playing his entire rookie season as a guard, Johnson took over the center position from an ailing Kareem ABDUL-JABBAR for the sixth game of the 1980 championship series against the Philadelphia 76ers. While the general consensus was that the Lakers would lose that game and return to

Magic Johnson helped revolutionize professional basketball during the 1980's by bringing exceptional team skills and enthusiasm to the game. *(Andrew D. Berstein/Courtesy of the Los Angeles Lakers)*

Los Angeles to win the seventh game with Abdul-Jabbar back in the lineup, Johnson scored forty-four points to lead the team to victory and was named most valuable player of the series. Throughout his NBA career, Johnson earned virtually every personal honor available, including three NBA most valuable player awards.

Johnson's 1991 Retirement

The primary phase of Johnson's career came to a sudden and reverberating end in November, 1991. As a result of having contracted the human immunodeficiency virus (HIV), the cause of the deadly ACQUIRED IMMUNODEFICIENCY SYNDROME (AIDS), Johnson was advised by doctors that he should no longer play professional basketball. He retired from the Los Angeles Lakers but returned to professional-level playing after he was selected to compete on the U.S. basketball team at the 1992 Olympic Games. After the "Dream Team" captured the gold medal, Johnson announced his decision to return to the Lakers.

However, controversy surrounded a minor injury that caused Johnson to bleed during an exhibition game in 1992. A number of NBA players threatened to boycott games against the Lakers unless the league took strong precautions to ensure against transmission of the AIDS virus. Johnson announced that he would retire once again. This second retirement decision touched off a fresh wave of concern about the disease that had already affected millions.

AIDS Activist

Magic Johnson was anything but inactive during the rest of the 1990's. A highly visible spokesperson in the fight against the virus associated with AIDS, Johnson served in a number of different fund-raising and governmental capacities. The profits of his 1992 book, *What You Can Do About AIDS*, were donated to AIDS research. Johnson showed remarkable courage in revealing intimate details about his personal life, despite criticism from the homosexual community for appearing to be unsympathetic to their experiences as victims of the virus. Johnson served on the Presidential Commission on the Human Immunodeficiency Virus Epidemic, but he resigned in October of 1992, citing a difference of opinion with policies promoted by the Bush administration. Johnson and his wife, Cookie, continued to campaign for AIDS awareness, education, and sexual responsibility, focusing much of their work on reaching out to members of the African American community.

Later Careers

Ongoing workouts and a daily regimen kept Johnson in excellent physical condition. He was also the principal founder and star of the Magic Johnson All-Stars, a barnstorming team consisting of former collegiate and professional players. He remained involved with the NBA as a part-owner of the Lakers and served as the team's interim coach for fifteen games near the end of the 1993-1994 season. Although he was offered the coaching job on a full-time basis, Johnson turned it down, citing the grueling NBA schedule as being too physically and emotionally taxing.

Johnson had to contend with attacks on his personal character. He was sued for gross negligence by Waymer Moore, a woman who claimed to have contracted HIV from Johnson as the result of a one-night sexual encounter in 1990. The lawyers based their case on Moore's claim that Johnson had never disclosed his promiscuous lifestyle to her before their encounter.

In July of 1995, Magic Johnson held a press conference in conjunction with the Laker organization. In a statement concerning his rumored return to the NBA, Johnson said that he enjoyed his retirement and wanted to continue barnstorming with his all-star team while leaving his schedule open for other appearances and his many business interests. He also expressed his desire to spend more time with his wife and children: a son, Earvin Johnson III (born in 1993), and daughter, Elisa (adopted in 1995).

Johnson became involved in large-scale property development, opening theaters, restaurants, and shopping centers in urban and inner-city areas. By 1996 his net worth was estimated to be about $100 million. In 1995 Johnson, through his Johnson Development Corporation, opened Magic Johnson Theatres, a motion picture complex in the predominantly middle-class black neighborhood of Baldwin Hills in Los Angeles. As a partnership with Sony Entertainment, Johnson's sixty-million-dollar, state-of-the-art theater complex was projected as the first of a chain of theaters designed to show films that appeal to black audiences. By 1999 Johnson had also opened theater complexes in Atlanta and Houston, and Johnson Development Corporation had purchased shopping centers in Los Angeles and Las Vegas.

On January 30, 1996, Johnson returned to the Los Angeles Lakers and again began competing in NBA games. Praised by many for his leadership, maturity, and confidence, he displayed impressive versatility during his return, but he was sometimes frustrated by the role assigned to him by the coaches and other players. He retired again in May, 1996. In 1997 Johnson's physicians reported that the AIDS virus in his body was being held to undetectable levels by medication. Johnson briefly hosted his own late-night talk show, *The Magic Johnson Hour*, on the Fox network in 1998.

—*Updated by Joel N. Rosen*

See also: Business and commerce; Olympic gold medal winners; Sports.

Suggested Readings:

Blatt, Howard. *Magic! Against the Odds*. New York: Pocket Books, 1996.

Johnson, Earvin. *My Life*. New York: Random House, 1992.

Johnson, Rick L. *Magic Johnson: Basketball's Smiling Superstar*. New York: Dillon, 1992.

Stauth, Cameron. *The Golden Boys*. New York: Pocket Books, 1992.

Johnson, Malvin Gray (January 28, 1896, Greensboro, North Carolina—October 4, 1934): Painter. Johnson worked as a commercial artist for a living. He enjoyed painting his native rural South and preferred African American subjects. He was one of the first African American artists to experiment with cubism and was said to use many of the styles of white painters. He was trained at the National Academy of Design and won the Otto H. Kahn Prize in 1928.

See also: Painters and illustrators.

Johnson, Michael (b. September 13, 1967, Dallas, Texas): Track and field sprinter. The youngest of five children born to Paul and Ruby Johnson, Michael Johnson grew up in the Oak Cliff section of Dallas. Michael and his siblings were encouraged to excel at school, and all five went on to graduate from college. Johnson initially decided to pursue track competitions as a way to guarantee entry into a good college. After graduating from Skyline High School in Dallas, Texas, he was accepted at Baylor University. At Baylor, Johnson was recruited to run relays and began training year-round in individual and team events. Johnson became a record-setting athlete while competing in NCAA events for Baylor; in 1990, he ended the year ranked first in the world in both the 200- and 400-meter events. That same year, he completed his bachelor's degree in business from Baylor.

In the 1990's, Johnson continued to improve his running times. In 1994 and again in 1995, Johnson was ranked first in the world in both events. He also established records as the first athlete to run 200 meters in less than 20 seconds and to run 400 meters in less than 44 seconds. At the 1995 National Championship Track and Field Meet, held in Sacramento, California, in June, Johnson became the first American athlete to win both the 200- and 400-meter competitions, surpassing the accomplishments of Carl Lewis. He repeated the feat at the World Championships held in Göteborg, Sweden, in August of 1995, becoming the first competitor to finish first in both events at an international meet. In addition to his world championship medals, Johnson was awarded a Mercedes-Benz automobile for each of his victories.

Johnson evolved an unorthodox running style, coming out of his mark to stand up straight, even bent slightly backward, almost immediately. He also takes short, choppy strides, rather than the long, graceful strides characteristic of many sprinters. Johnson's sprinting style has also been considered unusual because he does not use the high knee lifts common among other sprinters. Despite these differences, Johnson established new world records in the 200-meter event twice in 1994-1995 and won forty-one consecutive 400-meter events between 1990 and 1995. Previously, hurdler Edwin Moses was the only individual to achieve such a long winning streak.

Johnson did not have the expected success at the 1992 Summer Olympics in Barcelona, Spain. While in Barcelona he became ill with food poisoning and failed to qualify in the 400-meter event. He did recuperate in time to anchor the men's 1,600-meter relay team, which won the gold medal and established a new world record.

On the other hand, his performance in the 1996 Olympics in Atlanta, Georgia, was triumphant. He broke the world record in his tryout for the 200-meter. In the games themselves, he won the 400-meter race in record Olympic time, then won the 200-meter by breaking his own world record by more than 0.3 seconds; his time was a remarkable 19.32 seconds. U.S. team coach Erv Hunt referred to Johnson's abilities as "almost superhuman." In the 1997 World Track and Field Championships in Athens, he won his third world championship in the 400-meter race. Johnson also won the decathlon in the 1998 Goodwill Games.

—*Updated by John Jacob*

See also: Olympic gold medal winners.

Johnson, Mordecai Wyatt (January 12, 1890, Paris, Tennessee—September 10, 1976, Washington, D.C.): Clergyman and educator. Johnson enrolled at Morehouse College in Atlanta, Georgia, in the fall of 1905. He graduated from Morehouse with a B.A. in 1911 and received an appointment to teach English there. Johnson discovered that teaching English was not what he wanted to do, so he earned a second B.A. from the University of Chicago in the social sciences in 1913. Despite his success as a teacher at Morehouse, he left there in 1913 to enter Rochester Theological Seminary, from which he graduated in 1916. In 1923 he received the Master of Sacred Theology from Harvard; in 1928, he received the Doctor of Divinity from Gammon Theological Seminary.

Johnson's ambition was to become a minister. While he was enrolled at Rochester Theological Seminary, he was pastor of the Second Baptist Church in Mumford, New York. His gift as an orator, which manifested itself while he was in high school, complemented the ministry. For nine years, he pastored the First Baptist Church in Charleston, West Virginia, where he established himself firmly as a spiritual and civic leader.

In 1926 Johnson became the first African American to serve as president of Howard University. When he assumed the presidency, Howard was without academic distinction. By the time he retired in 1960, he had made the university strong and prominent.

Mordecai W. Johnson, the first African American president of Howard University. *(Associated Publishers, Inc.)*

The university was producing half of the nation's African American physicians, and its law school was in the forefront of CIVIL RIGHTS. Johnson was responsible for securing annual federal financial support for Howard. A recipient of numerous honorary degrees, Johnson also won the prestigious SPINGARN MEDAL (1929) for having contributed the most toward the progress of African Americans during the previous year.

Johnson, Robert (May 8, 1911, Hazlehurst, Mississippi—August 16, 1938, Greenwood, Mississippi): BLUES singer and guitarist. Johnson was the eleventh child of Julia Major Dodds (the wife of Charles Dodds), but his biological father was Noah Johnson. Julia Dodds later married a man named Willie "Dusty" Willis, and Robert lived for a time with Charles Dodds. Johnson was known by several names, including Robert Dodds, Robert Spencer (the surname adopted by Charles Dodds, who moved to Memphis), and a few others. He apparently did not use the surname "Johnson" until he was a teenager. He apparently had little formal schooling, but one of his brothers taught him some guitar basics. He also had some proficiency on the harmonica.

By the late 1920's, Johnson had married, but his wife, Virginia Travis, died in childbirth. He furthered his guitar playing techniques from an association with Eddie "Son" House in the 1930's. He was also influenced by Willie Brown, with whom he played at various MISSISSIPPI juke joints, fish fries, small clubs, and picnics. He moved around the country as an itinerant musician and migrant worker to places including Helena, ARKANSAS (where he met his common-law wife, Ester Lockwood), Illinois, Kentucky, Missouri, Michigan, New Jersey, New York, Texas, and North and South Dakota. Although he was regarded as a loner, he performed occasionally with other blues musicians such as Henry Townsend, Johnny SHINES (with whom he appeared on a local radio program in Detroit in 1937), Sonny Boy WILLIAMSON, HOWLIN' WOLF, and others.

Johnson's celebrated twenty-nine recordings for the Vocalion/American Record Company label were made in November, 1936, in San Antonio, Texas, and June, 1937, in Dallas. They included "Come On in My Kitchen," "Dust My Broom," "I'm a Steady Rollin' Man," "Kind Hearted Woman," "Terraplane Blues," "Crossroads Blues," "Me and the Devil Blues," and "Hellhound on My Trail." The last three songs formed the basis of legends regarding Johnson's obsession with the devil.

Myths surrounding Johnson's death in 1938 only added to the folklore surrounding his life. He was reportedly poisoned or stabbed during an engagement in Greenwood, Mississippi. Not until the early 1970's was his death certificate found. Johnson's vocal style was taut and nasalized, but not of the raspy quality of several older bluesmen such as Charley PATTON and Blind Lemon JEFFERSON.

Johnson, Sargent (October 7, 1888, Boston, Massachusetts—October 10, 1967, San Francisco, California): Artist. Johnson became well known in 1925, when his works were shown by the San Francisco Art Association. He won the Harmon Foundation award, as outstanding African American artist, three times. Johnson's most representative works are figures of African Americans. African art forms influenced his work, which consisted largely of ceramics and metal sculpture.
See also: Painters and illustrators.

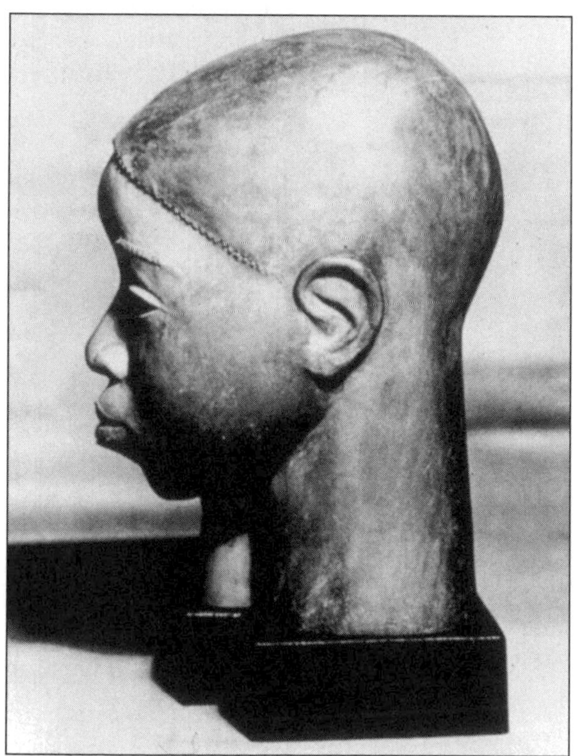

Sargent Johnson's sculpture *Chester* reflects the style of early Nigerian bronzes. *(National Archives)*

Self-portrait of William Henry Johnson. *(National Archives)*

Johnson, William Henry (1901, Florence, South Carolina—April 13, 1970, Long Island, New York): Painter. Johnson was a pioneer black modernist. During his long career, he explored several different styles, including abstract and expressionist. Although his work reflects the influence of Vincent Van Gogh and Georges Rouault, Johnson's paintings, most notably his studies of black life, are clearly American. He painted murals for the Works Progress Administration and was once jailed for painting in a South Carolina street.
See also: Painters and illustrators.

Johnson administration: Many African Americans supported the Democratic ticket of John F. Kennedy and Lyndon B. Johnson in the presidential election of 1960 because they trusted Kennedy's verbal commitment to CIVIL RIGHTS. Vice President Johnson became president upon Kennedy's assassination on November 22, 1963. Civil rights leaders worried that Johnson, who was from TEXAS, would be less enthusiastic than Kennedy about pushing civil rights initiatives. However, Johnson proved more aggressive than Kennedy had been, and the deep emotions stirred by Kennedy's assassination helped Johnson persuade Congress to pass landmark legislation. During his five years in office, Congress passed the most significant pieces of civil rights legislation since the RECONSTRUCTION era a century earlier.

In his first state of the union address, delivered in January, 1964, Johnson called for passage of a civil rights act that would provide "increased opportunity for all." During the following months, Johnson worked with congressional leaders to pass legislation that became known as the Civil Rights Act of 1964. The bill, which Johnson signed on July 2, 1964, outlawed literacy tests as a qualification for voting and prohibited segregation in restaurants, motels, theaters, stadiums, and other public places. The following year, Martin Luther KING, Jr.'s march from Selma to Montgomery, ALABAMA, dramatized the need for legislation to ensure the voting rights of African Americans. Johnson proposed and signed the VOTING RIGHTS ACT OF 1965, which attempted to eliminate the remaining barriers that prevented African Americans from voting in the South. In 1968 Johnson also signed legislation outlawing discrimination in housing.

During his tenure in office, Johnson also initiated an ambitious program to help America's poor. The WAR ON POVERTY, which provided federal funds for medical, educational, and social programs to serve the poor, assisted millions of Americans with incomes below the POVERTY line.

Two months after taking office, President Lyndon B. Johnson met with (left to right) Roy Wilkins of the NAACP, James Farmer of CORE, Martin Luther King, Jr., of the SCLC, and Whitney Young of the National Urban League. *(AP/Wide World Photos)*

Notable African American Appointees in the Johnson Administration

Robert C. Weaver	Secretary of Housing and Urban Development (the first African American cabinet member)
Andrew F. Brimmer	Assistant secretary of Commerce; member of Federal Reserve Board
Lisle Carter, Jr.	Assistant secretary of Health, Education, and Welfare
Mercer Cook	Ambassador to Senegal and Gambia
Patricia R. Harris	Ambassador to Luxembourg
Aileen Clarke Hernandez	Commissioner on Equal Employment Opportunity Commission
Samuel C. Jackson	Assistant secretary of Housing and Urban Development
Clinton Knox	Ambassador to Dahomey
Thurgood Marshall	Solicitor general
Elliot P. Skinner	Ambassador to Upper Volta (Burkina Faso)
Hugh H. Smythe	Ambassador to Syria
Hobart Taylor, Jr.	Vice chairman of the Equal Employment Opportunity Commission
Samuel Z. Westerfield	Deputy assistant secretary for economic affairs at Bureau of African Affairs (State Department)
Franklin Williams	U.S. representative to UNESCO; ambassador to Ghana

Johnson further demonstrated his commitment to civil rights by naming the first African American justice to the U.S. SUPREME COURT. In 1967 Johnson appointed to the Court Thurgood MARSHALL, who thirteen years before had spearheaded the legal team that successfully argued for an end to school segregation in the landmark 1954 case BROWN V. BOARD OF EDUCATION.

Despite Johnson's achievements in the area of civil rights, African Americans became increasingly discontented during Johnson's tenure in office. In 1965, a week after Johnson signed the Voting Rights Act, a race riot broke out in the WATTS section of Los Angeles. The riot, the immediate cause of which was an altercation between white policemen and African American residents, lasted five days and caused thirty-four deaths. Two summers later, in 1967, devastating race riots also occurred in Newark, Detroit, Cleveland, Milwaukee, and Memphis. The two most deadly were in NEWARK and DETROIT. The Detroit riot lasted a week and claimed forty-three lives. Rioting again broke out in urban centers across the United States after the assassination of Martin Luther King in April, 1968.

Johnson's presidential tenure, which ended in January, 1969, was also marred by the VIETNAM WAR. Johnson called for American involvement to be escalated repeatedly, until the war proved so divisive within the United States that it led him not to seek reelection in 1968. The war also drew funding away from his antipoverty programs. A disproportionate number of African Americans were fighting and dying in the war, leading many African Americans to criticize the war effort and call for an end to American fighting in Vietnam.

—*James Tackach*

See also: Housing discrimination; Selma to Montgomery march; Watts riots.

Suggested Readings:

Andrew, John A., III. *Lyndon Johnson and the Great Society*. Chicago: Ivan R. Dee, 1998.

Dallek, Robert. *Flawed Giant: Lyndon B. Johnson, 1960-1973*. New York: Oxford University Press, 1998.

Mann, Robert. *The Walls of Jericho: Lyndon Johnson, Hubert Humphrey, Richard Russell, and the Struggle for Civil Rights*. New York: Harvest Books, 1997.

Kearns, Doris. *Lyndon Johnson and the American Dream*. New York: Harper and Row, 1976.
Sikkoff, Harvard. *The Struggle for Black Equality, 1954-1980*. New York: Hill and Wang, 1981.

Publisher John H. Johnson. *(AP/Wide World Photos)*

Johnson Publishing Company: Magazine publisher. The world's largest African American-owned publishing company, Johnson is the leading publisher of African American magazines. In the late 1990's it was the second-largest African American-owned business in the United States.

Johnson Publishing was created in November, 1942, by twenty-four-year-old John Harold Johnson. Johnson, then the editor of the company newspaper at the African American-owned Supreme Life Insurance, compiled weekly news reports about African Americans to keep the company president informed. He turned this idea into a magazine, *Negro Digest*, which he started with a $500 loan procured with his mother's furniture as collateral. Johnson pre-sold copies, and after the first publication he encouraged friends to ask for the magazine at local newsstands to stimulate sales. The first issue offered articles and features by Carl Sandburg and Langston Hughes, among others. *Negro Digest* was published until 1975.

Johnson created Ebony magazine in 1945 and Jet in 1951. They were the sole African American-oriented magazines for about twenty years. Unable to find enough advertisers in the early days, Johnson started his own mail-order line of beauty products (which became Fashion Fair Cosmetics and Supreme Beauty Products). He advertised them in the magazines, and they became highly successful business operations. The company began to publish books and launched new magazines such as *Ebony Man* and *Ebony South Africa*. It bought interests in television and radio stations and became involved in various other enterprises.

Johnson Publishing Company is owned solely by the Johnson family. In the 1990's, John H. Johnson was publisher, chairman, and chief executive officer; his wife, Eunice W. Johnson, was secretary-treasurer; and their daughter Linda Johnson Rice was president and chief operating officer. Among the activities that the Johnson Publishing Company became involved in were sponsoring the American Black Achievement Awards and hosting the yearly Ebony Fashion Fair.

—*Michelle C. K. McKowen*

See also: Black press.

Johnston, Joshua (c. 1765—1830): Portrait artist. Johnston is one of the most celebrated African American painters. He may have been a slave or a West Indian immigrant. Some accounts tell that he purchased his freedom. Because his style resembles that of the Peale family of Maryland, it is also thought that he may have received artistic training from the family while their slave. His portraits include some of the wealthy and aristocratic slaveholding families in the BALTIMORE, MARYLAND, area. His only known black subject was found in the well-known *Portrait of a Cleric*. *See also:* Painters and illustrators.

Joint Center for Political and Economic Studies: Research center founded in 1970 in WASHINGTON, D.C. Originally known as the Joint Center for Political Studies, it was founded to focus on the concerns and problems of African Americans. Funded by foundation and corporate grants, and with a budget in the millions of dollars, the center has had distinguished black social scientists and intellectuals on its staff since its founding under the sponsorship of HOWARD UNIVERSITY. It also provides space for social scientists and scholars on loan or visiting from major colleges and universities.

Among the topics on which the center conducts research are rates of African American participation in the electoral process, through voting and running for office; the effectiveness of black elected officials; the effectiveness of public policy regarding black communities; and resources available to socially and economically disadvantaged communities. The center also publishes position papers and studies dealing with African American affairs as well as a monthly publication, *Joint Center for Political and Economic Studies—Focus*. These reports are widely consulted in liberal DEMOCRATIC PARTY circles. The center maintains a library focusing on black politics and conducts public policy forums that bring together experts from a variety of fields.

The center, although funded by a variety of groups including the Ford Foundation, is independent, nonpartisan, and nonprofit. It has retained its emphasis on the political process and on providing information to politicians, particularly African Americans, but it has expanded its research concerns to include energy, crime, community development, and revenue sharing. *See also:* Politics and government; Voters.

Jones, Absalom (November 6, 1746, Sussex, Delaware—February 13, 1818, Philadelphia, Pennsylvania): First African American priest of the Protestant Episcopal Church. From his humble beginnings of birth into slavery and of teaching himself to read, Jones became an educator, an author, and an abolitionist.

Jones worked hard to purchase his wife's, and later his own, freedom. Determined that physical and spiritual freedom must go together, he and Richard ALLEN became lay preachers among African Americans of St. George's Methodist Episcopal Church in PHILADELPHIA in 1786. In 1787 he, Allen, and fellow African Americans formed the FREE

Absalom Jones, the first African American Episcopalian priest. *(Associated Publishers, Inc.)*

AFRICAN SOCIETY, the first of its kind to practice nondenominational Christianity and to denounce slavery. Members also tried to discourage immorality, drunkenness, and gambling. The success of the society in Philadelphia encouraged the formation of similar ones in NEW YORK CITY, BOSTON, MASSACHUSETTS, and Newport, RHODE ISLAND.

The 1793 yellow fever epidemic in Philadelphia brought out the humanitarian and social qualities of Jones. He and Allen organized African Americans to work as nurses, health aides, and undertakers. After the epidemic, the formation of an African church with its own church building was pursued vigorously. Jones became the first leader of the church when it was dedicated in 1794 and was formally christened as the St. Thomas African Episcopal Church. In 1804 he was ordained to the priesthood formally, thus becoming the first African American Protestant Episcopal priest in the United States.

Jones constantly visited his parishioners and helped them with spiritual and material needs. Knowing the value of education, he built a school for both the religious and the secular instruction of African Americans. There was then no state-sponsored school for African Americans in PENNSYLVANIA. Jones also founded the African Friendly Society and the Female Benevolent Society and was elected to the position of Worshipful Master of the African Masonic Lodge of Philadelphia.

With Allen's help, he organized African Americans to petition the Pennsylvania legislature and the U.S. Congress to abolish slavery and, in 1808, he published a sermon on the same subject. During the WAR OF 1812, he helped form the Black Legion of three thousand African American soldiers, and in 1817, the year before his death, he actively organized a conference of African Americans to denounce the formation of the AMERICAN COLONIZATION SOCIETY, which sought to send free black people to Africa.

Jones, Bill T. (b. February 15, 1952, Bunnell, Florida): Dancer and choreographer. A post-modern student of DANCE and choreographer, he studied technique with Percival Borde, Pat Taylor Frye, Lois Welk, and Senta Driver. Beginning in the 1970's he performed in his own works and in those of his collaborators, Sheryl Sutton and Arnie Zane, combining his exciting stage presence with complex and intricate choreographed movements and verbalizations.

Jones, Elaine R. (b. March 2, 1944, Norfolk, Virginia): Attorney. Jones was selected as the first female director-counsel of the NATIONAL

Elaine R. Jones speaking on the occasion of the fortieth anniversary of the Supreme Court's *Brown v. Board of Education* decision in 1994. *(AP/Wide World Photos)*

Association for the Advancement of Colored People Legal Defense and Educational Fund in 1993. After completing her bachelor's degree at Howard University in 1965, Jones was the first African American female law student to attend the law school at the University of Virginia, where she received her law degree in 1970.

She joined the NAACP Legal Defense and Educational Fund immediately after finishing law school and became managing attorney of the organization's New York City office in 1973. After serving as special assistant to Secretary of Transportation William T. Coleman, Jr., from 1975 to 1977, Jones joined the legal staff of the NAACP's Washington, D.C., office. She was made deputy director-counsel in 1988 before succeeding Julius Chambers as full director in 1993. Jones had a strong connection to the Clinton White House as a result of her working relationship with Hillary Rodham Clinton when both had served together in the 1980's on an American Bar Association commission on women in the legal profession. She continued serving as director-counsel of the LDF through the 1990's. In 1999 she was given the American Bar Association's Spirit of Excellence Award.

National Urban League officer Eugene Kinckle Jones. *(Schomburg Center for Research in Black Culture, New York Public Library)*

Jones, Eugene Kinckle (July 30, 1885, Richmond, Virginia—January 11, 1954, New York, New York): Civil rights leader. Jones was executive secretary of the National Urban League from 1917 to 1941 and general secretary from 1941 to 1950. He was also Negro Affairs adviser to the U.S. Department of Commerce from 1933 to 1943 and chaired the Negro Advisory Committee for the Texas Centennial Exposition of 1936 and the World's Fair of 1939 in New York City.

Jones, Gayl (b. November 23, 1949, Lexington, Kentucky): Feminist author. Jones's work is in the tradition of fellow African American female writers Zora Neale Hurston and Alice Walker. Jones earned a doctorate from Brown University in 1975, the same year she published her first novel. Her early fiction in the 1970's—widely called bold and daring—is said to have been influential on the work of Walker, Toni Morrison, and Ntozake Shange. Jones's published works include the novel *Corregidora* (1975); a collection of stories, *White Rat* (1977); *Song for Anninho* (1981) and *Xarque and Other Poems* (1985), both of which are books of narrative poems; *The Healing* (1998); and *Mosquito* (1999), her first work of long fiction in twenty years.

Jones was an English professor at the University of Michigan at Ann Arbor from 1975 to 1983. In 1983 an arrest warrant was issued for her husband after he was accused of shooting at marchers during a gay rights event. Between 1983 and 1998 she and her husband lived in exile in Europe, then in hiding in KENTUCKY. In 1998 police found them. In a startling turn of events, Jones's husband slashed his own throat—in the presence of police and his wife—rather than surrender.

Jones, Hank (b. July 31, 1918, Vicksburg, Mississippi): JAZZ pianist. Reared in Pontiac, MICHIGAN, Henry "Hank" Jones developed a reputation as one of the finest of the modern jazz pianists. A product of a musical family, which included his brothers Thad and Elvin, both of whom became noted jazz artists, Jones started his professional career at the age of thirteen. He was influenced by the well-known pianists of the day such as Earl HINES, Fats WALLER, Art TATUM, and Teddy WILSON.

Jones migrated to NEW YORK CITY in 1944 to work with Luck Thompson and Hot Lips PAGE at the Onyx Club, where he absorbed the musical style of bop and worked with a host of 1940's jazz greats, including Coleman HAWKINS, Billy ECKSTINE, Andy Kirk, and Howard McGhee. In addition to taking part in Norman Granz's Jazz at the Philharmonic series in 1947, Jones worked as an accompanist for Ella FITZGERALD between 1948 and 1953. In 1959 Jones secured a staff position with CBS, a position he held for seventeen years. He worked with the Ray Block Orchestra as part of *The Ed Sullivan Show.*

A versatile, much sought accompanist, Jones preferred to work in trio settings during the 1970's, although he also performed in duo formats with pianists John Lewis and Tommy Flanagan. In 1976 he became part of the Great Jazz Trio, which originally included Ron Carter on bass and Tony Williams on drums. Jones also was musical conductor for *Ain't Misbehavin'*, a Broadway play of the late 1970's. In the 1980's, Jones toured Japan and was in residence at the Cafe Ziegfeld.

Jones can be heard on hundreds of recordings with such legendary figures as Milt Jackson, Lester YOUNG, Cannonball ADDERLEY, and Charlie PARKER. He recorded, with his brother Thad, *Presenting Thad Jones—Mel Lewis and the Jazz Orchestra* (1966). As soloist,

Jazz pianist Hank Jones at a recording session in 1996. *(Janet Sommer/ Archive Photos)*

he recorded *Have You Met Hank Jones?* (1956) and *Satin Doll* (1980). In the duo format, he recorded *Our Delights* (1978) with Tommy Flanagan and *An Evening with Two Grand Pianos* (1979) with John Lewis. As a leader, he recorded *Just for Fun* (1977) and *The Great Jazz Trio Revisited: At the Village Vanguard* (1980). Jones continued to record and perform in a variety of ensemble formats during the early 1990's.
See also: Bebop; Music.

Jones, James Earl (b. January 17, 1931, Arkabutla, Mississippi): Actor. The son of actor Robert Earl Jones (who appeared in the 1964 film *One Potato, Two Potato*), James Earl Jones was born in rural MISSISSIPPI in the midst of the GREAT DEPRESSION. He was reared by his maternal grandparents on a farm near Jackson, MICHIGAN, and attended the University of Michigan, where he at first planned to study medicine. Though he graduated cum laude from the university in 1953, during his years there he changed his interest from medicine to acting. After his graduation, Jones did military service at the U.S. Army's Cold Weather Mountain Training Command in COLORADO; on completion of his Army stint, he moved to NEW YORK CITY to pursue an acting career.

First Roles

In New York, Jones enrolled in the American Theatre Wing and worked alongside his father waxing floors while both father and son chased their acting goals. In 1957 the younger Jones made his first appearance on the New York stage, playing the role of Sergeant Blunt in an Off-Broadway production of *Wedding in Japan*. From that point on, Jones amassed a series of notable portrayals, including that of Oberon in *A Midsummer Night's Dream* for the New York Shakespeare Festival in 1961. In 1962 Jones portrayed Ephraim in John Errol's *Moon on a Rainbow Shawl* and undertook various Shakespearean roles, including Caliban in *The Tempest* and the Prince of Morocco in *The Merchant of Venice*. His early stage work was acknowledged with a number of awards, including a 1961 Obie Award and a 1961-1962 Daniel Blum Theatre World Award.

In the mid-1960's, Jones continued to make a name for himself on the stage by starring in such roles as Zachariah Pieterson in South African playwright Athol Fugard's acclaimed *The Blood Knot* and as the title role of the Delacorte Theatre production of *Othello*. In 1964 he made his FILM debut in Stanley Kubrick's *Dr. Strangelove*. In the mid-1960's, Jones also made his television debut, appearing as an African chieftain in *Tarzan*.

Rise to Prominence

In 1966 Jones undertook the role that would establish him as a star. He portrayed Jack JOHNSON, the early 1900's heavyweight boxing champion, in the Broadway production of *The Great White Hope*. The play was a smash, and Jones's performance was recognized as a tour de force. For his role in the long-running production, Jones received a 1969 Tony Award as best dramatic actor in a Broadway play and a Drama Desk Award as one of the 1968-1969 season's best actors. Jones also starred in the 1970 film version of the play and received an Oscar nomination for his performance.

Jones's success continued in the 1970's. In 1971 his alma mater, the University of Michigan, presented him with an honorary doctorate of humane letters. He gave highly praised performances in productions of Fugard's *Boesman and Lena* and Lorraine HANSBERRY's *Les Blancs*, and he began playing roles traditionally undertaken by white actors. He acted the role of Claudius in *Macbeth* and gave acclaimed performances in the title role of *King Lear* and as Lenny in a stage adaptation of John Steinbeck's *Of Mice and Men*. He also appeared again as Othello in a Mark Taper Forum production and acted in productions of Anton Chekov's *The Cherry Orchard* and Eugene O'Neill's *The Iceman Cometh*.

Jones's 1978 appearance in the one-man Broadway show *Paul Robeson* generated controversy; black critics claimed that the play was not an accurate reflection of Paul ROBESON's life. Drama critics, though, praised Jones's performance.

Actor James Earl Jones accepting a cable ACE award in 1991, with Cicely Tyson who also won an ACE that year. *(AP/Wide World Photos)*

Film and Television Career

In the 1970's, Jones moved increasingly into film and television roles. In 1972 he starred in *The Man*, a film about a black politician thrust into the presidency, and in 1974 he appeared opposite Diahann CARROLL in *Claudine*, a performance for which he received a Golden Globe Award nomination. He had roles in numerous other films in the mid-1970's, including *The Bingo Long Traveling All-Stars and Motor Kings* (1976) and the film version of Joseph Walker's acclaimed play *The River Niger* (1976). He also had an uncredited role as the voice of Darth Vader in *Star Wars* (1976). Also in 1976, Jones won election to the board of governors of the Academy of Motion Picture Arts and Sciences, and in 1977 he was inducted into the Black Filmmakers Hall of Fame.

Jones's 1970's television credits included roles as Alex HALEY in 1979's *Roots: The Next Generations* and as the star of the short-lived CBS police series *Paris*. He appeared on countless other shows, ranging from soap operas to public television documentaries.

Box-Office Stardom

Jones continued to be one of Hollywood's busiest and most sought-after stars through the 1980's. He reprised his role as the voice of Darth Vader in two hit sequels to *Star Wars*, *The Empire Strikes Back* (1980) and *Return of the Jedi* (1983); Jones's memorable, stentorian rendering of Darth Vader's utterances about "the Dark Side" became part of the national consciousness. He appeared as another villain, a sinister sorcerer, opposite Arnold Schwarzenegger in *Conan the Barbarian* (1982). Jones also returned to the stage in the 1980's in a 1981 production of Fugard's *Master Harold . . . and the Boys* and a 1985 version of August WILSON's Pulitzer Prize-winning drama *Fences*, for which Jones received a second Tony Award. In 1985, too, he was inducted into the Theatre Hall of Fame.

Jones appeared in a string of hit films in the late 1980's, including *Coming to America* (1988), in which he played Eddie MURPHY's father, an African king; *Field of Dreams* (1989), playing a reclusive writer; and *The Hunt for Red October* (1990), in the role of Admiral James Greer, a Central Intelligence Agency spy master. Jones reprised his role as Greer in *Patriot Games* (1992), a successful sequel to the earlier hit. In the early 1990's, Jones starred in *Gideon's Fire*, a short-lived television series that teamed him with Richard Crenna and Madge Sinclair. Other 1990's work included roles in the films *Cry the Beloved Country* (1995), *Gang Related* (1997), and *Summer's End* (1997) and in the television miniseries *Merlin* (1998).

—*Don Evans*

Painter Lois Mailou Jones. *(Associated Publishers, Inc.)*

Suggested Readings:

Bogle, Donald. *Blacks in American Films and Television*. New York: Garland, 1988.

Haskins, James. *Black Theater in America*. New York: Thomas Y. Crowell, 1982.

"James Earl Jones." *Current Biography* 55 (November, 1994): 34-39.

Jones, James Earl. "An Interview with James Earl Jones." Interview with Jeff Laffel. *Films in Review* 47 (September/October, 1996): 2-15.

Jones, James Earl, and Penelope Niven. *James Earl Jones: Voices and Silences*. New York: Scribner, 1993.

Jones, Lois Mailou (b. November 3, 1905, Boston, Massachusetts): Artist and educator. Jones studied art at Boston's School of the Museum of Fine Arts as well as in France, Haiti, and Africa. She worked as a costume and stage designer, a painter-illustrator, and a stained glass designer. She also designed fabrics. She exhibited in sixty solo exhibitions and in more than two hundred group exhibitions. Some of her notable paintings are *Negro Cabin* (1931), *The Ascent of Ethiopia* (1933), and *Jennie* (1943). Jones taught art at Howard University for forty-seven years.

See also: Painters and illustrators.

Jones, Quincy (b. March 14, 1933, Chicago, Illinois): Musician, composer, and record producer. Quincy Delight Jones, Jr., built a career that embodied the concept of "crossing over." His work crosses the lines of musical genres, from so-called serious music to popular music, including rap. From the early 1950's, Jones became a performer, composer, arranger, conductor, and record producer. By the 1990's he had also written more than fifty film scores. Most important, he crossed over from an African American audience to diverse ethnic and dominant cultural audiences. Jones brought cultural diversity to the music he wrote and produced, and he proved the commercial viability of multiculturalism in the United States. By the mid-1990's Jones had won twenty-six Grammy Awards and received more than seventy nominations.

A small sampling of the many great performers of U.S. twentieth-century popular music with whom Jones worked includes Lionel HAMPTON, Dizzy GILLESPIE, Count BASIE, Frank Sinatra, Ray CHARLES, Sammy DAVIS, Jr., Andy Williams, Peggy Lee, Aretha FRANKLIN, Diana Ross, Stevie WONDER, and Michael JACKSON.

Early Life

Born on CHICAGO's South Side, the son of Quincy Delight and Sarah Jones, Quincy Jones was reared by his father and his stepmother in Seattle and attended college in Seattle and Boston. Jones had already lived in the Midwest and on both U.S. coasts before he was out of his teens.

Musical Roots

Jones was a mid-twentieth century African American musical prodigy. In an interview published in EBONY magazine in June, 1972, Jones traced his musical roots back to his acquaintance as a child in Seattle in the early 1940's with Joseph Powe, who was with the gospel-singing Wings Over Jordan choir and who led a dance band in the Navy. Jones taught himself the rudiments of orchestration by poring over Powe's orchestration texts while he was babysitting Powe's children. While growing up in Seattle, Jones also met Ray Charles, who was three years older than him and who was destined to become one of the greatest singers of the twentieth century. Jones and Charles formed a combo and played local small clubs and weddings.

In 1948, when Jones was fifteen, he approached Lionel Hampton, who was passing through Seattle with his orchestra, and presented Hampton with a JAZZ suite he had composed; Hampton was so impressed that he performed the suite with his orchestra and invited the teenage Jones to join the orchestra as a trumpet player. Only the intervention of Hampton's wife, Gladys, kept Jones in high school, from which he graduated before he began college study at the University of Seattle, the Boston Conservatory, and the Berklee College of Music in Boston. Jones won a scholarship to Berklee; years later, in 1983, he received an honorary doctorate from the school for his many musical achievements during the more than thirty years since he had been a student there.

Composer Quincy Jones working in his home studio in 1974. *(AP/Wide World Photos)*

Composer and Record Executive
Jones played trumpet with famed bandleader Lionel Hampton from 1950 to 1953 and with jazz trumpeter Dizzy Gillespie in 1956. In 1960, while still in his twenties, Jones also led his own eighteen-member orchestra on a tour through Europe and the United States. After touring the world with Gillespie, Jones settled for a time in Europe. He lived in Paris and Stockholm, studying composition with the classical teachers Nadia Boulanger and Olivier Messiaen and associating with the expatriate African American writers Richard WRIGHT and James BALDWIN.

Jones returned to the United States in the early 1960's and soon after was named a vice president of Mercury Records. He was the first African American ever to hold a high executive position in a white-owned recording company. Another first followed soon after: Jones broke the color barrier that had long prevented African American composers from being hired to score major Hollywood films when film director Sidney Lumet chose him to compose music for *The Pawnbroker*, a 1965 film that dealt frankly with anti-Semitism and RACIAL PREJUDICE.

Music for Films
Jones was offered many opportunities to integrate entertainment and musical excellence with socially, racially, and educationally enlightened themes. He scored *In the Heat of the Night*, Norman Jewison's 1967 film starring Sidney POITIER as a police detective from Philadelphia who forges a bond with a white, small-town GEORGIA police chief. He also scored *MacKenna's Gold*, a 1969 film that included a love affair between an African American (Jim BROWN) and a white woman (Raquel Welch) and was the first major Hollywood film to address directly the subject of interracial sexuality.

Jones collaborated with Ray Charles on *Black Requiem* (1971), a musical history of the black liberation struggle scored for symphony orchestra and eighty-voice choir. He later scored the television miniseries *Roots* (1977), based on Alex HALEY's best-selling novel, which recounted the struggles of Haley's African American ancestors to free themselves from slavery, racism, and poverty in the American South.

In August, 1974, at the age of forty-one, Jones suffered a cerebral aneurysm—the bursting of blood vessels leading to the brain, an occurrence that is frequently fatal. Two surgeries repaired the damaged vessels, leaving several metal plates in Jones's head. Less than six months afterward, Jones was working on his music again. He scored *The Wiz*, the 1978 African American musical adaption of *The Wizard of Oz*; he then scored *The Color Purple*, director Steven Spielberg's 1985 film adaptation of Alice WALKER's novel about the oppression of African American women. Jones also wrote many signature themes for television shows, including *Ironside* and *Sanford and Son*.

Record Production
Among the many artists for whom Jones produced record albums is Michael Jackson. Jones produced Jackson's *Off the Wall* (1979) and the phenomenally successful *Thriller* (1982), which sold more albums worldwide than any other recording in history.

Jones's Own Recordings
Jones's career in recording—his own discography includes such major recordings as *You've Got it Bad, Girl* (1973), *Body Heat* (1974), *Mellow Madness* (1975), *I Heard That!* (1976), *The Dude* (1981), and *Quincy Jones, the Best* (1982)—reached a peak with the release in 1989 of *Back on the Block*. This recording combines Jones's many skills: composer, arranger, performer, and producer, as always, but also educator and historian of African American culture. The recording reaches back to the origins of African American music, sampling

(both musically and verbally) the work of many African American jazz greats—Charlie PARKER, Miles DAVIS, Dizzy GILLESPIE, Ella FITZGERALD, and Sarah VAUGHN—most of whom Jones had worked with at some point.

The recording also reaches forward, in particular to rap: In the title song, Jones joins rappers Big Daddy Kane, Ice-T, Melle Mel, and Kool Moe Dee in a rap celebration of African American cultural achievement that fuses rap with its earliest jazz and popular antecedents. Rap is represented again in "Birdland," in which rappers Kool Moe Dee and Big Daddy Kane perform what amounts to a rap history of African American music. Jones received six Grammy Awards for *Back on the Block*, including the award for album of the year.

The follow-up release to *Back on the Block* was *Q's Jook Joint*, released in 1995. ("Q" is Jones's nickname.) It is similarly eclectic and includes performances by artists ranging from Brandy to Ray Charles, Heavy D. to Toots Thielemans, Gloria Estefan to Stevie Wonder.

Business Ventures

Jones embarked on many ventures outside the recording studio and musical stage. He was a coproducer of the film *The Color Purple* and, in 1991, entered television production when he helped launch the Will SMITH series *The Fresh Prince of Bel Air*. He formed Quincy Jones-David Salzman Entertainment, or QDE, with David Salzman in 1993, and the company was involved with producing a number of television shows. In the mid-1990's QDE launched QD7 to create interactive products. Jones also founded his own record label, Qwest, and, with a group of businessmen and investors, founded Qwest Broadcasting, a minority-controlled company that owns a number of television stations.

Humanitarian Projects

Jones became active on behalf of African American causes early in his career. He participated in OPERATION BREADBASKET, an African American economic self-help organization founded in 1966 by Martin Luther KING, Jr., and taken over by Jesse JACKSON after King's assassination; Jones also served on the board of directors for OPERATION PUSH, an outgrowth of Operation Breadbasket, and was a founding member—with Donald Byrd, Roberta FLACK, Isaac Hayes, and Grady Tate—of the Institute for Black American Music (IBAM).

Jones also managed to find time to have a personal life. He married three times and became the father of five children: Kidada, Rashida, Jolie, Martina-Lisa, and Quincy III. His third marriage was to actor Peggy Lipton.

—*R. C. De Prospo*

See also: Broadcast licensing.

Suggested Readings:

Collie, Aldore. "After Forty Years, Fame and Fortune, Three Marriages, Brain Surgery, and an Emotional Breakdown, Quincy Jones Finds Peace." *Ebony* (April, 1990): 74.

Dougherty, Steve. "Quincy Jones." *People Weekly* (October 15, 1990): 103.

Horricks, Raymond. *Quincy Jones*. Spellmount, N.Y.: Hippocrene Books, 1985.

Ross, Courtney S., Frankfurt G. Balkind, and Nelson George, eds. *Listen Up: The Lives of Quincy Jones*. New York: Warner Books, 1990.

Sanders, Charles L. "With Quincy Jones." *Ebony* (October, 1985): 33-38.

Woodard, Josef. "Herbie and Quincy: Talkin' 'Bout the Music of These Times." *Down Beat* (January, 1990): 16.

Jones, Sissieretta (Matilda Sissieretta Joyner; January 5, 1869, Portsmouth, Virginia—June 24, 1933, Providence, Rhode Island): Singer. Jones studied music with keen interest at the Academy of Music in Providence, RHODE Is-

LAND, where she grew up. She furthered her music education at the New England Conservatory in BOSTON, MASSACHUSETTS. It was in Boston that she made her professional debut, becoming the first African American to perform at Wallack's Theatre.

Jones undertook a successful extensive performance tour of the Caribbean Islands and South America. She returned in 1892 to the United States and gave a rousing performance at Madison Square Garden in NEW YORK CITY. In February of that same year, she performed at the White House for President Benjamin Harrison and his guests. She then resumed her performance tour of major cities in the United States. In May, 1893, she gave a highly acclaimed performance in a grand concert at the Brooklyn Academy of Music. In recognition of her artistic contribution to New York City, the place she often returned to as home, an organization known as the Sons of New York presented her with a long diamond necklace, then valued at two thousand dollars, crafted by the Tiffany Company of New York City.

Jones next toured Europe, spending time in Italy, where she was given the nickname "Black Patti" as an affirmation of her rich singing style, similar to that of Italian soprano Adelina Patti. In Great Britain, she was honored by the British royal family, before whom she performed. She returned to the United States in 1896. In September of that year, she played to a packed house in New York City. She was billed as the most popular prima donna of all nations and races.

Jones's career reached its climax in 1896, when two white theatrical managers put together an all-African American troupe and named it after her. The Black Patti Troubadours toured the East and West coasts of the United States. Even at age forty, Jones was tireless, starring in the revue *A Trip to Africa* (1910).

See also: Music.

Jones v. Alfred H. Mayer Company: U.S. SUPREME COURT case on HOUSING DISCRIMINATION decided in 1968. Joseph Lee Jones sued the Alfred H. Mayer Company in 1965, claiming that the company refused to sell him a home in Paddock Woods in St. Louis County, MISSOURI, solely because he was an African American. Such a refusal, he argued, violated the federal Civil Rights Act of 1866, a provision of which stated that "all citizens of the United States shall have the same right, in every State and Territory, as is enjoyed by white citizens thereof to inherit, purchase, lease, sell, hold, and convey real and personal property."

The federal district court dismissed Jones's complaint, and the U.S. Court of Appeals affirmed the dismissal, holding that the relevant provision of the 1866 law applied only to state action, not to private discrimination. The Supreme Court reversed the lower court and ruled 7 to 2 that the law prohibits both public and private discrimination against blacks in the sale or rental of property. The decision marked an important step against HOUSING DISCRIMINATION.

—*Thomas J. Davis*

Joplin, Scott (November 24, 1868, Texarkana, Texas—April 1, 1917, New York, New York): RAGTIME music composer and pianist. The preeminent composer of the ragtime genre, Scott Joplin, was one of several children. Two of his brothers, Will and Robert, also had some musical training. The family lived in Texarkana, TEXAS, where his father was a violinist and his mother a banjoist. Joplin studied piano with a local immigrant German pianist and began a career as a "professa" (a pianist who played by rote instead of from the music). He also sang with a quartet which on occasion included his brothers.

In the mid-1880s, Joplin left Texarkana, and he eventually reached St. Louis, where he is believed to have met rag pianist Thomas

Nearly six decades after Scott Joplin died, his music helped the film *The Sting* win Academy Awards for best sound track and best song. *(Arkent Archive)*

Turpin. He attended the 1893 International World Exposition in Chicago, where he led a band and apparently was exposed to other compositional techniques. His first publications, two Victorian ballads entitled "A Picture of Her Face" and "Please Say You Will," appeared in 1895. His next publications were three piano works, "The Great Crush Collision March" (inspired by a major train accident in the Midwest), "Combination March," and "Harmony Waltz."

Joplin settled in Sedalia, Missouri, and entered the George Smith College for Negros, where he took courses in advanced music composition. He also taught piano to Arthur Marshall and Scott Hayden, two protégés who later distinguished themselves as ragtime composers and pianists. In 1899 he had his first piano rag works published (Joplin preferred the term "syncopated piano music" to "ragtime"). They were "Original Rag," published by Carl Hoffman, and "Maple Leaf Rag," published by John Stark. "Maple Leaf Rag" was by far Joplin's most successful piano work, selling close to half a million copies within ten years of its release. Stark published most of Joplin's piano works.

Joplin also produced a folk ballet, entitled *The Ragtime Dance*, in 1899. In 1903 Joplin began composing a ragtime opera, *A Guest of Honor*. The work received mixed reaction from the public and was then lost. Joplin continued to produce rag piano works such as "The Entertainer," "Weeping Willow Rag," and "Bethena Waltz." In 1908, after moving to New York, he produced *The School of Ragtime*, a piano manual featuring rag piano exercises.

Joplin was also at work on a second opera, *Treemonisha*, which he published at his own expense in 1911. In an attempt to gain financial backers for a full-scale production of *Treemonisha*, Joplin held a semistaged and costumed run-through of the work in 1915. It was the closest to a performance that Joplin ever saw. Joplin's bouts of depression later prompted his institutionalization in a sanitarium, where he died in 1917. *Treemonisha* was revived in the 1970's, first in concert form by the Atlanta Symphony and eventually in a fully staged performance by the Houston Grand Opera in 1975. Joplin's piano works similarly enjoyed a resurgence in the 1970's. "The Entertainer," along with other pieces, was featured in the 1973 film *The Sting*.

Jordan, Barbara (February 21, 1936, Houston, Texas—January 17, 1996, Austin, Texas): Attorney, educator, and Texas politician. Barbara Charline Jordan was born in racially segregated HOUSTON, the youngest of three daughters of Arlyne and Benjamin Jordan. Her father was a BAPTIST minister and warehouse clerk who influenced her to achieve great self-control and develop her intellect. Her mother had been a skilled public speaker prior to her marriage, and her maternal grandfather taught her to have high aspirations and to be unique.

Jordan attended segregated Phillis Wheatley High School, where, in her sophomore year, she was inspired by a "career day" speaker, African American lawyer Edith Simpson. Jordan graduated from high school and entered segregated Texas Southern University in Houston. As an undergraduate, she became a champion debater, developing her deep, commanding voice and excellent vocabulary. She graduated in 1956 magna cum laude with a bachelor's degree in government

Barbara Jordan at the Democratic National Convention in 1992. *(AP/Wide World Photos)*

and became the first black student admitted to Boston University Law School, where she earned a law degree in 1959.

Texas and Politics

Jordan decided to return to Texas, where her roots were and where she would have an opportunity to fight racial injustice firsthand. For a time, she practiced law out of her parents' dining room. Her involvement with politics began in 1960, when she worked for John F. Kennedy's presidential campaign, making speeches and directing a voting drive. The DEMOCRATIC PARTY vice presidential candidate, Texan Lyndon B. Johnson, became her mentor.

In 1962 Jordan began her own campaign for the Democratic nomination for the office of Texas state representative. She lost the election; in 1964, she ran again for the same position, losing a second time to the same opponent. Reapportionment of Texas house and senate districts made it more possible for Jordan to win election, as the new Eleventh State Senatorial District encompassed many blacks, Hispanics, and working-class whites. Jordan decided to run again and won the Democratic primary in 1966. Unopposed in the regular election, she was elected to the Texas senate and sworn in on January 10, 1967.

Jordan mastered the complicated, arcane Texas senate rules and earned the respect of powerful senators, who came to admire her intelligence and integrity. She spoke out against a proposed sales tax and fought a voter-registration bill that would have hampered registration of the poor. In 1968 she easily won reelection. During her second term, Jordan served on ten committees and was appointed chairman of the powerful Labor Committee. That committee was very productive, reporting out a minimum-wage bill and a bill to increase worker's-compensation benefits.

Jordan was unusually effective as a legislator, introducing many bills and seeing about half of them to passage. She usually followed a moderate path, seeking compromise rather than stalemate. In March of 1972, she was unanimously elected president pro tem of the Texas senate. An indication of her popularity and power in the Texas senate is the fact that her portrait hangs there alongside portraits of Lyndon B. Johnson, Jefferson Davis, and the Alamo defenders.

Washington Calls

Jordan had also begun to receive favorable attention outside her home state. As a result of the 1970 census, Texas was apportioned a new U.S. congressional seat. Jordan ran for the Democratic nomination for the new Eighteenth Congressional District position; her campaign emphasized her record of helping working people and the poor. She won 80 percent of the vote in the primary and in the November, 1972, election easily defeated her Republican opponent. Barbara Jordan became the first African American congresswoman from the South. With Andrew YOUNG of GEORGIA, she shared the honor of being the first African American representative from the South since 1901.

It was a tradition for freshman members to keep a low profile, but after three months of the NIXON ADMINISTRATION's cutbacks in programs such as welfare and education, Jordan spoke on the House floor about her concern that the executive branch had too much power. As the Watergate story began to unwind, she called for a thorough investigation, praised the press for exposing the scandal, and supported the appointment of an independent special prosecutor. Jordan had been appointed to the House Judiciary Committee early in her first term. When the Judiciary Committee held hearings on President Richard Nixon's nomination of Gerald Ford to replace Vice President Spiro Agnew, who had resigned in disgrace, she spoke against Ford's CIVIL RIGHTS record and voted against his confirmation.

Jordan's legislative duties left little time for the Washington social scene. She put in long hours and had a very high rate of roll-call participation. She easily won elections for second and third terms in Congress. As had happened in the Texas senate, she sponsored and cosponsored many bills that went on to be enacted. She successfully pushed for a broadening of the 1965 Voting Rights Act to cover language minorities and worked on a bill to abolish fair-trade laws, arguing that they caused consumers to pay more for price-fixed goods.

Jordan had critics during her years in office. While serving in the Texas senate, she was targeted by an Army intelligence investigation of VIETNAM WAR critics. She was also unpopular with some militant African Americans and some feminists because of her moderate stance.

Two Famous Speeches

Many Americans came to admire Jordan as a result of the televised hearings of the House Judiciary Committee in 1974. The committee explored the important constitutional issue of whether President Nixon should be impeached for his role in the Watergate scandal. In a six-month probe, the committee heard testimony on twenty-two articles of impeachment. Recordings of presidential conversations requested by the committee were withheld by the Nixon administration; Jordan criticized the White House and discussed the inquiry on many television shows. In televised hearings, each committee member gave a speech analyzing the impeachment issue. Jordan spoke on July 25, 1974. In powerful words, she described her faith in the Constitution and her unwillingness to have it subverted. Jordan was among the committee members voting for impeachment, a vote that contributed to Nixon's resignation. When President Ford pardoned the former president, Jordan criticized the move.

Jordan and Ohio senator John Glenn were chosen to be the keynote speakers at the Democratic National Convention in July of 1976. Jordan's speech was a highlight of the New York City gathering. She pointed out that the convention was unique in that for the first time in 144 years it had a black female as a keynote speaker. She received a lengthy standing ovation. Jordan supported the Jimmy Carter-Walter Mondale ticket selected by the convention and was considered for a cabinet appointment after Carter's victory, but she was not offered the one position she sought, U.S. attorney general.

Because of her active schedule as a legislator, Jordan had to turn down most offers to give public speeches. During her third term, she began to feel that her future role would be to instruct rather than to legislate. By retiring from public office, she would be able to devote more time to addressing national issues. Jordan decided not to run for a fourth term.

Texas Professorship

In 1978 Jordan returned to Texas and a position as a public service professor at the Lyndon Baines Johnson School of Public Affairs at the University of Texas. A scholar of the Constitution, Jordan taught political ethics. In addition to teaching and directing research, she gave speeches, wrote her autobiography, and served as a television commentator. In 1984 she was elected to the Orators Hall of Fame and received a Distinguished Alumnus Award from the American Association of State Colleges and Universities. In 1988 she delivered a nominating speech for vice presidential candidate Senator Lloyd Bentsen at the Atlanta Democratic Convention. By that time, she used a wheelchair as the result of muscle weakness caused by multiple sclerosis, and that same year she nearly drowned in a swimming pool accident. In April of 1990, still a professor at the University of Texas, Jordan was inducted into the National Women's Hall of Fame.

Continuing to maintain her political influence by taking a stand on tough issues, Jordan accepted an appointment from Governor Ann Richards of Texas to serve as an adviser on ethics in government. In 1992 she was one of three keynote speakers at the Democratic National Convention in New York City. That same year Jordan was awarded the prestigious SPINGARN MEDAL by the NATIONAL ASSOCIATION FOR THE ADVANCEMENT OF COLORED PEOPLE (NAACP). She was also voted one of the ten most influential American women of the twentieth century by the National Women's Hall of Fame, into which she was inducted in 1990.

During an interview that was aired on BLACK ENTERTAINMENT TELEVISION (BET) in 1993, Jordan maintained her conviction that circumstances of birth, race, or creed should not inhibit an individual from achieving greatness. Jordan's own battle with multiple sclerosis did not prevent her from demonstrating her immense talent as a public speaker. Diagnosed with leukemia, Jordan developed symptoms of viral pneumonia as a result of the disease and died in January of 1996, shortly before her sixtieth birthday.

—*Nancy Conn Terjesen*

—*Updated by Wendy Sacket*

See also: Congress members; Democratic Party; Politics and government.

Suggested Readings:

Byrant, Ira B. *Barbara Charline Jordan: From the Ghetto to the Capitol*. Houston, Tex.: D. Armstrong, 1977.

Davis, Marianna W., ed. *Contributions of Black Women to America, Volume 2: Civil Rights, Politics and Government, Education, Medicine, Science*. Columbia, S.C.: Kenday Press, 1982.

Haskins, James. *Barbara Jordan*. New York: Dial Press, 1977.

Jordan, Barbara, and Shelby Hearon. *Barbara Jordan: A Self Portrait*. Garden City, N.Y.: Doubleday, 1979.

Roberts, Naurice. *Barbara Jordan, the Great Lady from Texas*. Chicago: Childrens Press, 1984.
Rogers, Mary Beth. *Barbara Jordan: American Hero*. New York: Bantam Books, 1998.

Jordan, June (b. July 9, 1936, Harlem, New York): Educator, novelist, essayist, poet, and activist. Her first novel, *His Own Where* (1971), was on *The New York Times* List of Most Outstanding Books of 1971 and the American Library Association List of Best Books; it was also a National Book Award finalist. In 1984 Jordan won the National Black Journalists achievement award for international reporting, and in 1989 she won the MADRE Award for Leadership. Jordan became a professor of BLACK STUDIES at the University of California at Berkeley in 1997.

Jordan, Michael (b. February 17, 1963, Brooklyn, New York): Professional BASKETBALL player. Jordan grew up in Wilmington, NORTH CAROLINA. As a basketball player, he would push the limits of what was thought possible in the game. He established heights of performance that set new standards for comparison and evaluation. No one at the guard position had ever dominated the court—and public attention off the court—as Jordan did.

Early Years

As a child, Jordan aspired to be a BASEBALL player, but as he grew into his teens, basketball became his primary interest. After gaining determination and confidence from competition with his older brother Larry, Jordan decided to try out for the Laney High School varsity team as a sophomore. After being cut from the team, he grew five inches to come back as a six-foot three-inch junior and set a new school scoring record. In 1980, before the start of his senior year, in which he was named as a high school All-American, he decided to attend the University of North Carolina at Chapel Hill.

It was Jordan's jump shot that gave the North Carolina Tarheels the national championship in 1982. This championship gave him his first real recognition as a player. After being named college player of the year in 1983 and 1984 and winning a gold medal in the 1984 Olympic Games, he decided to enter the National Basketball Association (NBA).

Joining the Bulls

Jordan was drafted by the Chicago Bulls as the third pick of the first round. He brought a winning attitude and new intensity to a losing team in CHICAGO. The team steadily came together, guided by Jordan and coach Phil Jackson. The team's first NBA championship came in 1991. In the process of lifting the Bulls organization, Jordan was awarded virtually every individual honor the league had, from rookie of the year in 1985 to defensive player of the year in 1988 to league most valuable player in 1988 and 1991. He led the NBA in points averaged per game for five straight seasons, beginning in 1986-1987.

Jordan stunned the sports world with his 1993 decision to retire from professional basketball at the height of a remarkable career. The Chicago Bulls had just captured their third straight NBA championship, and Jordan claimed that his decision stemmed from a desire to leave the media spotlight at the height of his powers. Jordan, who had won seven consecutive scoring titles, also confessed that he felt that he had nothing left to prove as a player. Many insiders and fans were convinced that Jordan's abrupt announcement was largely attributable to the murder of his father, James Jordan, in North Carolina in July of 1993. There were also constant rumors that Jordan had a gambling addiction—rumors that had been fueled when Jordan was seen after hours in an Atlantic City casino shortly after the third game of the 1992 NBA semifinals

After returning to the NBA from his baseball hiatus in 1995, Michael Jordan briefly wore "45" on his jerseys. *(AP/Wide World Photos)*

in New York. There was also an allegation by one of Jordan's former golfing partners that Jordan had an outstanding debt of $57,000. Jordan admitted having bet substantial amounts on golf games.

Jordan Attempts a Baseball Career

Following his retirement, and after much media speculation regarding Jordan's future, Jordan's athletic career took another decidedly unusual turn: It was announced that he had signed a minor league baseball contract with the Chicago White Sox organization in March of 1994. Although he had not played baseball since his senior year of high school, Jordan was sent to the Double A level and spent the entire 1994 season in ALABAMA with the Birmingham Barons of the Southern League. While Jordan struggled to bring his game to a professional level, his fans and teammates were left to marvel at the media spectacle that surrounded Jordan's change of sport. Paid attendance at Birmingham games skyrocketed that season to an unprecedented 467,867.

Jordan's best showing as a professional baseball player came during a stint with the Scottsdale Scorpions of the Arizona Fall League in 1994. As a Scorpion, he hit .252, while his outfielding skills showed a marked improvement. Nevertheless, Jordan's impatience to improve, coupled with the realization that at thirty-one years of age he was considered to be too old to master the demands of the sport, proved to be too much for an athlete of Jordan's caliber and pride. By January of 1995, speculation began to build that Jordan would return to the NBA.

Return to Basketball

Citing both disgust with major league baseball's ongoing labor disputes and his desire to prove his place in NBA history, Jordan re-signed with the Chicago Bulls in mid-March. On March 19, 1995, in a nationally televised contest in Indianapolis against the Indiana Pacers, Jordan made his return to league play. Because the Bulls had retired his original number, 23, Jordan returned wearing a new number on his jersey—45. Jordan often showed flashes of his former brilliance, but his game had suffered somewhat from the effects of the seventeen-month layoff. He led the Bulls to the second round of the NBA playoffs. During the third game of the second round, Jordan once again donned his familiar number 23, a move that cost his team $25,000 in league fines but was also seen as his complete return to the league. Although the Bulls lost to eventual league runner-up Orlando, it was obvious to all that Jordan had brought a much-needed spark to the team.

Jordan and the Bulls went on to three remarkable seasons. In the phenomenal 1995-1996 season, the team finished the regular season with a record-breaking 72 wins, with 10 losses. Jordan became the tenth player in the NBA to score 25,000 points in his career, and the Bulls won their fourth championship of the 1990's. They won the championship again in the 1996-1997 and 1997-1998 seasons, and Jordan won his sixth NBA finals most valuble player award. Having led the Bulls to three straight championships, and six championships overall, Jordan announced his second retirement in early 1999.

Jordan's huge salary—earning $30 million in 1997 alone—and off-the-court business activities had made him a multimillionaire. He established his own golf-products company and gave his name to a successful line of cologne; he endorsed Air Jordan sneakers for Nike and other products. He even made a foray into film, costarring with Bugs Bunny in the live action/animated feature *Space Jam* (1996). Early in 1999, Jordan announced a program called Jordan Fundamentals through which he would donate $5 million over five years. Also in 1999, he backed out of negotiations to buy a 50 percent interest in the Charlotte Hornets, stating that the deal would not have allowed him control over business aspects of the basketball team. In January, 2000, he bought a part-ownership of the Washington Wizards and became head of the team's basketball operations. In March he announced he would be withdrawing from his still-heavy schedule of commercial endorsements.

—Updated by Joel N. Rosen

See also: Olympic gold medal winners; Sports.

Jordan, Vernon, Jr. (b. August 15, 1935, Atlanta, Georgia): NATIONAL URBAN LEAGUE official. Vernon Eulion Jordan, Jr., headed the National Urban League from 1972 to 1981, serving as president and executive director. He is remembered for his criticisms of the policies of the Nixon, Carter, and Reagan administrations and for citing the harmful effects that government policies had on African Americans.

Jordan graduated from DePauw University in 1957 and from HOWARD UNIVERSITY Law School in 1960. He also holds numerous honorary degrees. He passed the GEORGIA bar exam in 1960 and practiced law in ATLANTA until 1961. At that time, he became the Georgia field secretary for the NATIONAL ASSOCIATION FOR THE ADVANCEMENT OF COLORED PEOPLE (NAACP), a position he held until 1963. Jordan passed the ARKANSAS bar exam in 1964 and practiced in Pine Bluff from 1964 to 1965. He also directed the Southern Regional Council of the Voter Education Project from 1964 to 1968. After serving briefly as an attorney in the Office of Economic Opportunity in Atlanta, he was selected as executive director of the UNITED NEGRO COLLEGE FUND, serving in 1970 and 1971.

Under Jordan's leadership, the National Urban League expanded its focus to include such topics as energy and the environment while retaining its emphasis on social services. Jordan fought for government programs to promote full employment and to provide guaranteed minimum incomes. While criticizing government policies that he saw as harming the black community disproportionately, he continued to forge links to government leaders, softening the effects of proposed federal policies and bringing federal contracts to the black business community.

In a speech to the National Urban League in July of 1977, Jordan criticized President Jimmy Carter's policies to slow inflation, claiming that they harmed poor black people. Jordan's criticism was somewhat surprising given the fact that he was considered to be one of the black leaders closest to Carter. The president offered no apology for his administration's treatment of African Americans or the poor. Also in 1977, Jordan initiated the Black Leadership Forum, bringing together leaders of various groups to coordinate their efforts and to ease any strains among them.

On May 29, 1980, Jordan was shot and seriously wounded outside a hotel room in Fort Wayne, Indiana. Inquiries by the FEDERAL BUREAU OF INVESTIGATION founded evidence of premeditation in the attack. A white man who had been convicted of killing two black joggers and was known to hate black people was identified as a suspect, but not enough evidence was found to make an arrest.

Vernon Jordan (center) at a conference on civil rights held by President Gerald Ford (left) in October, 1974; Jesse Jackson (right) also attended. *(AP/Wide World Photos)*

Jordan made his last speech as president of the National Urban League on July 18, 1981, as the keynote speaker at its annual conference. In his speech, Jordan described the hardships imposed on poor black people by the policies of the Ronald REAGAN ADMINISTRATION and called for compassion in an era of conservatism. While praising past efforts at AFFIRMATIVE ACTION and set-aside programs for minority-owned businesses, he suggested a "return to basics" that would stress group programs and efforts throughout the black community.

Jordan called on that community to build coalitions, develop new strategies, challenge institutions, and protest when necessary. He rejected the idea that individual achievement was important when a large proportion of African Americans lived in poverty. Jordan announced plans to resign as executive director of the National Urban League on September 10, 1981, and stepped down on December 31 of that year to take a position in the WASHINGTON, D.C., office of the law firm Akin, Gump, Strauss, Hauer, and Feld. He was succeeded by John E. JACOB. In 1992 President-elect Bill Clinton appointed Jordan to chair his transition team.

Throughout the Clinton presidency, Jordan was a friend and confidante of Clinton. His close connections with the CLINTON ADMINISTRATION and with the legal and business communities of Washington made Jordan a powerful behind-the-scenes figure in the 1990's. In 1998 Jordan became embroiled in the Monica

Lewinsky scandal that tarnished the Clinton presidency. During the Clinton impeachment proceedings, he was questioned by attorneys representing House of Representatives prosecutors over his role in attempting to secure a job for Lewinsky, a White House intern who had an affair with President Clinton. In 2000 Jordan left his full-time position with the law firm and took a position as a senior managing partner with the New York investment banking firm Lazard Freres.

Josephite missionaries: ROMAN CATHOLIC religious society founded in 1893 to serve African Americans. They began with one black priest member and for many years severely restricted black membership and accepted the pattern of segregated parishes. The CIVIL RIGHTS movement of the 1960's stirred the Josephites, and they became far more activist. In the 1990's, they numbered about 150 members and worked mostly in the South.

Journal of Negro Education: Quarterly journal launched at HOWARD UNIVERSITY in 1932. The journal provides exhaustive, authoritative coverage of all topics of significance related to black EDUCATION.

Charles H. Thompson, the journal's founder, was the first African American to receive a Ph.D. in education. As editor during the journal's first thirty-one years, he published articles by more than twelve hundred scholars, including the best in the field. He ensured that the journal described and evaluated black education from the perspective of the classroom, state legislatures, curricula, publications, and professional associations. To many of the articles he added astute editorial comments; these were sometimes as substantial as the articles themselves.

Each issue of *Journal of Negro Education* includes scholarly, peer-reviewed articles, book and media reviews, data on college enrollment of blacks, and notices of doctoral research being done on blacks. Since its inception the journal has devoted its summer issue to a special topic. These include critiques of the black elementary school (1932), the black private and church-affiliated college (1960), education in black cities (1973), testing and achievement of black Americans (1980), the black child's home environment (1987), school reform (1993), a commemoration of BROWN V. BOARD OF EDUCATION (1994), and educating black children in a violent society (1996).

Articles from the many years of *Journal of Negro Education* are frequently cited in scholarly works on black education, history, politics, and biography, and the journal's content has been studied and analyzed for its reflection of the image of blacks.

—*Glenn Ellen Starr Stilling*

See also: Black press.

Journal of Negro History: Quarterly historical journal established in 1916. It was the official voice of the Association for the Study of Negro Life and History. Both the journal and the association were largely the creations of Carter G. WOODSON. Woodson, often cited as the "father of black history," almost single-handedly created the successful and acclaimed *Journal of Negro History*.

After the CIVIL WAR ended in 1865, African American freedmen were, in theory at least, able to pursue education. However, because of extreme segregation, very few academic institutions were open to them. Few white scholars were particularly interested in studying African American life and history, and those works that were published frequently contained serious, even outrageous, distortions. Many educated African Americans believed that a systematic and rigorous academic publication was needed to answer the many unanswered questions about black history. Black scholars hoped to use such a journal to advance their work and to begin to equalize their status with that of whites.

Quarterly publication of the *Journal of Negro History* began on January 1, 1916. Woodson published the first edition at his own expense. He remained the sole editor from the beginning until 1950. In the first half of the twentieth century, the vast majority of black historians belonged to the Association for the Study of Negro Life and History, and many had their work published in the journal. Black scholars continued to have a difficult time getting their work accepted by mainstream history journals—especially by southern publications, by whom they were still treated as inferiors.

The *Journal of Negro History* fostered the chronicling of the black experience in Africa as well as in the United States and helped make black history a respected field of academic study. It eventually began to serve as a research source for white historians.

—*Earl R. Andresen*

See also: Black History Month; Historiography.

Joyner-Kersee, Jackie (b. March 3, 1962, East St. Louis, Illinois): Track and field athlete. Widely regarded as the world's greatest woman athlete, Joyner-Kersee was the first woman to win the heptathlon in two Olympics although she was diagnosed as an asthmatic. After starting track competition at age nine, she won the first of four National Junior Championships in the pentathlon at age fourteen. In 1979 she won the long jump at the Pan American Junior Games. Although she jumped her personal best at the Olympic trials in 1980, the American boycott kept her from participating in the 1980 Summer Olympics in Moscow.

Following high school graduation in the top 10 percent of her class in 1980, she won a scholarship at the University of California at Los Angeles (UCLA). Under UCLA coach Bob

Jackie Joyner-Kersee long-jumping at an invitational meet in Los Angeles in 1987. *(AP/Wide World Photos)*

Kersee's direction, she competed in the World Track and Field Championships in Helsinki in 1983 but had to withdraw because of a pulled hamstring. In the 1984 Summer Olympics in Los Angeles, she finished second behind Australian Glynis Nunn in the heptathlon and won a silver medal.

Joyner-Kersee broke the American record for the long jump at Zurich, Switzerland, in 1985. She also established the collegiate long jump record and the collegiate heptathlon record. In 1986 she married Bob Kersee, graduated from UCLA, broke the world record in the heptathlon at the Moscow Goodwill Games, and placed first in the heptathlon, breaking the world record at the U.S. Olympic

Festival in Houston. In 1987 Joyner-Kersee tied the world record in the long jump at the Pan American Games in Indianapolis and won in both the long jump and heptathlon at the U.S. Olympic track and field trials, once again setting world records for the heptathlon and the indoor 55-meter hurdles.

Finally, in the 1988 Summer Olympics in Seoul, Korea, Joyner-Kersee obtained two well-deserved gold medals, in the long jump and the heptathlon, setting the world record for the heptathlon. On August 25, 1991, at the World Track and Field Championships in Tokyo, she twisted her ankle during a long-jump takeoff but still won the gold medal before withdrawing from the heptathlon. In February of 1992, she set a long jump record at the 85th Millrose Games at Madison Square Garden. Joyner-Kersee competed and won in the long jump and heptathlon at the 1992 Olympic trials in New Orleans. In the 1992 Summer Olympics, held in Barcelona, Spain, she became the first woman to win the heptathlon in two Olympics. In June of 1995, she again won the heptathlon at the U.S. Track and Field Championships, but two months later she withdrew from the event because of injuries at the World Track and Field Championships in Göteborg, Sweden.

Joyner-Kersee finished second in the heptathlon to Kelly Blair at the U.S. trials for the 1996 Olympics and won the long jump competition. At the Olympics, held in ATLANTA, GEORGIA, she suffered a thigh injury in the first event of the heptathlon; her husband had to go to her and convince her to withdraw. In the long jump she won the bronze medal.

Joyner-Kersee returned to BASKETBALL for the first season of the newly organized American Basketball League in 1996-1997, playing for the Richmond Rage. Her playing time on the court was limited, and her asthma hampered her performance. She did not care if she could be a basketball star, she commented; simply playing in a professional basketball league had been a dream of hers for many years.

In 1997 she took fifth place at the World Track and Field Championships, and in July, 1998, she announced her retirement. She had won more Olympic track and field medals than any other American woman. Joyner-Kersee also managed to find time to serve on the boards of several organizations, including the charitable organization known as the Jackie Joyner-Kersee Community Foundation, which she had started in 1988.

—Dorothy C. Salem

See also: Olympic gold medal winners.

Suggested Readings:

Davis, Michael. *Black American Women in Olympic Track and Field*. Jefferson, N.C.: McFarland, 1992.

Joyner-Kersee, Jacqueline. "*T&FN* Interview: Jackie Joyner-Kersee." Interview with Jon Hendershott. *Track and Field News* (September, 1990): 38-39.

Joyner-Kersee, Jacqueline, and Sonja Steptoe. *A Kind of Grace: The Autobiography of the World's Greatest Female Athlete*. New York: Warner Books, 1997.

Page, James. *Black Olympian Medalists*. Englewood, Colo.: Libraries Unlimited, 1991.

Woolum, Janet. *Outstanding Women Athletes: Who They Are and How They Influenced Sports in America*. Phoenix, Ariz.: Oryx Press, 1992.

Judges: Judges not only interpret the law but also arbitrate disputes, award damages, and prescribe penalties for lawbreakers. Although many judges pride themselves on their impartiality, judges' own backgrounds, cultures, and races affect their judicial decisions. Consequently, race often affects the workings of the American judicial system. CIVIL RIGHTS reform since 1950 has done much to make the American justice system more equitable, and the expansion of educational opportunities, the participation of blacks in the legal process, and the presence of African Americans on the bench have helped to promote racial justice in the courtroom. In 1983 there were about sixteen hundred black judges in the United States; by 1997 there were about two thousand.

Historical Overview

Historically, black robes were reserved for white men. The history of African Americans in the United States partly explains this problem. Prospective judges are typically lawyers, members of a profession that requires special training. Before the CIVIL WAR, only a few schools in the North provided educational training for blacks, and fewer still provided training in the law. Hence, an African American had little chance of becoming a judge.

After the Civil War, African Americans obtained greater opportunities to pursue college training, and many of them sought careers in law. They entered the legal profession through normal channels. Some did so after studying under mentors in the field of law, a common practice during the nineteenth century, while others pursued degrees in law. HOWARD UNIVERSITY, established in WASHINGTON, D.C., was the first HISTORICALLY BLACK COLLEGE to provide legal education for blacks. Its law school, founded in 1869 and headed by John Mercer Langston, an African American lawyer, trained 238 lawyers by 1900. The number of African American lawyers grew steadily after 1900, especially in the North. In 1910, for example, there were 798 African American lawyers in the North; there were only 361 black lawyers in the South. By 1950 there were 1,450 black lawyers in the North, but only 232 in the South. By 1970 there were more than 4,000 African American lawyers in the North, but only 600 in the South.

African American women early demonstrated an interest in law. In 1872 Charlotte Ray became the first woman to graduate from Howard's law school. In 1910 African American women made up 1.9 percent of all American female lawyers; black men constituted only 0.6 percent of the country's male lawyers. By 1960 this figure had increased to 2 percent for black women, but only to 1 percent for black men. Still, African American women faced the dual barriers of race and gender; fewer black women had been appointed or elected to high-level judgeships. From 1939 to 1974, there were only twenty-eight black women in state and federal judicial posts.

Conrad Mallett, Jr., chief justice of Michigan's state supreme court in 1997. *(AP/Wide World Photos)*

Early Jurists

Despite racial and educational obstacles, African Americans have been federal and state judges since the late 1800's. During the RECONSTRUCTION period after the Civil War, Johnathan Jasper Wright became the first African American to serve in a state or federal court in the United States. Born in Luzerne County, Pennsylvania, in 1840, Wright—like most African Americans of his era—came from a modest farming background. An excellent student, Wright attended Lancastrian University in Ithaca, New York, at a time when few members of his race pursued HIGHER EDUCATION. Afterward, he read law in Pennsylvania. After the Civil War, Wright looked for greater opportunities in the Reconstruction South. He became an organizer in the Republican Party. In 1868 he served in the SOUTH CAROLINA constitutional convention and was elected to the state senate that year.

Wright began his judicial career in 1870, when South Carolina's predominantly African American legislature elected him to the state supreme court. His initial election was to fill an unexpired vacancy on the bench. Once the term ended, the legislature elected him to a full term. His colleagues considered him to be a competent attorney and able judge; his tenure, though, was not without controversy. Justice Wright, a civil rights reformer, challenged the state's JIM CROW LAWS regulating transportation. A state statute provided for separate railroad cars for black and white passengers. Wright ignored the law; when forcibly removed from a coach reserved for whites, Wright sued and won. With the end of Reconstruction in 1877, however, the whites on the bench forced him into retirement. Obviously disillusioned by the disfranchisement of his race, Wright left the political scene permanently and died in Charleston in relative obscurity in 1887.

Wright was not the only African American to hold a judicial post before WORLD WAR I. Robert Heberton Terrell, born in 1857, was the first black judge of the twentieth century. Born in Charlottesville, VIRGINIA, he attended Groton Academy in Groton, Massachusetts. He graduated magna cum laude from Harvard University in 1889 and earned two law degrees from Howard Law School.

Terrell began his judicial career in 1901. A man of strong intellect, he had come to the attention of Booker T. WASHINGTON, the controversial African American leader and educator. Terrell shared Washington's self-help philosophy, and he believed that blacks should cross racial lines when possible. Like Washington, he believed in the politics of reconciliation, and he urged blacks to speak less about their race, emphasizing instead economic issues. He believed that if African Americans were diligent in education and business, they might achieve more in American society than if they continued to debate race-related issues. Washington liked Terrell's politics and urged President Theodore Roosevelt to appoint him to a federal post. Roosevelt acceded and named Terrell a justice of the peace in the District of Columbia. In 1910, at Washington's urging, President William Howard Taft elevated Terrell to the municipal court in the District of Columbia, a position he held until his death in 1925.

African American judges remained rare before 1960, despite the early tenures of Wright, Terrell, and William H. HASTIE, the first African American to sit on the U.S. Court of Appeals. There are obvious barriers facing prospective black judges. Some judicial posts are elective positions, and white voters have historically been cold to African American candidates. With few exceptions, African Americans have done poorly in predominantly white districts. African Americans are most likely to receive judgeships through presidential appointment or election by a state legislature, but these approaches to judgeships are dependent on the political party in control of the presidency and legislature. Historically, the DEMOCRATIC PARTY has had the best record in placing African Americans on the bench.

In 1983 U.S. District Court judge Barrington Parker presided over the trial of President Ronald Reagan's would-be assassin, John Hinckley, Jr. *(AP/Wide World Photos)*

Political Appointees

President John F. Kennedy launched the judicial career of Thurgood MARSHALL, a former civil rights lawyer, when he placed Marshall on the U.S. Court of Appeals. President Lyndon B. Johnson appointed Marshall to the U.S. SUPREME COURT in 1967. Constance Baker MOTLEY, Marshall's colleague in the civil rights crusade, was also a Johnson appointee. Starting her career as a U.S. district judge in 1966, she became the first black woman appointed to the U.S. District Court, where she rose to the position of senior judge.

A. Leon HIGGINBOTHAM and Nathaniel Jones are among the judges placed on federal courts by Democratic presidents. Higginbotham, a graduate of the Yale Law School, was appointed to the U.S. Court of Appeals, Third Circuit, by President Jimmy Carter in 1977. Jones, another Carter appointee, was appointed to the Sixth Circuit U.S. Court of Appeals. In addition to their appointments by Democratic presidents, these judges had another thing in common: They all presided over courts in cities with large African American populations. Cities such as Philadelphia, New York, Los Angeles, and Chicago are typical of areas where black judges have been appointed.

Republican leaders have trailed Democrats in placing African Americans in judicial posts. The party is largely conservative, and although by the 1990's black conservatism was growing, relatively few African Americans have supported its policies. Moreover, many blacks have the perception that Republicans are against programs that benefit minorities. Consequently, African Americans, who generally shy away from the REPUBLICAN PARTY, have little input into judicial appointments made by Republicans. Justice Clarence THOMAS, the second African American appointed to the U.S. Supreme Court (he was nominated by Republican president George Bush), was a highly controversial appointee. A strict conservative, Thomas led women to fear that he wanted to tear down abortion rights, and he appeared to liberals to be an enemy of AFFIRMATIVE ACTION. After one of the most sensational Senate confirmation hearings in American history, dominated by charges of Thomas's alleged sexual harassment of a former employee named Anita HILL, the Senate confirmed Thomas by a slim majority.

—*Stephen Middleton*

See also: Legal professions.

Suggested Readings:

Franklin, John Hope. *George Washington Williams: A Biography*. Chicago: University of Chicago Press, 1985.

Goldman, Roger. *Thurgood Marshall: Justice for All*. New York: Carroll & Graf, 1992.

Logan, Rayford, and Michael R. Winston, eds. *Dictionary of American Negro Biography*. New York: W. W. Norton, 1982.

McGuire, Phillip. *He Too Spoke for Democracy: Judge Hastie, World War II, and the Black Soldier*. Contributions in Afro-American and African Studies 110. New York: Greenwood Press, 1988.

Ware, Gilbert. *William Hastie: Grace Under Pressure*. New York: Oxford University Press, 1984.

Washington, Linn. *Black Judges on Justice: Perspectives from the Bench*. New York: New Press, 1994.

Julian, Hubert Fauntleroy (Huberto Fauntleroyana Juliano, b. 1897, Trinidad): Aviator. Julian, known as the Black Eagle, frequently flew stunts over Harlem and was the first African American to parachute from an airplane over NEW YORK CITY, in 1922. He invented a safety device related to the parachute and was the military governor of Ethiopia during the 1939 invasion by Italy.

Hubert Julian (left) and his assistant, William J. Powell in 1932. *(AP/Wide World Photos)*

Julian, Percy Lavon (April 11, 1899, Montgomery, Alabama—April 19, 1975, Waukegan, Illinois): Scientist and businessman. Julian was one of six children of Elizabeth Lena Julian and James Sumner Julian, a railway mail clerk. In 1916 Julian left ALABAMA and worked as a waiter in a white fraternity house to pay his tuition to De Pauw University. After being graduated in 1920 as valedictorian and a member of the Phi Beta Kappa honor society, Julian taught at FISK UNIVERSITY until 1922, when he was able to attend Harvard University to earn his master's degree in chemistry. He later taught at West Virginia State College for Negroes and at HOWARD UNIVERSITY. From 1929 to 1931, he studied at the University of Vienna, presenting his doctoral dissertation on alkaloids and free radicals in German.

Julian and an Austrian colleague, Dr. Josef Pikl, continued their research on synthesizing the physostigmine molecule as a drug for treating glaucoma. They presented their successful work, done in the United States, to the American Chemical Society in 1934. At the end of 1935, Julian married sociologist Anna Johnson and left academic life to become director of research for the Glidden Company, supervising a staff of fifty chemists. His work at Glidden focused on commercial applications of soybean extracts

Percy L. Julian in his lab. *(Associated Publishers, Inc.)*

and resulted in producing the foam fire extinguisher used by the U.S. Navy in World War II as well as synthetic cortisone for the treatment of rheumatoid arthritis.

Julian eventually was awarded 130 patents for chemical discoveries and, in 1954, opened his own research laboratory in Chicago, Illinois, with a manufacturing plant in Mexico City. He sold this business in 1961 to the Smith, Kline, and French pharmaceutical firm for $2.3 million. Julian also maintained an active role on the board of Chicago's Provident Hospital and with other charitable organizations. A supporter of the Civil Rights movement, Julian was awarded the Spingarn Medal by the National Association for the Advancement of Colored People (NAACP) in 1947. In 1967 he chaired a committee of black businessmen that raised a million dollars for the NAACP Legal Defense and Educational Fund. He remained actively involved in civic and educational organizations until his death.

See also: Business and commerce; Science and technology.

Juneteenth: Traditional celebration held on June nineteenth each year in many African American communities in Texas. The holiday commemorates the end of slavery in Texas and occurs on a different day from emancipation celebrations in other states. The date derives from General Gordon Granger's official announcement of emancipation in Texas at the end of the Civil War; Juneteenth has been celebrated since 1866.

Jury selection: Trial by jury is guaranteed in criminal cases by the Sixth Amendment to the U.S. Constitution and in civil cases by the Seventh Amendment. Legal scholars hold the jury selection process to be one of the most important aspects of a trial, largely because the jury molds the ultimate outcome of the trial through its role as fact-finder. The jury selection process has frequently involved discriminatory practices, often based on racial or gender stereotypes reflective of historical prejudices.

Jury Selection Procedure

The process of *voir dire* (a phrase which may be loosely translated as "to tell the truth") allows attorneys or court personnel to question the panel of potential jurors (the *venire*, meaning "you are called to come") in an effort to discover bias, prejudice, or any other basis that would keep a juror from rendering a fair and impartial verdict. Two types of reasons exist for removing a potential juror: challenges for cause, in which the basis for exclusion must be stated and approved by the judge, and peremptory challenges, in which no reason needs to be given. There is no limit to the number of challenges for cause that can be made. The number of peremptory challenges is limited, with the number determined by statute.

Challenges for cause might be justified by personal relationships between juror and litigant, preconceptions about the case or the parties involved, or prejudice against a particular racial, ethnic, or religious group. Because the reasons for the exercise of peremptory challenges do not have to be specified, lawyers often use them to obtain a partial rather than an impartial jury, seeking to exclude those potential jurors whom they believe will not find in their client's favor and retaining those who will. Studies have shown that almost one-third of all prospective jurors are eliminated through the peremptory challenge. According to such studies, defense attorneys usually exercise two or three times as many challenges as prosecutors, but prosecutors are more likely to challenge minorities than defense attorneys. Exercise of peremptory challenges gives attorneys power and opportunity to shape the racial and class compositions of the jury. Consequently, when racial and ethnic minorities are excluded, the result seldom resembles a fair cross-section of the community.

Racial Exclusion

Although overt discrimination in the jury selection process has been prohibited since the enactment of the Civil Rights Act of 1875, African Americans were rarely if ever summoned for jury duty in the South before the 1960's because it was common practice to limit jury lists to those who were registered to vote. In urban areas, juror names were often recommended to the court by prominent individuals in the community (the so-called Key Man list), eliminating all others. In CALIFORNIA, prospective jurors were required to take an intelligence

Although the Civil Rights Act of 1875 specifically prohibited racial discrimination in jury selection, few African Americans sat in juries in southern states until the 1960's. *(Library of Congress)*

test which they automatically failed if they did not complete it in ten minutes. Such strictures eliminated 14.5 percent of upper-income individuals and 81 percent of GHETTO residents. (That law was declared unconstitutional in 1968.) These and other similar practices resulted in the subordination or exclusion of racial and ethnic minorities.

The constitutional requirements regarding trials are twofold: There must be a trial by a jury of one's peers, and the trial must be held in the district in which the crime occurred. With regard to the first condition, there is no necessity that each jury must represent all groups in the community. Rather, no group may be systematically excluded from the jury panel. Theoretically, a random selection of potential jurors summoned for service through this system should result in a jury that represents the composition of the community.

With regard to the second condition, conducting trials in the district where the crime or incident occurred engenders a sense of communal justice because those familiar with local norms and practices are better able to place the dispute in context. A change of venue for a trial may be granted if the court is of the opinion that excessive pretrial publicity would preclude a jury from rendering a fair and impartial verdict. Cost and convenience are additional factors to be weighed in selecting an alternate site. In the case of a racially sensitive trial, such as the 1992 case concerning the beating of Rodney KING, however, an additional factor apparently emerged: the demographic similarity of the new location to the scene of the crime. Critics contend that demographic concerns raise the socially divisive issue of quotas; proponents counter that because different racial and ethnic groups reach different conclusions in the jury room based on their life experiences, demographic composition is a valid consideration.

The Federal Jury Selection Act of 1968 sought to make juries more representative by increasing the diversity of the pools from which juries are drawn, expanding the pool to include not only registered voters but also licensed drivers, users of public utilities, and individuals listed in local telephone directories. At the same time, however, the size of juries was reduced from twelve to eight or six in some states without a corresponding reduction in the number of peremptory challenges allowed. As a result, it became easier to remove all members of racial minorities from jury service. Likewise, certain juries were no longer required to reach a unanimous decision, so even if one or two minority members remained on a jury, their votes would not necessarily result in a hung jury.

Certain high-profile cases in the 1960's and 1970's pitted black defendants against predominantly white juries, because the prosecution deliberately used peremptory challenges to eliminate black jurors from the panel. Notable among these cases are the trials of Black Panther Huey P. NEWTON in 1968 and University of California professor Angela DAVIS in 1972.

Changes in the Law

Until 1986 state and federal court relied on the U.S. SUPREME COURT's reasoning in SWAIN V. ALABAMA (1965), in which the Court ruled that prosecutors had the right to remove African Americans from juries unless such actions happened in virtually all the cases in the district. Because of the widespread practice of using peremptory challenges to exclude minorities, the Court later overturned *Swain*, ruling in *Batson v. Kentucky* (1986) that the use of peremptory challenges to remove blacks from juries was unconstitutional and discriminatory, constituting a denial of equal protection under the law. In the line of cases that followed, the Supreme Court found that selection procedures that purposely exclude African Americans from juries affect the entire community, undermining "public confidence in the fairness of our system of justice." The Court concluded that a person's race is "unrelated to his fitness as a juror."

Critics and dissenters warned that the Court's decision in *Batson* and subsequent rulings could make the peremptory challenge so difficult to administer that its abolition would necessarily follow. The Supreme Court and lower courts have praised the peremptory challenge as being well designed to ensure that juries are impartial. Abolition of such challenges would focus jury selection entirely on the challenge for cause, thus heightening judges' power by permitting them to shape the jury, whose purpose is to offset the class bias and "elitism" of the judiciary. In the highly publicized trial of O. J. SIMPSON, many of the jurors and alternates were summarily dismissed after being empaneled. Because a number of the dismissed jurors were African Americans, the defense accused the prosecution of racism and intentional tampering with the jury by targeting minorities for dismissal. Peremptory challenges aimed at excluding minorities were later declared unconstitutional in civil cases. In 1994 intentional discrimination on the basis of gender was also declared unconstitutional.

—*Marcia J. Weiss*

See also: Crime and the criminal justice system; Demography.

Suggested Readings:

Alschuler, Albert W. *Racial Quotas and the Jury*. Chicago: Law School, University of Chicago, 1995.

Babcock, Barbara A. "Jury Service and Community Representation." In *Verdict: Assessing the Civil Jury System*, edited by Robert E. Litan. Washington, D.C.: Brookings Institution, 1993.

Fukurai, Hiroshi, Edgar W. Butler, and Richard Krooth. *Race and the Jury: Racial Disenfranchisement and the Search for Justice*. New York: Plenum Press, 1993.

Guinther, John. *The Jury in America*. New York: Facts on File, 1988.

Hans, Valerie P., and Neil Vidmar. *Judging the Jury*. New York: Plenum Press, 1986.

Just, Ernest Everett (August 14, 1883, Charleston, South Carolina—October 27, 1941, Washington, D.C.): Biologist. Just was acclaimed for his pioneering work on cell structure. He developed several new concepts related to cell life and metabolism.

Ernest Just was the product of the all-black Industrial Elementary School of Orangeburg, SOUTH CAROLINA. His father died when he was four years old, and his mother supported her family by teaching school. The poor quality of education available to African Americans in Charleston compelled his mother to send the promising Ernest to New York. In four weeks, he earned enough money to at-

In 1915 Ernest E. Just was the first recipient of the NAACP's prestigious Spingarn Medal. *(Associated Publishers, Inc.)*

tend Kimball Academy in NEW HAMPSHIRE. There, in 1903, he completed the four-year program in three years, winning academic honors.

He was admitted to Dartmouth College. In 1907 he graduated with honors in zoology and history, the only magna cum laude in his class and president of Phi Beta Kappa. He began to teach at HOWARD UNIVERSITY, spending his summers conducting research at the Marine Biological Laboratory at Woods Hole, MASSACHUSETTS, under Frank Lillie, head of the Biology Department at the University of Chicago. Just received his Ph.D. from the University of Chicago in 1916. He had already published six papers based on his work at Woods Hole. Before his death from cancer, he published two major books and more than sixty articles.

Just was noted for his work on egg fertilization and cellular biology. He ushered in a new school of thought concerning cell life and metabolism and was sought by biologists from all over the world. He was awarded the SPINGARN MEDAL by the NATIONAL ASSOCIATION FOR THE ADVANCEMENT OF COLORED PEOPLE (NAACP) in 1951.

—*Rita Smith-Wade-El*

See also: Science, technology, and discovery.

Juvenile and young adult fiction: In *The Negro in American Fiction* (1937), writer Sterling A. BROWN wrote about children's LITERATURE, "Negro children have generally been written of in the same terms as their mothers and fathers, as quaint, living jokes, designed to make white children laugh." Brown's generalization essentially held true for another two decades; children's literature in America, until after the mid-twentieth century, nearly excluded African American children. When black children were depicted, the characterizations were often condescending, stereotypical, and racist. Since the CIVIL RIGHTS movement, however, this situation has changed considerably, and both African American and white writers of juvenile fiction have shown a new understanding of and respect for young people of all races. Writers of African American children's fiction are likely to avoid stereotypes and to confront the political and sociological issues of race in America.

Historical Background

Although literature for white children burgeoned in the nineteenth century, black children's literature remained essentially unwritten. When black characters appeared in children's fiction, their literary purpose was usually to "educate" white children about African Americans. This literature was created primarily by white authors for a white readership; predictably, the literature tended toward stereotyping and simplistic characterization. For example, in one exceptionally popular nineteenth-century children's novel, Thomas Bailey Aldrich's *The Story of a Bad Boy* (1867), the slave character Little Black Sam happily endures his master's abuse (presented in supposedly charitable terms) and escapes to Canada only after he is sold and separated from his beloved mother. In Louisa May Alcott's classic novel *Little Women* (1868), the only black character is the cook, Hannah, who is directed by the four March daughters, though Alcott makes a point of the March family's beneficence and generosity in treating Hannah more as a friend than as a servant. In 1890 Louis Pendleton published *King Tom and the Runaways*, which features Jim—a remarkably cheerful but unintelligent black.

In the early twentieth century, the depiction of African Americans in children's fiction was only somewhat improved. The racist caricature of African Americans as lazy, stupid, or mindlessly cheerful was tempered by various authors' attempts to emphasize the "universality" of human experience. Since "universalizing" a novel's characters often meant depriving them of their racial identity, however, the results of such efforts were at best dubious. Perhaps the most egregious example of denuding an African American of racial identity occurs in Hugh Lofting's famous *The Story of Doctor Dolittle* (1920). Prince Bumpo, the black character, searches for a sleeping princess and wakes her with his kiss, but he deplores his color when the princess rejects his marriage proposal on the basis of his race. A good man, Prince Bumpo pleads with Dr. Dolittle to change his race so that he can marry the princess; when Dolittle complies, Bumpo frees Dolittle and gives him half of his kingdom.

Addressing Racial Issues

In the work of some writers, however, the racial issues of African Americans are treated somewhat more realistically. For example, Florence Crannell Means explores the pressure black children often feel to conform to a white majority—not only in behavior but also in racial appearance. In *Shuttered Windows* (1938), Harriet and Mossie resent the burden of straightening their hair to conform to white preconceptions of feminine beauty; the topic of hair-straightening and color is again developed in Means's *Great Day in the Morning* (1946), when Lilybelle wishes for a magic tonic that would straighten hair and lighten skin. Means's fiction also examines vocational goals to which African American children in a segregated society might reasonably aspire. Harriet, the protagonist of *Shuttered Windows*, dreams of becoming a concert pianist; confronted by the abysmal conditions of an impoverished southern black school, however, Harriet relinquishes her dreams and becomes a teacher of home economics. In *Great Day in the Morning*, Lilybelle renounces her dream of teaching (which is associated in the book with her class prejudices) and becomes a practical nurse in the South. Means is politically conservative and an accommodationist in her portrayal of racial progress, but she nevertheless dramatizes racial topics in children's literature with a directness unusual for the time.

Arna Bontemps also helped change the direction of African American children's fiction. Her *Chariot in the Sky* (1951) deals with the difficulties encountered by blacks in the antebellum South, the Civil War, and the Reconstruction period. The main character, Caleb, is a slave who escapes from his plantation but is captured, returned to his master, and apprenticed. He eventually becomes free and attends Fisk University. This historical novel is notable in children's fiction because Bontemps dramatizes the problems with which African Americans were confronted: the family disintegration caused by slavery, the maintenance of pride in racial heritage despite slavery, the severity of black America's plight during Reconstruction, the threat of the Ku Klux Klan, and intraracial conflict.

Fiction Since the 1960's

As a result of the prominence of the Civil Rights movement and the emergence of Black Power and black studies movements, children's and young adult literature changed dramatically. With varying degrees of success, authors have explored in fictional terms the cultural history of African Americans, neither rationalizing nor excusing the legacy of racism in the United States. Sometimes with uncompromising realism, authors have presented the conditions of ghetto life: the poverty, the sometimes chaotic family structures, the violence, and the "nonstandard" English spoken by main characters.

John Steptoe's *Stevie* (1969) is a crucial event in the history of African American young-adult literature. *Stevie* is one of the first major novels set in the ghetto; Steptoe's intimate knowledge of ghetto culture—the incipient violence, unpredictable family arrangements, discrimination, and urban slang—brings considerable emotional power to his narrative. The novel is also important because the characters' dialogue is "nonstandard"; to make characters express their deepest feelings in BLACK ENGLISH imparts dignity and integrity not only to the characters but also to their language.

Related to *Stevie* is June JORDAN's controversial *His Own Where* (1971). Like *Stevie*, Jordan's novel is set in the ghetto. Jordan's realism is as uncompromising as Steptoe's: Buddy, a sixteen-year-old boy whose father is dying, loves Angela (age fourteen), who has been beaten and thrown out of her house by her father. The two young lovers decide to inhabit a deserted shed near a cemetery (called "His Own Where") and look forward to having children. However uneasy the reader may feel about Angela's presumptive pregnancy, the stylistic innovations in Jordan's novel are startling. Jordan chooses to write a "stream-of-consciousness" narrative in Black English. That is, she imitates without mediation the thought processes of her characters, who think exactly as they speak; the reader receives the characters' unconnected thoughts and reflections, and the reader is expected to supply those connections.

Julius Lester's work has done much to advance contemporary African American children's and young adult literature. His literature is primarily historical and documentary, yet his influence on subsequent fiction is seminal; his work has irrevocably changed fiction that treats African Americans. Lester's books are grounded in actual events, are recounted by slaves or eyewitnesses, or are retellings of African American folktales. Lester recovers African American folktales with his *Black Folktales* (1969) and *The Knee-High Man, and Other Tales* (1972), celebrating not only the vivid imagination of the slaves of the South (presumably, the origin of many of the tales is the slaves, as they dealt with their situations) but also tribal tales of African origin. The dominant tone of the two books is pride and affirmation of both black folk culture and the African heritage black Americans share.

Perhaps Lester's most famous book is *To Be a Slave* (1968). Lester collects and edits the actual words of former slaves, who tell about their capture in Africa, the Middle Passage, plantation life, and their experience during Reconstruction. Throughout the book, he intersperses his own commentary on slave life and implies how slave conditions led to social conditions in twentieth-century America. Before Lester, the experience of the slave had been sentimentalized or ignored; Lester's book forces the reader to confront the brutality of slavery and to honor the spiritual strength of blacks who withstood it. Lester's book, with its emphasis on courage and perseverance as the black heritage, heavily influences children's and young adult literature published afterward.

Mildred Taylor and Virginia Hamilton

Lester's model of strength in adversity is repeated by many subsequent novelists who treat the history of the black experience. One historical novelist in particular who celebrates black perseverance as heroic is Mildred Taylor, whose trilogy of books about the Logan family chronicles life in MISSISSIPPI during the Depression. Her Logan family novels are *Song of the Trees* (1975); *Roll of Thunder, Hear My Cry* (1976), which won the Newbery Medal; and *Let the Circle Be Unbroken* (1981). The main character, nine-year-old Cassie, witnesses her parents' resilience in the face of the depredations of the economy, the brutality of white supremacists, LYNCHING, intraracial strife, voter registration struggles, and the injustice of unions. Taylor also wrote *The Gold Cadillac* (1987), about life in OHIO during the 1940's. Taylor explained that she was influenced by her father's stories of black experience in the South. In all of her work, she emphasizes how African Americans confronted racial injustice with dignity and self-respect.

Virginia HAMILTON, the first African American writer to win the Newbery Medal—

for *M. C. Higgins, the Great* (1974)—also demonstrates the influence of Julius Lester. Hamilton subtly informs her novels with black FOLKLORE and mythology; in fact, African American folktales provide the substratum of her literature. For example, *M. C. Higgins, the Great* combines children's fantasy literature with black mythology about witches: red-haired blacks are often seen as witches, for example, and snakes are sometimes identified as witches. The plot, however, is idiosyncratic and unconventional; the book is about a boy who observes the world while sitting on a forty-foot pole in the mountains. In recovering and retelling black folktales, Hamilton specifically recalls Lester in her book *The People Could Fly: American Black Folktales* (1985), a collection of twenty-four beautifully illustrated African American folktales. Other folklore-based books by Hamilton include *The Dark Way* (1990) and *A Ring of Tricksters* (1997).

Perhaps Hamilton is best known for her Justice trilogy: *Justice and Her Brothers* (1978), *Dustland* (1980), and *The Gathering* (1981). The trilogy is about an eleven-year-old black girl, Justice, and her twin brothers and a friend; they discover they have powers to mind-travel into the future. Hamilton's trilogy is not explicitly racial in theme. Instead, she explores topics such as ecology, communication between children and their parents, Oedipal conflicts, and the philosophy of freedom. Her science fiction (or fantasy) is challenging and intellectually multidimensional. Hamilton continued writing children's stories in the late 1990's, publishing *Second Cousins* in 1998 and *Bluish* in 1999.

Hamilton's work may signal yet another change of direction in African American fiction for children and young adults. She writes with a confidence that many racial battles against injustice have already been fought, and the fictive landscape she sets out to describe does not necessarily make race and racial conflict its predominant features. Nevertheless, all of her literature is grounded firmly in black culture. To read Hamilton, and to read many other post-1960's black authors, is to be aware of a greater range of literary topics than was available in the past, but always to recognize that the African American sensibility—expressed often in myth, dream, history, and folklore—forms the bedrock of the literature.

—*Gary Storhoff*

See also: Children; Children's literature.

Suggested Readings:

Apseloff, Marilyn. *Virginia Hamilton: Ohio Explorer in the World of Imagination*. Columbus: The State Library of Ohio, 1979.

Kutenplon, Deborah, and Ellen Olmstead. *Young Adult Fiction by African American Writers, 1968-1993: A Critical and Annotated Guide*. New York: Garland, 1996.

MacCann, Donnarae, and Gloria Woodward, eds. *The Black American in Books for Children: Readings in Racism*. Metuchen, N.J.: Scarecrow Press, 1972.

Mikkelsen, Nina. *Virginia Hamilton*. New York: Twayne, 1994.

Rees, David. "Long Ride Through a Painted Desert: Virginia Hamilton." In *Painted Desert, Green Shade: Essays on Contemporary Writers of Fiction for Children and Young Adults*. Boston: The Horn Book, 1984.

Rollock, Barbara. *Black Authors and Illustrators of Children's Books: A Bibliographic Dictionary*. New York: Garland, 1988.

Sims, Rudine. *Shadow and Substance: Afro-American Experience in Contemporary Children's Fiction*. Urbana, Ill.: National Council of Teachers of English, 1982.

K

Kansas: According to estimates of the Census of the United States, about 2.6 million people were living in the state of Kansas in 1997. Of this number 153,000, or about 6 percent, were African Americans.

Some of the most important events in American racial history have involved Kansas. In 1854 Congress passed the Kansas-Nebraska Act. According to this law, two territories, Kansas and Nebraska, would be admitted to the union as states. Whether they would be admitted as slave states or free states was to be left up to the people who lived in the territories. Therefore, the Kansas Territory became a battleground between antislavery and proslavery forces. Eventually Kansas was admitted to the union as a free state. Prior to this admission, there were many fights between the opposing groups. Kansas was referred to by newspaper writers of the time as "bloody Kansas" or "bleeding Kansas."

One interesting figure of the bloody Kansas era was John Brown, who moved from Ohio to Kansas in 1855. Brown, a white man but a fierce opponent of slavery, led the murder of five proslavery men on the banks of the Pottawatomie River in Kansas. Then, having formulated an ill-conceived plan to spark a slave rebellion, Brown captured the arsenal of the U.S. Army at Harpers Ferry, Virginia (later part of West Virginia), in 1859. He was executed shortly thereafter.

Another interesting part of the African American history of Kansas was the buffalo soldiers. In 1866 two regiments of African American soldiers were added to the U.S. Cavalry, the Ninth Cavalry and Tenth Cavalry. The Tenth Cavalry Regiment was sta-

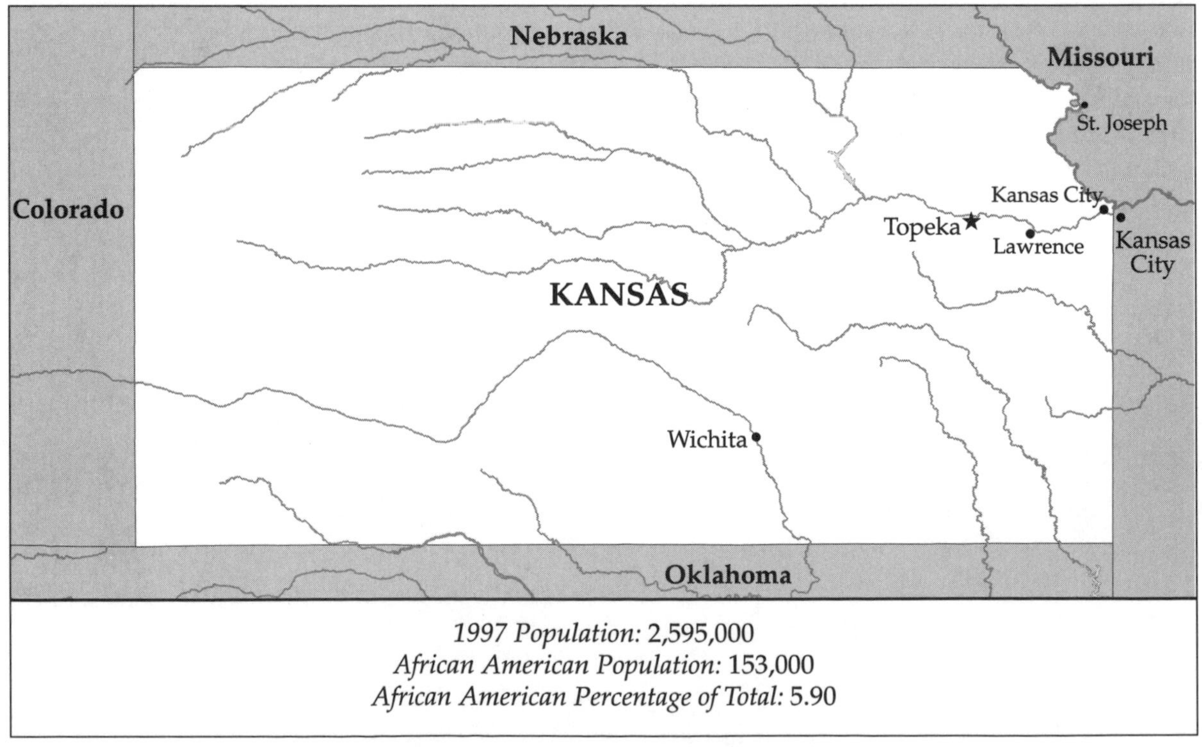

1997 Population: 2,595,000
African American Population: 153,000
African American Percentage of Total: 5.90

Ho for Kansas!

Brethren, Friends, & Fellow Citizens:
I feel thankful to inform you that the
REAL ESTATE
AND
Homestead Association,
Will Leave Here the
15th of April, 1878,
In pursuit of Homes in the Southwestern Lands of America, at Transportation Rates, cheaper than ever was known before.
For full information inquire of
Benj. Singleton, better known as old Pap,
NO. 5 NORTH FRONT STREET.
Beware of Speculators and Adventurers, as it is a dangerous thing to fall in their hands.
Nashville, Tenn., March 18, 1878.

Typical nineteenth-century broadside encouraging African Americans to leave the South and homestead in Kansas. *(Library of Congress)*

tioned at Fort Leavenworth, Kansas, under the command of Colonel Benjamin Grierson. For more than twenty years this regiment patrolled the American frontier from Montana to Texas, along the Rio Grande, and in Arizona. The Plains Indians referred to members of the regiment as buffalo soldiers, a nickname that stuck. Later this group fought in Cuba during the Spanish-American War and was involved in the charge up San Juan Hill. In 1941, when the United States entered World War II, the Ninth Cavalry from Louisiana and the Tenth Cavalry of Kansas were combined to form the Fourth Cavalry Brigade under the command of General Benjamin O. Davis. In 1944 the brigade was disbanded.

In 1954 Kansas again contributed to the history of African Americans. In that year the U.S. Supreme Court decided the case *Brown v. Board of Education of Topeka, Kansas*, generally known simply as Brown v. Board of Education. The Court held that the schools of Topeka, Kansas, must become racially integrated because racially segregated schools are inherently unequal. The decision had immense implications for all American school systems and for all American social institutions. As a result of this decision, virtually all social institutions in the United States were eventually desegregated.

Many famous African Americans were born or lived in Kansas. Poet Gwendolyn Brooks, the first African American to win the Pulitzer Prize, was a native of Kansas. Writer Langston Hughes was not born in Kansas, but he spent much of his childhood there with his grandmother and mother. He wrote a novel, *Not Without Laughter* (1930), about a boy growing up in Kansas. Influential jazz musician Charlie "Yardbird" Parker was born in Kansas, and he spent much of his adult life there.

—Annita Marie Ward

Pulitzer Prize-winning poet Gwendolyn Brooks was a native of Kansas. *(AP/Wide World Photos)*

See also: Exodusters and homesteaders; Frontier Society; Frontier marshals and sheriffs; Frontier wars; Nicodemus, Kansas.

Kansas-Nebraska Act: Legislation passed by Congress on May 30, 1854, to create the territories of KANSAS and NEBRASKA. The U.S. annexation of this area, which was intended to be used to establish new routes for the transcontinental railroad, was complicated by the bitter controversy over the status of SLAVERY. Proslavery congressmen did not want a free territory established west of Missouri and had defeated four previous attempts to organize the land there as a single territory. As the West rapidly expanded, an agreement between the pro- and antislavery forces had to be reached.

Senator Stephen A. Douglas of Illinois, chair of the Senate Committee on Territories, offered a compromise. He suggested that two new territories be created, with the question of slavery to be left to the settlers themselves when they applied for statehood. Douglas called this principle "popular sovereignty." This was in total opposition to the MISSOURI COMPROMISE OF 1820, which prohibited slavery in both territories, so Douglas also included a provision in the Kansas-Nebraska Act specifically to repeal the Missouri Compromise.

Antislavery forces in Congress were outraged, but after three months of bitter debate, and with the support of southern Democrats and President Franklin Pierce, the act was adopted. Douglas genuinely believed that popular sovereignty was a democratic solution to the slavery dilemma in new territories, but he failed to understand that slavery was no longer merely a political problem but was also considered to be a serious moral issue. Northern opponents were not content with leaving the slavery question up to the citizens of the territory themselves, because they believed that this would only encourage the spread of slavery, especially in Kansas.

The passage of the act caused an outbreak of violence between pro- and antislavery forces in the Kansas Territory in 1855, a tragedy which led to the nick-name "Bleeding Kansas." In 1854 the REPUBLICAN PARTY came into being, founded by opponents of the bill and expansion of slavery. The effect of the Kansas-Nebraska Act, which was seen by most southerners as a reasonable attempt to settle the slavery issue in the territories, instead intensified the tensions between North and South and led the country ever closer to CIVIL WAR.

Karenga, Maulana Ron (Ronald McKinley Everett; b. 1941, Parsonburg, Maryland): Black nationalist. Karenga founded the US Cultural Organization, generally called US, in 1965, following the WATTS RIOTS in LOS ANGELES. At the time, he was a graduate student in African studies at the University of California at Los Angeles (UCLA). He created the KWANZAA holiday and founded the Kawaida movement, which stressed seven "principles of blackness." Both were important parts of the US organization. Karenga argued for the need of black art to bring about rebellion and for a separate black aesthetic. US urged black people to adopt the Swahili language, which did not belong to any particular African tribe or group of people but instead represented AFRICA. Karenga helped plan and convene black power conferences in 1966, 1967, and 1968.

Karenga is known by the Swahili title of "Maulana," or master teacher. He was credited by Los Angeles politicians with helping to calm black anger in the city and prevent riots after the assassination of Martin Luther KING, Jr., in 1968. He and US were not always supported by law enforcement agencies. Increasingly bitter confrontations between his followers and BLACK PANTHER PARTY members led to the shooting deaths of two Black Panthers at UCLA in 1969; three US members were

Black nationalist leader Ron Karenga during the late 1960's. *(© Roy Lewis Archives)*

convicted of the crime. Many years later the FEDERAL BUREAU OF INVESTIGATION (FBI) admitted that its underground agents had encouraged and helped the warfare between US and the Black Panthers.

In 1971 Karenga was arrested on charges of assaulting a female member of his group. He was found guilty and given a sentence of six months to ten years. The US group, without his leadership, formally disbanded in 1974. Karenga was paroled in May of 1975. While in prison at California Men's Colony in San Luis Obispo he wrote articles on subjects ranging from feminism to PAN-AFRICANISM.

Karenga continued to be active in the 1980's and 1990's, becoming an advocate of socialism, receiving two doctorates, the second in social ethics from the University of Southern California in 1993, and supporting AFROCENTRICITY. In the 1990's he chaired the Black Studies Department at California State University, Long Beach, and served as director of the African American Cultural Center in Los Angeles. Karenga's books include *Introduction to Black Studies* (1982) and *Kemet, the African World View: Research and Restoration* (1986). His writing often appeared in *Black Scholar.*

Kaufman, Bob (April 18, 1925, New Orleans, Louisiana—January 12, 1986, San Francisco, California): One of the great JAZZ poets, Bob Garnell Kaufman, wrote poetry that challenges the political and cultural establishment of the United States.

Kaufman was known to many as "the original BEBOP man." His poems include love poems, jazz poems, and poems of political and social protest. Often they are infused with jazz sounds and rhythms and are meant to have musical accompaniment. Kaufman made his poetic orations part of the occasion at hand, and his poems were inseparable from the activities of his daily life. During his oral recitations of poetry, Kaufman generated a direct interplay between himself and the audience, the hallmark of a lyric poet. The oral dimension of Kaufman's poetry is particularly characteristic of the poetry of the beat generation, which he helped to shape.

Kaufman ran away from home at the age of thirteen, and after serving in the Merchant Marine for twenty years he began his poetic career in San Francisco in 1958. At first, Kaufman only recited his improvisational verses at bars and coffee houses. In 1959 he and three others founded *Beatitude* magazine in order to publish unknown but talented poets. Kaufman himself published poems in *Beatitude*; collections of his work include *Solitudes Crowded with Loneliness* (1965), *The Golden Sardine* (1967), and *Ancient Rain: Poems 1956-1978* (1981). In 1981 he received an award from the National Endowment for the Arts.

—*Alvin K. Benson*

See also: Literature.

Kelley, William Melvin (b. November 1, 1937, Bronx, New York): Writer. Kelley is best known for his novel *A Different Drummer* (1962), a deft and sly exposure of the attitudes toward race that exist in the United States. Kelley combines a powerful sense of place that has been compared with William Faulkner's with an almost Dickensian ability to re-create the quirks of human character.

Kelley grew up in NEW YORK CITY, where he attended the Fieldston School, an integrated but largely white private school, where he excelled both in academic courses and in athletics. He studied law at Harvard University, but he found writing more interesting after being taught by the poet Archibald MacLeish and the novelist John Hawkes.

A Different Drummer, Kelley's debut novel, is generally considered his finest work. His use of multiple narrators and the sophistication of his prose stimulated comparisons with great modernist writers such as James Joyce. Kelley's fiction deals with the legacy of SLAVERY, the African American tradition in music—particularly important in his second novel, *A Drop of Patience* (1965)—and political issues, although he largely avoided these in his first works.

By 1970 Kelley had written two other novels, *dem* (1967) and *Dunfords Travels Everywheres* (1970), and a collection of short stories, *Dancers on the Shore* (1964). He stopped publishing after 1970. Among Kelley's positions teaching literature and writing were posts at the New School for Social Research in New York City, the State University of New York at Geneseo, and the University of Paris, Nanterre.

—*Carl Rollyson*

See also: Literature.

Kelly, Leontine (b. March 5, 1920, Washington, D.C.): METHODIST cleric. Kelly had been a schoolteacher and lay speaker of a congregation before entering the ministry in 1969. In 1984 she became the first black woman to be elected bishop of the United Methodist Church. Credited with expanding the role of African Americans and women in the church, Kelly received the SOUTHERN CHRISTIAN LEADERSHIP CONFERENCE (SCLC) "Drum Major for Justice" award in 1987.

Kelly, Sharon Pratt (b. January 30, 1944, Washington, D.C.): Mayor of WASHINGTON, D.C., from 1991 to 1995. Also known as Sharon Pratt Dixon, the name she used when she took office. At the end of her first year in office, she married James Kelly and took his last name. She was born Sharon Pratt.

When Kelly was four years old, her mother died of cancer. She, her younger sister, and her father subsequently went to live with her paternal grandmother and aunt. Some years later, her father remarried, and Kelly moved to a new home with her father and her stepmother. Kelly attended public schools in the District of Columbia and graduated from Roosevelt High School with honors. She earned a bachelor's degree with honors in political science from HOWARD UNIVERSITY in 1965 and a law degree from Howard's law school in 1968.

Professional Career

Soon after her graduation, Kelly became involved in protecting the rights of children and their families. She also taught business law part time. In 1972 she accepted a position as an instructor at Washington's Antioch Law School. She remained there until 1976 and was promoted to the rank of professor. In addition, Kelly was appointed vice president of the District of Columbia Law Revision Commission. As such, she assisted in transferring supervision of the district's Criminal Code Authority from Congress to the District of Columbia City Council.

During the middle 1970's, Kelly left Antioch to work for the Potomac Electric Power

Sharon Pratt Dixon (later Kelly) and her campaign manager, David Byrd, raise their arms triumphantly when she was elected mayor of Washington, D.C., in November, 1990. *(Reuters/Mike Theiler/Archive Photos)*

Company (PEPCO). From 1976 to 1979, she was an attorney in the company's general counsel's office. Kelly became the company's director of consumer affairs in 1979, remaining in that post until 1983, when she became the organization's vice president for consumer affairs. She was the first African American woman to serve as a vice president at PEPCO. In 1986 she became the company's vice president for public policy. In the latter two posts, Kelly launched several financial and operational programs designed to assist low- and fixed-income residents in the District of Columbia. She also worked to decentralize PEPCO and to create job opportunities throughout the community by providing satellite branches of the utility company in various neighborhoods.

Political Career

In the middle 1970's, too, Kelly became a leader in the Democratic Party. Politics was not new to her; her first husband, Arrington Dixon (whom she married in 1966 and from whom she was divorced in 1982), had served as chairman of the District of Columbia City Council. When she was at home with her young children, Kelly had managed her husband's political campaigns, and she herself was active in the drive for home rule in the District of Columbia. In 1985 she became the first African American woman to be appointed treasurer of the Democratic National Committee. Kelly served four consecutive terms on the committee and held a seat on the party's executive committee.

Election as Mayor

On November 6, 1990, Sharon Pratt Kelly was elected mayor of Washington, D.C. She was the first black woman to become mayor of a major American city. Moreover, she joined the relatively short list of women heading state and local governments. Kelly, who was elected with 86 percent of the vote, was also the first native Washingtonian to be elected the city's mayor.

Kelly's limited political experience and her campaign pledge to clean house had special appeal for many voters who had grown weary of the charges of political corruption associated with the administration of the city's previous mayor, Marion S. Barry, Jr. Kelly's no-nonsense style and her promise to clean up the city government convinced many voters that her lack of previous experience as an elected official would not compromise her effectiveness as mayor.

Washington, like many major American cities, had a multitude of problems, including urban decay, high unemployment, drug trafficking and other crime, and homelessness. In addition, the district had experienced an epidemic of violence in the decade before her election; there were 483 homicides reported in 1990. Equally disturbing was the financial crisis that caused Washington to have a deficit as high as $300 million at the end of the 1990 fiscal year.

Reforms Thwarted

The city's dire financial situation caused Kelly to seek economic relief soon after assuming office. Members of the U.S. Congress agreed to appropriate $100 million in congressional emergency funding for the fiscal year 1991. Kelly admonished local government agencies to curb spending and to redirect resources toward improving city services. She directed particular attention to the government of the District of Columbia, which had been accused of gross mismanagement. She argued that a comprehensive overhaul was needed.

During her first year as mayor, both her grandmother and a trusted aide died; late in 1991 she married businessman James R. Kelly III. By her second year, Kelly had run into political trouble. She was unable to gain real control of the city's government; many in the government still felt loyalty to former mayor Barry. Kelly tended not to trust the advice she received, and her new husband did not seem to be lending her any public support. Former mayor Barry caused her further trouble when his supporters led an effort to recall her. Though the effort soon failed, it led Kelly to back away from the reforms she had promised.

Kelly blamed Congress for Washington's financial problems and then further alienated Congress by providing it with sketchy and even false information about the city's finances. As her administration continued, political observers increasingly saw her lack of experience as a major problem. The District's voters became disillusioned, and in the 1994 Democratic primary campaign, Marion Barry staged a comeback and defeated Kelly for the nomination. Barry was subsequently elected mayor.

Kelly received a number of awards in the 1980's and 1990's. In 1985 she was honored for distinguished leadership by the UNITED NEGRO COLLEGE FUND. In 1986 she was the recipient of an award for distinguished service from the Federation of Women's Clubs. In 1991 she won EBONY magazine's achievement award and the Mary McLeod Bethune-W. E. B. Du Bois Award. The mayor received honorary degrees from Howard University and George Washington University.

—*Betty L. Plummer*

See also: Mayors; Politics and government.

Suggested Readings:

Baker, James N. "Minority Against Minority: Rioting in D.C. Tests the New Mayor's Resolve." *Newsweek* (May 20, 1991): 28.

Borger, Gloria. "People to Watch: Sharon Dixon." *U.S. News and World Report* (December 31, 1990): 72-73.

French, Mary Ann. "Who Is Sharon Pratt Dixon?" *Essence* (April, 1991): 54.

Jaffe, Harry. "Running on Empty." *Washingtonian* (January, 1992): 50.

Jaffe, Harry, and Tom Sherwood. "Trust Me." *Washingtonian* (May, 1991): 69.

Kenan, Randall G. (b. March 12, 1963, Brooklyn, New York): Writer. Although born in Brooklyn, Kenan spent most of his childhood and adolescence with relatives in Chinquapin, NORTH CAROLINA. He graduated from East Duplin High School in Beulahville, North Carolina, in 1981. Kenan incorporated these early formative experiences in a small, rural African American town into his fiction. Having spent a summer at Oxford University, Kenan graduated from the University of North Carolina at Chapel Hill in December of 1984 with a bachelor's degree in English. Kenan soon moved to New York City where, with the help of a former college instructor, he found employment in the publishing industry. He first worked as an editor with Random House and then worked at Alfred A. Knopf, a Random House subsidiary. Since 1989, Kenan has been a lecturer at Sarah Lawrence College and has also taught writing at Columbia University.

Deeply influenced by the work of Toni Morrison, William Faulkner, Gabriel García Márquez, and James Baldwin, among other writers, Kenan fashioned his fiction from familiar experiences and environments. Kenan's novel *A Visitation of Spirits* (1989) and short-story collection *Let the Dead Bury Their Dead* (1992) are both set in the fictional North Carolina town of Tims Creek.

A Visitation of Spirits explores a young man's experiences of growing up black and gay in Tims Creek, a rural community with a largely fundamentalist Christian population. Widely praised by critics for its experimental style and rich prose, the novel not only focuses on the black gay experience but also portrays, in a constant movement between realism and fantasy, how regional, racial, and religious identities also shape the characters' lives. The seeming opposition between reality and fantasy is fruitfully explored and broken down by Kenan, not only in this novel but also in *Let the Dead Bury Their Dead.*

A Visitation of Spirits sold well for a first novel and received critical acclaim. In addition, *Let the Dead Bury Their Dead* was nominated for the 1992 National Book Critics Circle Award in fiction.

Kenan's work represents a new voice in African American gay literature, since he does not set his fictional works, as many of his colleagues do, in large urban environments. Instead, he gives voice to experiences that so far have remained on the margins of gay black literature. Moreover, labeling Kenan a "gay black writer" is too restrictive, since he also emphasizes the importance played by regional as well as racial characteristics in the formation of identity. For him, sexual orientation ultimately is only one aspect of a character's identity.

See also: Homosexuality; Literature.

Suggested Readings:

Harris, Trudier. *The Power of the Porch: The Storyteller's Craft in Zora Neale Hurston, Gloria Naylor, and Randall Kenan*. Athens: University of Georgia Press, 1996.

McRuer, Robert. "A Visitation of Difference: Randall Kenan and Black Queer Theory." In *Critical Essays: Gay and Lesbian Writers of Color*, edited by Emmanuel S. Nelson. New York: Haworth Press, 1993.

Kennedy, Adrienne (b. September 13, 1931, Pittsburgh, Pennsylvania): Dramatist. Winner of an Obie Award in 1964 for her first play, *Funnyhouse of a Negro*, Kennedy experimented with an abstract style that was a radical change from the traditional social realism of African American drama. She continued her stylistic experiments in plays such as *A Rat's Mass* (1966), which criticizes organized religion and examines the effects of oppression on the individual.

Kennedy graduated from Ohio State University in 1953 and then went to New York City to write. A visit to Ghana during its period of early nationhood, Kennedy said, freed her to create plays in experimental forms. Breaking with the African American dramatic tradition of social realism, Kennedy's one-act plays present the inner world of a central character in external form in order to portray the impact of racism and sexism on the unconscious. To express this inner world, Kennedy's works create a powerful theatrical experience that is surrealistic and dreamlike, usually suggesting nightmares.

Her abstract techniques—such as the use of grotesque masks and symbolic settings and

Playwright Adrienne Kennedy.

costumes—convey to viewers the inner confusion and pain felt by the victims of racism and sexism. Kennedy expresses conflict not through dialogue but through the power of images such black-and-white stage settings and costumes. Frequently her characters are symbols of ideas and cross boundaries of time and space. Thus, Queen Victoria and Patrice Lumumba appear in *Funnyhouse of a Negro*, set in the 1960's in New York City. More than fifty critical studies of Kennedy's work have been published. Among her other plays are *A Movie Star Has to Star in Black and White* (1976), *The Alexander Plays* (a collection of four related plays published together in 1992), and *Sleep Deprivation Chamber* (1996), written with her son, Adam Patrice Kennedy.

—*Francine Dempsey*

See also: Literature.

Kennedy administration: President John F. Kennedy, in office from January, 1961, to November, 1963, enforced federal laws against discrimination and segregation and paved the way for the eventual approval of the Civil Rights Act of 1964.

In the November, 1960, presidential election, John F. Kennedy barely defeated Richard M. Nixon. More than 70 percent of African American voters in that election supported Senator Kennedy, and this strong support enabled him to eke out victories in the key states of Illinois and Texas. African Americans had high hopes that President Kennedy would take significant steps to end to segregation and discrimination in the United States.

In 1961 and 1962, Kennedy issued executive orders that forbade discrimination in federal employment, and he appointed a number of African Americans to high governmental positions. He also sent federal troops to the Universities of Mississippi and Alabama when governors of those states refused to obey court orders requiring the integration of state universities. Regarding civil rights legislation, Kennedy moved cautiously. By June, 1963, he had finally obtained bipartisan support in both houses of Congress, and he proposed federal legislation to ban discrimination in employment and housing.

Notable African American Appointees in the Kennedy Administration

Arthur A. Chapin	Director of the Equal Employment Opportunity Commission
Mercer Cook	Ambassador to Niger
Andrew T. Hatcher	Associate press secretary
Melvin Humphrey	Acting director and deputy director of Housing and Urban Development
Clifton F. Wharton, Sr.	Ambassador to Norway

Malcolm X at a May, 1963, press conference at which he criticized the Kennedy administration's handling of civil rights problems. Malcolm's caustic remarks about Kennedy's assassination later that year provoked widespread controversy. *(AP/Wide World Photos)*

On August 28, 1963, the day of the famous MARCH ON WASHINGTON, he met at the White House with Dr. Martin Luther KING, Jr., and other African American leaders and expressed his support for civil rights. Shortly before Kennedy's assassination on November 22, 1963, his civil rights proposals were approved by the House Judiciary Committee. When Lyndon B. Johnson became president after Kennedy's death, he made passage of civil rights legislation a top priority. He was able to use the powerful emotions of shock and grief that swept the country after the assassination to persuade Congress to pass the sweeping Civil Rights Act of 1964, legislation that was even stronger than the Kennedy proposal.

—Edmund J. Campion

See also: Johnson administration.

Kentucky: Kentucky entered the union as the fifteenth state on June 1, 1792. Of the state's 1997 population of 3.9 million, as estimated by the CENSUS OF THE UNITED STATES, 7.2 percent, or about 283,000 people, were African American. The state's black population is more highly urbanized than the white population, and the largest concentrations of African Americans are in the Louisville, Lexington, and Hopkinsville areas.

In the years preceding the CIVIL WAR, the COMPROMISE OF 1820 divided the slave states from the free states; Kentucky was among the slave states. Interracial marriage was illegal in Kentucky, as it was in sixteen other states. A fine of $500 to $1,000 was imposed; continued violation resulted in a three-month to twelve-month prison term. (However, compared with ALABAMA's law, for example, which imposed a two- to seven-year prison term, Kentucky's law was relatively lenient.) Because Kentucky was a border state between North and South, many slaves trying to reach OHIO to gain freedom passed through Kentucky, which contained primary passageways of the UNDERGROUND RAILROAD. This was an organized network for helping runaway slaves proceed from one point to another en route to the North; sympathizers provided room and board for the night before the slave went on to the next station.

During the Civil War (1861-1865), Kentucky maintained neutrality. However, the state legislature created a military force to drive Confederates out, thereby placing the state on the side of the North in practical terms. Many Kentuckians sympathized with the South, and members of some families fought on opposite sides; seventy-five thou-

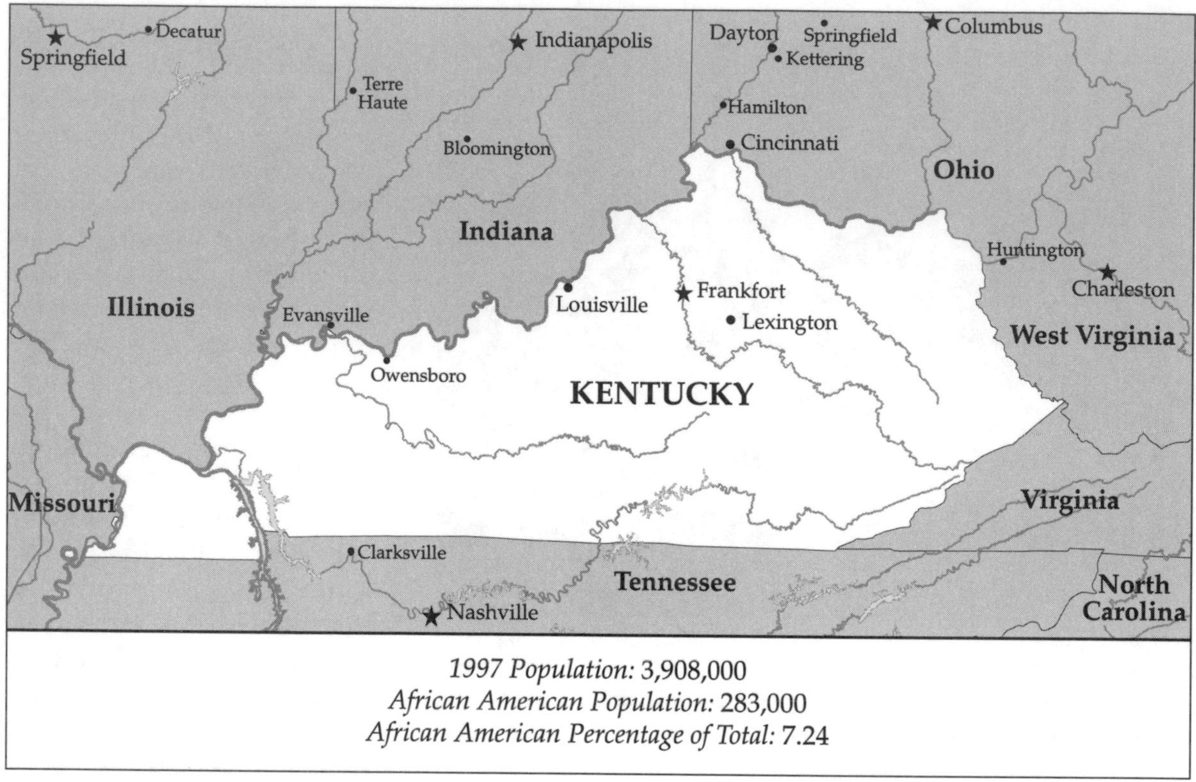

1997 Population: 3,908,000
African American Population: 283,000
African American Percentage of Total: 7.24

sand Kentucky soldiers fought for the North, thirty-five thousand for the South.

Kentucky passed a Jim Crow segregation law in 1892, and in 1914 Louisville passed a housing ordinance forbidding blacks from moving into predominantly white blocks (and whites from moving into primarily black blocks). The U.S. SUPREME COURT, in BUCHANAN V. WARLEY (1917), held the Louisville ordinance to be unconstitutional.

As African Americans in Kentucky continued to struggle for true freedom after the Civil War, educational opportunity became a prime focus. In 1904 the Kentucky legislature passed a "day law" prohibiting black and white students from studying on the same campus; enforced segregation prevailed for many decades. In 1948 a student's lawsuit forced the University of Kentucky to admit qualified African American students. Three years later, the all-black Louisville Municipal College was closed. With the U.S. Supreme Court decision BROWN V. BOARD OF EDUCATION (1954) mandating school desegregation, the governor of Kentucky announced that Kentucky would do whatever was necessary to comply with the law. There was relatively little trouble making the transition to integrated schools.

By the mid-1970's, however the flight of whites from schools in thirteen Kentucky counties had resulted in resegregation. The controversial BUSING plan that was put in place to achieve desegregation resulted in near-riot conditions in Louisville. African Americans throughout Kentucky also faced housing problems. Urban renewal projects during the 1960's amounted to "urban removal" for many. In 1968 Kentucky became the first state in the South to enact statewide housing laws. Nonetheless, the problem of resegregation because of changing housing patterns recurred during the 1970's.

By the 1960's, African Americans had been elected to public office as legislators, mayors and other city and county officials, school board members, and law enforcement officials. Kentucky has been home to a number of notable figures, among them Abraham Lincoln, boxer Muhammad ALI, and Whitney M. YOUNG, Jr., who was the executive director of the NATIONAL URBAN LEAGUE until his death in 1971. In 1967 Georgia Davis became the first African American, and the first woman, elected to the state senate.

—*Victoria Price*

See also: Jim Crow laws.

Kerner Report: The Kerner Report was the work of the National Advisory Commission on Civil Disorders (Kerner Commission) named by President Lyndon B. Johnson on July 29, 1967, to investigate RACE RIOTS that had occurred with increasing frequency from 1963 to 1967. The commission focused on disorders in Tampa, Cincinnati, ATLANTA, northern NEW JERSEY, and DETROIT. The commission and the report were popularly referred to by the name of the commission's chairman, Otto Kerner, the governor of Illinois; the commission's vice chairman was John V. Lindsay, NEW YORK CITY's mayor. The other nine commissioners included representatives of CIVIL RIGHTS organizations, labor, industry, government, and police. The commission delivered its final report on March 1, 1968; the report viewed white racism as the root cause of urban unrest. The report was pessimistic in tone and warned that the country was headed toward an unequal, racially separate society. The report gave the commission's view of what had occurred during the riots, what the causes were, and what could be done to prevent the recurrence of such disorders.

The Riots

The commission reported that the incidents had followed a pattern from city to city. Unlike the white-perpetrated violence against blacks that had often occurred in the late nineteenth and early twentieth centuries, the 1960's disorders were property-oriented actions. Symbols of white society in GHETTO areas, such as white-owned businesses, were targeted. The typical rioter was a male adolescent or young adult African American who was a high school dropout and a lifelong resident of the city. Rioters generally distrusted the political system and were hostile toward middle-class blacks and all whites; the rioters' goal was not a revolutionary transformation of society but fuller participation in that society and a share of its rewards.

The riots happened in racially segregated slum neighborhoods with impoverished residents, high crime rates, and deteriorated housing. The disorders often began with a triggering incident involving police, but the underlying causes lay in old grievances held by African American communities.

Sorting out the Causes

The commission rejected the popular theory that the riots were caused by outside agitators stirring up trouble. Instead, the causes lay in the grim realities of ghetto life, which left rioters feeling frustrated and hopeless. The report also noted troubled relationships between ghetto dwellers and police, city hall, neighborhood merchants, and the press. Underlying all of these patterns was white prejudice and discrimination. In this section of its report, the commission also traced the historical roots of protest to the colonial period and compared the experience of African Americans with the experience of white immigrants.

The report noted that ghetto residents experienced great difficulty making a living as a result of high unemployment, underemployment, and discrimination in promotions. Ghetto education often took place in de facto segregated schools in which children were processed rather than truly educated. Teachers often had negative attitudes toward and low expectations of inner-city pupils. The schools themselves were often overcrowded and poorly equipped. Poor African Americans were concentrated in dangerous neighborhoods where they often lived in unhealthy, substandard housing. Whites were fleeing to the suburbs and leaving central cities in financial crisis. The welfare system denied help to many truly needy families, set assistance amounts too low for decent living, and was administered in a way that encouraged dependency and destroyed welfare recipients' self-respect.

The report also pointed to the existence of an abrasive relationship between ghetto residents and the police. Ghetto residents felt they had been harassed by police and denied prompt protection. They complained of being exploited by retail merchants who charged high prices and demanded high interest rates on credit sales. Ghetto dwellers lacked confidence in city governments as the result of poor communication and past failures of city governments to solve ghetto problems. Newspaper and television reporters gave only sporadic coverage to African American life, and such coverage, when it occurred, emphasized negative, violent incidents.

In addition to these specific grievances, the Kerner Report stated that the stage for violence was set by more general trends such as a national climate favoring violence and ghetto residents' growing sense of powerlessness, feelings of deprivation resulting from exposure to middle-class lifestyles, and frustration stemming from unmet expectations. Legislation and court victories in the 1960's had caused ghetto dwellers' hopes to be raised, yet few tangible improvements had appeared in their lives.

Steps to Prevent Recurrence

The commission noted that its recommendations were on a large scale, in proportion to the large scale of the problems uncovered. Such extensive changes, the report said, would be possible in light of the rich nation's abundant resources, but it was important to select pro-

President Lyndon B. Johnson opens the first meeting of the Kerner Commission. *(National Archives)*

grams that could yield significant, rapid results in order to end the pattern of hopelessness. The report rejected both the continuation of present policies and the enrichment of ghetto areas without a push for racial integration. A combination of programs that could both enrich ghetto life and lead to integration was proposed.

To remedy problems in the area of employment, the report recommended creating new jobs in both the public and private sectors. The commission also stressed the need for job-training programs and for strict enforcement of laws against employment discrimination. Solutions to education problems lay in smaller classes, more teacher training, and multicultural education; techniques such as the creation of magnet schools were recommended to promote integration in schools. The commission also proposed a new linkage between the ghetto community and its schools. Centralized planning was desirable, but community control could be implemented for many aspects of education. Solutions proposed for the housing crisis included the creation of scattered-site public housing, the construction of more low-income housing, passage of a federal fair-housing law, and the use of programs such as rent supplements and federal mortgage subsidies to enable low-income citizens to afford decent housing. The report also proposed reforms of the welfare system and recommended uniform national standards for assistance, work incentives, job training, and day-care centers. The commission advocated a national system of income supplementation that would put a floor under the income of all Americans at a level sufficient to assure decent living.

Other Recommendations

The Kerner Commission's report also recommended programs to improve the economic climate in POVERTY areas, such as offering tax credits to entice business and industry to locate in such neighborhoods and enlarging the Small Business Administration's role in encouraging African American entrepreneurship. Police departments were advised to hire more African American officers and to improve police-community relations with grievance mechanisms independent of the police departments. City governments were urged to institute neighborhood action task forces.

The report also contained recommendations for improved control of future disorders, with special emphasis on the roles of police and fire departments, the National Guard, and the Army. The commission emphasized the importance of the training of personnel and the coordination of control agencies. Rumor-control tactics were discussed, and legal aspects of riot control were addressed. Underlying all the report's specific recommendations was the Kerner Commission's desire to see an end to racism on the part of the country's white majority.

The Report's Aftermath

There was no special ceremony at the White House marking receipt of the report. The Johnson administration's response consisted largely of silence. Many government officials publicly rejected the charge of white racism. Congress passed antiriot legislation rather than the kinds of social programs advocated in the Kerner Report. In 1969 the Urban Coalition and Urban America assessed what followed the report in the book *One Year Later* and concluded that the country had not adopted the goals and strategies recommended by the Kerner Commission.

The Kerner Report was extensively discussed in the press. More than two million copies of the report were sold, including paperback, hardback, and government-issue editions. Many people were surprised by the report's analysis and recommendations, expecting a report in bland, bureaucratic style that would place blame upon riot participants alone and advocate small-scale reforms. Instead, the public read the report's strong and often elegant prose, its startling conclusion about racial polarization, and its recommendations for extensive social change. While many people were familiar with the report's analysis, however, not all were convinced of its accuracy. A Louis Harris poll conducted just after the report's release found that more than half the white respondents did not agree that white racism was the main cause of the civil disorders.

There was limited further civil disorder in African American communities in the 1960's following the publication of the Kerner Report. Violence occurred in 1968 following the assassination of Martin Luther King, Jr. In all, there were more than one hundred such incidents during the period, leading to more than forty deaths. After that, the nation's focus changed; the next serious civil disorders involved white-perpetrated violence at the Chicago Democratic National Convention in 1968.

—*Nancy Conn Terjesen*

See also: De facto segregation; Employment and unemployment; Race, racism, and race relations; Racial discrimination; Racial prejudice; Racial violence and hatred.

Suggested Readings:

Barnhart, William E., Bill Barnhart, and Eugene F. Schlickman. *Kerner: The Conflict of Intangible Rights*. Champaign: University of Illinois Press, 1999.

Harris, Fred R., and Roger W. Wilkins, eds. *Quiet Riots: Race and Poverty in the United States*. New York: Pantheon Books, 1988.

Masotti, Louis H., Jeffrey K. Hadden, Kenneth F. Seminatore, and Jerome R. Corsi. *A Time to Burn? An Evaluation of the Present Crisis in Race Relations*. Chicago: Rand McNally, 1969.

Ritchie, Barbara. *The Riot Report: A Shortened Version of the Report of the National Advisory Commission on Civil Disorders*. New York: Viking Press, 1969.

Rossi, Peter, ed. *Ghetto Riots*. Chicago: Aldine, 1970.

Urban America and The Urban Coalition. *One Year Later: An Assessment of the Nation's Response to the Crisis Described by the National Advisory Commission on Civil Disorders*. New York: Praeger, 1969.

U.S. Kerner Commission. *Report of the National Advisory Commission on Civil Disorders*. Washington, D.C.: U.S. Govenment Printing Office, 1968.

Killens, John Oliver (January 14, 1916, Macon, Georgia—October 27, 1987, Brooklyn, New York): Novelist, dramatist, essay writer, and university lecturer. Killens began writing seriously after World War II, first having served as a staff member of the National Labor Relations Board and in the U.S. Army. His first novel, *Youngblood* (1954), is the story of a family struggling against racism in a small Georgia town during the early twentieth century. Although the novel has sometimes been criticized for being didactic, its characters and portrayal of racism earned it praise.

In *And Then We Heard the Thunder* (1963), Killens tells the story of a black soldier in World War II, who finds that racism in the American military is his most immediate enemy. This novel was a Pulitzer Prize nominee. The struggle to ensure black voting rights is the subject matter of *'Sippi*, Killens's 1967 novel, which generally is considered to be less successful artistically.

The Cotillion: Or, One Good Bull Is Half the Herd (1971) brought Killens another Pulitzer Prize nomination. Told from multiple points of view, the novel conveys a vivid sense of Harlem street life contrasted with the more staid world of the Brooklyn black women's club that sponsors the cotillion. Even the texture of the prose makes clear that Killens values the former over the latter, but Killens underscores the point with direct commentary and plot outcome.

Killens wrote several plays, including *Lower Than the Angels* (pr. 1965) and *Cotillion* (pr. 1975), adapted from his novel. He also wrote two screenplays: *Odds Against Tomorrow* (1959), written with Nelson Gidding and starring Harry Belafonte, and *Slaves* (1969), written with Herbert J. Biberman.

In the late 1960's and early 1970's, Killens traveled to Africa, China, and the Soviet Union, where he developed an interest in the Russian writer of partial Ethiopian descent, Alexander Pushkin, about whom he later wrote the novel *Great Black Russian: A Novel on the Life and Times of Alexander Pushkin* (1989). Killens also wrote *Black Man's Burden* (1965)—a collection of political essays—and two books for young adults, *Great Gittin' Up Morning* (1972), a biography of Denmark Vesey, and *A Man Ain't Nothin' but a Man: The Adventures of John Henry* (1975). He began teaching creative writing in 1946.
See also: Literature.

Kimbro, Warren: Member of the New Haven, Connecticut, chapter of the Black Panther Party. In mid-1969, Kimbro helped interrogate Alex Rackley, a New York Panther suspected of informing to police. After a decision was made to execute Rackley, Kimbro helped implement the order. The victim's body was discovered on May 21. Kimbro was arrested for murder, along with ten others, including Bobby Seale. On January 16, 1970, Kimbro unexpectedly pled guilty to shooting Rackley and testified against Seale and fellow Panthers. Ironically, Kimbro received a life sentence for second-degree murder while charges eventually were dropped against Seale.

Kincaid, Jamaica (Elaine Potter Richardson; b. May 25, 1949, St. Johns, Antigua): Writer. Jamaica Kincaid is believed by many to be the most important woman writer of her time from the West Indies. Born Elaine Potter Richardson, she bagan her life in obscurity on the island of Antigua. Eventually, she won recognition from the New York literary establishment and then from the American public. Kincaid's books explore family problems, and they depict the damage done by colonialism, racial prejudice, and gender discrimination.

Jamaica Kincaid. (*Sigrid Estrada*)

Though her family was not well-to-do, in her early years Richardson enjoyed the full attention of her mother, who taught her to love literature. That closeness ended after her brothers were born, and eventually a very real hostility developed between mother and daughter. At age seventeen she went to New York, where she worked as an au pair, took some courses, renamed herself Jamaica Kincaid, and began submitting articles to magazines and newspapers.

Kincaid's chance at success came through George Trow, a contributor to *The New Yorker*, who introduced her to his editor, William Shawn. The magazine began publishing Kincaid's work and in 1976 hired her as a staff writer. Encouraged by Trow, Kincaid tried her hand at fiction. Her first effort, the short story "Girl," was published in *The New Yorker* in 1978 and later was included in Kincaid's award-winning collection, *At the Bottom of the River* (1983). Most of the other short fiction in the book had also appeared in *The New Yorker.*

Responding to critics who found her stories puzzling and difficult, Kincaid chose a more conventional pattern for *Annie John* (1985), her first novel. *Annie John* is typical of Kincaid's fiction in that it is highly autobiographical and uses a West Indian setting. Like the two novels that followed, *Lucy* (1990) and *The Autobiography of My Mother* (1996), *Annie John* describes a mother's emotional withdrawal from her daughter. As critics have noted, the withdrawal parallels the betrayal of natives by their colonial overlords. Only by leaving her island, with its colonial past, its racism, and its gender discrimination, can the protagonist of *Annie John* find her own identity. The process is neither pleasant nor easy.

Kincaid settled in rural VERMONT with her husband, Allen Shawn, and their two children but continued to write about dark realities. Just as her novels tend to focus on failed relationships, her travel book, *A Small Place* (1998), is an indictment of colonialism, and *My Brother's Keeper* (1998) is not so much the story of her youngest brother's death from ACQUIRED IMMUNODEFICIENCY SYNDROME (AIDS) as a description of an empty life. In her work Kincaid is a crusader against false optimism and easy answers.

—*Rosemary M. Canfield Reisman*

See also: West Indian heritage.

Suggested Readings:

Birbalsingh, Frank. "Jamaica Kincaid: From Antigua to America." In *Frontiers of Caribbean Literatures in English*, edited by Frank Birbalsingh. New York: St. Martin's Press, 1996.

Ferguson, Moira. *Jamaica Kincaid: Where the Land Meets the Body*. Charlottesville: University Press of Virginia, 1994.

Simmons, Diane. *Jamaica Kincaid*. New York: Twayne, 1994.

B. B. King (left) and fellow bluesman Rufus Thomas in 1995. *(AP/ Wide World Photos)*

King, B. B. (b. September 16, 1925, Itta Bena, Mississippi): BLUES singer and guitarist. Riley "B. B." King sang in church from the age of four and formed a high school spiritual quartet. He worked in the fields from his childhood, even when he was making some money playing guitar on weekends and at night, until he went to MEMPHIS, TENNESSEE. He spent some time there with an older bluesman cousin, Booker T. "Bukka" White.

King became a popular performer on Memphis's Beale Street, and was billed for his work as a disc jockey on a local radio station as the Beale Street Blues Boy, which allegedly led to the name "B. B." He began recording in 1949. He acknowledged the early influence of Blind Lemon Jefferson and Lonnie Johnson, so it is not surprising that his single-string runs have drawn comment from blues critics.

King worked all over the South, in blues-loving cities such as Chicago, Illinois, and St. Louis, Missouri, in rural honky-tonks, and in segregated theaters such as the Regal in Chicago. As a young musician, King listened to the great jazz guitarists and to singer Jimmy Rushing, whose recordings with Count Basie gave King the idea, he once said, for the structure of his own band, particularly for his driving trumpet section.

King's *Live at the Regal* (1965) is considered to be one of the definitive blues albums, offering an interchange between performer and audience. King frequently performed live, playing 342 one-night shows in 1956 alone. The blues revival of the mid-1960's brought his music to the attention of white audiences, and he began to play regularly on rock concert circuits. He continued to record powerful blues albums, playing his guitar, Lucille. In 1981 he won a Grammy Award for *There Must Be a Better World Somewhere*. His authorized biography, *The Arrival of B. B. King*, was written by Charles Sawyer in 1980.
See also: Music.

King, Coretta Scott (b. April 27, 1927, Marion, Alabama): Civil rights leader and widow of Martin Luther King, Jr. Born Coretta Scott, she was one of three children in a family that had farmed its own land since Reconstruction. She majored in education and music at Antioch College, attending on a scholarship. She considered a career in teaching but became disillusioned when the city of Yellow Springs, Ohio, where Antioch College was located, would not let her do her student teaching there. The city said that no black person had ever taught in its public schools.

After her husband was assassinated in 1968, Coretta Scott King became a major civil rights figure in her own right. *(Library of Congress)*

After her graduation from Antioch College, she did graduate work at the New England Conservatory of Music in Boston, Massachusetts. It was while she was a student there that she met Martin Luther King, Jr., then a student at Boston University. They were married on June 18, 1953. In April, 1954, her husband accepted a position as pastor of Dexter Avenue Baptist Church in Montgomery, Alabama. King earned her degree in voice from the New England Conservatory of Music in June of that year, and her husband finished work for his doctorate in August. They moved to Montgomery in September.

By 1964 the couple had four children—Yolanda, Martin Luther, III, Dexter Scott, and Bernice Albertine. During this time, King served mostly as a dedicated mother and wife while her husband engaged in his activities on behalf of civil rights. She did use her musical interest and training to develop a format for a freedom concert, incorporating hymns and spirituals in addition to freedom songs that narrated the civil rights struggle.

After the assassination of Martin Luther King, Jr., on April 4, 1968, Coretta became much more involved in civil rights work. She was the keynote speaker at the Lincoln Memorial on May 12, 1968, during the Poor People's Campaign, also leading a march of welfare mothers during that gathering in Washington, D.C. Her speech on Solidarity Day (June 19, 1968) often is identified as an example of her work. That same year, she became the first woman to deliver a commencement address at Harvard University. In 1969 she lent her support to striking hospital workers in Charleston, South Carolina. She called on American women to unite to fight racism, poverty, and war, and was part of the National Commission on the Observance of International Women's Year, created by executive order of President Gerald Ford in 1975. In 1983 she won the Franklin D. Roosevelt Freedom Medal for epitomizing his four freedoms—of worship, of speech, from want, and from fear.

King also established the Martin Luther King, Jr., Center for Social Change in Atlanta, Georgia. The center gives an annual prize to a practitioner of nonviolent efforts to further peace and civil rights. King resigned as president of the center in 1989 but kept her titles as chief executive officer and spokesperson. Her son Dexter Scott took over the presidency but resigned by the end of the year, citing power struggles among the center's leadership.

Arm-in-arm with her son Martin Luther King III, Coretta Scott King leads the annual reenactment of the historic Selma-to-Montgomery march in 1999. *(AP/Wide World Photos)*

Among her other work, King traveled to Africa and in 1985 was arrested with two of her children for demonstrating outside the South African embassy in Washington, D.C. She spoke frequently about women's rights and human rights and wrote a syndicated weekly newspaper column. She was cochair of the National Committee for Full Employment and the Full Employment Action Council. Her reminiscences, *My Life with Martin Luther King, Jr.*, were published in 1969.
See also: King, Martin Luther, Jr.; Martin Luther King, Jr., Day.

King, Martin Luther, Jr. (January 15, 1929, Atlanta, Georgia—April 4, 1968, Memphis, Tennessee): Southern BAPTIST minister and CIVIL RIGHTS leader. During his lifetime, Martin Luther King, Jr., was instrumental in leading mass civil rights movements in the stride toward peace, freedom, and democracy. In 1964 King became the youngest recipient of the Nobel Peace Prize. He received hundreds of awards and honors, all of which he sometimes referred to as the "shallow things" in life. On occasion, he would say the real rewards in life are justice and equality. To honor King's legacy, the U.S. Congress passed a bill to observe his birthday as a national holiday on the third Monday of each January beginning in 1986.

Nobel laureate Martin Luther King, Jr., in 1964. *(Nobel Foundation)*

Family Background
King was the second child and first son of the Reverend Michael Luther KING, Sr., and Alberta Williams King. He was originally christened Michael Luther King, Jr., but his father changed both their names to Martin in 1933 to honor the wishes of his late father, who insisted that he had originally given that name to his son in the days when birth certificates were rare for blacks. The family had a long history of religious commitment; both King's father and his maternal grandfather, Adam Daniel Williams, were Baptist preachers who served as pastors of EBENEZER BAPTIST CHURCH in Atlanta.

Education, Religion, and Philosophy
King received his elementary and secondary education in the public schools of Atlanta. At the age of fifteen, he was accepted as an early-admissions student at Atlanta's Morehouse College under a special program for the gifted; he graduated in 1948 at age nineteen with a bachelor of arts degree in sociology. His earlier interests in college had been in medicine and law, but following his father's guidance, King decided to enter the ministry. On February 25, 1948, he was ordained as a Baptist minister. In September of that year, he was admitted to Crozer Theological Seminary in Chester, PENNSYLVANIA. While at Crozer, King became the first African American to be elected the

school's student body president and graduated with the highest grade point average in his class.

After hearing sermons on the life of Mohandas Gandhi and his philosophy of nonviolence, King began to devote himself to the study of Gandhi's teachings. After completing the work for his bachelor of divinity degree in 1951, King pursued a doctorate in systematic theology at Boston University. King's religious studies deepened his interest in the great philosophers of the world and led him to explore the works of such thinkers as Paul Tillich, Henry Nelson Wieman, Reinhold Niebuhr, and Walter Rauschenbusch.

Marriage and Graduation

While in Boston, King met Coretta Scott, a student at the New England Conservatory of Music. King's father performed their wedding ceremony at Coretta's home in Marion, ALABAMA, on June 18, 1953. In 1954, while he was completing his work on his doctoral dissertation, King was offered the pastorship at Dexter Avenue Baptist Church in Montgomery, Alabama. King accepted and was installed as pastor by his father on October 31, 1954.

In May of 1954, the U.S. SUPREME COURT had issued a landmark decision in BROWN V. BOARD OF EDUCATION outlawing segregation in public schools and overturning the "SEPARATE BUT EQUAL" doctrine that had been established in 1896 by PLESSY V. FERGUSON. King hailed the Court's ruling as "a world-shaking decree." Slightly more than a year after accepting the pastorship, King found himself thrust into the forefront of the Civil Rights movement. On December 1, 1955, Rosa PARKS, a garment seamstress, refused to give up her seat on a Montgomery bus to a white passenger as instructed by the bus driver. As a result, Parks was placed under arrest for violating the city's ordinance on segregation. Community leaders such as E. D. Nixon and Ralph ABERNATHY formed the Montgomery Improvement Association (MIA) to spearhead a boycott of the transit company and chose King as their leader.

Employing a strategy of nonviolence and noncooperation, more than fifty thousand African Americans refused to ride the buses for 381 days. Determined to bring bus segregation to an end, the protestors found alternative means of transportation—they walked, organized carpools, and were transported at reduced fares by taxicabs owned and operated by African Americans. The MIA made several attempts to negotiate an agreement with the Montgomery bus company, but to no avail. The agreement presented by the MIA called for three demands: that seating of passengers be made on a first-come-first-served basis, that all passengers receive courteous treatment by white bus drivers, and that African Americans be hired as bus drivers. A series of court cases ensued, climaxing with the U.S. SUPREME COURT's ruling on November 13, 1956, declaring the Alabama state and local laws requiring segregation on buses to be unconstitutional. On December 21, 1956, the buses were desegregated.

Nonviolent Doctrine

In February of 1957 in New Orleans, King helped to organize the SOUTHERN CHRISTIAN LEADERSHIP CONFERENCE (SCLC); he served as the SCLC's president for the remainder of his life. King gained international recognition for his work with the SCLC promoting a doctrine of nonviolent direct action. The group's primary goal was to attract the masses of African Americans into the struggle for freedom by expanding "the Montgomery way" throughout the South. The SCLC concentrated on a "spiritual strategy" that would raise the moral consciousness of the nation.

With King at its helm, the SCLC became the driving force in liberating the psyche of African Americans from white racism. Through King's leadership, the SCLC sought to dismantle the system of segregation in the South while at the same time bringing empowerment to the African American community. The SCLC involved itself in numerous programs, including efforts in voter registration, political education, leadership training, education in nonviolent methods, and economic development. The organization became the springboard from which King launched his campaign for freedom, lecturing throughout the country to gain support for the civil rights of African Americans and peace and justice for all people.

From February 2 to March 10, 1959, King and his wife, Coretta, visited India, studying the Gandhian techniques of nonviolence while they were the guests of Prime Minister Jawaharlal Nehru. Upon his return to the United States, King became even more convinced that nonviolent protest was the best approach to liberate oppressed people. In his first book, *Stride Toward Freedom: The Montgomery Story* (1958), King outlined the six principles of nonviolence: active resistance to evil, the winning of one's opponent through understanding, directing one's attack against forces of evil rather than against persons performing such acts, willingness to accept suffering without retaliation, refusal to hate one's opponent, and the conviction that the universe is on the side of justice. Thus, all policy guiding the movement was developed from this prevailing philosophy.

The growing demands of the Civil Rights movement forced King to make the difficult decision to move back to Atlanta, where he became copastor, with his father, of the Ebenezer Baptist Church. From this vantage point, he felt better able to orchestrate the affairs of the SCLC and the Civil Rights movement. The tactics of active nonviolent resistance (SIT-INS, marches, FREEDOM RIDES, pray-ins, and other forms of protest) had mass appeal to both African Americans and liberal whites throughout the country.

National attention was once again drawn to the movement when King was arrested on October 19, 1960, along with a group of stu-

King being arrested in Montgomery, Alabama, in 1958. *(AP/Wide World Photos)*

King led marchers across the Alabama River bridge at Selma on March 21, 1965. *(AP/Wide World Photos)*

dents for participating in a sit-in at a segregated lunch counter in an Atlanta department store in violation of the state's trespassing law. Although the charges were dropped, King was sentenced to the Reidsville State Prison on charges that he had violated his probation with reference to a traffic arrest case. The nation was appalled at the arrest of King. The failure of President Dwight Eisenhower to intervene, however, presented an opportunity for the Democratic presidential candidate John F. Kennedy to intercede, and King was released on a two-thousand-dollar bond. Many believe that this move by Kennedy contributed directly to his close victory in the presidential elections a few days later.

High Point in King's Leadership

The period between 1960 and 1965 proved to be the acme of King's leadership. He gained support for the movement worldwide as well as from Presidents Kennedy and Lyndon B. Johnson. Throughout this period, the Civil Rights movement conducted many successful campaigns but also experienced some relative failures. For example, the 1961-1962 Albany, Georgia, campaign to desegregate public facilities was deemed a failure and a lesson learned. Other campaigns or movements, though, were highly successful. The Birmingham movement in the spring of 1963, which campaigned against segregated public accommodations, gave renewed impetus to the quest for freedom and justice.

For the first time, King used schoolchildren in protest marches; despite the children's presence, and despite the peaceful nature of the demonstrations, the director of public safety in Birmingham, Eugene "Bull" Connor, ordered the use of police dogs and fire hoses to stop the marching protesters. King, along with hundreds of supporters, was arrested for protesting segregation of Birmingham's eating facilities. From his jail cell on April 16, 1963, King wrote his profound "Letter from a Birmingham Jail," in which he addressed those who were critical of his insistence on mass demonstrations. The letter from Birmingham became the centerpiece for his next book, *Why We Can't Wait* (1964).

Before the Birmingham campaign was completed, King was already planning, with other civil rights leaders, the historic mass March on Washington. At the foot of the Lincoln Memorial, on August 28, 1963, an interracial audience of more than 250,000 gathered to listen to a number of speakers calling for justice and equality in all aspects of life for all Americans regardless of race, color, creed, or social status. The most electrifying speech of the day was King's famous "I Have a Dream" address. The essence of King's speech was his hope that one day all people would be judged by the "content of their character" and not by the color of their skin. Afterward, King and a delegation of other civil rights leaders met with President Kennedy in the White House to discuss support for strong civil rights legislation. Despite Kennedy's death in November, 1963, Congress passed the Civil Rights Act of 1964 the following summer, giving the federal government the power to enforce desegregation of public places and outlawing discrimination in employment. In December, 1964, King was awarded the Nobel Peace Prize.

The Selma, Alabama, movement was, King said, "particularly gratifying" in that it was an ecumenical involvement of Protestants, Catholics, Jews, and other religious groups that had come together to dramatize the need for a federal voting-rights law. However gratifying it might have been, the Selma campaign had its high and low points. On March 7, 1965, known as "bloody Sunday," marching demonstrators were beaten back by Sheriff Jim Clark and his deputies as they attempted to cross a bridge en route from Selma to Montgomery. A second attempt to cross was turned around by King. The third attempt was successful, and twenty-five thousand marchers assembled to hear King speak on voting rights. In the interim, President Johnson addressed Congress on the need for a federal voting rights bill, concluding his remarks with the theme of the Civil Rights movement, "and we shall overcome." On August 6, the Voting

The day before he was assassinated on the balcony of Memphis's Lorraine Motel, King (second from right) was photographed in the same location, along with Hosea Williams, Jesse Jackson, and Ralph Abernathy. *(AP/Wide World Photos)*

Rights Act of 1965 was signed into law.

The race riots occurring in northern cities were, in part, a response to racially discriminatory practices and other problems plaguing the inner cities. In 1966 King attempted to address this growing concern by launching a campaign for open housing in Chicago. He was pelted with stones as he led marchers through Gage Park in Chicago, where he described white mobs as being more hostile than those faced in Mississippi. An agreement for open housing was reached but later reneged on after King and his aides left town.

Undaunted, King continued to lead campaigns throughout the North and South, addressing broader issues to improve the quality of life for all people. On April 4, 1967, King delivered a speech at the Riverside Church in New York City entitled "Beyond Vietnam." He was criticized for this speech, and as he became more outspoken on the war question, the criticisms mounted. King explained, however, that his moral convictions would not allow him to remain silent. Therefore, he continued to speak out in opposition to the war and delivered a major sermon in February of 1968 at Ebenezer Baptist Church entitled "Why I Opposed the War in Vietnam."

King and the SCLC then set out to organize a multiracial poor people's campaign to be staged in Washington, D.C., employing the tactics of civil disobedience and nonviolence. The Poor People's Campaign was interrupted when King was called to Memphis, Tennessee, to lend support to a garbage workers' strike. On April 3, 1968, King delivered his final speech, "I've Been to the Mountaintop," which he closed with the following prophetic words: "I may not get there with you, but I want you to know tonight that we as a people will get to the promised land." The following day, while standing on the balcony of the Lorraine Motel, King was shot to death by James Earl Ray.

—Robert S. Mikell

See also: Johnson administration; Kennedy administration; King, Coretta Scott; King, Martin Luther, Sr.; Martin Luther King, Jr., Day; Segregation and integration.

Suggested Readings:

Abernathy, Donzaleigh. *Partners to History: Martin Luther King, Jr., Ralph David Abernathy, and the Civil Rights Movement*. Los Angeles: General, 1998.

Abernathy, Ralph D. *And the Walls Came Tumbling Down: An Autobiography*. New York: Harper & Row, 1989.

Branch, Taylor. *Parting the Waters: America in the King Years, 1954-1963*. New York: Simon & Schuster, 1988.

______. *Pillar of Fire: America in the King Years, 1963-65*. New York: Simon & Schuster, 1998.

Garrow, David J. *Bearing the Cross: Martin Luther King, Jr., and the Southern Christian Leadership Conference*. New York: William Morrow, 1986.

______, ed. *We Shall Overcome: The Civil Rights Movement in the United States in the 1950's and 1960's*. 3 vols. New York: Carlson, 1989.

Harding, Vincent. *Martin Luther King: The Inconvenient Hero*. Maryknoll, N.Y.: Orbis Books, 1996.

King, Martin Luther, Jr. *The Autobiography of Martin Luther King, Jr.* Edited by Clayborne Carson. New York: Warner Books, 1998.

Lischer, Richard. *The Preacher King: Martin Luther King, Jr. and the Word That Moved America*. New York: Oxford University Press, 1995.

McKnight, Gerald. *The Last Crusade: Martin Luther King, Jr., the FBI, and the Poor People's Campaign*. Boulder, Colo.: Westview Press, 1998.

Moses, Greg. *Revolution of Conscience: Martin Luther King, Jr., and the Philosophy of Nonviolence*. New York: Guilford Press, 1997.

Posner, Gerald L. *Killing the Dream: James Earl Ray and the Assassination of Martin Luther King, Jr.* New York: Random House, 1998.

Ward, Brian, and Tony Badger, eds. *The Making of Martin Luther King and the Civil Rights Movement*. New York: New York University Press, 1996.

King, Martin Luther, Sr. (December 19, 1899, Stockbridge, Georgia—November 11, 1984, Atlanta, Georgia): Baptist clergyman. King is best known as the father of civil rights leader Martin Luther King, Jr., but was active in civil rights and community leadership efforts of his own. He was pastor of Ebenezer Baptist Church in Atlanta, one of the largest Baptist churches in the South, from 1932 to 1975.

King was the oldest of ten children in a household of sharecroppers. He changed his first name in recognition of Martin Luther, the founder of Protestantism. He graduated from Morehouse College in Atlanta in 1930, with a bachelor's degree in theology. While attending Morehouse College, he met and married Alberta Williams, the daughter of the Reverend A. D. Williams, whom he would soon replace as pastor at Ebenezer Baptist Church.

As pastor at Ebenezer Baptist Church, King worked in food programs for the needy and preached nonviolence, racial equality, and concern for the poor, as well as faith in God. He unofficially added two commandments to the standard ten. "Thou shalt own thy own home" and "Thou shalt send thy sons to college." In 1936 he led hundreds of protesters on a march to Atlanta's city hall to demand voting rights.

King served on the board of directors of the Southern Christian Leadership Council. He also was a member of the Social Action Committee of the National Association for the Advancement of Colored People (NAACP) and played a leading role in the battle to equalize salaries of black and white teachers in Atlanta. He fought to desegregate elevators in courthouses so that African Americans could have access to voter registration. In 1972 King was named Clergyman of the Year by the Georgia Region of the National Conference of Christians and Jews.

Martin Luther King, Jr., was assassinated in 1968. King's only other son, A. D. Williams, drowned in 1969. Alberta King was shot to death in 1974 while playing the organ at a service at Ebenezer Baptist Church.

See also: King, Coretta Scott; Martin Luther King, Jr., Day.

King, Melvin H. (b. October 20, 1928, Boston, Massachusetts): Politician and community activist. In 1979 King mounted his first campaign for mayor of Boston, Massachusetts, and finished third in a six-way primary election. King ran as a socialist candidate in the

Melvin H. King during his campaign for Congress in 1986. *(AP/Wide World Photos)*

1983 Boston mayoral campaign and constructed his own RAINBOW COALITION of supporters among Boston's liberal white, black, Hispanic, and Asian voters. In the campaign, he stressed his commitment to increasing the number of jobs, providing better public housing, and requiring city developers to contribute more of their profits to help renovate Boston's aging residential neighborhoods. King finished first among eight candidates in the primary but lost the run-off election to Raymond L. Flynn, whose populist message appealed to the same constituents that supported King. King had beaten Flynn by ninety-eight votes in the primary.

Before his mayoral campaign, King had an extended career as a community activist and educator. He was a youth worker and organizer with the United South End Settlements for fifteen years, and in 1967 he was named as executive director of the Urban League of Greater Boston. He also chaired the Bishop's Housing Action Group and Low-Cost Housing, Inc. As an educator, he taught mathematics in the Boston public schools, at Northeastern University, and at Boston University's Metropolitan College. In 1971 he joined the faculty of the Massachusetts Institute of Technology as a lecturer in the Department of Urban Studies. He was promoted to adjunct professor and director of the Community Fellows Program in 1975. King was elected to the Commonwealth of MASSACHUSETTS legislature in 1973 and served until 1982.

See also: Politics and government.

King, Rodney, arrest and beating: On the night of March 3, 1991, four LOS ANGELES, CALIFORNIA police officers arrested and severely beat Rodney Glenn King, a twenty-four-year-old unemployed construction worker. King had led police on a fifteen-minute automobile chase that reached speeds of 115 miles per hour. When King stopped his car, he was initially questioned by two California Highway Patrol officers before officers from the Los Angeles Police Department (LAPD) took over the investigation.

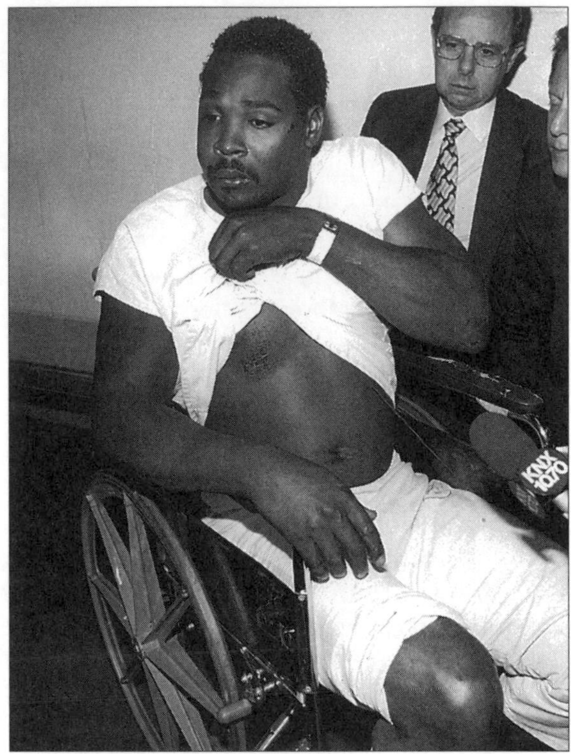

Rodney King shows reporters the injuries he received from his beating by Los Angeles police officers. *(AP/Wide World Photos)*

The LAPD officers handcuffed King and shot him with a Taser electric stun gun. They then beat him with aluminum batons and kicked him so severely that he required two days of hospitalization. Doctors reported that King suffered a skull fracture, a broken leg, a shattered eye socket and cheekbone, and brain damage. Eleven other officers witnessed the brutality, and no one intervened to stop it. Unknown to the police, a citizen had videotaped the beating from his balcony window. On March 4, national news programs broadcast the 81-second videotape, generating enormous public sympathy for King. In the aftermath of this publicity, the LAPD Internal Affairs Division launched an investigation into the incident. On March 14, a Los Angeles County grand jury indicted four LAPD officers for assault with a deadly weapon and for attempting to cover up the incident.

The trial of the police began in April of 1992, in suburban Simi Valley Superior Court, in Ventura County, across the northwestern boundary of Los Angeles. This change of venue was granted by the California Court of Appeals, which ruled that pretrial publicity prevented the officers from receiving a fair trial in Los Angeles. During the trial, King was advised not to testify on his own behalf. On April 29, the Simi Valley jury acquitted the four officers of all but one charge, accepting the opinion that the videotape showed what one defense attorney called "a controlled application of baton strikes" in order to subdue King. The verdict surprised and outraged many Americans. Tom Bradley, the African American mayor of Los Angeles, said, "Today the system failed us."

Within hours after the verdict was announced, looting and violence broke out in predominantly African American and Latino South Central Los Angeles. By nightfall, more than a hundred fires raged and a dozen people were dead. Around midnight, Governor Pete Wilson announced plans to send in National Guard troops to help quell the violence. The riot lasted for four days, from April 30 to May 3, with fifty-eight deaths and damage to property reaching $1 billion. President George H. W. Bush authorized the deployment of U.S. Army soldiers to patrol the streets before the chaos ended. After the first day of rioting, Rodney King talked to reporters for the first time and made an emotional plea for order. "People," he implored, "I just want to say, you know, can we, can we all get along?"

Almost twelve thousand people were arrested in the riots and charged with burglary and looting. More than ten thousand stores were burned, and more than four thousand people were injured. When investigators totaled all the losses, the riot stood as the bloodiest and most destructive in American history. The Justice Department filed federal civil rights charges against the four police officers for violating Rodney King's right to due process. This federal trial resulted in the conviction of police sergeant Stacey Koon and officer Laurence Powell, both of whom received short prison sentences in August of 1993.

In May of 1994, Rodney King received $3.8 million in compensatory damages through a civil suit filed against the city of Los Angeles. Despite his intent to put his troubles behind him, King had repeated encounters with local law enforcement agencies throughout the 1990's.

See also: Race riots.

King Curtis (Curtis Ousley; February 7, 1934, Fort Worth, Texas—August 13, 1971, New York, New York): Saxophonist and bandleader. Inspired by the sounds of saxophonist Lester Young, Curtis began playing the saxophone at the age of twelve, appearing in various jazz, rhythm-and-blues, and pop bands around the Fort Worth area until he joined vibraphonist Lionel Hampton's band in the early 1950's. After his experience with Hampton's outfit, Curtis went on to session work, appearing on tracks with fellow Texan Buddy Holly, Nat "King" Cole, Brook Benton, and the Coasters, who featured Curtis's "chicken-scratching" solo on their 1957 hit "Yakety-Yak." By the mid-1950's, Curtis had formed his own band, originally the Noble Knights and ultimately the Kingpins, along with guitarist Eric Gale and keyboardist Brother Jack McDuff. This jazz outfit recorded for Prestige through the latter part of the decade.

Curtis began to cross over into the rhythm-and-blues and pop markets. Although he continued to record jazz for Prestige in the early 1960's with pianist Wynton Kelly, bassist Paul

Chambers, and cornetist Nat Adderley, he was becoming a force in the more mainstream genres. His first mainstream hits included soul standards, such as "Night Train" and "Honky Tonk," and an original piece, "Soul Serenade." In 1962 he cut "Soul Twist," capitalizing on the twist craze in vogue during this period.

Between the years 1962 and 1971, Curtis released fifteen singles that hit the pop or rhythm-and-blues charts for various labels, including Atco, Capitol, and Status. His most profitable alliance was with Atlantic, which used him both as a headliner and as a sideman. He played backup on singer Aretha Franklin's releases and recorded tracks with a number of favored sidemen, including keyboardist Richard Tee and guitarist Cornell Dupree. With his 1971 release, *King Curtis at the Fillmore West*, Curtis reached a milestone in both popular appeal and critical acclaim. Atlantic gave him further responsibility, tabbing him as Aretha Franklin's musical director while she continued to advance into stardom. His success was short-lived. On the evening of August 31, 1971, he was stabbed to death by an unknown assailant in front of an apartment building he owned in New York City.

See also: Franklin, Aretha; Hampton, Lionel; Music.

Kings of Harmony: Gospel quartet. Inspiring the many male gospel music quartets that came out of Alabama in the 1930's and 1940's, the Kings of Harmony left a legend against which all such groups are measured. They made few recordings, preferring instead to give live performances, gaining for themselves a reputation as "house wreckers" and a prominent place in the history of gospel music.

Jefferson County, Alabama, was the cradle of the hard gospel quartet style, which evolved from the Jubilee quartet style. The primary development of hard gospel was the use of a powerful lead vocal backed by tenor, baritone, and bass harmonies. Groups such as the Foster Singers, the Birmingham Jubilee Singers, and Silas Steele's Famous Blue Jay Singers were among the pioneers of this style. The Kings of Harmony, widely considered the "grandfathers" of the hard gospel quartet, originally were a Jubilee quartet. When the Kings' tenor-baritone, Carey "Squeakey" Bradley, heard the Soul Stirrers, however, the group began to innovate.

A newspaper reported in 1943 that during a performance at Radio Church, Bradley became so "overheated" that he was carried from the stage, too weak to continue. "House wrecking" or "church wrecking" was not new to gospel music; the Kings of Harmony, however, were especially gifted with the ability to cause members of the audience (and sometimes members of the quartet) to faint or otherwise succumb to the overwhelming power of the music. Gospel music is foremost a religious practice, and the audience is as much congregation as spectator. When the Kings of Harmony sang, the spirit did not move the church to applaud politely; it called for fervent participation and, sometimes, collapse.

Although the group left few recordings, the ones it did leave remain significant. In 1939 the Kings of Harmony was the first group to record on Herman Lubinsky's Savoy label. This was a brilliant start for a company that would record many of the finest singers in gospel music. "Poor Pilgrim of Sorrow" and "Give Me Wings" were hits. The Kings of Harmony entered the recording studio again in 1946 to record Thomas Andrew Dorsey's "Precious Lord" and "God Shall Wipe All Tears Away." These recordings attest the legendary power of the Kings of Harmony.

Kirk, Rahsaan Roland (August 7, 1936, Columbus, Ohio—December 5, 1977, Bloomington, Indiana): Jazz instrumentalist. Kirk was

Rahsaan Roland Kirk practicing with his saxophone at home in early 1977. *(AP/Wide World Photos)*

blind from age two. Primarily a tenor saxophonist, he is also known for playing such exotic reed instruments as the manzello and stritch in addition to the clarinet, flute, and trumpet. He sometimes played two or even three of the reed instruments at one time; he might play two moving parts or drone on one instrument while fingering the other two. Occasionally he would engage in startling counterpoint, as when he played "Sentimental Journey" and "Going Home" simultaneously at a live performance in 1970.

Those more impressed by appearance than substance considered Kirk to be an oddity or a freak, especially early in his career. Those people were mistaken. Kirk was a major instrumentalist who developed his own musical vocabulary and whose sound is immediately identifiable. Although he flirted with the avant garde, he kept his roots firmly in the jazz tradition. To illustrate his debt to the past, at various times he recorded original compositions honoring trumpeters Clifford Brown and Dizzy GILLESPIE, saxophonists Sidney BECHET, Don BYAS, Charlie PARKER, and Lester YOUNG, and pianist Thelonious MONK, among others.

Kirk recorded mostly as a leader, with numerous albums for Mercury and then for Atlantic Records. He also recorded with other people's groups, however. At one recording session led by bassist Charles MINGUS in 1961, Kirk gave one of his most impassioned performances, especially on "Ecclusiastics." Later that decade, as if his versatility and eclecticism needed to sbe proved, he played (but did not record) with rock guitarists Jimi HENDRIX and Frank Zappa.

In his playing and in his speaking between performances in clubs, Kirk was one of the more humorous modern jazzmen, and he is remembered by many for his comic asides. Although Kirk suffered a stroke in 1975, he continued playing during the remaining two years of his life.

See also: Music.

Kirwan v. Podberesky: U.S. SUPREME COURT decision declining to review the constitutionality of race-based, minority scholarships. In a ruling issued on May 20, 1995, the Court rejected the CLINTON ADMINISTRATION's request to overturn a 1994 circuit court of appeals decision that had invalidated a scholarship program at the University of Maryland at College Park because it was open only to African American students. The program was a merit-based program with eligibility limited to African American students. By denying review of the appellate decision without comment, the Supreme Court let stand the decision by the court of appeals that the scholarship program was unconstitutional.

Kitt, Eartha (b. January 26, 1928, North, South Carolina): Actor and singer. Kitt is known for her campy yet sultry, performance style and her penchant for exotic and sensational costumes. As a nightclub singer, she performed throughout the world.

Kitt worked as a child in the cotton fields alongside other family members. She moved to NEW YORK CITY to live with her aunt while still a young child. She dropped out of high school to work as a seamstress, but soon left that job to join the Katherine DUNHAM Dance Troupe. After traveling throughout Europe and MEXICO with the company, Kitt returned to the United States as a featured entertainer in the revue *New Faces of 1952*. Her performance drew rave reviews from critics, especially her rendition of the song "Monotonous." She earned a starring role in the drama *Mrs. Patterson* (1954) and appeared in several other plays by the end of the decade.

Kitt reached a wider audience as a recording artist with such hits as "C'est Si Bon" (1953) and "Santa Baby" (1953). She appeared as a frequent guest on television talk and variety shows and had a recurring role as the Catwoman on the *Batman* series (1967). Her film credits include *St. Louis Blues* (1958), the title role in *Anna Lucasta* (1959), *Friday Foster* (1975), and *Erik, the Viking* (1989).

Outspoken on political and social issues, Kitt publicly embarrassed the JOHNSON ADMINISTRATION by criticizing the government during a nonpolitical White House luncheon hosted by Lady Bird Johnson. Public anger over the incident led to a drastic reduction in work opportunities for Kitt for nearly a decade, until her triumphant return to the stage in *Timbuktu* (1978). An adaptation of the musical *Kismet*, by Geoffrey Holder, the play earned popular and critical acclaim for Kitt in her starring role as Sahleem-La-Lume.

See also: Film; Music.

Knight, Gladys, and the Pips: One of the most durable and successful soul groups of the 1960's, 1970's, and 1980's. The group's lead singer, Gladys Knight, began singing gospel early in her life. In 1952, at the age of seven, she won the top prize on the *Ted Mack Amateur Hour*. Knight formed a group from among her family in her native ATLANTA, GEORGIA. They became known as the Pips, after a cousin, James "Pip" Woods, who was their first manager. When the group's membership finally stabilized in 1961, it consisted of Knight, her brother Merald "Bubba" Knight, her cousin William Guest, and Edward Patten, who had joined the group in

Eartha Kitt (center) sings to the piano accompaniment of Nat "King" Cole in the 1957 film *St. Louis Blues. (Museum of Modern Art, Film Stills Archive)*

1957. Their first hit, "Every Beat of My Heart," was released by two separate record companies in 1961, one of which (Fury) renamed the group Gladys Knight and the Pips. Thereafter, the group made a successful living on the RHYTHM-AND-BLUES circuit but remained relatively obscure until being signed by MOTOWN Records in 1967.

The group's career at Motown was mixed. Their first Motown hit, "I Heard It Through the Grapevine," was a short time later recorded by the same label's Marvin GAYE, who had written the song, and it came to be thought of as his song. Motown also tried unsuccessfully to change the group's name, disliking the sound of "Pips." The quartet produced a number of hits at Motown, including "If I Were Your Woman" (1970) and "Help Me Make it Through the Night" (1972), but they never quite meshed with the company's management.

In 1972 Gladys Knight and the Pips moved to Buddah Records, where they enjoyed their greatest successes, particularly "Midnight Train to Georgia" (1973), "The Best Thing That Ever Happened to Me" (1974), and "On and On" (1974). The group did the sound track for the film *Claudine* (1974), and Gladys Knight made her movie debut in 1976 in *Pipe Dreams* with then-husband Barry Hankerson. Legal troubles in the later 1970's forced Knight to record separately for a while, but the group reunited in 1980 and celebrated thirty-five years of working together in 1988. The following year, Knight left to embark on a solo career, and she continued performing throughout the 1990's.

See also: Gospel music and spirituals; Music.

Knight, Marie: GOSPEL MUSIC singer. Throughout the years she toured with Sister Rosetta THARPE, Knight sang for capacity crowds at huge venues. An imprudent foray into BLUES recording left her without an audience.

Rosetta Tharpe had been a force in gospel music since the late 1930's. With her flamboyant, foot-stomping style and her guitar (very unusual for a female singer, let alone a female gospel singer), Tharpe was able, as no other gospel singer ever was, to balance her Sunday gospel singing with weeknight JAZZ. Her heart, however, was in gospel, and, in 1946, she teamed up with Marie Knight of the Oakwood Avenue Baptist Church in NEWARK, NEW JERSEY. They were a striking pair of opposites. Tharpe was plump, campy, and effusive, and she sang and played in a bluesy, syncopated style; Knight was elegant, and her voice was fervent and disciplined. They played off each other musically, and they volleyed witticisms and charmed their audiences. Drawing capacity crowds across the United States, Knight and Tharpe's popularity reached its apex in 1950 as they played to an audience of twenty-seven thousand at Griffith Stadium in WASHINGTON, D.C. Tharpe's wedding the following year was attended by almost that many guests.

The unforgiving gospel community, which had managed to overlook Tharpe's previous dabbling in the "devil's music," felt betrayed when the adored duo released a blues record. Tharpe, resilient and dedicated to gospel, survived the rebuff but was forced to seek engagements in Europe and, later, in small-town churches where she still was appreciated. Knight, as a solo act spurned by the gospel circuit, made a pathetic and unsuccessful attempt at cultivating a blues career. Her magnificent voice, which always had been in striking counterpoint to Tharpe's bending, bluesy wail, was wasted. She made an unnatural blues shouter, and her singing career soon ended.

Although Knight eventually resorted to employment as a telephone operator in Brooklyn, New York, she was not forgotten entirely. She remained on friendly terms with Tharpe, despite the tensions aroused by the disastrous blues recording that led to their breakup, and in 1973 she sang "Peace in the Valley" at Tharpe's funeral.

Knights of Peter Claver: Fraternal society for black men who are ROMAN CATHOLICS. The organization was founded in 1909, when African Americans were excluded from the Knights of Columbus, the major Catholic fraternal society. By the 1990's, the Knights of Peter Claver had about thirty-five thousand members and more than four hundred local branches. Besides social and religious activities, it sponsored educational programs, awarded scholarships, and had a charitable program. From early conservatism, it evolved to support CIVIL RIGHTS activism.

Kodesh Church of Immanuel: Pentecostal denomination. The Reverend Frank Russell Killingsworth founded the church in October, 1929, and incorporated it in 1930. The church is interracial but primarily black. The denomination forbids the use of alcohol and tobacco, Sabbath desecration, and attendance by members at theatrical presentations that it considers immoral. It practices divine healing but not to the exclusion of science or medicine. In the 1980's the denomination claimed about four thousand members in six churches in PENNSYLVANIA, OHIO, and Virginia.
See also: Pentecostalism.

Komunyakaa, Yusef (b. April 29, 1947, Bogalusa, Louisiana) Poet. Author of one of the most intense poetical accounts of the black soldier's experience in the VIETNAM WAR, Komunyakaa also writes powerfully of his LOUISIANA childhood and his experience as a black man in the deep South.

Born James Willie Brown, the eldest son of a Louisiana carpenter, Komunyakaa took his West African name from his grandfather. Entering the U.S. Army shortly after graduation from high school in 1965, Komunyakaa served in Vietnam in 1969 and 1970 as a war correspondent and editor of a military newspaper. After leaving the Army, he started college at the University of Colorado, where he began writing poetry in 1973. He ultimately earned a master of fine arts in creative writing from the University of California at Irvine, in 1980.

Komunyakaa published several books of poetry before a 1988 collection called *Dien Cai Dau* finally focused on his Vietnam experience. His poetic reputation soared in 1994 when his book *Neon Vernacular* (1993) won a Pulitzer Prize and a $50,000 award from the Claremont Graduate School—to that time the largest monetary award ever given for a book of poetry. Most of his poems reflect on his childhood in Louisiana and his struggles with racism in the South; many also refer to his military experience in Vietnam. His poetry is marked by short lines, an everyday vocabulary, and frequently surrealistic images that create an intense and often obscure complexity of thought and feeling. In 1985 Komunyakaa began teaching creative writing at Indiana University.

—*Terry Nienhuis*

See also: Literature; Military; Vietnam War.

Korean-African American relations: Relations between African Americans and Asian Americans in general have ranged from antagonistic to comradely, depending on the point in time and prevailing political and economic conditions.

Before Korean immigrants began arriving in the United States in significant numbers in the mid-1960's, Japanese and Chinese immigrants had come, beginning in the late 1880's. Chinese and Japanese immigrants established ethnic enclaves in major cities along the West Coast; African Americans also migrated to

Korean Americans preparing to defend their businesses during the 1992 Los Angeles riots. *(AP/Wide World Photos)*

western cities after the abolition of SLAVERY. Both Asian American and African American communities were located in deteriorated areas because of housing segregation. Although both groups were discriminated against by whites, conflicts and tensions frequently occurred between Asian and African American communities.

The middleman minority theory, developed by Edna Bonacich, explains some of the reasons for these conflicts, which occurred with Korean Americans as well after the 1960's. Although many racial and ethnic groups suffered from discrimination by whites, Asian immigrants and their descendants found an economic niche between the dominant group (whites) and other minority groups. The so-called middleman minority groups are the target of hostility from groups below them in racial and economic hierarchies.

Asian and African American relations improved somewhat after the CIVIL RIGHTS movement. For example, the NATIONAL ASSOCIATION FOR THE ADVANCEMENT OF COLORED PEOPLE (NAACP) and many black leaders helped Japanese Americans in successfully lobbying the federal government for reparations to those who were interned during WORLD WAR II.

Large numbers of Koreans began to immigrate to the United States after 1965, when a new U.S. immigration policy went into effect. They established Korean communities in major cities. Although many Koreans are Christians, differences in culture, language, and race made Koreans targets of discrimination.

Korean Americans established rotating credit associations, groups that would lend money to individual members to start small businesses. In the 1970's and 1980's, many Koreans bought small stores they could afford in inner-city areas, primarily in Los ANGELES and NEW YORK CITY. The Korean owners often did not live nearby, living either in Korean enclaves or in the suburbs. Tensions quickly grew between the Korean store owners and their predominantly African American customers.

The Koreans, as recent immigrants, often had poor command of English and could not communicate well with their customers; they also tended to have members of their own families working in their stores. Many African Americans came to view the Korean merchants as exploiters, feeling that they were charging high prices for sometimes low-quality goods, treating their customers discourteously, not hiring any blacks, and not investing in local neighborhoods. The merchants grew wary, even uneasy, about their customers, and the customers grew resentful of the merchants. Each group knew little if anything about the other's background or culture.

Eventually some well-publicized incidents occurred; in Brooklyn, New York (home of a larger black community than Harlem), in 1992, blacks boycotted Korean stores for nine months after a store owner allegedly harassed an African American shopper. In Los Angeles in 1991, a woman Korean shop owner shot and killed a fifteen-year-old African American girl named Latasha Harlins after a dispute about a bottle of orange juice. African Americans in Los Angeles were shocked, and a year later, when a judge granted the shop owner probation instead of a jail sentence, they were outraged.

The timing could not have been worse. About two weeks later, the verdict was announced in the Rodney KING case: Four white policemen were found not guilty in the beating of King, an African American man (the beating had been videotaped). The LOS ANGELES RIOTS broke out in South Central Los Angeles. Whole areas burned out of control. Korean businesses were an immediate target of people's anger and resentment. Hundreds of small Korean businesses were destroyed, and more were looted.

After the disastrous riots, African American and Korean leaders in New York and Los Angeles attempted to improve relations between the groups. The Black-Korean Alliance was formed in Los Angeles; in New York the Korean-American Grocers' Association sought ways to bring the communities closer together. The efforts made some headway. However, as long as central cities in the United States are places of poverty and unemployment with virtually no economic opportunities, tensions between various racial and ethnic groups will undoubtedly recur.

—*Hisako Matsuo*

See also: Race, racism, and race relations.

Korean War: Soon after WORLD WAR II, the U.S. War Department made the decision to continue to use African Americans in the armed services in proportion to their percentage of the United States' population. Previously, the armed forces had generally tried to limit black participation in the MILITARY. Black soldiers, however, were still assigned to segregated units.

Pressured by CIVIL RIGHTS groups, President Harry S Truman in 1948 created the Committee on Equality of Treatment and Opportunity in the Armed Services. The president also issued EXECUTIVE ORDER 9981, announcing that the executive branch wanted equality of treatment and opportunities for all people in the armed forces and that the new policy was to be implemented as rapidly as possible.

Two years later, Truman's committee also recommended that all forms of discrimination and segregation be eliminated in the military. Although the military hierarchy was slow in implementing Truman's order, a racial first oc-

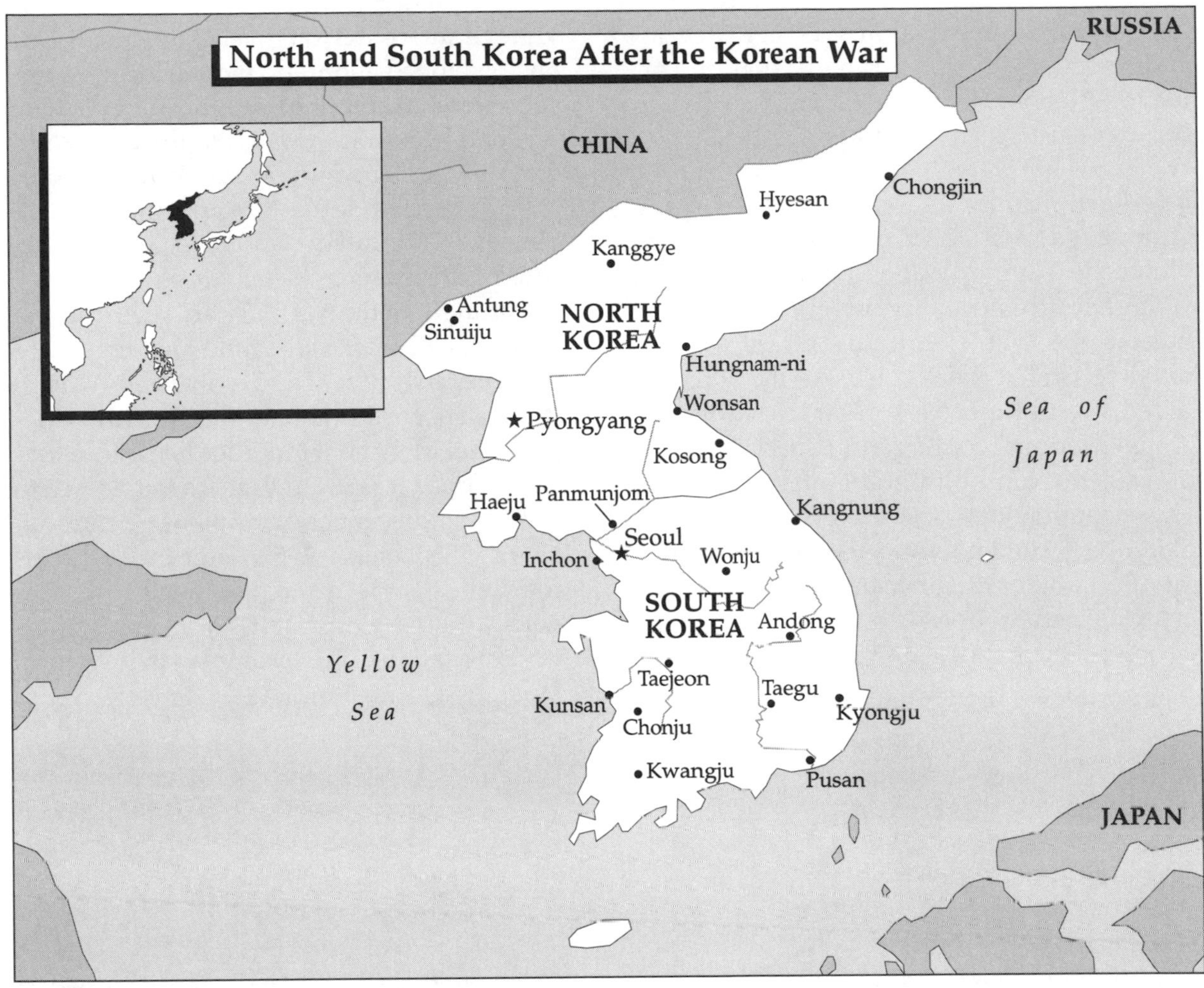

curred that year when First Lieutenant Nancy Leftenant became the first African American woman officer in the regular Army Nurse Corps. In 1950 the Army abolished its racial quota system. Some training camps were being integrated just as the Korean War began; still, the first African American soldiers to reach Korea went in segregated units.

Black Units in Action

The largest of the all-black units was the Twenty-fourth Infantry Regiment of the Twenty-fifth Infantry Division. The Twenty-fourth Infantry Regiment landed in Korea on July 13, 1950, and on July 20 saw its first battle. Yechon, an important transportation hub, had fallen to the North Korean army, and the Twenty-fifth Division was ordered to retake it. The all-black Twenty-fourth Regiment spearheaded the drive that successfully pushed the North Koreans out of the area and reoccupied the town.

Witnesses of the battle reported that the soldiers of the Twenty-fourth Regiment showed great valor under fire; they fought a furious sixteen-hour battle to retake Yechon. Further, they won a victory at a time when American-United Nations military successes had been few; the success lifted morale. Later, when other units—white and black—engaged the enemy, Americans often shouted "Remember Yechon." By August of 1950, several other all-black units had arrived in Korea, including infantry regiments and battalions, artillery battalions, the Sixty-fourth Tank Battalion, and various service units.

Integration of Units

Although delays occurred, the hardships to which the Korean War subjected American soldiers spurred military integration onward. Indeed, the war eventually ended institutional racism in the service. As the war seesawed, North Korean forces struck hard at the United Nations' contingent. Especially hard-hit was the U.S. Ninth Infantry Regiment, whose commander, desperate for men, began taking replacements from the all-black Third Battalion, integrating because military necessity was paramount. The battlefield experiment worked, as African Americans and their white counterparts fought side by side. As the war developed, more and more African Americans were taken out of support units (where they had been concentrated in the two world wars) and assigned to combat. By mid-May of 1951, 20 percent of the African American soldiers were in integrated units, with three-fifths of the number in combat.

Throughout the war, African American soldiers proved their valor time and again. For example, in June of 1951, Private William Thompson posthumously received the Congressional Medal of Honor for heroism under enemy fire. It was the first such award given to a black soldier since the Spanish-American War of 1898. Later, in 1952, Sergeant Cornelius Charlton also received the medal posthumously. Some entire units won meritorious service citations. For example, the Twenty-

An integrated machine-gun crew of the Second Infantry Division of the U.S. Army holds its position during the Korean War—the first U.S. conflict fought with fully integrated units. *(National Archives)*

fifth Infantry Division, of which the all-black Twenty-fourth Regiment was a part, received two Republic of Korea Presidential Unit Citations.

In November of 1951, military historian General S. L. A. Marshall was serving as an infantry operations analyst for the Eighth Army. He witnessed integrated units making fighting retreats from the Yalu River and became convinced that integration was a complete success and that the entire Army should integrate. Not all white officers shared Marshall's sentiments, however, and many still believed that African Americans were poor soldiers and were not to be trusted. Such negative sentiments extended all the way up to General Douglas MacArthur's headquarters. MacArthur was cool to the idea of integration; his headquarters staff also reflected that attitude and, when possible, obstructed integration efforts. One field commander, General Edward M. Almond of the Tenth Corps, ordered the resegregation of black soldiers who had previously been integrated into his unit, and MacArthur took no action to correct Almond.

Removal of MacArthur

President Truman, however, removed MacArthur from command on April 11, 1951, for insubordination (for reasons having nothing to do with integration) and named Lieutenant General Matthew B. Ridgeway as the new commander. Ridgeway quickly asked for and secured permission from the War Department to integrate all the American forces in Korea. Under Ridgeway, integration proceeded with relative speed. During the summer and fall, most of the African American units were either disbanded, as men were deployed to previously all-white units, or were infused with white personnel. By July of 1953, 90 percent of the African American personnel in Korea were serving in integrated units.

When the public in the United States learned of Army integration in Korea, many white southerners (especially those in Congress) expressed concern. One southern senator attached an amendment to a draft-extension bill; the amendment would have allowed soldiers a choice of serving in integrated or segregated units. The amendment was easily defeated, as was a similar measure introduced in the House of Representatives.

Thankful that another mark of second-class citizenship was being erased, the African American community stateside applauded the Army's decision to integrate. The *Pittsburgh Courier* noted a twinge of regret when the all-black "Remember Yechon" Twenty-fourth Regiment was disbanded but nevertheless supported the decision to integrate.

Black military strength in the U.S. Army in Korea and Japan increased fourfold during the war. On July 1, 1950, 201 African American officers (including 24 female nurses) and 12,427 enlisted men were serving. By July 1, 1953, the numbers had grown to 955 officers (including 36 women), 146 warrant officers, and 50,646 enlisted personnel, including 199 enlisted black women. African Americans killed in action numbered 3,223—9.3 percent of the American total. In 1955 the War Department announced that it had abolished every segregated unit.

Broader Effects of Army Integration

There was an unexpected side effect of the integration efforts of the Army during the Korean War: Some Army commanders in areas outside the Far East began unauthorized integration on their own. On the West Coast and in Alaska, for example, commanders integrated forces. General J. W. Cunningham, commanding forces in Alaska, told his superiors that he had developed a harmonious system of complete desegregation.

Furthermore, social scientists on assignment for the Army studied the performance of African Americans in desegregated units and concluded that black soldiers were happier and performed better than in their old segregated units. Additionally, a poll was taken among the Army's officers showing that six out of seven believed that white and black soldiers performed equally well in battle.

Impact on Other Branches of Military

The example of integration in the Army encouraged other branches of the service to integrate. Actually, the Air Force had already taken the lead and was integrating as the Korean War began. Further, the Marine Corps began integrating, especially because of the pressure to build from scratch the First Marine Division in time for MacArthur's Inchon invasion. In 1950 the Marine Corps had only 2 black officers and 1,965 black enlisted men; by 1953, it had 19 black officers and 24,468 black enlisted personnel.

The Navy proved recalcitrant. With only a few exceptions, it assigned its black personnel to the messmen's branch or to other service units. A noted exception was Ensign Jesse L. Brown, an aviator assigned to the aircraft carrier U.S.S. *Leyte*, who was shot down and killed in December of 1950. The Navy did not fully integrate until the 1960's.

Although the Navy lagged behind, integration in the other branches during the Korean War proved to be a tremendous success. Racial incidents also decreased in integrated units. Such success provided a powerful argument for liberals to use against political conservatives in the United States who insisted that a government could not legislate mores. Desegregation of the military stood as an important precedent when the federal government began assuming a more active role in upholding civil rights in the 1950's and 1960's. Moreover, military integration alone marked the attainment of a goal for which African Americans had been striving since the American Revolution.

—*James Smallwood*

See also: Quotas; Segregation and integration.

Suggested Readings:

Bowers, William T., William M. Hammond, and George L. Garrigle. *Black Soldier, White Army: The Twenty-fourth Infantry Regiment in Korea*. Washington, D.C.: U.S. Government Printing Office, 1996.

Bussey, Charles M. *Firefight at Yechon: Courage and Racism in the Korean War*. Washington, D.C.: Brassey's, 1991.

Dalfiume, Richard M. *Desegregation of the U.S. Armed Forces: Fighting on Two Fronts, 1939-1953*. Columbus: University of Missouri Press, 1969.

Foner, Jack D. *Blacks and the Military in American History*. New York: Praeger, 1974.

Lanning, Michael L. *The African American Soldier from Crispus Attucks to Colin Powell*. Seacaucus, N.J.: Birch Lane Press, 1997.

Morrow, Curtis. *What's a Commie Ever Done to Black People?: A Korean War Memoir of Fighting in the U.S. Army's Last All Negro Unit*. Jefferson, N.C.: McFarland & Company, 1997.

Powell, Colin L. *President Truman and the Desegregation of the Armed Forces: A Fiftieth Anniversary View of Executive Order 9981*. Washington, D.C.: National Legal Center for the Public Interest, 1998.

Rishell, Lyle. *With a Black Platoon in Combat: A Year in Korea*. College Station: Texas A & M University Press, 1993.

Summers, Harry G. *Korean War Almanac*. New York: Facts On File, 1990.

Kotto, Yaphet (b. November 15, 1937, New York, New York): Actor. One of the few African American actors to have worked consistently in Hollywood from the 1960's to the 1990's, Yaphet Fredrick Kotto appeared regularly in feature films beginning in 1964. His first film role was in *Nothing but a Man* (1964). His film appearances include *The Liberation of L. B. Jones* (1970), *Across 110th Street* (1972), *Live and Let Die* (1973), *Truck Turner* (1974), *Report to* *the Commissioner* (1975), *Sharks' Treasure* (1975), *Friday Foster* (1975), *Drum* (1976), *Monkey Hustle* (1977), *Alien* (1979), *Brubaker* (1980), *Fighting Back* (1982), *The Star Chamber* (1983), and *Midnight Run* (1988). Kotto often portrayed simple working-class people looking for uncomplicated lives with some small pleasures.

Kotto is also known as an accomplished stage actor, having performed both on and off Broadway in plays such as *The Great White Hope*, *Zula and the Zayda*, *The Blood Knot*, *Black Monday*, *In White America*, and *A Good Place to Raise a Boy*. As a television actor, Kotto was seen in the series *Tour of Duty* and as Sergeant James "China" Bell, a Vietnam veteran and embittered former boxer, in the series *For Love and Honor*, set in the early 1980's at an Army training camp. Made-for-television movie appearances include *Raid on Entebbe* (1977), *Rage* (1980), *Women of San Quentin* (1983), *Badge of the Assassin* (1985), and *Harem* (1986). Kotto served as the chair of the Foundation of Research and Education for Sickle Cell Disease, and he established New Era Communications.

Two decades after replacing James Earl Jones as boxer Jack Johnson in *The Great White Hope* on Broadway, Kotto played the lead in a 1990 staging of August Wilson's play *Fences*—again replacing Jones. The role of Troy Maxson, a former Negro League baseball player trying desperately to keep his family together, marked a change from the tough characters the actor had frequently been portraying on television and in films.

Kotto's film work in the 1990's included a part in *Freddy's Dead: The Final Nightmare* (1991), an installment of the *Nightmare on Elm Street* horror series. Kotto also appeared in the made-for-television films *After the Shock* (1990), a dramatization of the aftermath of the 1989 San Francisco earthquake; *Chrome Soldiers* (1992), a revenge tale involving Vietnam veterans; and *The American Clock* (1993), an adaptation of Arthur Miller's 1980 play recalling the Depression years.

Yaphet Kotto in 1994. *(AP/Wide World Photos)*

In 1993 Kotto first appeared as Lieutenant Al Giardello with the debut of the NBC television crime drama *Homicide: Life on the Streets*. The series earned critical acclaim for its gritty realism and its sensitive handling of racial issues. Kotto appeared in a supporting role in the 1996 film *Two if by Sea*. While Kotto's career undeniably profited from the success of blaxploitation films and the resulting demand for African American actors in the 1970's, he turned down offers to play the stereotypically negative characters common in the genre. "I swore when I was nineteen," Kotto explained in an interview, "I was not going to leave an image of people to feel ashamed of." While filming *Alien* (1979), Kotto began writing his autobiography, *The Royalty*, which was published in 1990.

—*Updated by Amy Adelstein*

Krigwa Players: Theater group formed in 1924 by W. E. B. Du Bois in New York City. The group was sponsored by The Crisis, the magazine of the NATIONAL ASSOCIATION FOR THE ADVANCEMENT OF COLORED PEOPLE (NAACP), and had member groups nationwide. The Krigwa Players was formed to produce for African American audiences plays about African Americans that were written, performed, and directed by African Americans.

Ku Klux Klan: White supremacist vigilante organization. The Ku Klux Klan (KKK) was formed in MEMPHIS, TENNESSEE, in 1866 by six bored young men returning from the CIVIL WAR. While waiting in an attorney's office, out of idleness, they created a social club, which they named in imitation of the Greek word *Kuklos*, adopted by a then-popular fraternity, Kuklos Adelphon. *Kuklos* is Greek for "circle." The founders did not have any political motivations or racial designs. They created a secret lodge near Pulaski, TENNESSEE, adopted mystic titles for the officers, and had fun making mischief and playing pranks at night, wandering in ghostly costumes made of white bedsheets and pillow covers.

Racist Emphasis

The birth of the KKK as a radical racist organization was a conscious afterthought. The political and social realities of the South immediately after the Civil War provided a congenial atmosphere for the transformation of the KKK. Southerners had not yet reconciled to the ban on SLAVERY and were skeptical of congressional legislation granting civil rights, political equality, and new opportunities for blacks. Many hate groups were formed around this time in defense of what many people perceived to be the American way of life. Thus, the KKK was to become a secret army of hooded terrorists battling for the cause of white supremacy.

In 1867 the KKK was formally instituted as an organization at a convention of delegates from southern states at Nashville. A constitution was prepared, and Nathan Bedford Forrest, a former slave trader and a Confederate general, was chosen to be the group's first leader, or Imperial Wizard.

Beginning in the late 1880's, branches of the KKK began to spring up in states outside the South. Klan leadership, however, remained mainly in the hands of southerners. In the South, the Klan also received the patronage of the DEMOCRATIC PARTY. Because of the group's secret style of operation, the leadership could not have much direct communication with the rank-and-file national membership. The result was a loosely knit organization without much centralized control or direction.

The basic style of the Klan's operation was uniform in all states: night-riding violence. Initially, the targets of the Klan's rhetoric and violence were the REPUBLICAN PARTY, U.S. Army or state militia officers, integrationist white schoolteachers, and blacks who registered to vote or attended schools. Later, gang rapes, LYNCHING, burning, and other forms of violence were added to the Klan's arsenal, bringing nationwide notoriety to Klan members.

The KKK formed close links with the anti-immigrant Know-Nothing Movement and the Knights of the Golden Circle, a band of former Confederate soldiers. By 1870 there were about forty thousand Klan members in Tennessee alone, and some 550,000 across the South. Yet the success of the KKK also led to its downfall. The lack of centralized control, congressional investigations into the Klan's criminal activities, and the jailing of several Klansmen in the early 1870's led to the KKK's disbanding under Forrest. In 1871 Congress declared night riding a crime. While the Klan as a united organization was disbanded, however, the idea of the Klan lingered on in the memories of many southerners. Novelist Thomas Dixon perpetuated its memory in his work *The Clansman: A Historical Romance of the Ku Klux Klan*, published in 1905.

Revival of the Ku Klux Klan

During and after WORLD WAR I, the KKK reemerged with greater political clout and popularity among a wider section of society. In October, 1915, the first cross burning took place. The Klan's popularity and notoriety spread with the release of the first epic motion picture, THE BIRTH OF A NATION (1915, directed by D. W. Griffith). The film was based on Dixon's novel, and it portrayed blacks as stereotypical buffoons and wastrels and showed the Klan in a heroic light. The film was protested heatedly. Both the White House and the U.S. SUPREME COURT upheld its constitutional right to be shown.

Since the RECONSTRUCTION era, the Klan has had periods of high success and sudden downfalls, but it has never completely disappeared. Its revival as a unified organization and its swings in popularity have been related to a combination of historical settings, shifts in the economy, and varying degrees of societal tolerance.

The early twentieth century witnessed upheavals caused by an influx of eastern and southern European immigrants and the migration of southern blacks to the North and West. American society of the period was characterized by general intolerance and extreme conservatism coupled with a worsening economy. The results were anti-immigrant feelings, anti-Asian legislation, growing racism, and racial riots. It was also a time when the popularity of the Klan rose. The revived Klan added to its hit list new victims: ROMAN CATHOLICS, Jews, most immigrants, and labor unions. By 1924 Klan membership rose to perhaps four million, up from one million in 1921.

Height of Klan's Popularity

By the mid-1920's, the KKK had become a national phenomenon with a murky political, religious, racial, and social-revivalist identity. The popularity of the Klan was demonstrated when, in August, 1925, some forty thousand Klan members in hooded uniforms marched down Pennsylvania Avenue in WASHINGTON, D.C. The Klan had also begun to exert influence in electoral politics at both the national and state levels.

The success of the Klan, however, coincided with the beginning of its decline. By 1929 the group's membership had fallen to about one million nationwide. Once again, the violence, extremism, and hooliganism of the Klan brought about its downfall. Stories of corruption, brutal violence, and immorality drove away thousands of members, and a series of arrests and jail sentences for Klansmen discouraged others. The Klan was never again to attain such large-scale success.

In the 1940's and 1950's, efforts were made to revive the Klan around anticommunist themes. The Internal Revenue Service, however, broke the backbone of the Klan by filing a lien for $685,000 against it in 1944, and the Klan was disbanded. The Klan, however, survived in a diffuse and fragmented form. A number of Klan-related organizations reemerged under varied names in different states, without a centralized leadership or control. Friction and conflict among Klansmen often led to splits, resulting in a proliferation of Klan organizations.

The Klan After the 1960's

The beginning of the CIVIL RIGHTS movement, particularly the aftermath of the Supreme Court's 1954 decision in the BROWN V. BOARD OF EDUCATION case outlawing segregation in public schools, provided a new opportunity for the Klan to thrive in the South. Southern opponents of integration, however, split along economic class lines; while the white gentry fought integration through citizens' councils, the Klan had appeal only to the lower classes. Blacks, integrated schools, Jews, and the federal government became the main targets of attack, both rhetorical and violent.

Louisiana Klansmen burn a cross in 1962 in what was reportedly the first big Klan demonstration in the state in three decades. *(AP/Wide World Photos)*

In the 1960's, the Klan was challenged by a number of rival white supremacist organizations such as the National States Rights Party and the American Nazi Party. The national membership of the Klan in the early 1960's had fallen to about fifty thousand.

Acts of racial violence against blacks in the South during the Civil Rights movement were internationally televised, generating bad publicity for the Klan's criminal acts. As civil rights legislation was passed during the 1960's and early 1970's, a number of Klansmen who were involved in murders, burnings, and other forms of violence began to receive severe prison sentences. The Klan's popularity dwindled further; its membership had declined to about fifteen hundred by the early 1970's.

The beginning of the 1980's witnessed a growing conservatism in the United States, and the tone set by the REAGAN ADMINISTRATION, with its far-right leanings, gave a new boost to the KKK and to a number of other racist groups. In 1980 the Klan's membership was estimated to be close to twelve thousand. Without a strong and committed leadership on top, however, the Klan became more diffuse in its organization and philosophy. It veered closer to neo-Nazi groups and continued its acts of violence in the name of Christianity and the doctrine of supremacy of the Aryan race.

Proliferation of New Groups

The late 1980's and the early 1990's saw a proliferation of racial hate groups of many varieties. The KKK also reasserted its identity, reaffirming the Klan ties at national and local levels in the form of multiplying organizations such as the Invisible Empire, the Knights of the Ku Klux Klan, the Alabama Knights, the California Knights, the Louisiana Knights, the North Carolina Knights, the Texas Knights, the White Patriot Party, the National Association of White People, the White Aryan Resistance, and many others.

—*Indu Vohra*

See also: Hate crime; Racial prejudice; Racial violence and hatred.

Suggested Readings:

Bullard, Sara, et al., eds. *The Ku Klux Klan: A History of Racism and Violence*. 3d ed. Montgomery, Ala.: Klanwatch, 1988.

Chalmers, David M. *Hooded Americanism: The History of the Ku Klux Klan*. 3d ed. Durham, N.C.: Duke University Press, 1987.

Ezekiel, Raphael S. *The Racist Mind: Portraits of American Neo-Nazis and Klansmen*. New York: Viking Press, 1995.

Katz, William Loren. *The Invisible Empire: The Ku Klux Klan's Impact on History*. Washington, D.C.: Open Hand, 1986.

Maclean, Nancy. *Behind the Mask of Chivalry: The Making of the Second Ku Klux Klan*. New York: Oxford University Press, 1994.

Quarles, Chester L. *The Ku Klux Klan and Related American Racialist and Antisemitic Organizations: A History and Analysis*. Jefferson, N.C.: McFarland, 1999.

Ruiz, Jim. *The Black Hood of the Ku Klux Klan*. San Francisco: Austin & Winfield, 1998.

Sims, Patsy. *The Klan*. 2d ed. Lexington: University Press of Kentucky, 1996.

Stanton, Bill. *Klanwatch: Bringing the Ku Klux Klan to Justice*. New York: Weidenfeld, 1991.

Tucker, Richard K. *The Dragon and the Cross: The Rise and Fall of the Ku Klux Klan in Middle America*. Hamden, Conn.: Archon Books, 1991.

Wade, Wyn C. *The Fiery Cross: The Ku Klux Klan in America*. New York: Oxford University Press, 1998.

Kwanzaa: Cultural holiday celebrated each year between December 26 and January 1. Created by Maulana Ron KARENGA during the 1960's, Kwanzaa provides a set of positive values for African Americans based on traditional African values. The word *kwanzaa* itself comes from an East African Swahili word for "first fruits," in celebration of harvesting the first crops in traditional African society.

As a nonreligious holiday, Kwanzaa is celebrated in the United States as an opportunity for African American families and communities to come together to commemorate the fruits of their labors during the past year. The seven-day holiday period is a time for reflecting, reassessing, recommitting, rewarding, and rejoicing in a festive atmosphere of peace, love, and unity.

The Seven Principles of Kwanzaa

Taking their names from Swahili words, each of the seven days of Kwanzaa has a particular meaning; collectively the meanings are known as the Nguzo Saba (the seven principles). Umoja (unity), celebrated on December 26, means "to strive for and maintain unity in the family, community, nation and race." Kujichagulia (self-determination), celebrated on December 27, means "to define ourselves, name ourselves, and speak for ourselves." Ujima (collective work and responsibility), celebrated on December 28, means "to build and maintain our community together and make our sisters' and brothers' problems our problems and to solve them together." Ujamaa (cooperative economics), celebrated on December 29, means "to build and maintain our own stores, shops, and other businesses and to profit from them collectively."

Nia (purpose), celebrated on December 30, means "to make our collective vocation the building and developing of our community in order to restore our people to their traditional greatness." Kuumba (creativity), celebrated on December 31, means "to do always as much as we can, in the way we can, in order to leave our community more beautiful and beneficial than we inherited it." Finally, Imani (faith), celebrated on January 1, means "to believe with all our heart in our people, our parents, our teachers, our leaders, and the righteousness and victory of our struggle." The seventh day of Kwanzaa is also a special day for children. They are given gifts in symbolic recognition of their importance in the continuation of the family.

The Kwanzaa Observance

According to Karenga, the private and public observance of the holiday takes place as follows: Everyone is seated in a circle, representing unity. A libation is poured into a communal cup and shared among family members and guests while the libation statement (tamshi la tambiko) is offered to honor the group's African ancestors. Their names are recited and honored. Next, the eldest group members of both genders are acknowledged.

Then the seven symbols of Kwanzaa are presented and explained. These include the mkeka, or straw mat, the foundation on which all the items are placed; the kinara, or candle holder that holds the seven candles and represents the first stalk from which all people originated; the mishumaa saba, or seven candles representing the seven principles of Kwanzaa (the Nguzo Saba); the vibunzi, or ears of corn representing the offspring of the stalk (children of the father of the house); the kikombe cha umoja, or Unity Cup, that holds the libation and represents Umoja—the first principle of Kwanzaa; the zawadi, or gifts representing the fruits of labor of the parents as well as the rewards of the seeds sown by the children; and the karamu, or feast, which symbolizes the festive celebration that brings the community together to exchange gifts and to give thanks to the Creator.

The red, black, and green liberation flag, or bendera ya taifa, is displayed. Created by black nationalist leader Marcus GARVEY, the bendera has a special meaning. Red symbolizes the blood shed by African peoples; green stands for hope and the bountiful landscape of the Motherland; and black represents the face of African peoples. Next, the seven principles of Kwanzaa (Nguzo Saba) are recited and explained.

On the first day of Kwanzaa, the black Kwanzaa candle is lit and placed in the center

Chi Wara, the antelope representing the new year (right), dances to launch a Kwanzaa celebration in Los Angeles in 1997. *(AP/Wide World Photos)*

of the kinara. On each following day, an additional candle is lit, alternately from left to right, with the three green candles placed on the left and the three red candles placed on the right. The Nguzo Saba is reviewed by the group while the candles are being lit. Then, a designated speaker discusses the meaning and significance of the Kwanzaa principle associated with that particular day. Those celebrating the holiday are invited to make a brief comment on the principle of that day. Next, the Unity Cup is offered to all in attendance, or a distinguished guest is invited to sip from the cup in honor of all those present. Members of the group are invited to participate in various cultural expressions, including poetry reading, singing, and dancing.

Following these presentations on December 31, the Kwanzaa feast begins. Whether guests are seated around a table or spread out for potluck dining, they follow a specific order of serving. Elders are served first, followed by expectant women, then children, and finally the remaining guests. At the conclusion of the meal, a farewell statement (tamshi la tutaonana) is given: "African people be proud, be strong, create, work, and practice the seven principles of Kwanzaa." All guests then shout the word "harambee," meaning "we must all pull together," seven times, holding the final shout as long as possible.

—Kwame Nantambu

See also: Afrocentricity; Black nationalism.

L

LaBelle, Patti (Patricia Louise Holte; b. October 4, 1944, Philadelphia, Pennsylvania): Singer, songwriter, bandleader, and actor. Music fans know LaBelle as a frenetic showwoman who often wears space-age attire. LaBelle grew up as an introspective and lonely child who did not realize the talent she possessed until she took to the stage as a teenager.

Motivated by the recordings of singers Nina SIMONE, Dakota Staton, and Gloria Lynne, LaBelle joined the Ordettes, a vocal group featuring Cindy Birdsong (who later was Florence Ballard's replacement in the SUPREMES). LaBelle, Birdsong, and singers Nona Hendryx and Sarah Dash signed with Newton Records and became the Blue Belles, named for Bluebelle Records, a subsidiary of the Newton label. After the group reached the top twenty in 1962 with "I Sold My Heart to the Junkman," it was renamed Patti LaBelle and the Blue Belles.

After a number of label changes, the group's big break came when it was asked to open for the Who during the latter's 1968 U.S. tour. The trio (Birdsong had left in 1967 to join the Supremes) became a respected concert and recording act and a highly sought session group. The group was rechristened Labelle in 1971. In 1973, with Nona Hendryx writing most of the music, LaBelle reached the top ten with the *Nightbirds* album and number one with the single "Lady Marmalade." That song was introduced in a 1974 appearance at New York's Metropolitan Opera House, where Labelle was the first black band ever to appear.

Soon after Hendryx left the band in midtour in 1976, a somewhat traumatized yet determined LaBelle decided to go solo, recording two albums for Epic to close out the 1970's and exploring other options in film, television, and stage. In 1982 she costarred with singer Al GREEN in a revival of *Your Arms Too Short to Box with God* on Broadway. She never strayed far from her music career, however, enjoying chart success through duets with Grover Washington, Jr., and Bobby Womack and being a part of many other musical ventures.

Frenetic entertainer Patti LaBelle. *(MCA Records)*

LaBelle had successful singles in 1985 and 1986, the first being "New Attitude" from the *Beverly Hills Cop* sound track, and the second a duet with Michael McDonald, "On My Own." Among her releases in the 1990's were a Christmas album in 1990, *Burnin'* in 1991, for which she won a Grammy Award for Best R&B Female Vocal Performance, and the collection *Gems* in 1994.

LaBelle's rousing appearance in her hometown in support of the 1985 *Live Aid* concert brought her acclaim as a spirited activist, and in the 1980's and 1990's she was linked to a number of social and charitable organizations ranging from Big Sisters to the United Negro College Fund to many urban renewal and homelessness projects in the Northeast.
See also: Music; Rhythm and blues.

Lafontant, Jewel (b. April 28, 1922, Chicago, Illinois): Government official. Richard Nixon, whose presidential nomination Lafontant seconded in 1960, appointed her as deputy solicitor general and United Nations representative in 1973. She served in the former post until 1975. In 1989 President George Bush appointed her as an ambassador and coordinator for refugee affairs. A strong promoter of black entrepreneurs, Lafontant served as director of several major corporations and on the National Council of Minority Business Enterprise.
See also: Diplomats; Politics and government.

Jewel Lafontant, a government appointee under the Nixon and Bush administrations. *(Library of Congress)*

Lane, William Henry "Master Juba" (1825, New York?, New York—1853, London, England): Dancer. Lane has been variously described as the Greatest Dancer in the World, the Wonder of the World, and the King of All Dancers. No record of his early life is available. He was tutored in dance by Jim Lowe. Master Juba, or Juba, the stage name by which Lane became popular, is derived from *Giouba*, an African step-dance.

Like his mentor, Lowe, Lane was not permitted to appear in regular theaters. He found a place in dance halls operated by African Americans in New York City. There he displayed his creative dance talent in such an outstanding manner that his name soon spread across the United States. His fame brought a demand for and an acceptance of Lane in mainstream theaters, and he acted with performers and before audiences of all races.

By 1845 Lane had become a member of the Ethiopian Minstrels and was their main box office attraction. Lane's popularity angered John Diamond, a highly talented white dancer. He challenged Lane to a series of dance contests. Future advertisements billed Lane as the winner of three contests which were performed in New York.

The Georgia Champions, another minstrel group, also sought Lane's services. He went on a performance tour of New England with the members. His performances with the group were described as intricate and beautiful beyond words. It is believed that British novelist Charles Dickens saw a performance by Lane and that it is he whom Dickens captures so vividly in his *American Journals*.

Lane's last performances were in London. He had gone there in 1848 to join Pell's Ethiopian Serenaders. He met the same critical ac-

claim that he had enjoyed in the United States. It was while in London that he met and married a British woman. His short life and highly successful career came to an end in 1852 in London. Lane had opened the door for African Americans to perform with white minstrels and for African Americans to perform in all theaters.
See also: Dance.

Laney, Lucy Craft (April 13, 1854, Macon, Georgia—October 23, 1933, Augusta, Georgia): Educator. Laney's father, David Laney, was born a slave in South Carolina. A skilled carpenter, he purchased his freedom. After moving to Macon, he was hired to teach his trade to slaves. He purchased his wife, Louisa, from her owners, the Campbells, a prominent family in Macon. This ensured the freedom of the ten children the Laneys were to have.

One of the Campbell family members was instrumental in developing the early literacy skills of Lucy Laney. She learned to read by the age of four. Eventually, she graduated from the Lewis High School, which was later known as Ballad Normal School. With aid from the Campbell family and the American Missionary Association, Laney entered Atlanta University and became one of the first four graduates of its higher normal department.

After her graduation in 1873, Laney taught in public schools in several cities for ten years. In 1883 the Presbyterian Board of Missions helped Laney open up a school in the lecture room of the Christ Presbyterian Church in Augusta, Georgia. The board, however, did not fund the school, which was chartered by the state of Georgia on January 6, 1886. Laney sought financial assistance from the General Assembly of the Presbyterian Church at its 1887 meeting in Minneapolis, Minnesota. At this meeting, she met Francina E. H. Haines of Milwaukee, Wisconsin, who persuaded others to support the school. Later, the school which Laney founded was named Haines Normal and Industrial Institute in honor of Haines.

Laney set high standards for herself, for the teachers employed at her school, and for the students enrolled there. She took courses during the summer at the University of Chicago. Mary McLeod Bethune, the cofounder of Bethune-Cookman College in Daytona Beach, Florida, started her teaching career at Haines. John Hope, a distinguished student, was greatly influenced by Laney's training. Despite many financial difficulties, Haines made valuable contributions to the education of African Americans, but it closed in 1979. Lucy Laney High School was built on the site after the Haines buildings were razed.
See also: Education; Presbyterians.

Langston, John Mercer (December 14, 1829, Louisa County, Virginia—November 15, 1897, Washington, D.C.): Educator and public official. Langston was the son of a white Virginian, Ralph Quarles, and a part-African, part-Indian slave named Lucy Langston. Langston's parents lived together as husband and wife for many years, and Quarles left all of his money and property to their children. Langston was emancipated at the age of five. Like his older brothers, Charles and Gideon, he went to Oberlin College, where he earned three degrees. While living in Ohio, he was admitted to the Ohio bar and was one of the first African Americans elected to office, as clerk of Brownhelm Township in 1855. He was also clerk of Oberlin from 1865 to 1867. He organized the National Equal Rights League in 1864 and served as its first president.

After the Civil War, Langston served as school inspector general of the Freedmen's Bureau and as professor of law, dean, and acting president of Howard University (1869-1876). He was the United States' minister to Haiti and chargé d'affaires to Santo Domingo

(1877-1885) and was made president of Virginia Normal and Collegiate Institute in Petersburg, VIRGINIA, in 1885. In 1890 he was seated in the U.S. House of Representatives, after a challenge that took nearly two years to the 1888 vote. He served from September 23, 1890, to March 3, 1891.

The African American town of LANGSTON, OKLAHOMA, was named for him. Langston Colored Agricultural and Normal University, later Langston University, opened in 1898 as a land-grant college. Langston's brother Charles married Mary Leary, widow of Lewis Sheridan Leary, who was killed in John BROWN's Raid on HARPERS FERRY. Their daughter's son was author Langston HUGHES.

Langston, Oklahoma: Founded in 1890, the town was one of more than twenty African American communities established in the OKLAHOMA Territory. Named after educator John Mercer LANGSTON, it was planned by Edward P. McCabe to be part of a future all-black state. It failed to develop as such, but it did become the home of Oklahoma's state-supported black agricultural and mechanical college, Langston University (formerly Langston Colored Agricultural and Normal University).

Larsen, Nella (April 13, 1891, Chicago, Illinois—March 30, 1964, New York, New York): Novelist. Larsen depicts middle-class heroines contending with gender and racial issues; her work is often compared thematically with that of Jesse Redmon FAUSET.

Larsen received recognition as a writer during the HARLEM RENAISSANCE, culminating in the publication of her only two novels, *Quicksand* (1928) and *Passing* (1929). At the height of her career, she was awarded the Harmon Foundation's bronze medal for literary achievement in 1929. In 1930 she became the first African American woman awarded a Guggenheim Fellowship.

Born Nellie Walker, Larsen was the child of a Danish mother and a West Indian father. After the death of her father when she was two years old, Larsen's mother remarried a Danish man, and Larsen came to feel like an outsider in her own family. Much like the heroine of *Quicksand*, Helga Crane, Larsen spent the rest of her life trying to come to terms with her racial identity. She was considered one of the Harlem Renaissance's most promising young writers, but Larsen was dealt a series of professional and personal setbacks. In 1930 she was accused of plagiarism regarding her short story "Sanctuary," a charge of which she was later cleared. In 1933 she underwent a painful divorce, sensationalized in the press, from physicist Elmer S. Imes.

By the late 1930's, Larsen stopped writing professionally and dropped out of all literary circles. Virtually forgotten as a writer, Larsen lived her final years in Manhattan working as a night-shift nursing supervisor. Larsen's literary reputation and writing, like those of Zora Neale HURSTON, were restored to their proper place in the literary canon by African American and feminist critics of the 1970's and 1980's.

—*Kevin Eyster*

See also: Literature.

Last Poets: Avant-garde group of musicians and poets based in NEW YORK CITY. Their first two albums were *The Last Poets* (1970) and *This Is Madness* (1971). The Last Poets were never popular with a mass audience, but they influenced a generation of African American musicians. The three original group members were Jalal Mansur Nuriddin, Omar Ben Hassan, and Abiodun Oyewole. Oyewole was convicted of robbery in 1970 and replaced by Nilajah. In 1972 Suliman El Hadi replaced Hassan.

The Last Poets' approach can be seen as a seminal form of RAP, featuring recitations (they originally called them "spiels") over rhythmic backgrounds. The group was strongly influenced by the radical pop culture of the era. It integrated political and social themes into its lyrics, which were set to the background of congas and other drums. The Last Poets' songs included lyrics describing inner-city culture and contained references to drugs and sex.

The original group was active for a few years in the late 1960's and early 1970's, then was absent from the music scene for the rest of the decade. In the 1980's, as rap and HIP-HOP became increasingly popular—and as many rap artists acknowledged the genre's debt to the Last Poets—the group's importance was recognized. Members subsequently released a number of group and solo recordings in the 1980's and 1990's; in the mid-1990's two former members were using the name Last Poets for their separate projects.

Latimer, Lewis Howard (September 4, 1848, Chelsea, Massachusetts—December 11, 1928, Flushing, New York): Scientist and inventor. Lewis Latimer was widely known as a member of Thomas Alva Edison's research team and as a major contributor to the development and commercialization of the incandescent light bulb. Latimer was also a humanitarian who participated in many projects that benefited immigrants and other disadvantaged people of all races. Furthermore, he was a zealous advocate of CIVIL RIGHTS for African Americans and a dedicated husband and father.

Early Life

The son of a former slave, Lewis Howard Latimer was born in Chelsea, MASSACHUSETTS, in 1848 and reared in the city of BOSTON. Louis was one of George Latimer's four children. In 1848 George Latimer, unable to make a decent living in Boston, reacted by deserting his family.

Fatherless, the ten-year-old Lewis was thus catapulted into becoming a major economic provider for his single-parent family. He quit school and went to work at whatever jobs he could find. These included selling copies of the *Liberator*, a newspaper written by the fiery abolitionist William Lloyd GARRISON, who had participated in Latimer's father's emancipation. Lewis also found his own employment prospects poor, and at the age of sixteen, in the midst of the CIVIL WAR, he joined the U.S. Navy. Throughout the rest of the Civil War, Lewis served in the Navy, first as a cabin boy and then as a seaman. After his honorable discharge from the Navy in 1865, Lewis Latimer returned to Boston, where his basic skill in drawing led him to obtain a job with Crosby and Gould, a reputable firm of patent lawyers.

Employment as a Draftsman

At first, Latimer was used only as an assistant to the Crosby and Gould draftsmen, who made detailed patent diagrams for the firm's clients. As Latimer's skill at mechanical draftsmanship increased (as a result of much effort on his part), his position in the firm was slowly elevated, until he became the firm's chief patent draftsman. Also, during that time, Lewis Latimer married Mary Wilson, the beloved wife with whom he had two daughters.

In 1876 Alexander Graham Bell needed a skilled draftsman to prepare the patent blueprints for his newly invented telephone. Bell went to Crosby and Gould for help, and Latimer was assigned to execute the drawings on the Bell telephone patent. At that time, Latimer had also begun to invent things himself. For example, his first invention, patented in 1873, was a "water closet" (a bathroom) to be used in railroad cars. Unsatisfied with his employment at Crosby and Gould, Latimer left the company in 1880.

Latimer's next employment was with Hiram Maxim, who had invented the first rapid-fire machine gun and had headed the U.S. Electric Lighting Company of Bridgeport, Connecticut. The move was dictated by Latimer's belief that electricity, in its infancy at the time, had a great future. At the U.S. Electric Lighting Company, Latimer began his real lifework.

Further Development of Patents

Working with Maxim's company (which was then competing with the company of Thomas Alva Edison, because Maxim claimed prior discovery of the incandescent lamp), Latimer began his endeavors by improving the quality and lifespan of the carbon filaments then used in all incandescent bulbs. Latimer received patents for his most important inventions: improved processes for the joining of an incandescent light bulb's internal carbon filaments to the fine wires at the base of the bulb and the manufacture of a superior form of carbon filaments. Latimer's carbon filaments, made from the cellulose of cotton thread or from treated bamboo slivers, were a state-of-the-art contribution to the development and commercialization of the early incandescent light bulbs.

Latimer assigned these patents, and the others he obtained, to the U.S. Electric Lighting Company. Among the later Latimer patents was one for the design of the threaded sockets still used in most light bulbs. According to some sources, Maxim was prejudiced against African Americans, and Latimer quickly left his employ for that reason. Certainly, despite the fact that Latimer's inventions were quite profitable for the U.S. Electric Lighting Company, Maxim made no mention of this very valuable employee in his autobiography.

Joining Edison's Research Team

In 1884, after working briefly for several other electric companies, Latimer joined the Edison Electric Light Company. He did a great deal of research on the incandescent light bulb and related processes at Edison's engineering division in New York City. Another important aspect of Latimer's career was his participation in the installation of the Edison Company's citywide carbon-filament incandescent lighting systems in New York City, Philadelphia, and many other metropolitan areas. Latimer's research efforts culminated in the book *Incandescent Electric Lighting* (1890), which became a valuable guide for a generation of lighting engineers.

Highly thought of in the electric industry, Latimer was soon transferred to the legal department of the Edison Company, where he served as an expert witness, defending the patents on Edison's inventions in many important legal battles. Reportedly, Latimer's phenomenal knowledge of the vast body of electrical patents saved the Edison Company many millions of dollars in patent battles with Maxim's company and with Westinghouse Electric.

During that time, the Edison Electric Light Company went through a series of mergers and other changes that converted it into the General Electric Company. In 1890 the General Electric Company and Westinghouse formed a joint board of patent control, to prevent further expensive patent battles and to prevent patent infringements by other companies. Latimer was appointed chief draftsman and expert witness for the patent board and served in that capacity until the board was dissolved thirty-one years later. At that time, Latimer went back to working with patent lawyers, becoming associated with the firm of Hammer and Schwartz, where he remained until retirement.

Humanitarian Interests

Latimer was a devoted family man, spending much effort on family matters and the rearing of his children. He was also active in many humanitarian community activities. One of these activities was Latimer's diligent labor in the area of civil rights for the African American. Latimer's humanitarian efforts did not stop there, however, as he was interested in many other good works. For example, he participated widely and diligently in teaching recent immigrants and other disadvantaged Americans the English language and mechanical drawing at New York's famous Henry Street Settlement House. Throughout his life, Latimer also continued to invent, and his later inventions included both a forerunner of the refrigerator and a book rest.

In 1918 a group of scientists, engineers, and inventors who had been involved with Thomas Alva Edison during his creative period formed an organization called the Edison Pioneers. Latimer was one of the charter members of the organization and the only African American participant in the group. In 1924, however, Latimer became seriously ill, and he was forced to retire from all activity in the business world and from his other pursuits.

Lewis Latimer died four years later at his home in Flushing, New York. Latimer's death was mourned by many who felt that he had brought light into the world, both literally, in his many endeavors with the Edison Company, and figuratively, by being a humanitarian and a benefactor to many people. The Edison Pioneers eulogized Latimer as broad-minded, versatile in intellectual and culural activities, and a devoted husband and father. A lasting honor dedicated to his memory was the May, 1968, naming of the Lewis H. Latimer Public School in Brooklyn, New York.

—*Sanford S. Singer*

See also: Science and technology.

Suggested Readings:

Harris, M. A. *The Story of Lewis Latimer*. Brooklyn, N.Y.: Negro History Associates, 1964.

Hayden, Robert C. *Eight Black American Inventors*. Reading, Mass.: Addison-Wesley, 1972.

Jenkins, Edward S. *To Fathom More: African American Scientists and Inventors*. Lanham, Md.: University Press of America, 1996.

Klein, Aaron E. *The Hidden Contributors: Black Scientists and Inventors in America*. Garden City, N.Y.: Doubleday, 1971.

Sammons, Vivian O. *Blacks in Science and Medicine*. New York: Hemisphere, 1990.

Lattimer, Agnes Delores (b. May 13, 1928, Memphis, Tennessee): Physician. Lattimer received her bachelor's degree from Fisk University and her M.D. from the Chicago Medical School. A distinguished pediatrician, Lattimer taught in the department of pediatrics at Chicago Medical School, was a fellow of the American Academy of Pediatrics, and served on the Chicago Board of Health. She also wrote many scholarly articles in her field.

See also: Health care professionals; Medicine.

Law enforcement: The first historical records of African Americans serving as police officers occur as early as 1861 in Washington, D.C., and 1872 in Chicago, Illinois. However, prior to World War II, the number of African American law enforcement officers at any level (local, state, or national) was very small. Moreover, the early experiences of African Americans in law enforcement were not pleasant ones: Job assignments were restricted, promotions were unlikely, patrol assignments were generally in black neighborhoods, specialized assignments were rarely given, and arrest powers were limited.

Since the 1970's, the representation of African Americans in law enforcement has steadily increased. In some of the nation's large cities, African Americans have representation within law enforcement that is proportional to their presence in the populations they serve.

By the 1990's, African Americans could be found in all ranks and at all levels of law enforcement. African American police chiefs had been appointed in some of the largest U.S. cities, including Chicago, Atlanta, Detroit, Philadelphia, Miami, and Los Angeles. Yet nationwide, in the early 1990's, African Americans were still underrepresented in law enforcement in terms of their percentage of the total U.S. population. While African Americans constituted approximately 12.3 percent of the total U.S. population in the early to mid-1990's, they constituted only about 10 to 11 percent of all officers in local police departments.

During the 1980's and 1990's the percentage of African Americans employed as police officers and detectives in public service rose dramatically. *(Robert W. Ginn/Unicorn Stock Photos)*

By 1997, however, according to the U.S. Bureau of Labor Statistics, African Americans made up 13.4 percent of the roughly 579,000 persons employed as police officers and detectives in public service, up from 9.5 percent in 1983. In addition, blacks constituted about 18.6 percent of "sheriffs, bailiffs, and other law enforcement officers" and 27.4 percent of correctional institution officers. Notwithstanding these significant advancements in the numbers of African Americans in law enforcement, changes in racial attitudes within agencies developed more slowly, and blacks have continued to be notably underrepresented in managerial positions.

Civil Rights and Law Enforcement Careers

The Civil Rights movement led to the passage of the 1964 Civil Rights Act by the U.S. Congress. Title VII of this landmark law concerns employment opportunities and prohibits discrimination because of sex, race, color, or national origin. The law established the EQUAL EMPLOYMENT OPPORTUNITY COMMISSION (EEOC) for administration and gave the commission authority to establish guidelines. This law had little impact on law enforcement agencies because it did not affect state and local governments; it affected only private business. In 1972 Congress passed the Equal Opportunity Act, which modified Title VII to include state and local units of government with fifteen or more employees. The act prohibits discrimination based on sex, race, color, religion, or national origin in employment of any kind—public or private, local, state, or federal.

The EEOC took its mandate seriously and forcefully supported AFFIRMATIVE ACTION (deliberate effort to increase minority representation, such as in a workforce or student body) in order to establish an ethnically integrated and highly productive workforce at all levels of government. Few topics in law enforcement have generated more debate than hiring QUOTAS and affirmative action.

In the 1970's, in a number of cities across

the nation, courts ordered the implementation of quota systems for police department hiring. Quota hiring represented an effort to bring women and minorities into a police department once it had been determined that they were unrepresented compared with their population in the community.

Recruitment and Selection

The recruitment and selection of law enforcement officers is only partially dictated by Title VII law and court decisions: State and local statutes and requirements may limit the pool of potential applicants. Therefore, specific restrictions and qualifications may dictate a department's recruitment pool and become part of the department's minimal selection requirements. Prior to 1972, many law enforcement agencies had height, weight, strength, and other entrance requirements; most of these, whether intentionally or unintentionally, discriminated against women and minorities. When lawsuits were filed protesting such requirements, the courts found them not to be job related, so they were eliminated from the selection criteria.

A number of other issues soon surfaced. In the 1980's and 1990's, minimal education requirements for police officers came under attack. Critics debated the relationship between education level and police performance. Those who believed that there is no direct relationship between education and police performance claimed that requirements of HIGHER EDUCATION discriminate against African Americans who cannot afford to attend col-

In the 1967 film *In the Heat of the Night*, Rod Steiger (right) played the racist police chief of a southern town who cannot solve a local murder case without the expert help of an African American police detective (Sidney Poitier, left) visiting from the North. *(Museum of Modern Art, Film Stills Archive)*

lege. Another hiring issue is that written examinations have been found to be culturally biased against minorities. Background investigations and oral interviews have also been found to be very subjective in evaluating the qualifications of minority applicants. These evaluations have sometimes been found to be discriminatory by the courts. In an attempt to avoid years of litigation, many agencies entered into consent decrees. These decrees typically include short-term and long-term plans to revamp recruiting, entrance criteria, and the hiring of minorities.

The problems of recruitment and selection are complex. Even if there were no biased or prejudiced police personnel who do not want to hire, work with, or promote minority officers, there could be difficulties in finding a pool of sufficiently qualified minority applicants from which to hire new officers. If a department does not have an adequate number of acceptably qualified applicants, then it must hire less qualified applicants.

There are a number of reasons why recruiting African American officers can be difficult. African American citizens often have a negative view of the police, viewing them as a symbol of oppression. For decades, the police have been charged with—and sometimes found guilty of—using brutality against minority suspects and treating minorities with disrespect. In some cases, officers have been accused of failing to come to the aid of minority victims. Some African Americans believe that the police department will not treat them fairly if they become officers, and there is historical evidence to support this belief. African Americans who want to become law enforcement officers may also face discouragement from friends and relatives who consider police work to be "selling out."

Special Problems of Black Officers

In his classic work *Black in Blue* (1969), Nicholas Alex introduced the concept of "double marginality" to describe the position of African American police officers. Since they are black, these officers do not feel a part of the white police culture. As police officers, they feel segregated from their racial peers, many of whom distrust police officers. Added to this is the loneliness and isolation from the general population that most police officers feel. Many subsequent studies of police officers conducted in the 1970's, 1980's, and 1990's have supported this view of "double marginality." At least one researcher, Valencia Campbell, questioned this concept, however. In a 1980 study, Campbell argued that, partly as a result of the BLACK POWER MOVEMENT of the 1960's, African American officers in the 1970's were more positive and self-assured than in the past and were less willing to accept the discriminatory practices of law enforcement agencies.

While "double marginality" has been introduced to explain the position of black male law enforcement officers, the concept of "double jeopardy" has been introduced to explain the position of black female law enforcement officers. According to a 1995 study by Susan Martin, African American female officers must contend with both sexism and racism on the job.

African American officers have associations and support groups, at both the local and national levels, for patrol and command-level officers. The National Black Policeman's Association is composed of patrol officers. The National Organization of Black Law Enforcement Executives (NOBLE) was established in the mid-1970's. NOBLE's goals include increasing the number of minority officers hired, increasing the quality of justice, improving community relations, and increasing crime protection in some areas. Such national black organizations, along with similar organizations at the state and local levels, have been effective in combating discrimination.

African American police officers face difficult decisions concerning the types of organizations they decide to join. An African American officer may be seen as an "Uncle Tom" by the black community if he or she selects a white police organization. On the other hand, the department may consider black officers to be outsiders if they choose to join a black organization.

Job Assignments and Promotions

In numerous incidents, courts have found that law enforcement agencies have discriminated against minorities when giving job assignments, giving performance evaluations, and granting promotions. Some courts have stated that the law enforcement agencies in the cases generally assigned minority officers to routine patrol duties while giving the more favorable assignments to whites.

Relatively few African Americans are given civilian-clothed anticrime or undercover assignments, and in general some minority officers claim that white officers are much more likely to be put in assignments that groom them for administrative level jobs. Minority officers are given routine patrol assignments or undercover jobs in minority areas.

African Americans are grossly underrepresented above the patrol level. This situation is probably attributable partly to discrimination and partly to the fact that blacks for so long were not even well represented at the patrol level. An additional problem is that the best and brightest black candidates are often recruited by federal agencies (nicknamed "federal raiders") and taken from municipal police departments. Federal jobs offer excellent salaries and benefits and are considered prestigious. Therefore, some observers have noted, the black officers who have the greatest potential for promotion may be leaving the municipal police departments.

Federal agencies, such as the FEDERAL BUREAU OF INVESTIGATION (FBI), Central Intelligence Agency (CIA), Drug Enforcement Administration (DEA), Secret Service, Marshals Service, Immigration and Naturalization Service (INS), and the Bureau of Prisons actively recruit minorities with targeted advertising. Some federal agencies offer special incentives to minority students in college and graduate programs, and some have markedly improved their grievance procedures and promotion policies. The FBI, once the target of severe criticism for its lack of response to the concerns of its minority agents, decided in the 1980's and 1990's to review its procedures for selecting agents for promotion, and it established grievance procedures in an effort toward equal opportunity.

Other problems that have hindered minority promotions are biased promotional exams, lack of access to the political network in the department, and the general lack of higher education among minority officers. Police organizations have tried to remedy the promotion problem for minorities by using quotas for promotion and employing "rank-jumping" (in which officers are promoted two steps above their current positions rather than the usual one-step promotion) in order to move toward equity in promotion. These practices, however, have caused a WHITE BACKLASH in which white officers argue that less qualified officers are being promoted ahead of them.

Experts have noted that hiring women and minorities for law enforcement careers is practical and beneficial. For example, hiring individuals more reflective of an area's population, particularly in large urban areas, enhances understanding and communication between the police and the community, prevents conflicts, and may gradually change the negative feelings toward law enforcement officers that many young minority men share.

For members of minorities themselves, a career in law enforcement can be a way to move into the middle class. Policing can provide a reasonable salary, job security, and a pension.

—Marylee Reynolds

See also: Crime and the criminal justice system; Racial discrimination; Racial prejudice.

Suggested Readings:

Alex, Nicholas. *New York Cops Talk Back: A Study of a Beleaguered Minority*. New York: John Wiley & Sons, 1976.

Campbell, Valencia. "Double Marginality of Black Policemen: A Reassessment." *Criminology* 17, no. 4 (1980): 477-484.

Dolan, Edward F., and Margaret M. Scariano. *The Police in American Society*. New York: Franklin Watts, 1988.

Kuykendall, Jack, and David Burns. "The Black Police Officer: An Historical Perspective." *Journal of Contemporary Criminal Justice* 1, no. 4 (1980): 103-113.

Leinen, Stephen. *Black Police, White Society*. New York: New York University Press, 1984.

Martin, Susan E. "The Interactive Effects of Race and Sex on Women Police Officers." In *The Criminal Justice System and Women: Offenders, Victims, and Workers*, edited by Barbara Raffel Price and Natalie J. Sokoloff. 2d ed. New York: McGraw-Hill, 1995.

Moore, Harry W. *Special Topics in Policing*. Cincinnati, Ohio: Anderson, 1992.

Ross, Lee E. *African American Criminologists, 1970-1996: An Annotated Bibliography*. Westport, Conn: Greenwood Press, 1998.

Stratton, John G. *Police Passages*. Manhattan Beach, Calif.: Glennon, 1984.

Sullivan, Peggy S. "Minority Officers Current Issues." In *Critical Issues in Policing: Contemporary Readings*, edited by Roger G. Dunham and Geoffrey P. Alpert. Prospect Heights, Ill.: Waveland Press, 1989.

Lawless, Theodore K. (December 6, 1892, New Orleans, Louisiana—May 1, 1971, Chicago, Illinois): Medical doctor. Lawless received degrees from Talladega College in ALABAMA and from Harvard University before receiving his M.D. from Northwestern University. His medical specialty was dermatology. He made a number of important contributions to the treatment of syphilis and leprosy, and taught at Northwestern's school of medicine from 1924 to 1941.
See also: Medicine.

Dermatologist Theodore K. Lawless. *(Associated Publishers, Inc.)*

Lawrence, Jacob (September 7, 1917, Atlantic City, New Jersey—June 9, 2000, Seattle Washington): Artist and educator. Lawrence studied at the American Artists School (1938-1939) and the Harlem Art Workshop (1937-1939). He received a Rosenwald Fellowship, a Guggenheim Fellowship, and an American Academy of Arts and Letters grant. Lawrence became a full professor at the University of Washington in 1971. He exhibited at the Museum of Modern Art (1963), the Metropolitan Museum (1963), and the Seattle Art Museum (1986). In 1990 Lawrence received the National Medal of Arts.

Jacob Lawrence's painting depicting John Brown and Frederick Douglass arguing over plans for the raid on Harpers Ferry. *(National Archives)*

Perhaps the best-known African American postwar painter, Lawrence maintained an allegiance to African American themes of history and culture throughout his career. He explored the theme of integration as a member of the Federal Arts Work Project (1939-1940). His initial recognition came with the publication of his migration series in *Fortune* magazine in 1941. Lawrence established a style of working out a textual theme through a pictorial series early in his career. These series may have been influenced by the historical antecedents of Egyptian wall painting and Mexican murals. The Toussaint-L'Ouverture series (1937-1938) was his first. The Frederick Douglass series (1938-1939) established his pattern, and between the years 1940 and 1943 he completed the Harriet Tubman, the John Brown, and the Harlem series. During World War II, he served with the U.S. Coast Guard and finished the war series (1946), a cycle of paintings not based on a specific text.

Lawrence was a master craftsman able to merge narration, figuration, and abstract design into striking statements. He illustrated poet Langston Hughes's *One Way Ticket* (1949). Concerned with African American history, culture, and social injustice, Lawrence depicts historical figures and black communal life with harsh angular movement and explosive colors. His distorted but highly intuitive paintings combine elements of expressionism and cubism with African American themes. In paintings such as *Street Scene #1* (1936) and *Three Family Toilet* (1943), Lawrence affirmed his commitment to the bitter struggle of black people for personal dignity and freedom.

Lawrence painted murals for the Kingdome stadium in Seattle (*Games*, 1979) and a public building in Jamaica, New York (*Community*, 1989). In 1990 he completed his fifteenth series, *Eight Sermons from Genesis*. Lawrence taught at the Pratt Institute Art School, Art Students League, and the University of Washington at Seattle.
See also: Painters and illustrators.

Lawrence, Robert H., Jr. (October 2, 1935, Chicago, Illinois—December 8, 1967, Edwards Air Force Base, California): First African American astronaut designate. Lawrence was one of four pilots selected to begin training for thirty-day space flights, as part of the national space program. His selection was announced on June 30, 1967, by the U.S. Air Force. Lawrence had been a research scientist with the Air Force Weapons Laboratory at Kirtland Air Force Base in New Mexico. He was killed in a crash during a routine proficiency flight in an F-104.
See also: Aviators and astronauts.

Robert H. Lawrence, Jr., the first African American astronaut, died during a training mission. *(AP/Wide World Photos)*

Lawrence-Lightfoot, Sara (b. August, 1944, Nashville, Tennessee): Sociologist. Educated at Swarthmore College, the Bank Street College of Education, and Harvard University, Lawrence-Lightfoot became a sociologist like her father, Charles Lawrence. Asked to join the faculty of Harvard the year she completed her degree, Lawrence-Lightfoot became only the second tenured African American female professor in the institution's history.

When told she had been awarded the prestigious MacArthur Prize in 1984, Lawrence-Lightfoot replied, "Now I can write about my mother." She went on to write *Balm in Gilead: Portrait of a Healer* (1988), which relates the life and career of Margaret Morgan Lawrence, one of the first African American child psychiatrists in the United States.

Born in Vicksburg, Mississippi, Morgan moved to New York to pursue her dream of becoming a doctor. Helping to finance her undergraduate education at Cornell University by working as a maid, she was denied admittance to its medical school because of her race. Despite her disappointment, Morgan received her medical degree from Columbia University and became distinguished for her work in child therapy.

Balm in Gilead is not merely the story of Morgan or four generations of the Morgan family; it is also a portrait of life in the black middle class. The work is thought by some to be part of a new literary genre, combining biography, oral history, and sociology. Unique in its interactive "storytelling" between mother and daughter, *Balm in Gilead*, like Lawrence-Lightfoot's other works, extends the boundaries of conventional sociology. It won the Christopher Award for "literary merit and humanitarian achievement," and led to Lawrence-Lightfoot's being awarded Harvard's George Ledlie Prize for "the most valuable contribution to science and the benefit of mankind."

Balm in Gilead was not Lawrence-Lightfoot's first work of note; she had written three others. *Worlds Apart: Relationships Between Families and Schools* (1978), a book of case studies about schools and families, disputes the notion that children's failure in school is the fault of the family. *Beyond Bias: Perspectives on Classrooms* (1979), written with Jean Carew, continues Lawrence-Lightfoot's exploration of schools. Her third work, *The Good High School: Portraits of Character and Culture* (1983), examined six high schools and introduced the method Lawrence-Lightfoot named "portraiture"—rendering "individual faces and voices . . . to tell a larger story." *The Good High School* won the 1984 outstanding book award of the American Educational Research Association and was the work for which Lawrence-Lightfoot received the MacArthur Prize.

Lawrence-Lightfoot's 1994 work, *I've Known Rivers: Lives of Loss and Liberation*, is her response to E. Franklin FRAZIER's classic study on the black middle class, *Black Bourgeoisie* (1957). In his work, Frazier argued that African Americans, uprooted from their racial tradition, become neither black nor white. In *I've Known Rivers*, Lawrence-Lightfoot acknowledges that there is loss but states that there is also liberation. African Americans can become successful and maintain connections with their culture. Relating the stories of six middle-aged, middle-class African Americans, three men and three women, Lawrence-Lightfoot in this book continues the methods of portraiture and storytelling that have become her trademarks.

See also: Literature; Oral and family history.

Lawson, John: CIVIL WAR hero. Born a free man in PENNSYLVANIA in 1837, Lawson entered the Union Navy during the Civil War and served under Admiral David Farragut aboard the USS *Hartford*. Lawson participated

Congressional Medal of Honor winner John Lawson. *(National Archives)*

in numerous campaigns, including the battle against Fort Morgan at Mobile Bay, in ALABAMA. He was wounded in that battle but refused to seek medical treatment, continuing to fight at his station. Lawson received the Naval Medal of Honor for his actions at Mobile Bay.

In the last years of his life, Leadbelly recorded folk and work songs that might otherwise have been lost to posterity. *(AP/Wide World Photos)*

Leadbelly (Huddie Ledbetter; January 20, 1889, Mooringsport, Louisiana—December 6, 1949, New York, New York): BLUES singer and guitarist. Leadbelly represents an aspect of American experience, especially southern rural experience, that has long vanished from American life, the importance of the traveling musician and the audiences for his kinds of music. By the time Leadbelly was in his early teens, he was known in his area as a musician. In the early part of the twentieth century, he accompanied folk singer and guitarist Blind Lemon JEFFERSON in the streets and bars of TEXAS.

Twice sentenced and jailed, for murder in Texas and then for attempted homicide in LOUISIANA, he was discovered by folklorist John Lomax, who recorded his songs for the Library of Congress and was instrumental in securing Leadbelly's parole in 1934. After his parole was granted, Leadbelly went to New York with Lomax and eventually built up an audience, especially among JAZZ fans, who regarded him as an exciting and significant figure in the history and evolution of the blues. He also played and sang for college audiences and was respected and admired as perhaps the best remaining example of a dying tradition.

In the last years of his life, at the urging of folklorists, he recorded folk and work songs and sang and played on records with virtuoso harmonica player Sonny Terry, another musician of the wandering minstrel genre. Anyone who has heard his records quickly remembers Leadbelly's gravelly voice and matter-of-fact spoken discourse to his audiences. His twelve-string guitar playing was equally individualized: rhythmic, highly innovative, and harmonically complex.

Leadbelly is said to have possessed a repertoire of more than five hundred songs. He is considered to be one of the most important and commercially untainted representatives of African American song traditions, most notably the blues and the work songs of the rural South. Considering his great gifts and contributions to his culture and his people, it is perhaps ironic that he is best known for his song "Goodnight Irene," which bears little ethnic identity as most people know it.

Lee, Canada (Leonard Lionel Cornelius Canegata; May 3, 1907, New York, New York—May 9, 1952, New York, New York): Actor. Lee's family name of Canegata was Danish, taken by his West Indian ancestors. By age seven, he was studying the violin; by age fourteen, he was a jockey at the racetrack in Saratoga, New York; and by age seventeen, he had turned to BOXING. Within a short time, he had won ninety out of one hundred amateur fights and the national amateur lightweight title. He turned professional in 1926 and became a leading contender for the welterweight championship. It was as a boxer that he picked up his professional name of Canada Lee. He was forced to quit boxing in 1933 because of a detached retina.

In 1934 he led his own JAZZ band for a brief time. He was soon cast in the Works Progress Administration's production of *Brother Mose*. He then appeared as Blacksnake in *Stevedore*, as Banquo in Orson Welles's Federal Theatre production of *Macbeth* (with an all-African American cast), as Jean Christophe in *Haiti*, and as Drayton in *Mamba's Daughter*, with Ethel WATERS.

Actor Canada Lee speaking at a 1945 rally to save the Fair Employment Practice Commission. *(AP/Wide World Photos)*

Lee's first major recognition came in 1941, when he appeared as Bigger Thomas in the stage version of Richard WRIGHT's *Native Son*. He was praised for giving one of the season's best performances and for being a magnetic actor. In 1944 Lee appeared in Alfred Hitchcock's film *Lifeboat*. He served as the narrator on the radio program *New World A-Comin'*, as well as appearing on other radio shows that served to heighten public awareness of the African American cause. He also performed on stage in *Anna Lucasta*.

In the following years, Lee made a series of appearances on Broadway: as Caliban in *The Tempest* (1945), as David Bennett in *On Whitman Avenue* (1946), as Bosola in *The Duchess of Malfi* (1946), and as George in *Set My People Free* (1948). During these years, he was also politically active. Shortly before his death, he starred in the film *Cry the Beloved Country* (1951), based on Alan Paton's tragic novel about race relations in South Africa.